TO
CHAIN THE
DOG OF
WAR

TO CHAIN THE DOG OF WAR

The War Power of Congress in History and Law

Francis D. Wormuth and Edwin B. Firmage
with
Francis P. Butler, Contributing Author

SOUTHERN METHODIST UNIVERSITY PRESS • 1986

Library of Congress Cataloguing-In-Publication Data

Wormuth, Francis Dunham, 1909–
    To chain the dog of war.

    Bibliography: p.
    Includes index.
    1. War, Declaration of—United States—History.
2. War and emergency powers—United States—History.
I. Firmage, Edwin Brown. II. Title.
KF4941.W67   1985   342.73'062   85–14249
ISBN 0-87074-206-X   347.30262

Contents

Preface

Ordinarily, the term *war power* denotes the power to initiate and prosecute a war and includes all the implied powers considered necessary and proper for the conduct of the war, such as allocation of raw materials, price-fixing, and payment of pensions. Here the term is used in a much narrower sense; this book examines the power to initiate war in American constitutional law and the history of the uses of that power. Other, broader meanings of the term are discussed only as they pertain to this issue.

The Constitution assigns the power to initiate war solely to the Congress, one of the wisest of the many checks and balances built into our political system; but, throughout our history, Presidents have committed acts of war without congressional authorization. The question of where to assign the power to initiate and conduct war was thoroughly debated during the writing of the Constitution, and the outcome of that debate was a document that clearly did not give the President unlimited war power but in fact separated the power to conduct war from the power to initiate it.

Acts of war, acts of reprisal, acts of self-defense—all have been taken by past Presidents, but seldom without consideration of the legal implications of their actions. The records of executive debate on the limitations of war power are extensive. Often, as we shall see, a President has refused to act on the grounds that he could not act within the legal boundaries of the Constitution. At a time of national crisis, notably during the Civil War, the President has acted illegally and depended upon Congress to ratify his action after the fact. In the latter half of the twentieth century, however, a major change in the concept of the war power began to be promulgated. Beginning with the Korean War, Presidents, congressmen, and publicists claimed for the executive the power to initiate war without the consent of Congress. The war in Korea, the Indochina war embracing Vietnam, Laos, Thailand, and Cambodia, and many lesser actions required justification, and so the Department of State, the Department of Justice, the Library of Congress, several members of Congress, lawyers, law professors, and historians have attempted to revise the understanding of the Constitution, changing its meaning as universally held during the first one hundred and sixty years of our history.

Significant congressional reaction to the erosion of congressional power and to the corresponding arrangement of presidential power resulted in the Fulbright proviso and the War Powers Resolution of 1973. In this broader perspective of presidential and congressional power, the Watergate crisis and its aftermath—impeachment proceedings, presidential resignation, attempts to bring the intelligence community more tightly under the rule of law—all reinforce the growing perception that Whiggish understandings of power and the necessity of its containment are as relevant and wise in the twentieth as in the eighteenth century.

Since Vietnam and Watergate, and the reaction against overwhelming presidential power, the pendulum of reaction has swung again. Presidents continue to use the armed forces without congressional approval in the Middle East and in Latin America; the presidential and congressional interpretation of the War Powers Resolution is unnecessarily narrow, threatening to render it meaningless; the legal restraints upon the intelligence community have been relaxed; and public opinion, forgetting Vietnam and Watergate, approves and applauds.

It has been argued that the technology of the nuclear era makes impossible the policy of congressional deliberation as reflected in the original understanding of the war powers. Missiles from one side of the earth may reach the other side in minutes. The advantage of surprise first strike with nuclear weaponry would be enormous, perhaps decisive. In this book, we will respond that the element of modern technology cuts the other way, in awesome proportion. The consequence of nuclear war is likely to be devastation beyond experience, beyond belief or comprehension, beyond the capacity of our civilization to respond and repair. Such technology demands more restraint, not less, on the way we go to war.

This book examines our nation's experience with the initiation of war from the beginning of the Republic through that most costly and most tragic violation of our Constitution, the Vietnam War, which from its obscure beginning to its inglorious conclusion was carried on by the executive without proper congressional sanction. By analyzing the President's powers as commander in chief of the armed forces—through a careful study of the political and legal meaning of war in a national and international context, distinguishing between declared and undeclared, de facto war—we will find a pattern of intent and interpretation, supported by numerous statements of the founding fathers, past Presidents, and supreme courts. By examining acts of self-defense in our military dealings with piracy, threats to United States citizens on foreign soil, and Indian raids, we will see that the many modern lists of the wars supposedly initiated by the executive—lists official and unofficial, originating from the military, from historians, and from executive and congressional studies—are misleading because they include many actions that were in fact authorized by Congress, such as the naval landings described in Chapter 10.

There have been cases of executive action without approval prior to 1950. There have been Presidents who have acted autonomously with military force, convinced of their rectitude, sometimes convinced as well of their anointment as leaders and saviors of America and the world: Theodore Roosevelt, Andrew Jackson, and others, particularly since the beginning of World War II. Some, Congress has reprimanded, some not. Congress has been willing to endorse and ratify some illegal actions in retrospect and has pronounced a most ambiguous benediction on others by appropriating funds to continue the action illegally begun.

This book examines the legal questions of ratification by appropriation, delegation of the power to make war, the nature of "conditional war," and separation of powers in foreign relations. It begins by examining the nature of the presidency historically and concludes by portraying the presidency as an ideal. Such an examination can lead us only to praise the wisdom of the framers of the Constitution in their decision to sever the power to initiate war from the power to conduct it. When those powers rest in the same single pair of hands, legally or de facto through congressional abrogation of duty, the nation and the world should be uneasy.

While over ninety percent of the contents of this volume have never before been published, Chapter 15, "The Doctrine of Political Questions," is based largely upon an article by Edwin Firmage published in the *University of Colorado Law Review* and is published here with permission. Chapter 18, "The Presidency as an Ideal Type" was taken from an article by Francis Wormuth originally published by *Fortuna*. It is reprinted here with the kindly permission of the editor, Fulvio Fenucci. Small portions of the argument of this volume are taken from earlier publications by Francis D. Wormuth and Edwin B. Firmage. These are scattered throughout parts of the argument and cannot be conveniently identified. Professor Wormuth's materials are used here with the permission of the copyright holders: The Center for the Study of Democratic Institutions, which published *The Vietnam War: The President versus the Constitution* (1968); and the *California Law Review*, which published "The Nixon Theory of the War Power: A Critique" (1972). The Fred B. Rothman Co. obligingly concurred in the consent of the *California Law Review*. The Princeton University Press kindly agreed to the publication of passages from Professor Firmage's article, "Law and the Indochina War: A Retrospective View," published in Richard Falk, ed., *The Vietnam War and International Law*, Vol. 4 (1976).

We would like to thank Francis Butler, who contributed Chapter 9, "Lists of Wars." This chapter adds so substantially to our volume that we thought it only fair that Colonel Butler's name be on this volume as a contributing author. Special thanks are also due Stephen C. Clark for his help on Chapters 16 and 17. We make grateful acknowledgment for contributions of data and other assistance to Frank Plymale Butler, Richard Goldberger, William C. Barnhart, Thomas B. McAffee, Oscar Kraines, Morris D. Forkosch, and

Harvey Wheeler. Mick McAllister and D. Teddy Diggs provided invaluable editorial assistance. Lora Lee Petersen and Elizabeth Kirschen deserve special thanks for typing so many drafts of so many chapters so very cheerfully and well.

A word of explanation on our footnoting will be helpful. References are treated three ways. Material that required footnoting will be found at the bottom of the page. Simple page references, however, are keyed to the Bibliography with parenthetical references in the text—the item number in italic, followed by Roman numeral volume reference if applicable, and then the page number ([item] *181*, [vol.] IV, [page] 36, is Richardson's *Messages*). References to cases, statutes, and various common government documents, such as *Congressional Record*, are collected separately and are indicated in the text with an asterisk.

FRANCIS D. WORMUTH
EDWIN B. FIRMAGE

Professor Francis D. Wormuth (1909–1980)

Francis Wormuth died as this volume neared completion. I am deeply grateful to have been able to work with Professor Wormuth since the mid-1970s on these chapters, and I completed the final revision of the entire manuscript, including the addition of Chapters 16 and 17, during the past years without him but, I hope, in harmony with his beliefs.

He was born at Port Leyden, New York, on May 23, 1909, and he received his formal education at Cornell University, where he earned his bachelor's master's, and doctoral degrees.

Francis's brilliance was recognized early; he received as many honors as the academic world can bestow upon its very best. While a student at Cornell, he was awarded the Messenger Memorial Prize for his essay, "The History of English Thought"; the Guilford Prize for "Macaulay"; and the Sherman–Bennett Prize in Government for his paper, "The Constitutional Theory of Sir Edward Coke."

Francis was a Boldt Fellow at Cornell, a Sterling Fellow at Yale, a Guggenheim Fellow, a Ford Fellow at Yale Law School, and a Fulbright Lecturer at Johns Hopkins University, Bologna Italy Center.

At the University of Utah, Professor Wormuth was named Distinguished Research Professor for 1971–72; he served from 1975 until his death as Distinguished Professor.

Among Francis Wormuth's scores of books and monographs, perhaps his most notable were *The Origins of Modern Constitutionalism*, published in 1948;

The Royal Prerogative, published a decade before; and now *To Chain the Dog of War: The War Power of Congress in History and Law*.

His most original, deeply perceptive writings in constitutional law and political theory have led his colleagues to compare him, both in brilliance and in significance of contribution, to Harold Laski, Charles Merriam, C. J. Friedrich, and Charles McIlwàin.

Francis was not only a scholar of the first rank, of international reputation, but also a brilliant teacher whose students sound like a Who's Who of university professors throughout our country. He made disciples of his students, but not with any intent to create a personal following. Rather, his brilliance, his integrity and utter candor, his fearless exposition simply drew us to him as our colleague and mentor and friend.

EDWIN B. FIRMAGE

University of Utah
Salt Lake City, 1985

Chapter 1

THE PRESIDENCY
IN ITS HISTORICAL SETTING

It is usually said that the United States has contributed two inventions to political science: federalism and judicial review. And this is more or less true. But two other ideas which have played a great part in our constitutional history were not American in origin: checks and balances and the separation of powers.

Herodotus, writing in the fifth century B.C., established the familiar classification of governments—the government of the one, of the few, and of the many. In the next century Aristotle reported that "some, indeed, say that the best constitution is a combination of all existing forms, and they praise the Lacedaemonian because it is made up of oligarchy, monarchy, and democracy, the king forming the monarchy, and the council of elders the oligarchy, while the democratic element is represented by the Ephors for the Ephors are selected from the people." (*243*, 20) Thereafter the idea of the mixed state, as it has come to be called, became common. Polybius gave final expression to the classical conception in the second century B.C. Accepting Plato's theory of an inevitable cycle of revolutions throughout the three simple forms, he said that Lycurgus had contrived a mixed government for Sparta.

The royal power was prevented from growing insolent by fear of the people, which had also assigned to it an adequate share in the constitution. The people in their turn were restrained from a bold contempt of the kings by fear of the Gerousia: the members of which, being selected on grounds of merit, were certain to throw their influence on the side of justice in every question that arose; and thus the party placed at a disadvantage by its conservative tendency was always strengthened and supported by the weight and influence of the Gerousia. The result of this combination has been that the Lacedaemonians retained their freedom for the longest period of any people with which we are acquainted. (*149*, I, 467)

The constitution that Lycurgus had invented by "the light of reason," the Romans had achieved "through many struggles and difficulties, and by continually adopting reforms from knowledge gained in disaster."

> As for the Roman constitution, it had three elements, each of them possessing sovereign powers: and their respective share of power in the whole state had been regulated with such a scrupulous regard to equality and equilibrium, that no one could say for certain, not even a native, whether the constitution as a whole were an aristocracy or democracy or despotism. . . .
>
> When any one of the three classes becomes puffed up, and manifests an inclination to be contentious and unduly encroaching, the mutual interdependency of all the three, and the possibility of the pretensions of any one being checked and thwarted by the others, must plainly check this tendency: and so the proper equilibrium is maintained by the impulsiveness of the one part being checked by the fear of the other. . . . (*149*, I, 473)

Julius Caesar destroyed the Roman mixed state, and Caesar Augustus erected what amounted to an absolute monarchy on the ruins. Thereafter, for more than sixteen centuries, the mixed state lived a purely literary life, and a very attenuated one; it was mentioned—rarely—as a possible form of government or—very rarely—as a characterization of an actual institutional system. It was restored to the field of active political discussion by Charles I in 1642, at the outbreak of the English Civil Wars, in his reply to the Nineteen Propositions of Parliament.

> There being three kinds of government amongst men, absolute monarchy, aristocracy, and democracy, and all these having their particular conveniences and inconveniences. . . .
>
> The ill of absolute monarchy is tyranny, the ill of aristocracy is faction and division, the ills of democracy are tumults, violence, and licentiousness. The good of monarchy is the uniting of a nation under one head to resist invasion from abroad, and insurrection at home: the good of aristocracy is the conjunction of counsel in the ablest persons of a state for the public benefit: the good of democracy is liberty, and the courage and industry which liberty begets. (*243*, 52–53)

The King was, of course, the monarchical element, the House of Lords the aristocratic, the House of Commons the democratic. The King was charged with the conduct of foreign relations, the power of appointment, the pardoning power, and other functions; the Lords had power of judicature; the Commons possessed the sole right to propose taxes and to impeach. All three participated in legislation.

The theory of the mixed state immediately became the usual characterization of the English constitutional system. Oliver Cromwell's second written constitution, the Humble Petition and Advice, was a copy of the Stuart constitution. This plan governed England from May 1657 to May 1659 with Oliver Cromwell—and, after his death, his son Richard—as Lord Protector, an elective House of Commons, and an "other House" of appointed members as a surrogate for the Lords. Nathaniel Fiennes, one of Cromwell's Commissioners of the Great Seal, addressed the Parliament of the new government in 1658. He praised the plan because the power of legislation was divided among the three branches. "If anything inconvenient should chance to slip out at one door, must it not pass two more, before it come abroad, to the detriment of the people?" (243, 123) An eminent lawyer, Sir John Maynard, who sat in the House of Commons, echoed Fiennes: "I would give my negative, if it were put, that we should have a free legislature within these walls. . . . There is nothing can be well done by man. A check is necessary upon us." (243, 126)

The Humble Petition and Advice was scuttled by the army in 1659; yet after a series of republican expedients failed, Charles Stuart was recalled from exile as King. For two hundred years thereafter England was a mixed monarchy. Sir William Blackstone, for example, wrote in his *Commentaries on the Laws of England*:

> And herein indeed consists the true excellence of the English government, that all parts of it form a mutual check upon each other. In the legislature, the people are a check upon the nobility, and the nobility a check upon the people, by the mutual privilege of rejecting what the other has resolved: while the king is a check upon both, which preserves the executive power from encroachments. And this very executive power is again checked and kept within bounds by the two houses, through the privilege they have of inquiring into, impeaching and punishing the conduct (not indeed of the king, which would destroy his constitutional independence; but, which is more beneficial to the public) of his evil and pernicious counsellors. . . . Like three distinct powers in mechanics, they jointly impel the machine of government in a direction different from what either, acting by itself, would have done; but at the same time in a direction partaking of each, and formed out of all; a direction which constitutes the true line of the liberty and happiness of the community. (243, 176)

But in the latter part of the eighteenth century it came to be recognized by the more acute observers that the King was dependent on the Commons and must appoint ministers acceptable to that body. And the King, under pressure from the Commons, could bring the Lords to terms by threatening to create more peers. Finally, in 1869 Walter Bagehot reported the extinction of the mixed state. "The ultimate authority in the English Constitution is a newly-elected House of Commons." (*11*, 201)

Matters went quite otherwise in the United States. During the colonial period the virtues of the mixed state and of checks and balances were learned from the mother country. In 1784 John Adams published his *Defence of the Constitutions of the United States*. Adams lauded the partition of power established by all the state constitutions of the revolutionary period; Luther Martin, in his report to the Maryland legislature on the Constitutional Convention, said that the reviewers had justly observed that Adams "appears to be as fond of *checks* and *balances* as Lord Chesterfield of the Graces." (*53*, III, 192) But Martin himself thought checks and balances appropriate to a state government; he merely protested that bicameralism was unnecessary to a simple confederation of states, which the United States had been under the Articles of Confederation and which he hoped they would con-tinue to be.

In England, checks and balances reflected social divisions: monarchy, the aristocracy, and the commonalty. But in the United States there was neither a monarchy nor an aristocracy. In No. 14 of the *Federalist* James Madison asserted that America had shown that representation might be made the basis of "unmixed and extensive republics." He might have added that America had also shown that checks and balances might exist in an unmixed republic, balancing institutions rather than social classes against each other. The institutions that the framers of the Constitution counterpoised were determined by the theory of the separation of powers.

Frank J. Goodnow observed in 1914 that there were only two functions of government—the formulation of policy and the execution of policy. (*68*) This analysis had first been stated during the English Civil Wars: the formulation of policy was assigned to the legislative power, and the execution of policy was attributed to what was called either the executive or the judicial power. At its first appearance the separation of powers was therefore a twofold separation.

The proposition that the two powers should be in separate hands was first stated by John Lilburne, the leader of the Levellers, a democratic political faction during the Civil Wars. In 1645 he was arrested and interrogated by a committee of the House of Commons; he insisted that he should be dealt with according to known rules of law. This could be insured only if those who made the law had no power to execute it. In 1649 he was interrogated by the Council of State, which was in effect a committee of the Rump House of Commons, and he offered a further argument for distinct personnel in the executive branch: Parliament should correct errors of the executive, but the benefit would be lost if the members of the executive sat in Parliament and judged the appeals. (*243*, 65–66)

Thereafter the propriety of separating the legislative power from the executive or judicial function became universally accepted. Both Cromwel·lian constitutions—the Instrument of Government, which was put into effect in 1653, and the Humble Petition and Advice, which was adopted in 1658—were praised for observing the twofold separation of powers. In 1660, on the eve of the Stuart Restoration, Sir Roger L'Estrange praised the Stuart monarchy as a mixed state that practiced the separation of powers. The distinction of "the legislative from the ministerial authority" was "the most vital part of freedom." (243, 71)

John Locke, in his *Two Treatises of Government*, offers us a view of the Stuart constitution as modified by the radical political theory that had developed during the Civil Wars: the doctrines of social contract, of individualism and equality, and of the separation of powers. The principal omission is the theory of the mixed state. Locke wrote the major part of the book between 1679 and 1683 to express the philosophy of the Whig party in its contest with Charles II, and he may have stated a case for a legislative chamber of hereditary members in the major portion of the manuscript that was destroyed before the book was published, updated, and revised in 1690. That publication was extremely influential; it not only justified the Glorious Revolution but also helped shape constitutional discussion in England and America in the eighteenth century.

Locke wrote:

> In all Cases, whilst the Government subsists, *the Legislative is the Supream Power*. For what can give Laws to another, must needs be superior to him: and since the Legislative is no otherwise Legislative of the Society, but by the right it has to make Laws for all the parts and for every Member of the Society, prescribing Rules to their actions, and giving power of Execution, where they are transgressed, the *Legislative* must needs be the *Supream*, and all other Powers in any Members or parts of the Society, derived from and subordinate to it. (*104*, 385–86)

There are two other powers of government.

> But because the Laws, that are at once, and in a short time made, have a constant and lasting force, and need a *perpetual Execution*, or an attendance thereunto: Therefore 'tis necessary there should be a *Power always in being*, which should see to the *Execution* of the Laws that are made, and remain in force. And thus the *Legislative* and *Executive* Power come often to be separated.
>
> There is another Power in every Commonwealth, which one may call *natural*, because it answers to the Power every Man naturally had before he entered into Society. For though in a Commonwealth the Members of it are distinct Persons still in reference to one another, and as such as governed by the Laws of Society; yet in reference to the rest of Mankind, they make one Body, which is, as every Member of it before was, still in the State of Nature with the rest of Mankind. Hence it is, that the Controversies that happen between any Man of the Society with those that are out of it, are managed by the publick; and an injury done to a Member of their Body, engages in whole in the reparation of it. So that

under this Consideration, the whole community is one Body in the State of Nature, in respect of all other States of Persons out of its Community.

This therefore contains the Power of War and Peace, Leagues and Alliances, and all the Transactions, with all Persons and Communities without the Commonwealth, and may be called *Federative*, if any one pleases. So the thing be understood, I am indifferent to the name. (*104*, 382)

The executive power may be placed in the hands of several persons or of one, who may also have a share in the legislative power. But he is merely the "*Supream Executor* of the Law," and if he violates law "and acts by his own private Will, he degrades himself, and is but a single private person without power, and without Will, that has any right to *Obedience*; the Members owing no Obedience but to the publick Will of the Society." (*104*, 386)

Locke, although he, like Lilburne, believed that "the Ruling Power ought to govern by *declared* and *received Laws*, and not by extemporary Dictates and undetermined Resolutions" (*104*, 378), trusted the legislative supremacy to accomplish this result. (*104*, 387)

There was one feature of the Stuart constitution that Locke felt unable to disavow. The King had long claimed a "prerogative" to act outside—that is, contrary to—the law in cases of necessity. Locke wrote that

there is a latitude left to the Executive power, to do many things of choice, which the Laws do not prescribe. . . . (*104*, 393)

The old Question will be asked, in this matter of *Prerogative*, But *who shall be Judge* when this Power is made a right use of? I answer: Between an Executive Power in being, and a Legislative that depends upon his will for their convening, there can be no *Judge on Earth*: As there can be none, between the Legislative, and the People, should either the Executive, or the Legislative, when they have got the Power in their hands, design, or go about to enslave, or destroy them. The People have no other remedy in this, as in all other cases where they have no Judge on Earth, but to *appeal to Heaven*. (*104*, 397)

It may strike the reader that Locke made a bad choice in granting a prerogative to violate the law for the public good and leaving no remedy for abuse of this power other than revolution. The inconveniences of the absence of prerogative are surely outweighed by the inconveniences of revolution. But the alternatives were those suggested by seventeenth-century English history. As we shall see, American law has made a better choice than either.

The federative power survived as a distinct power only until Montesquieu. The judicial power as a third power of government appears to owe its origin to the course of events in the struggle between King and Lords, and also to the King. But the King could control the advice of Lords, and its decisions in lawsuits, by appointing pliant judges and removing those who proved obdurate, for the judges' commissions appointed them only *durante beneplacito*, to hold office at the King's pleasure, rather than *quam diu se bene gesserint*, while they conducted themselves well. This of course allowed the King to decide constitutional disputes in his own favor. The independence of the judiciary was not insured until the passage of the Act of Settlement in 1701. This act provided that "judges' commissions be made *quam diu se bene gesserint*, and their salaries ascertained and established, but upon the addresses of both houses of parliament it may be lawful to remove them. . . ."* The act did not deny that the judges were executive officers but passed on the assumption that special considerations should guarantee them security of tenure.

Montesquieu spent eighteen months in England between 1729 and 1731. There he became acquainted with English political doctrine—the political value of liberty, the separation of powers, the mixed state. These he worked into *The Spirit of Laws*, which was published in 1748. He rather muddled the subject. (*106*, 201–3) He begins with Locke's threefold division of powers: legislative, executive, and federative; but the federative power—the executive power in matters governed by the law of nations—disappears from Montesquieu's discussion almost immediately, and the executive power proper is subdivided.[1] This gives us our present threefold analysis of powers. The political value of liberty requires that these three be separated.

> When the legislative and executive powers are united in the same person, or in the same body of magistracy, there can be no liberty; because apprehensions may arise, lest the same monarch or senate should enact tyrannical laws, to execute them in a tyrannical manner.
>
> Again, there is no liberty, if the power of judging be not separated from the legislative and executive powers. Were it joined with the legislative, the life and liberty of the subject would be exposed to arbitrary control; for the judge would then be the legislator. Were it joined to the executive power, the judge might behave with all the violence of an oppressor. (*116*, 202)

---

[1] In the *Essex Result*, reporting the action of the County of Essex in 1778 in rejecting a proposed constitution for Massachusetts, the delegates spoke of the legislative and judicial powers and observed:

The executive power is sometimes divided into the external executive and internal executive. The former comprehends war, peace, the sending and receiving ambassadors, and whatever concerns the transactions of the state with any other independent state. The confederation of the United States hath lopped off this branch of the executive, and place it in Congress. We have therefore only to consider the internal executive power, which is employed in the peace, security and protection of the subject and his property, and in the defence of the state. The executive power is to marshal and command her militia and armies for her defence, to enforce the law, and to carry into execution all the orders of the legislative powers. (*72*, 337)

Lilburne's primary motive for the separation of powers was to insure impartiality: the legislature should be confined to the making of general rules, and the executive to the enforcement of these rules. Locke shared this view, but his principal purpose in separating the executive from the legislature was to make the King subject to the representative body, the Parliament. The first paragraph quoted from Montesquieu suggests Lilburne's view, but not clearly. Montesquieu may be repeating an English political axiom without thoroughly understanding it. Nor is he clear on the judicial power. He begins by putting it in the hands of the prince or magistrate but then separates it, lest the judge "behave with all the violence of an oppressor." Then he goes on to place the judicial power not in the hands of the magistrate, but in the control of a jury. And he concludes the whole discussion by saying: "Of the three powers above-mentioned the judiciary is *en quelque facon nulle* [in a way nothing]. There remain therefore only two; and as they have need of a regulating power to temper them, the part of the legislative body composed of the nobility, is extremely proper for this very purpose." (*116*, 206) Montesquieu then expatiates on the virtues of British mixed monarchy, where the executive power is in the King, and the legislative power in the King and a bicameral Parliament.

In his *Commentaries on the Laws of England*, Sir William Blackstone used the idea of checks and balances and the seventeenth-century twofold separation of powers, joined with the rule that counseled the independence of the judiciary. In his famous argument in the *Case of Writs of Assistance* in 1761, James Otis employed the same analysis and said that the "executive courts" must pass into disuse acts of Parliament that violated the British constitution. (*243*, 199) The first New Hampshire constitution, of 1776, spoke of the "executive courts." As late as 1827 Chief Justice John Marshall spoke of "the judicial power as part of the executive."

But Montesquieu's was the dominant analysis in America. The first constitutions of Virginia, Maryland, North Carolina, Georgia, and Massachu-setts, and the second constitution of New Hampshire, decreed that the legislative, executive, and judicial powers were and should remain distinct. This was more easily decreed than accomplished. In his *Notes on the State of Virginia*, first published in 1785, Thomas Jefferson, a former governor of the state, complained of "very capital defects" in the constitution. The principal defect was the fact that the constitution had been adopted by the legislature, and its provisions might be altered by any subsequent act of the legislature.

> The judiciary and the executive were left dependent on the legislative, for their subsistence in office, and some of them for their continuance in it. If therefore the legislature assumes executive and judiciary powers, no opposition is likely to be made; nor, if made, can it be effectual; because in that case they may put their proceedings into the form of an act of assembly, which will render them obligatory on the other branches. They have, accordingly, in many instances, decided rights which should

have been left to judicial controversy: and the direction of the executive, during the whole time of their session, is becoming habitual and familiar. (*86*, 120)

To remedy this defect, Jefferson proposed that "the powers of government should be so divided and balanced among several bodies of magistracy, as that no one could transcend their legal limits, without being effectually checked and restrained by the others." So Jefferson called in checks and balances—not, as previously, of social classes, but of govern-mental institutions—to safeguard the separation of powers. Madison adopted the same argument in No. 48 of the *Federalist*, describing the arrangements he thought would perhaps accomplish the desired result. (*34*, 332) The executive, legislative, and judicial officers should draw their authority from the people through channels having no communication with one another; the method of choosing the judiciary, however, offered difficulties. The legislature should consist of two branches chosen by different methods of election; perhaps the weaker branch of the legislature, the Senate, should have "some qualified connection" with the executive to assist it in defending its rights against the more popular branch of the legislature. In addition, the executive should have a "qualified veto" over acts of legislation. To these internal checks of the national government he added the states as further checks, and he revived the argument of No. 10 of the *Federalist*: in an extensive republic, interests would be so numerous that a tyrannical majority would not come into existence.

In No. 78 of the *Federalist* Alexander Hamilton completed the argument on checks and balances. In a discussion of the judiciary he quoted Montesquieu, "There is no liberty, if the power of judging be not separated from the legislative and executive powers." In a constitution that limits legislative power, the judiciary must pronounce legislative acts contrary to the constitution as void, for the constitution is a fundamental law, and the courts must prefer it to a statute inconsistent with it. Jefferson had expressed the same opinion two years earlier in his answer to the inquiries of Jean Nicolas Démeunier, who was compiling an article on the United States for the *Encyclopédie Méthodique*. Repeating his complaint that people considered the constitution of Virginia an ordinary statute because it had been created by the legislature, and therefore many laws inconsistent with the constitution had been passed, Jefferson said, "I have not heard that in the other states they have ever infringed their constitutions; and I suppose they have not done it; as the judges would consider any law void, which was contrary to the constitution." (*87*, X, 18 & XIV, 658)

Like Madison, Jefferson believed that "the tyranny of the legislature is the most formidable dread at present." (*87*, XIV, 661) But at the Constitutional Convention of 1787 the liveliest apprehension centered on the executive. The Convention began its task with a consideration of the Virginia plan presented by Governor Edmund Randolph of Virginia. This called for a National Executive chosen by the National Legislature, but it did not specify as to whether the executive should consist of one or several persons. Randolph, however, "opposed a unity" in the executive. He regarded it as "the foetus of monarchy." (53, I, 66) James Wilson, the most vigorous champion of placing the executive power in a single person, argued, "Unity in the Executive instead of being the foetus of Monarchy would be the best safeguard against tyranny." The New Jersey plan provided for a collegial executive, but the plan offered by Charles Pinckney of South Carolina called for a President. At various times during the Convention, Randolph and George Mason spoke for a collegial executive but lost on two votes. (53, I, 96 & II, 22) However, some of the most influential members of the Convention favored associating a council with the President. The Virginia plan had proposed a Council of Revision to exercise a qualified veto over legislation. This was not adopted, but James Madison, Benjamin Franklin, Gouverneur Morris, Elbridge Gerry, Roger Sherman, and John F. Mercer spoke for an executive council or Privy Council or Council of State. There was no agreement on the composition of the body or its powers. Most of the members seem to have thought of it as advisory, but Madison would have given the President "liberty to depart from their Opinion at his peril." (53, I, 70) Morris would have created a Council of State composed of the chief justice and the secretaries of named departments. (53, II, 343-44) His proposal shrank into the passage in Article II, Section 2 of the Constitution. "He [the President] may require the Opinion, in writing, of the principal Officer in each of the executive Departments, upon any Subject relating to the duties of their respective Offices. . . ."

In addition, the Convention gave the Senate participation in certain executive functions, namely treaty making and presidential appointments. The use of the Senate to perform part of the task intended for an executive council shocked some of the members of the Convention. Gerry, who was the first to propose an executive council, refused to sign the Constitution and justified his action in a letter to the presiding officers of the two houses of the Massachusetts legislature. Among his objections was "that the executive is blended with, and will have an undue influence over, the legislature." (53, III, 128) Among the faults that caused Randolph of Virginia to refuse to sign was "the substitution of the Senate in place of an Executive Council." (53, III, 135) The third nonsigner, Mason of Virginia, had many objections to the Constitution. Among other things he complained that "the President of the United States has no Constitutional Council, a thing unknown in any safe and regular government" (53, II, 638), and he expressed his apprehensions that the President "will become a tool to the Senate." Luther Martin of Maryland had no opportunity to sign, since he left the Convention fifteen days before adjournment, but he made a very hostile report to the Maryland legislature which included the assertion that the Senate, "being constituted a privy council to the President," could not be expected to convict the

President during impeachment. (53, III, 219)

Both checks and balances and the separation of powers were to a considerable degree frustrated by a circumstance that Madison had assured the country could not occur in an extensive country with a multiplicity of interests—the development of political parties. During the first Washington administration the Federalist party coalesced about the secretary of the treasury, Alexander Hamilton, and the Republican party about the secretary of state, Thomas Jefferson. Washington was re-elected without opposition, but the third presidential election, which was won by John Adams in 1796, was fought on party lines. The existence of parties transformed the framers' plan for choosing the President. The Constitution made a provision for a distinct electoral base for the executive, in order to preserve the separation of powers; if he were chosen by the national legislature, as was proposed early in the Convention, he would be dependent on it. Therefore each state was allotted a number of electors equal to the number of its senators and representatives; each elector was to vote for two men for President. The candidate with the most votes, if the number was a majority of the electors, should become President. But in the absence of a party system it was unlikely that any candidate after George Washington would have a majority. In case two candidates had a majority and an equal number of votes, the House of Representatives, with each state having one vote, should choose a President from those two. If there was no majority, the House should choose a President from the five highest on the list. After the President was chosen, the person with the largest number of votes was to be Vice-President. The electors were expected to exercise their best personal judgment, and consequently the possibility that no candidate would receive a majority of votes was very real. No doubt the framers expected that after the retirement of Washington the function of the electors would be primarily to nominate five candidates among whom the House of Representatives would choose.

But with the emergence of the two-party system, the caucus of the senators and representatives of each party began to nominate candidates, and the electors became the usual body for the election of the President; only twice in our history has the House of Representatives chosen a President. From 1796, when Jefferson was nominated by the congressional caucus of the Republican party, to 1824, the caucus was the most common instrument of nomination. It was an admirable device. The members of the caucus chose as a presidential candidate a leader of their party whom they knew and respected, a man with experience in national affairs. But the caucus system collapsed in 1824 because of the disappearance of the Federalist party. For the election of 1832 all parties nominated their candidates by national conventions, and this method has persisted. This threw the center of gravity in the nominating process to state political machines, which were dominated by men who had had no involvement in national government and who were likely to place the highest value on the candidate that would help them carry their states. Since popular election of the presidential electors was by now the usual method, presidential elections became popularity contests between the nominees of the two parties.

Presidents have made highly inflated claims regarding the significance of the popular vote. With less plausibility than many Presidents, James Buchanan asserted that the President "is the only direct representative on earth of the people of all and each of the sovereign States." (*182*, 209) The true meaning of this representative character was shown by the boast of Theodore Roosevelt, "Half my blood is Southern and I have lived in the West, so that I feel I can represent the whole country." (*199*, 44)

Commentators on the presidency have for the most part accepted and enlarged upon these self-characterizations. So Theodore C. Sorensen wrote: "For only one man under our system is President. Only one man bears all the burdens of responsibility. Only one man, with his running mate, is accountable to all the people." And he says of the President's advisors, "Their views and visions of where the world is moving are far less grand than his." (*203*, 82) Reviewing the similar claims of Charles Evans Hughes as governor of New York, Edward Stanwood asked: "But after all is it not the argument for a 'good despot'? If despots had all been good, mankind would never have invented and established republics." (*205*, 333)

The President has become more than the executor of the laws; he is now the leader of a party and of the nation. There have been similar developments in other countries—Amaury de Riencourt has written of an evolution toward executive aggrandisement of power in *The Coming Caesars*. (*41*) But our system of checks and balances has thus far proved to be an insuperable obstacle to the permanence of American Caesarism.

Attempts have been made to revive the Stuart conception of an emergency power of the King, which John Locke recognized under the name of prerogative. In his dissenting opinion in the *Steel Seizure Case*, Chief Justice Fred Vinson spoke vaguely of "the leadership contemplated by the Framers" and claimed a limited emergency power for the President. "With or without statutory authorization, Presidents have at such times dealt with national emergencies by acting promptly and resolutely to enforce legislative programs, at least to save those programs until Congress could act."* In 1971 Secretary of State William P. Rogers asserted that "in emergency situations, the President has the power and responsibility to use the armed forces to protect the nation's security." (*185*, 1194, 1197) The only evidence he cites is the framers' agreement that under the Constitution the President might use the armed forces to repel a sudden attack on the United States, since such an attack would initiate a state of war without a congressional joint resolution.

Of course the existence of an emergency does not redistribute the powers of government allocated by the Constitution. In 1869, Justice Samuel Miller held that the action of the secretary of war (imputed to the President)—accepting without statutory authority bills of exchange in order to buy necessary supplies for the army—was illegal. Miller remarked, "We have no officers in this government from the President down to the most subordinate agent, who does not hold office under the law, with prescribed duties and limited authority."* The two dissenting justices argued that the statute authorizing the secretary to make contracts implicitly authorized him to accept the bills. Miller also wrote the unanimous opinion in *United States v. Lee*, decided in 1882, an ejection action against two army officers in possession of the Lee estate in Virginia. Miller said:

> Shall it be said, in the face of all this, . . . that the courts cannot give remedy when the citizen has been deprived of his property by force, his estate seized and converted to the use of the government without any lawful authority, because the president has ordered it and his officers are in possession? If such be the law, it sanctions a tyranny which has no existence in the monarchies of Europe, nor in any other government which has a just claim to well-regulated liberty and the protection of personal rights.*

And in 1935, in *Schechter Poultry Corp. v. United States*, Chief Justice Charles Evans Hughes said for eight justices (the ninth wrote a separate, concurring opinion), "Extraordinary conditions do not create or enlarge governmental power."*

Of course it is true that a government of limited and divided powers does not grant an instant decision for every question that anyone, or even a large number of people, may believe requires instant decision. The price we pay for renouncing autocracy is the absence of autocracy.

Locke's prerogative, the "power to act according to discretion, for the publick good, without the prescription of the Law, and sometimes even against it," if it had endured, would have overthrown his whole system. Albert V. Dicey described the solution to problems of emergency that eventually emerged in English law: "There are times of tumult and invasion when for the sake of legality itself the rules must be broken. The course which the government must then take is clear. The ministry must break the law and trust for protection to an act of immunity." (*44*, 513–14)

American law followed the same course. The first decision was the case of the *Appollon*, decided unanimously in 1824 by the Supreme Court in an opinion by Justice Joseph Story.* In 1820 Congress had levied a tonnage duty on French vessels. The *Appollon* was a French ship bound for Charleston, but on arrival off the port of Charleston the master learned that Congress had imposed the duty. He therefore sailed for Amelia Island, in Spanish territory, intending "to transship his cargo into the United States, and to receive from thence a cargo of cotton, without subjecting himself to the payment of the French tonnage duty." The collector of the port of St. Mary's caused the *Appollon* to be seized while in Spanish waters and brought to St. Mary's. The master of the vessel sued the collector for damages and recovered. Justice Story wrote:

> It cannot, however, escape observation, that this court has a plain path of duty marked out for it, and that is, to administer the law as it finds it. . . . Whatever may be the rights of the government, upon principles of the law of nations, to redress wrongs of this nature, and whatever the power of Congress to pass suitable laws to cure any defects in the present system, our duty lies in a more narrow compass; and we must administer the laws as they exist, without straining them to reach public mischiefs which they were never designed to remedy. It may be fit and proper for the government, in the exercise of the high discretion confided to the Executive, for great public purposes, to act on a sudden emergency, or to prevent an irreparable mischief, by summary measures which are not found in the text of laws. Such measures are properly matters of state, and if the responsibility is taken, under justifiable circumstances, the legislature will doubtless apply a proper indemnity.*

The Prize Cases, decided in 1863, upheld the blockade of southern ports proclaimed by President Lincoln in 1861. Having held that the "sudden attack" of the seceding states instituted a state of war in which the President's action was constitutionally justified, Justice Robert Grier said:

> If it were necessary to the technical existence of a war, that it should have a legislative sanction, we find it in almost every Act passed at the extraordinary session of the Legislature of 1861. . . . And finally, in 1861 we find Congress "*ex majore cautela*," and in anticipation of such astute objections, passing an Act "approving, legalizing and making valid all the acts, proclamations, and orders of the President, &c., as if they had been done under the previous express authority and direction of the Congress of the United States."
>
> Without admitting that such an Act was necessary under the circumstances, it is plain that if the President had in any manner assumed powers which it was necessary should have the authority or sanction of Congress, that on the well known principle of law, "*omnis ratihabitio et mandata equiparatur*," this ratification has operated to perfectly cure the defect.*

Limited retroactive acts of immunity were passed for the protection of Union soldiers during and after the Civil War and were upheld.* In 1913 the Supreme Court upheld the governor general of the Philippines in a damage suit by an alien whom he had unlawfully ordered deported because the territorial legislature had subsequently passed an act saying that his action was "approved and ratified and confirmed, and in all respects declared legal, and not subject to question or review." Justice Oliver Wendell Holmes said for a unanimous Court that

> it generally is recognized that in cases like the present, where the act originally purports to be done in the name and by the authority of the

state, a defect in that authority may be cured by the subsequent adoption of the act.*

There is, then, a solution to the problem of emergency. If the President believes that the necessity is sufficiently great, he should act illegally and look to Congress for ratification of his actions. He should not claim an emergency power to act against the law for the good of the nation, nor should he claim the exclusive right to determine what is good for the nation. In 1973 Congress administered a tardy rebuke for the actions of two Presidents in the War Powers Resolution, which reads in part:

> The constitutional powers of the President as Commander-in-Chief to introduce United States Armed Forces into hostilities, or into situations where imminent involvement in hostilities is clearly indicated by the circumstances, are exercised only pursuant to (1) a declaration of war, (2) specific statutory authorization, or (3) a national emergency created by attack upon the United States, its territory or possessions, or its armed forces.*

Chapter 2

THE WAR CLAUSE

The War Clause of the Constitution reads, "The Congress shall have power . . . To declare war, grant letters of marque and reprisal, and make rules concerning captures on land and water. . . ." The corresponding provision of the Articles of Confederation, under which the United States was governed from March 2, 1781, to 1789, said, "The United States in Congress assembled shall have the sole and exclusive power of determining on peace and war, except in the cases mentioned in the sixth article. . . ." The sixth article authorized the states to engage in war only if invaded or menaced with invasion by an Indian tribe.

On May 29, 1787, Governor Randolph of Virginia presented to the Constitutional Convention a plan for a constitution in fifteen numbered paragraphs. The seventh paragraph proposed "that a National Executive be instituted" and that the Executive "ought to enjoy the Executive rights vested in Congress by the Confederation." (53, I, 21) The Convention resolved itself into a committee of the whole to consider the Randolph plan. When the proposal to give the National Executive the executive powers possessed by the Continental Congress came before the Convention as a resolution on June 1, Charles Pinckney objected that "the Executive powers of [the existing] Congress might extend to peace & war which would render the Executive a Monarchy, of the worst kind, towit an elective one." (53, I, 65) James Wilson reassured him, "Making peace and war are generally determined by writers on the Laws of Nations to be legislative powers." (53, I, 73–74) James Madison conceded that the war power was legislative, but he nevertheless thought the resolution too broad. Rufus King noted: "Mad: agrees wth. Wilson in his definition of executive powers—executive powers ex vi termini, do not

include the Rights of war & peace &c. but the powers should confined and
defined—if large we shall have the Evils of elective Monarchies. . . ." (*53*,
I, 70) Randolph did not defend his resolution but directed his advocacy to
a plural executive. "A unity of the Executive he observed would savor too
much of a monarchy." (*53*, I, 74) The resolution was not brought to a vote.
Nevertheless the interchange seems to show a consensus that "determining
on war"—which can only mean a decision to initiate war—was a legislative power.

Accordingly, the Committee of Detail distributed a printed draft
constitution on August 6 providing, "The legislature of the United States shall
have the power . . . To make war. . . ." When this clause came up for
debate on August 17, Pinckney opposed vesting the power in Congress;
proceedings would be too slow. "The Senate would be the best depositary,
being more acquainted with foreign affairs, and most capable of proper
resolutions." Pierce Butler said that "he was for vesting the power in the
President, who will have all the requisite qualities, and will not make war
but when the Nation will support it." This drew from Elbridge Gerry the
rejoinder that he "never expected to hear in a republic a motion to empower
the Executive alone to declare war." (*53*, II, 318) Butler's motion received
no second.

Butler was the only member of the Convention ever to suggest that the
President should be given the power to initiate war. But Madison and Gerry
were not quite satisfied with the proposal of the Committee of Detail that
the legislature be given the power to make war. They moved to substitute
declare for *make*, "leaving to the Executive the power to repel sudden attacks."
The meaning of the motion was clear. The power to initiate war was left to
Congress, with the reservation that the President need not await authorization from Congress to repel a sudden attack on the United States. The
reservation on sudden attacks met with general approbation, but there was
a difference of opinion as to whether the change of language effected the
desired result. Roger Sherman of Connecticut opined: "The Executive shd.
be able to repel and not to commence war. 'Make' much better than 'declare'
the latter narrowing the power [of the Legislature] too much." (*53*, II, 318)
The records of the Convention noted that George Mason of Virginia "was
agst giving the power of war to the Executive, because not [safely] to be
trusted with it; or to the Senate, because not so constructed as to be entitled
to it. He was for clogging rather than facilitating war; but he was for
facilitating peace. He preferred '*declare*' to '*make*.' " Madison's motion was
carried by a vote of seven states to two. Then King observed that the verb
make might be interpreted as authorizing Congress not only to initiate but
also to conduct war, and Connecticut changed its vote, so that the verb *declare*
was adopted by a vote of eight to one. (*53*, II, 319n)

This is all the information we have on the debate. On the same day
Congress was given the power to "make rules concerning captures on land

and water," and on September 5 it was given the power to "grant letters of marque and reprisal." This completed the war clause.

The declaration of war in 1812 said, "That war be and the same is declared to exist between the United Kingdom of Great Britain and Ireland and the dependencies thereof, and the United States of America and their territories. . . ."* The same form was followed in all subsequent declarations of general war.

Emerich de Vattel, the most influential writer on the law of nations—which we call international law—at the time of the adoption of the Constitution, called such a declaration a "declaration of war pure and simple." (*43*, 254) It was desirable because it gave notice to the adversary, to neutral nations, and to the subjects of the sovereign initiating the war. It ought properly to be preceded by a "conditional declaration of war"—an ultimatum demanding the satisfaction of grievances—which would first offer an alternative to war. (*43*, 254–57) But it was possible to enter into the state of war without making either a conditional declaration or a declaration pure and simple. The state under attack was automatically at war. And by omitting the declaration, the attacking state gained the advantage of surprise.

The Dutch jurist Cornelius Van Bynkershoek, writing in 1737, said:

> Writers on the law of nations have laid down various elements that are essential in a lawful war, and among these is the requirement that a war should be openly declared either by a special proclamation or by sending a herald; and this opinion accords with the practices of the modern nations of Europe. (*227*, 18)

But compliance with this practice, he said, was "not demanded by any exigency of reason." "War may begin by a declaration, but it may also begin by mutual hostilities." (*227*, 19) In 1779, in the case of the *Maria Magdalena*, the British High Court of Admiralty held that the fact of hostilities made war.

> Where is the difference, whether a war is proclaimed by a Herald at the Royal Exchange, with his trumpets, and on the Pont Neuf at Paris, and by reading and affixing a printed paper on public buildings; or whether war is announced by royal ships, and whole fleets, at the mouths of cannon? . . . If learned authorities are to be quoted, Bynkershoek has a whole chapter to prove, from the history of Europe, that a lawful and perfect state of war may exist without proclamation.[1]

---

[1]Hay & M. 247, 252–53, 165 Eng. Repr. 57, 58. Great Britain and the United States, 36 Stat. 2259, 2271 (1910), with thirty-six other countries, have ratified or adhered to the Third Convention of the Second Hague Conference. Article I reads, "The Contracting Powers recognize that hostilities between them must not commence without previous and explicit warning, in the form either of a reasoned declaration of war or of an ultimatum with conditional declaration of war."

Whether the United States shall remain passive under these progressive usurpations and these accumulating wrongs, or, opposing force to force in defense of their national rights, shall commit a just cause into the hands of the Almighty Disposer of Events, avoiding all connections which might entangle it in the contest or views of other powers, and preserving a constant readiness to concur in an honorable reestablishment of peace and friendship, is a solemn question which the Constitution wisely confides to the legislative department of the Government. In recommending it to their early deliberations I am happy in the assurance that the decision will be worthy the enlightened and patriotic councils of a virtuous, a free, and a powerful nation.[3]

The acts of war—impressment of seamen and seizure of vessels—of which Madison complained would justify a declaration of war but did not in themselves amount to a generalized institution of hostilities, like the invasion that Justice Paterson had postulated. In the case of both war and acts of war, the American forces involved have the right at international law to defend themselves. But only in a state of war, whether initiated by hostile invasion or by congressional declaration, does the President have the right to go beyond self-defense and initiate offensive action.[4] There is reason for the distinction. In the case of individual acts of war, such as the seizure of a seaman or a ship, nothing is lost by resorting to diplomacy and delaying

---

[3]*181*, I, 489–90. The joint resolution declaring war against Germany in 1917, 40 Stat. 1, reads:

Whereas the Imperial German Government has committed repeated acts of war against the Government and the people of the United States of America: Therefore, be it

Resolved . . . That the state of war between the United States and the Imperial German Government which has thus been thrust upon the United States is hereby formally declared; and that the President be, and he is hereby, authorized and directed to employ the entire naval and military forces of the United States to carry on war against the Imperial German Government. . . .

[4]In the War Powers Resolution, 87 Stat. 555 (1973), Congress confused wars with acts of war. The resolution declares that the President has constitutional authority to introduce the armed forces into hostilities only pursuant to a declaration of war or specific statutory authorization or when there exists "a national emergency created by attack upon the United States, its territories or possessions, or its armed forces." If the third contingency contemplates only a "sudden attack" that launches a general war, as the expression "national emergency" implies, then the President is forbidden to resist a limited military stroke, an act of war, like the attack of the *Leopard* on the *Chesapeake*. But it is well settled that he may practice self-defense in such a case. On the other hand, if the rubric "national emergency" in the resolution includes both an act of war and invasion or a similar event that launches a general war, the President not only may repel an attack that is a mere act of war but also may respond with offensive war. But the Constitution does not permit him to initiate offensive war in response to an act of war without congressional authorization. Congress may not take away the President's constitutional power. Nor may it delegate its own constitutional power to the President by such a resolution; see Chapter 13.

a military response until Congress has acted. But when an enemy has launched a general war, as by invasion, it may be necessary to meet this danger by immediate recourse to all the practices of war that international law and municipal law permit. This does not mean that there is no role for Congress to play in such a case. The President's power to respond to a sudden attack with offensive war amounting to general war is an emergency power which exists only by virtue of the suddenness of the attack, and it is for Congress to take over the direction of policy as soon as possible. This distinction between an act of war and an invasion that institutes general war is illustrated by two events in American history.

During the first administration of Thomas Jefferson, the pasha of Tripoli made demands for tribute from the United States, and after various acts of harassment he declared war on May 14, 1801. On May 21, 1801, before he learned of this, President Jefferson had written the pasha that he was sending a "squadron of observation" to the Mediterranean "to superintendent the safety of our commerce, and to exercise our seamen in martial duties"; "we mean to rest the safety of our commerce on the resources of our own strength and bravery in every sea." (222, 135) The ships were instructed not to initiate hostilities, but two Tripolitan ships were blockaded in Gibraltar.[5] Attacked by a Tripolitan vessel, Captain Sterrett of the *Enterprise* reduced the Tripolitan ship to a shambles; then he disarmed and released it. In his first annual message to Congress on December 8, 1801, Jefferson observed:

> To this state of general peace with which we have been blessed, only one exception exists. Tripoli, the least considerable of the Barbary States, had come forward with demands unfounded either in right or in compact, and had permitted itself to denounce war on our failure to comply before a given day. The style of the demand admitted but one answer. I sent a small squadron of frigates into the Mediterranean, with assurances to that power of our sincere desire to remain in peace, but with orders to protect our commerce salutary. The Bey had already declared war. His cruisers were out. Two had arrived at Gibraltar. Our commerce in the Mediterranean was blockaded and that of the Atlantic in peril. The arrival of our squadron dispelled the danger. One of the Tripolitan cruisers having fallen in with and engaged the small schooner *Enterprise* . . . was captured, after a heavy slaughter of her men, without the loss of a single

[5]Although the ships were instructed not to "initiate" hostilities, they were given authority to determine if the situation warranted offensive responses to Tripoli's "declaring war or committing hostilities." If Commodore Richard Dale discovered that Tripoli and the other Barbary powers had declared war on the United States, he was instructed to "chastise their insolence—by sinking, burning, or destroying their ships and vessels wherever you shall find them." *Naval Documents Related to the United States War with the Barbary Powers*, quoted in Sofaer, *201*, 210. Sofaer concludes that "the orders to Dale seem to permit the squadron to capture and destroy ships that attacked American commerce even if war had not been declared, and the statement in the orders that prisoners be put ashore suggests that the capture and destruction of vessels were contemplated."

one on our part. . . . Unauthorized by the Constitution, without the sanction of Congress, to go beyond the line of defense, the vessel, being disabled from committing further hostilities, was liberated with its crew. The Legislature will doubtless consider whether, by authorizing measures of offense also, they will place our force on an equal footing with that of its adversaries. I communicate all material information on this sub-ject, that in the exercise of this important function confided by the Constitution to the Legislature exclusively their judgment may form itself on a knowledge and consideration of every circumstance of weight.[6]

Alexander Hamilton made a violent attack on Jefferson's legal theory. He focused his argument on the release of the Tripolitan ship.

It will readily be allowed, that the constitution of a particular country may limit the organ charged with the direction of the public force, in the use or application of that force, even in time of actual war; but nothing short of the strongest negative words, of the most express prohibitions, can be admitted to restrain that organ from so employing it, as to de-prive the fruits of actual victory, by making prisoners of the persons and detaining the property of a vanquished enemy. Our Constitution, happily, is not chargeable with so great an absurdity. The framers of it would have blushed at a provision, so repugnant to good sense, so inconsistent with national safety and convenience. That instrument has only provided affirmatively, that, "the Congress shall have power to declare war"; the plain meaning of which is, that it is the peculiar and exclusive province of Congress, *when the nation is at peace*, to change that state into a state of war; whether from calculations of policy, or from provocations or injuries received; in other words, it belongs to Congress only, *to go to war*. But when a foreign nation declares or openly and avowedly makes war upon the United States, they are then by the very fact *already at war*, and any declaration on the part of Congress is nugatory; it is at least unnecessary. . . .

Till the Congress should assemble and declare war, which would require time, our ships might, according to the hypothesis of the message, be sent by the President to fight those of the enemy as often as they should be attacked, but not to capture and detain them; if beaten, both vessels and crews would be lost to the United States; if successful, they could only disarm those they had overcome, and must suffer them to return to the place of common rendezvous, there to equip anew, for the purpose

[6]*181*, IV, 314–15. Jefferson's account to Congress was less than candid. Captain Sterrett had been instructed by Commodore Dale to capture any vessel he engaged on his return trip from Malta to the squadron's station off Tripoli. He had been warned, however, that on the way to Malta he should avoid actions that would deplete the ship's meager water supply. Despite his receipt of a full report from Sterrett and Dale, Jefferson did not make available to Congress materials that would have indicated that Sterrett had been authorized to take offensive measures and that the release of the Tripolitan vessel was a purely tactical decision. See Sofaer, *201*, 211–13.

of resuming their depredations on our towns and our trade. (71, VIII, 249–52)

Hamilton's complaint seems to have been a partisan effort to score at the President's expense. By 1798 he himself had adopted the Jeffersonian position. American shipping had repeatedly been seized by the French. On April 27, 1798, Congress had provided for enlarging the navy, and apparently Secretary of War James McHenry, who was eager for war with France, had asked Hamilton whether this action would justify the President in under-taking naval hostilities. On May 17 Hamilton had replied:

> Not having seen the law which provides the *naval armament*, I cannot tell whether it gives any new power to the President; that is, any power whatever with regard to the employment of the ships. If not, and he is left at the foot of the Constitution, as I understand to be the case, I am not ready to say that he has any other power than merely to employ the ships as convoys, with authority to *repel* force by *force* (but not to capture) and to repress hostilities within our waters, including a marine league from our coasts. Anything beyond this must fall under the idea of *reprisals*, and required the sanctions of that department which is to declare *or make war*. (71, X, 281–82)

Jefferson's position seems to have been correct. The Tripolitan attack ended with the defeat of the vessel, which did not raise a continuing threat, as a sudden invasion would have done. Consequently it was constitutionally mandatory for the President in 1801, as in 1798, to refer the question of whether a past .event should be made the occasion for war to "that department which is to declare *or make war*."

The question of the President's power in the case of a sudden attack that precipitated general war came before the Supreme Court for the first time in *The Prize Cases* in 1863.* On February 8, 1861, the Confederate States of America was established. On April 12 Fort Sumter was attacked. On April 15 President Lincoln called out militia under his statutory authority. On April 17 the Confederate States began the issuance of letters of marque; on the same day President Lincoln proclaimed a blockade of the seven states that had seceded. On April 30 he extended the blockade to Virginia and North Carolina, which had seceded in the meantime.

The Prize Cases were proceedings for the condemnation of a British vessel, the *Hiawatha*, and a Mexican vessel, the *Brilliante*, seized as neutral ships for violation of a blockade before the congressional authorization of the blockade on July 13, and of two Virginia vessels, the *Crenshaw* and the *Army Warwick*, seized as enemy property under the same circumstances. Justice Grier wrote the opinion of the Court upholding the blockade. He said:

> By the Constitution, Congress alone has the power to declare a national or foreign war. . . .
> If a war be made by invasion of a foreign nation, the President is not only authorized but bound to resist force, by force. He does not initiate

the war, but is bound to accept the challenge without waiting for any special legislative authority. And whether the hostile party be a foreign invader, or States organized in rebellion, it is none the less a war, although the declaration of it be *"unilateral."**

Justice Rensselaer Nelson wrote a dissenting opinion in the case of the *Hiawatha*, the argument of which covered all the seizures.

> . . . I am compelled to the conclusion that no civil war existed between this Government and the States in insurrection till recognized by the act of Congress 13th July, 1861; that the President does not possess the power under the Constitution to declare war or to recognize its existence within the meaning of the law of nations, which carries with it belligerent rights, and thus change the country and all its citizens from a state of peace to a state of war; that his power belongs exclusively to the Congress of the United States and, consequently, that the President of the United States had no power to set on foot a blockade under the law of nations, and the capture of the vessel and cargo in this case, and in all the cases before us in which the capture occurred before the 13th July, 1861, for breach of blockade, or as enemy property, are illegal and void, and that the decrees of condemnation should be reversed and the vessel and cargo restored.*

Until the act of July 13,* which not merely authorized a blockade but in effect declared that the seceding states were in a state of insurrection, there was for Nelson no civil war, for the President could not establish this legal status. There was a "personal war" against "the individuals engaged in resisting the authority of the government." In carrying on this war under the act of 1795,* which authorized him to use the militia, and the act of 1807,* which authorized him to use the land and naval forces to suppress insurrection, the President had acted properly in executing municipal law, but his actions had no effect at the law of nations. The act of Congress of July 13, however, converted the war against persons into a territorial war and also explicitly legitimized the blockade.

Chief Justice Roger B. Taney and Justices Nelson, John Catron, and Nathan Clifford dissented without opinion in the case of the *Brilliante*. This is perplexing. Although we have no record of votes to confirm it, we are entitled to conclude that all three accepted Nelson's opinion in the case of the *Hiawatha*, holding the seizure both of foreign vessels and of vessels owned by Virginians not shown to be disloyal illegal because Congress had not instituted a state of war. Justice Catron wrote on behalf of all four dissenters to James M. Carlisle on the day after his argument for the libellee in the case of the *Brilliante*, asking for a copy of this concluding speech to be included in the report of the case and expressing his own views.

> It is idle to disguise the fact that the claim set up to forfeit these ships and cargoes, *by the force of a proclimation* [*sic*], is not founded on constitutional power, but on a power assumed to be *created* by Military

necessity. *Necessity* is an old plea—old as the reign of Tibereas [*sic*]; its limits should be looked for in Tacitus. It is the commander's will. The End, we are told is to crush out the Rebellion; that the whole means are at the Presdt's discretion and that he is the sole Judge in the selection of the means to accomplish the End. This is a rejection of the Constitution with its limitations.[7]

This seems unrealistic. A large part of the territory of the United States had been occupied by a political organization which claimed sovereignty over this area and was attempting to expel the United States from it. The consequences were identical with those of a hostile invasion by a foreign power. The minority argued that until Congress had an opportunity to act, the President must allow this enemy access to the sea and must permit it to supply itself and to establish foreign credits for the prosecution of the war. In fact, rebellion had created a continuing emergency when Congress was not in session. When Congress convened, President Lincoln very properly referred the whole issue to Congress, which ratified and adopted his policies. The situation was not at all like the Tripolitan attack upon the American *Enterprise*, which raised a danger that disappeared at the end of the engagement.

The United States may enter into the state of war in only two ways: by a joint resolution or act of Congress, and by the declaration or invasion of an enemy. The President has no legal authority to initiate war. This was decided by a circuit court as early as 1806 in *United States v. Smith*. Colonel William S. Smith was alleged to have assisted a General Miranda to outfit an expedition in New York against the Spanish province of Caracas and was indicted under a statute that forbade setting on foot a military expedition against a nation with which the United States was at peace. Smith subpoenaed the secretary of state, the secretary of the navy, and two other officers. They refused to appear on the ground that the President had specifically told them that he could not dispense with their services at that time. Smith moved for an attachment to compel them to attend, making affidavit that he hoped to prove by the testimony of these witnesses that the expedition "was begun, prepared, and set on foot with the knowledge and approbation of the president of the United States, and with the knowledge and approbation of the secretary of state of the United States." Justice Paterson, sitting on circuit in New York, ruled for himself and District Judge Matthias B. Tallmadge that the trial should proceed without these witnesses because the testimony sought would be irrelevant.

> Supposing then that every syllable of the affidavit is true, of what avail can it be to the defendant on the present occasion? . . . Does it speak by way of justification? The president of the United States cannot control the statute, nor dispense with its execution, and still less can he authorize

[7]*Legal Historian*, 1 (1958), pp. 51–52.

a person to do what the law forbids. . . . Does he possess the power of making war? That power is exclusively vested in Congress. . . .

> There is a manifest distinction between our going to war with a nation at peace, and a war made against us by an actual invasion, or a formal declaration. In the former case, it is the exclusive province of Congress to change a state of peace into a state of war.[8]

Until 1950, no judge, no President, no legislator, no commentator ever suggested that the President had legal authority to initiate war. The controversialists who have introduced the novel theory supporting such authority have been obliged to revise the war clause. Several reinterpretations have been attempted.

In defending President Harry Truman's unauthorized entry into the Korean War, Senator Paul Douglas argued that large wars must be declared by Congress but that the President may initiate small wars.

> There is indeed good reason, besides the need for speed, why the President should have been permitted to use force in these cases without a formal declaration of war by Congress. That is because international situations frequently call for the retail use of force in localized situations which are not sufficiently serious to justify the wholesale and widespread use of force which a formal declaration of war would require.
>
> In other words, it may be desirable to create a situation which is half-way between complete peace, or the absence of all force, and outright war marked by the exercise of tremendous force on a wholesale scale. This is most notably the case when big powers deal with small countries, and in situations where only a relatively temporary application of force is needed to restore order and to remove the threat of aggression. It would be below the dignity of the United States to declare war on a

---

[8]United States v. Smith, 1196–97. Smith was acquitted by the jury, United States v. Smith, 27 F. Cas. 1233, 1245 (C.D.N.Y. 1806). On October 4, 1809, in a letter to the new Spanish minister, ex-President Jefferson said:

Your predecessor, soured on a question of etiquette against the administration of this country, wished to impute wrong to them in all their actions, even where he did not believe it himself. In this spirit, he wished it to be believed that we were in unjustifiable co-operation in Miranda's expedition. I solemnly, and on my personal truth and honor, declare to you that this was without foundation, and that there was neither co-operation, nor connivance on our part. He informed us that he was about to attempt the liberation of his native country from bondage, and intimated a hope of our aid, or connivance at least. He was at once informed, that although we had great cause of complaint against Spain, and even of war, yet whenever we should think proper to act as her enemy, it should be openly and above board, and that our hostility should never be exercised by such petty means. We had no suspicion that he expected to engage men here, but merely military stores. Against this there was not law, nor consequently any authority for us to interpose obstacles. On the other hand, we deemed it improper to betray his voluntary communication to Spain. (89, XII, 167)

pigmy state, but it might be necessary to apply force in such a case in order to prevent attacks on American lives and property.*

Similarly, Secretary of State William P. Rogers has suggested that unauthorized executive coercion of small countries might be validated by their defenselessness as, "there being no risk of major war, one could argue that there was no violation of Congress' power to declare war." (*185*, 1200) On this principle, the President might on his own initiative destroy the state of Israel with nuclear rockets because it has no powerful friends to resent the action.

Professor John Norton Moore suggested that "as a dividing line for presidential authority in the use of force abroad, one test might be to require congressional authorization in all cases where regular combat units are committed to sustained hostilities." (*121*, II, 814) Perhaps he wishes to permit the President to wage war with special forces, saboteurs, and mercenaries. But the existence of war does not depend on the table of organization of the armed forces. Moore may be thinking of episodic adventures as opposed to sustained combat, acts of war as opposed to war. Yet even acts of war may not be undertaken by the President without congressional authorization.

In defending President Lyndon Johnson's entry into war in Vietnam in a memorandum published in 1966, Leonard Meeker, the legal adviser of the State Department, argued that the President had a constitutional power to repel a sudden attack by North Vietnam on South Vietnam.

> In 1787 the world was a far larger place, and the framers probably had in mind attacks upon the United States. In the 20th century, the world has grown much smaller. An attack on a country far from our shores can impinge directly on the nation's security. In the SEATO Treaty, for example, it is formally declared that an armed attack against Vietnam would endanger the peace and safety of the United States. (*113*, 484)

It is not probable, but certain, that the sudden attack which Madison and Gerry would permit the President to repel was an attack upon the United States. When they attributed this power to him, they did not impute to him the right to intervene in any foreign war in which one state had attacked another. They did not give him the right to choose between war and peace, or the right to make a judgment concerning the security of the United States. They instead recognized that foreign countries are able to institute a state of war and provided for the President to act in the defense of the country until Congress could assemble and act under its constitutional war power.

Senator Barry Goldwater may have the most original interpretation of the war clause. He believes that when the Convention struck from the draft constitution the authorization of Congress to *make* war, "the Framers intended to leave the 'making of war' with the President."* If it wishes, Congress may declare (that is, announce) the war. Thus, the President is a sovereign, and Congress acts as herald to proclaim his action. This, of course, reverses the customary procedure by which Congress declares war, and the President then proclaims the existence of a state of war.

There are better authorities than these on the meaning of the war clause. After the Constitutional Convention had substituted the words *declare war* for *make war*, Butler "moved to give the Legislature power of peace, as they were to have that of war." (*53*, II, 319) Gerry seconded the motion, but it failed, undoubtedly because it would have curtailed the treaty power of the Senate. Butler described to the South Carolina legislature the Convention's rejection of Pinckney's motion to give "the sole power of making war and peace" to the Senate and then the rejection of his own motion to vest it in the President. "Some gentlemen were inclined to give this power to the President, but it was objected to, as throwing into his hands the influence of a monarch, having an opportunity of involving his country in a war whenever he wished to promote her destruction." (*53*, III, 250)

In 1787 Wilson, a member of the Constitutional Convention and one of the ablest lawyers of his day, assured the Pennsylvania ratifying convention:

> This system will not hurry us into war; it is calculated to guard against it. It will not be in the power of a single man, or a single body of men, to involve us in such distress; for the important power of declaring war is vested in the legislature at large: this declaration must be made with the concurrence of the House of Representatives: from this circumstance we may draw a certain conclusion that nothing but our national interest can draw us into a war. (*49*, II, 528)

In 1793 President Washington concluded that the treaty of alliance of 1778 with France did not bind the United States to defend French territory in America from Great Britain in the current war; he declared the United States neutral. Alexander Hamilton justified the neutrality proclamation in these terms:

> If the Legislature have a right to make war on the one hand—it is on the other the duty of the Executive to preserve Peace till war is declared; and in fulfilling that duty, it must necessarily possess a right of judging what is the nature of the obligations which the treaties of the Country impose on the Government; and when in pursuance of that right it has concluded that there is nothing in them inconsistent with a *state* of neutrality, it becomes both its province and its duty to enforce the laws incident to that state of the Nation. (*70*, XV, 40)

In reply James Madison argued that by construing a treaty dealing with war the President usurped the war power of Congress. This is rather captious, but it is noteworthy that both these delegates to the Convention agreed that it was for Congress alone to initiate war. Madison said:

> Every just view that can be taken of this subject admonishes the public of the necessity of a rigid adherence to the simple, the received, and the fundamental doctrine of the constitution, that the power to declare war,

including the power of judging of the causes of war, is *fully* and *exclusively* vested in the legislature; that the executive has no right, in any case, to decide the question, whether there is or is not cause for declaring war; that the right of convening and informing congress, whenever such a question seems to call for a decision, is all the right which the constitution has deemed requisite or proper; and that for such, more than for any other contingency, this right was specially given to the executive. (*111*, II, 642–43)

In 1803 Morris, who had helped give the Constitution its final shape, described the superior position of the Senate. "One important point, however, that of making war, was divided between the Senate and the House of Representatives." (*53*, III, 405)

William Paterson was a delegate to the Convention from New Jersey and was subsequently an associate justice of the Supreme Court. As we have seen, in the latter capacity he ruled in *United States v. Smith* in 1806 that "it is the exclusive province of congress to change a state of peace into a state of war." No delegate to the Convention, and no delegate to any state ratifying convention, gave a different interpretation to the war clause. These authorities, rather than modern theorists, should determine the proper constitutional interpretation of that clause.

Chapter 3

ACTS OF WAR

In an address on "The Control of the Foreign Relations of the United States," the most eminent American scholar in international law, John Bassett Moore, said:

> There is yet another question to which I feel obliged to advert, and that is the question of the President's power to use force in our foreign relations. By the constitution of the United States, the power to declare war is vested in the Congress. Sometimes orators and writers speak of "recognizing the existence of a state of war," as if this differed from declaring war; but the co-existence of the two phrases may be ascribed to motives of political strategy rather than to any belief or supposition that they denoted different legal conceptions. In reality the word "war" comprehends two meanings. It denotes (1) acts of war, and (2) the international condition of things called a "state of war." Acts of war do not always or necessarily develop into the general international condition of things called a state of war, but they are nevertheless war and involve the "making" of war in a legal sense.
>
> There can hardly be room for doubt that the framers of the constitution, when they vested in Congress the power to declare war, never imagined that they were leaving it to the executive to use the military and naval forces of the United States all over the world for the purpose of actually coercing other nations, occupying their territory, and killing their soldiers and citizens, all according to his own notion of the fitness of things, as long as he refrained from calling his action war or persisted in calling it peace. (*118*, V, 195–96)

In contrast to a state of war, an act of war is a self-contained episode to which the injured party has the right to respond with war. A number of considerations, one of which is of course the weakness of the injured party, may prevent retaliatory action. But an act of war, even when it can be perpetrated with impunity, does not cease to be an act of war.

The President does not have the right to initiate the state of war by offensive action. He may enter this state without congressional authorization only when it has been thrust upon the nation with an invasion, or conceivably other sudden attack, by a foreign state, under circumstances which give the President no opportunity to consult Congress. And he must consult Congress as soon as possible so that it can exercise its constitutional power whether to declare war or not.

Likewise, the President does not have the right to commit acts of war although, as we have seen, he may respond to acts of war with self–defense. Of course, the distinction between an offensive act of war and a defensive act of war might be significantly blurred by circumstances. In general practice, the distinction has been kept clear, except in the case of Mexico and the Central American and Caribbean states. Our conduct in those areas has been so lawless that William Howard Taft said, with some complacency, "The unstable condition as to law and order of some of the Central American Republics seems to create different rules of international law from those that obtain in governments that can be depended upon to maintain their own peace and order." (213, 95) Taft did not explain how the internal conditions in those states could alter the constitutional law of the United States.

Prominent among acts of war are military and naval attacks. But international law also recognizes as acts of war some actions that do not directly initiate hostilities. Those too are forbidden to the President. In our history the issue of presidential abstinence from acts of war has arisen most prominently in connection with recognition, reprisal, blockade, visitation and search on the high seas, and military trespass on foreign territory. Only these topics will be considered here.

Even where the Constitution does vest a power in the President, if exercising this power will be an act of war the President may not proceed without the concurrence of Congress. For example, the President's right to receive foreign ambassadors is merely ceremonial, but the reception of an ambassador is also a recognition of the sovereignty of the state represented. If the President receives the ambassador of a rebellious colony of a foreign state, he is recognizing the independence of the colony and thereby denying the sovereignty of the parent state. This is an act of war. Almost always, when the problem of war has been real, our Presidents have refused to recognize the independence of colonies without the consent of the war–making power, Congress. The commentators have regarded such consent as mandatory.

On March 25, 1818, Henry Clay introduced in the House of Representatives a bill appropriating funds to send a minister to the United Provinces of the Rio de la Plata when the President should deem it expedient.

> There was great reason, Mr. C. contended, from the peculiar character of the American Government, in there being a perfect

understanding between the legislative and Executive branches, in the acknowledgement of a new Power. Everywhere else the power of declaring war resided with the Executive. Here it was deposited with the Legislature. If, contrary to his opinion, there was even a risk that the acknowledgement of a new State might lead to war, it was advisable that the step should not be taken, without a previous knowledge of the will of the war–making branch.*

Henry St. George Tucker, who subsequently became a noted legal scholar and president of the Supreme Court of Appeals of Virginia, supported Clay. He explained that congressional participation was proper in the case of the rebellious Spanish colonies.

The action of the Executive *here* might have the effect of a declaration of war, which it is within the Constitutional powers of the Legislature alone to make. . . . How . . . embarrassing if, in the exercise of its constitutional powers [of recognition], the Executive should involve the nation in a war against the wishes of its Representatives.*

The bill encountered a number of objections and failed, but in a message on March 8, 1822, in response to a request from the House for information about the status of the former Spanish colonies, President James Monroe proposed that Congress concur with him in recognizing the new states by passing an appropriation act.

When the result of such a contest is manifestly settled, the new governments have a claim to recognition by other powers which ought not to be resisted. . . . The delay which has been observed in making a decision on this important subject will, it is presumed, have afforded an unequivocal proof to Spain, as it must have done to other powers, of the high respect entertained by the United States for her rights and of their determination not to interfere with them. . . .

In proposing this measure it is not contemplated to change thereby in the slightest manner our friendly relations with either of the parties, but to observe in all respects, as heretofore, should the war be continued, the most perfect neutrality between them. . . . Should Congress concur in the view herein presented, they will doubtless see the propriety of making the necessary appropriations for carrying it into effect. (*181*, I, 686–87)

On May 4, 1822, Congress appropriated $100,000 "for such missions to the independent nations of the American continent as the President of the United States may deem proper."*

In 1835 Texas declared its independence of Mexico. In 1836 the two houses of Congress passed separate resolutions recommending recognition of the Republic of Texas as soon as it should appear that it had "in successful operation a civil government capable of performing the duties and fulfilling the obligations of an independent power." (*119*, I, 98) In his message of

December 21, 1836, President Andrew Jackson took notice of these resolutions. He acknowledged the propriety of congressional participation in the invocation of a "power the exercise of which is equivalent, under some circumstances, to a declaration of war," but he recommended caution, since Mexico was by no means reconciled to the secession of Texas. (*119*, I, 100) In an appropriation act of March 3, 1837, Congress provided "for the outfit and salary of a diplomatic agent to be sent to the Republic of Texas, whenever the President of the United States may receive satisfactory evidence that Texas is an independent power, and shall deem it expedient to appoint such minister."* On March 7 President Martin Van Buren recognized Texas by the appointment of a chargé d'affaires.

In his annual message of December 7, 1875, President Ulysses Grant said that the state of affairs in Cuba did not warrant a recognition of the insurgents as an independent state or even as belligerents; moreover, either of these steps would lead "if not to abuses, certainly to collisions perilous to the peaceful relations" of the United States and Spain. (*181*, VI, 4293) President Grover Cleveland adopted the same position but made no reference to the relation between recognition and war. (*181*, VIII, 6151)

In his first annual message of December 6, 1897, President William McKinley quoted with approval President Grant's refusal to grant belligerent rights to the Cuban insurgents. (*181*, VIII, 6259) But on April 11, 1898, he reported to Congress that a "grave crisis" had arisen between the United States and Spain, principally as a result of the sinking of the *Maine*. He adverted to recognition and its relation to war. He did not recommend recognition, however, for another reason. He did not wish to endorse the existing Cuban political organization. Instead, he asked for war with Spain. (*181*, VIII, 6292)

President Theodore Roosevelt broke the earlier pattern. He was disgruntled at the delay of Colombia in ratifying the Hay–Herran treaty for the construction of the Panama Canal. With apparent foreknowledge of the Panamanian Revolution, he ordered three American warships—the day before the revolt—to insure freedom of transit across the isthmus. Marines were interposed to exclude Colombian troops, and Colombia was unable to subdue the rebellious province. On November 6, 1903, three days into the rebellion, Roosevelt recognized the sovereign state of Panama. In 1922 the United States agreed to pay Colombia twenty-five million dollars "to remove all misunderstandings growing out of the political events in Panama in November 1903."*

The practice of naval reprisal dates from the Middle Ages. When nationals of one state were plundered at sea by nationals of another state, the sovereign of the plundered ship might provide letters of marque and reprisal authorizing a recoupment of losses at the expense of whatever nationals of the offending state the ship should come across. By the seventeenth century it had become customary for states to augment their navies by issuing letters of marque and reprisal to privateers; these privately owned vessels were authorized to prey upon the shipping of the enemy, not for the purpose of recovering losses but for the sake of plunder. The practice of issuing letters of marque and reprisal was renounced by the signatories of the Declaration of Paris after the Crimean War in 1856 and subsequently by other states. This prohibition on privateering has in consequence attained the status of customary international law. (*131*, II, 460–61)

But reprisal also has a broader meaning. It is an official act of retaliation on another state, or on the nationals of another state, for some injury for which that state is held responsible. It may be a seizure of property to satisfy a claim, or it may be punitive, the infliction of a reciprocal injury. In the first case the reprisal is measured by the claim; in the latter case, it is equal to, or some multiple of, the original injury. Although the only form of reprisal assigned to Congress by the Constitution is the issuance of letters of marque and reprisal, every act of reprisal is an act of war and therefore requires congressional authorization.

In 1793 Secretary of State Thomas Jefferson wrote:

> The making of a reprisal on a nation is a very serious thing. Remonstrance and refusal of satisfaction ought to precede; and when reprisal follows, it is considered an act of war, and never failed to produce it in the case of a nation able to make war; besides, if the case were important and ripe for that step, Congress must be called upon to take it; the right of reprisal being expressly lodged with them by the Constitution, and not with the executive. (*119*, VII, 123)

In 1798 Alexander Hamilton advised Secretary of War James McHenry that the authorization of reprisals was an act of war and belonged to Congress. On March 3, 1799, Congress provided that if the President should find that American seamen impressed on the ships of the enemies of France and captured by the French were maltreated, he must cause "the most rigorous retaliation" to be inflicted on French prisoners.*

In 1825 President Monroe suggested that he be authorized to make reprisal on the property of the inhabitants of Spanish islands from which pirates raided American shipping, or to order pursuit on land or blockade, but Congress withheld authorization. (*181*, II, 848)

In 1834 President Jackson complained that France had not yet paid claims concededly due to Americans and asked Congress for power to make reprisals on French shipping if the French Chambers should not make an appropriation to discharge the claims at their next session. In 1835 his request was unanimously rejected by the Senate on the basis of a report by Senator Henry Clay for the Committee on Foreign Relations which said that reprisals did not institute a state of war but frequently provoked war; therefore, the authorization of reprisals belonged to Congress, and Congress could not delegate this power.

The most famous reprisal in American history occurred in 1854, the bombardment of Greytown, Nicaragua. The mouth of the San Juan River marked the eastern terminus of one of the routes across the isthmus. Great Britain claimed a protectorate over the "Mosquito Coast," and under a charter from the Mosquito King a company of American and European adventurers set up a transit company to conduct travelers over the isthmus. In 1852, with the consent of the Mosquito King and under the patronage of the British consul, this group established the sovereign state of Greytown. A rival enterprise, the Accessory Transit Company, held a charter from the Nicaraguan government and enjoyed the patronage of the United States government; it had its seat directly across the river in Punta Arenas. Inevitably friction arose. During a visit in May of 1853, Captain George Nichols Hollins of the U.S.S. *Cyane* temporarily placed a marine guard on Accessory Transit Company property that the Greytown authorities had ordered cleared. After his departure, in the course of one of several incidents, the American minister to Central America suffered a slight cut from a bottle thrown by a member of a Greytown mob. The secretary of the navy ordered Hollins to return and obtain redress for the damages suffered by the Accessory Transit Company and an apology for the attack upon the minister. His instructions were ambiguous. The people of Greytown, he noted,

> should be taught that the United States will not tolerate these outrages, and that they have the power and the determination to check them. It is, however, very much to be hoped that you can effect the purposes of your visit without a resort to violence and destruction of property and loss of life. The presence of your vessel will, no doubt, work much good. The Department reposes much in your prudence and good sense. (*119*, VII, 113–14)

Upon his arrival on July 12, 1854, Captain Hollins demanded an indemnity of twenty-four thousand dollars for the Accessory Transit Company, an apology for the attack on the minister, and assurances of good behavior. Greytown did not comply. On July 13 Hollins shelled the town intermittently throughout the day, and at four o'clock he sent a party ashore to burn what remained. He reported:

> The execution done by our shot and shell amounted to the almost total destruction of the buildings; but it was thought best to make the punishment of such a character as to inculcate a lesson never to be forgotten by those who have for so long a time set at defiance all warnings, and satisfy the whole world that the United States have the power and determination to enforce that reparation and respect due to them as a Government in whatever quarter the outrages may be committed. (*119*, VII, 114)

This episode is frequently paraded today as an illustration of the constitutional powers of the President; it was not regarded so at the time. The leading study of the affair reports:

Hollins's action met with strong condemnation from the American press and people. The New York *Times* was particularly bitter, and, assuming that the action was directed or approved by the government, intimated that the terms of the Clayton–Bulwer treaty had been broken, and denounced President Pierce for a violation of the Constitution of the United States, on the ground that Congress alone could declare war. The *Times* was an opposition paper, but the best elements of the Democrats themselves felt that they could not honestly defend the deed. (*239*, 179–80)

The minister to Great Britain, James Buchanan, assured the British government that Hollins's action was unauthorized and would be disavowed by the United States. (*239*, 181) Secretary of State William Marcy, however, saw no way of repudiating Hollins's act. At the same time, he dared not endorse it. When the British ambassador approached him he said that he could not express an opinion because the matter was under the consideration of the government. (*239*, 181) Both the Senate and the House demanded information on the bombardment. In the meantime, France, the German Confederation, and Nicaragua demanded indemnification for the destruction of the property of their nationals.

On August 8 Marcy wrote to Buchanan: "The occurrence at Greytown is an embarrassing affair. The place merited chastisement, but the severity of the one inflicted exceeded our expectations. The government will, however, I think, stand by Capt. Hollins." The government had no choice. To admit the impropriety of Hollins's action, which was more or less warranted by his instructions, would put the administration in a hopeless position in domestic politics and would oblige it to satisfy the foreign claims.

President Franklin Pierce finally broke the official silence in his annual message to Congress on December 4, 1854. He brazened the matter out. After making a tendentious and highly colored report of the events that were alleged to have justified the destruction of Greytown, he undertook to remove the action from the category of war by denying Greytown the status of an organized society, representing the community instead as a band of outlaws or pirates.

> Not standing before the world in the attitude of an organized political society, being neither competent to exercise the rights nor to discharge the obligations of a government, it was, in fact, a marauding establishment too dangerous to be disregarded and too guilty to pass unpunished, and yet incapable of being treated in any other way than as a piratical resort of outlaws or a camp of savages depredating on emigrant trains or caravans and the frontier settlements of civilized states. (*181*, IV, 2815)

This language bore no relation to fact. There had been no complaint whatever that Greytown had plundered or abused travelers. Neither the twenty–four thousand dollars at stake between Greytown and the Accessory

Transit Company nor the insult to the American minister involved any act of piracy or depredation. Pierce therefore supplemented his analogy to piracy with an analogy to acts of reprisal by European states. (*181*, IV, 2817) But Pierce offered no precedent in which the United States had inflicted injury on such a scale as this without an act of Congress.

In 1860 an American citizen named Durand, whose property had been destroyed in the bombardment of Greytown, sued Captain Hollins for damages. Justice Nelson of the Supreme Court, sitting on circuit in New York, ruled that the President's action was legal.

> As the executive head of the nation, the president is made the only legitimate organ of the general government, to open and carry on correspondence or negotiations with foreign nations, in matters concerning the interests of the country or its citizens. It is to him, also, the citizens abroad must look for protection of person and of property and for the faithful execution of laws existing and intended for their protection. For this purpose, the whole executive power of the country is placed in his hands, under the Constitution, and the laws passed in pursuance thereof; and different departments of government have been organized, through which this power may be most conveniently executed, whether by negotiation or by force—a department of state and a department of the navy.
>
> Now, as it respects the interposition of the executive abroad, for the protection of the lives or property of the citizen, the duty must, of necessity, rest in the discretion of the president. Acts of lawless violence, or of threatened violence to the citizen or his property, cannot be anticipated and provided for; and the protection, to be effectual or of any avail, may, not infrequently, require the most prompt and decided action. Under our system of government, the citizen abroad is as much entitled to protection as the citizen at home. The great object and duty of government is the protection of the lives, liberty, and property of the people composing it, whether abroad or at home; and any government failing in the accomplishment of the object, or the performance of the duty, is not worth preserving.
>
> I have said, that the interposition of the president abroad, for the protection of the citizens, must necessarily rest in his discretion; and it is quite clear that, in all cases where a public act or order rests in executive discretion neither he nor his authorized agent is personally civilly responsible for the consequences.[1]

---

[1]Durand v. Hollins, 8 F. Cas. 111, 112 (S.D.N.Y. 1860). In Perrin v. United States, 4 Ct. Cl. 543, 547 (1868), in an action against the United States by a French subject who had suffered loss in the destruction of Greytown, the court of claims ruled that it lacked jurisdiction in such a suit.

The claimant's case must necessarily rest upon the assumption that the bombardment and destruction of Greytown was illegal and not justified by the law of nations. And hinging upon that, it will readily be seen that the questions raised are such as can only be determined between the United States and the governments whose citizens it is alleged have been injured by the injurious acts

It would be hard to find an opinion further from the mark. The property purportedly protected was not American but that of a Nicaraguan corporation. Hollins's action, however, destroyed American property, that of the plaintiff. Despite what Justice Nelson said, there was no feature of emergency or urgency, for Hollins received his orders in Washington, D.C. Finally, what occurred was not what Nelson justified—interposition to protect citizens or their property from impending harm; it was reprisal for past injury, punitive rather than preventive. Justice Nelson was a strongly partisan Democrat, and in *Durand v. Hollins* he undertook to vindicate the conduct of a Democratic President. Only three years later, in *The Prize Cases*, he would deny the right of Republican President Lincoln to blockade the seceding states.

On April 9, 1914, a boat's crew from the U.S.S. *Dolphin* landed in Tampico to pick up supplies. They were arrested by a squad of soldiers under the command of a Mexican colonel, were paraded through the streets for a short time, and then were released. Apology was made, and President Victoriano Huerta expressed regret, but Admiral Henry Thomas Mayo, who commanded the American vessels at Tampico, demanded a twenty-one gun salute to the American flag. President Woodrow Wilson endorsed this demand. On April 17 an administration spokesman said that the Mexican salute to the flag of the United States would be followed by an American salute to the Mexican flag, and Huerta signified acceptance of the proposal. (*New York Times*, April 14, 1914) But the State Department then announced that the United States would make no such commitment, and on April 20 President Wilson addressed Congress, asking authority for a reprisal.

> No doubt I could do what is necessary in the circumstances to enforce respect for our Government without recourse to the Congress and yet not exceed my constitutional powers as President, but I do not wish to act in a matter possibly of so grave consequence except in close conference and cooperation with both the Senate and House. I therefore come to ask your approval that I should use the armed forces of the United States in such ways and to such an extent as may be necessary to obtain from Gen. Huerta and his adherents the fullest recognition of the rights and dignity of the United States, even admidst the distressing conditions now unhappily obtaining in Mexico.*

A joint resolution demanding amends from General Huerta passed the House on April 21.

On April 21 a cablegram from the American consul at Veracruz reported that a German vessel was about to land machine guns and munitions for

---

of this government. They are international political questions, which no court of this country in a case of this kind is authorized or empowered to decide.

It is true that under existing statutes neither the court of claims nor any other court had jurisdiction of such a claim against the United States and that the only remedy was by the route of diplomatic negotiation.

President Huerta. Wilson, who hated Huerta, ordered the marine commander at Veracruz to seize the customshouse and prevent the arms from being landed. This was done, and the German vessel sailed down the coast to discharge its cargo at another port. But, in the meantime, the American marines in Veracruz had encountered resistance. The ships at Tampico were hastily sent to Veracruz, and American forces occupied the whole city. On April 22 the Senate passed a joint resolution which was accepted by the House and was signed by the President on the same day. This extremely vague instrument disclaimed any intention "to make war on Mexico" but said that the President "is justified in the employment of the armed forces to enforce his demands for unequivocal amends for the affronts and indignities committed against the United States."*

Ten weeks after the seizure of Veracruz, Huerta resigned, but American relations with his rival and successor, Venustiano Carranza, were just as strained. On November 23, 1914, American forces evacuated Veracruz. Although the joint resolution had not been intended for the practical purpose of keeping machine guns from Huerta but rather for extorting a symbolic submission, without the resolution the occupation would have been illegal, and the resolution is therefore considered a ratification of the action. (*213*, 96)

On August 2 and August 4, 1964, according to announcements by the Johnson administration—which the Senate Committee on Foreign Relations was later unable to verify—North Vietnamese torpedo boats made futile attacks on two American destroyers in the Gulf of Tonkin. In reprisal, President Lyndon Johnson ordered the bombing of the naval bases from which the attacks had been launched; then he induced Congress to pass the Tonkin Gulf Resolution.* This resolution ratified the reprisals. In addition, it contained words so general as to authorize the President to initiate war in Indochina and elsewhere at will. This latter feature of the act was one of the justifications offered for the President's massive commitment of troops to South Vietnam, begun on February 7, 1965. With equal justification, Johnson could have landed troops in North Vietnam. He was unwilling to face the political consequences of such an action, however, so the conception of "sustained reprisal" was introduced. For some months a "Phase II" operation against North Vietnam, consisting of a "continuous program of progressively more serious air strikes running from two to six months," had been under discussion in a "working group" of the National Security Council. (*148*, III, 289) On the same day as the debarkation in South Vietnam, the White House announced that "retaliatory attacks" had been carried out against North Vietnam in reprisal for attacks by South Vietnamese guerrillas on "two South Vietnamese airfields, two U.S. barracks areas, several villages and one town in South Vietnam." (*New York Times*, Feb. 8, 1965)[2] On February

---

[2]Neither attacks on North Vietnam because of the conduct of the South Vietnamese, who the United States stubbornly insisted were nationals of a state called

8, the Joint Chiefs of Staff predicted: "As this program continues the realistic need for precise event association in this reprisal context will progressively diminish. A wide range of activities are within the scope of what may be stated to be provocations justifying reprisal." (*148*, III, 319) This proved to be true. "Sustained reprisal" continued for eight years. Of course "sustained reprisal" is not what international law knows as reprisal but what it knows as a state of war.

Until 1827, blockade occurred only as an aspect of a general war. When, during a war, an effective blockade was maintained and appropriate notice was given, neutral vessels attempting to trade with the blockaded state might be seized by the blockader. But such seizure in the absence of a state of war would be an act of war against the third party. As the Supreme Court said in *The Prize Cases*, "To legitimate the capture of a neutral vessel or property on the high seas, a war must exist *de facto*."*

In 1827 Great Britain, France, and Russia introduced the conception of the "pacific blockade." While insisting that they remained at peace with Turkey, they blockaded the Turkish armies in Greece. (*119*, VII, 135) A number of later pacific blockades were instituted by European states in the nineteenth and early twentieth centuries. (*119*, VII, 135–42; *131*, II, 146–48) There might be two reasons for confining hostilities to blockade. The blockading state might have limited objectives, such as reprisal, that could be fully satisfied by a blockade. Or the blockading state might wish to reassure other interested states as to its intentions; the concern of the United States when Latin American states were blockaded might be assuaged if the blockade were "peaceful."

The seizure of the shipping of a state under pacific blockade was, of course, an act of war, but if the blockaded state did not accept the challenge, the state of war did not come into existence, and the blockader lost the benefits of the law of war. If it seized or coerced the shipping of a third state trading with the blockaded state, that third state could treat this action as an act of war. Although some blockading states have excluded the vessels of third states under what they called a pacific blockade, this was then generally and is today universally considered a violation of international law. (*131*, II, 147) Throughout its history, with the notable exception of the Cuban blockade in 1962, the United States has insisted that under a pacific blockade there is no right to exclude the vessels of third states.

In 1838, when the French minister asked for the restitution of the American schooner *Lone*, which had been seized in a French pacific blockade of Mexico and had been rescued and brought to New Orleans, Acting Secretary of State Aaron Vail replied, "The writers on international law have not enumerated blockade as one of the peaceable remedies to which an injured nation might resort, but have classed it among the usual means of

---

South Vietnam, nor retaliation by the United States for attacks on South Vietnamese airfields, villages, and towns qualified as reprisal.

direct hostility." (*119*, VII, 135) In 1897 the United States refused to acknowledge a blockade of the Greek troops on Crete by Austria–Hungary, France, Germany, Great Britain, Italy, and Russia. The blockade was soon lifted. When Great Britain, Germany, and Italy blockaded Venezuela in 1902, Secretary of State John Hay announced that the United States did "not acquiesce in any extension of the doctrine of pacific blockade which may adversely affect the rights of states not parties to the controversy, or discriminate against the commerce of neutral nations." (*119*, VII, 140) He offered the good offices of the United States, and the issues were arbitrated.

In 1941, when there was a threat of a blockade of Siberian ports by Japan, Acting Secretary of State Sumner Welles protested: "A blockade of Siberian ports by Japan could only be regarded as legal under international law in the event that a state of war existed between Japan and Russia and that such a blockade had been declared a concomitant part of such a state of war." And in 1948, Ambassador Warren Austin of the United States said in the Security Council of the United Nations: "It is elementary that a proclamation of a blockade constitutes a claim of belligerent rights. The exercise of belligerent rights depends on the existence of war, whether it be international war or civil war. The claim to exercise belligerent rights must rest upon a recognition of the belligerency of the opposing party." (*237*, X, 868–69) In 1954, eleven members of the United States Air Force and two American civilians were shot down over China while on a flight, so it was said, from Korea to Japan. They were tried and convicted as spies. President Dwight D. Eisenhower contended that the Americans in uniform should be treated as prisoners of war, but he rejected the proposal that he seek their release by blockading China.

> It is possible that a blockade is conceivable without war; I have never read of it historically. A blockade is an act of war intended to bring your adversary to your way of thinking or to his knees. . . . So far as I am concerned, if ever we come to a place that I feel a step of war is necessary, it is going to be brought about not by any impulsive individualistic act of my own, but I am going before the Congress in the constitutional method set up in this country, and lay the problem before them with my recommendation as to whatever it may be. (*155*, 1076–77)

Secretary of State John Foster Dulles concurred, "Our first duty is to exhaust peaceful means of sustaining our international rights and those of our citizens, rather than now resorting to war action such as a naval and air blockade of Red China." (*237*, X, 869) The United Nations obtained the release of the prisoners in 1955.

In 1961 President John F. Kennedy, without congressional authorization, initiated a war against Cuba by invasion at the Bay of Pigs by mercenaries armed and paid by the United States, and then he abandoned his war. On October 3, 1962, Congress passed the so-called Cuba resolution, which recited that "the United States is determined" to do three things: (a) "to prevent by whatever means may be necessary, including the use of arms, the Marxist–Leninist regime in Cuba from extending, by force and the threat of force, its aggressive and subversive activities to any part of this hemisphere"; (b) "to prevent in Cuba the creation or use of an externally supported military capability capable of endangering the security of the United States"; and (c) "to work with the Organization of American States and with freedom-loving Cubans to support the aspirations of the Cuban people for self-determination."* After learning of the Soviet installation of nuclear missiles in Cuba, President Kennedy issued a proclamation on October 23, 1962, ordering "the forces under my command" to interdict "the delivery of offensive weapons and associated material to Cuba." (156, 242) The proclamation listed as offensive weapons the principal instruments of modern war and authorized the secretary of defense to add other classes of materiel. It further declared that all vessels proceeding to Cuba might be stopped and searched; vessels that failed to submit, and vessels that might be carrying the prohibited materiel and refused to change their course as directed, should be taken into custody.

For authorization President Kennedy appealed to the joint resolution of October 3, but that resolution had no legal effect. It merely expressed the determination of the United States to accomplish three goals. It said that the United States was determined—presumably by some future act of Congress—to employ arms, if need be, to accomplish the first goal. But to achieve the second goal, the prevention of the importation of arms by Cuba, Congress did not threaten to use force and conspicuously refrained from authorizing the President to establish a blockade.

On October 27, Soviet Premier Nikita Khrushchev offered to withdraw the missiles if the United States withdrew its nuclear missiles from Turkey. The Kennedy administration publicly rejected this offer (*Facts on File*, Oct. 25-31, 1962, p. 374), but after the Soviet Union removed its missiles from Cuba the United States removed the missiles in Turkey, saying that they were obsolete. Premier Khrushchev also said, "The United States has given a pledge not to invade Cuba." (*Facts on File*, Dec. 6-12, 1962, p. 437)

Since the United States has never recognized the right to exclude the vessels of a third state in a pacific blockade, the State Department was hard-pressed to justify the threat to the vessels of the Soviet Union. It undertook to do this by substituting the word *quarantine* for *blockade*.

To the extent that traditional blockade implies and requires a state of belligerency or war, the United States did not seek to justify the quarantine as a blockade. There was no assertion of a state of war or belligerency. Such conditions would not form the sole basis for measures such as the defensive quarantine. Another concept in traditional international law is that of "pacific blockade." Whatever the views that may be held as to the availability of such a doctrine, the United States did not rest its case on that ground. (112, 515)

Of course *quarantine* has never had any other meaning at international law than that of an exclusionary health measure imposed by the state experiencing the quarantine. (*119*, II, 142–60)

At a news conference on March 6, 1963, President Kennedy was asked whether it would not be possible to prevent our "allies" from transporting Soviet oil to Cuba. The President replied:

> There isn't any doubt that over a long period of time that denial of oil would make a difference. To deny the oil would require, of course, a blockade, and a blockade is an act of war, and you should be prepared to go for it. . . .
>
> But you should not be under any impression that a blockade is not an act of war, because when a ship refuses to stop, and you then sink ⁺he ship, there is usually a military response by the country involved. (*157*, 242)

In his proclamation of October 23, 1962, President Kennedy had ordered the visitation and search of vessels bound for Cuba. At international law, visitation and search of merchant vessels of another state on the high seas in time of peace is a derogation of sovereignty and is an act of war. Chief Justice John Marshall endorsed the opinion of Sir William Scott, "It is a right strictly belligerent in its character, which can never be exercised by a nation at peace, except against professed pirates, who are the enemies of the human race."* Moore has shown that the American position on this question has been asserted repeatedly and invariably from the beginning of our history. (*119*, II, 886–951)

When one state sends a military force into the territory of another, this also is a derogation of sovereignty and a delict at international law. It may give rise to war and therefore can be authorized only by the war–making authority. In ruling that a foreign ship of war had an implied license to enter American ports, Chief Justice Marshall observed that the case was entirely different with land forces.*

When an American vessel was seized as a prize in Spanish waters by an American gunboat for violation of the nonintercourse act of 1809, Chief Justice Marshall said, "The Seizure of an American vessel within the territorial jurisdiction of a foreign power is certainly an offense against that power which must be adjusted between the two governments."*

On May 15, 1820, in retaliation for unequal treatment of American shipping, Congress levied a tonnage duty of eighteen dollars per ton to be collected from all French vessels entering ports of the United States. As noted earlier (*see* Chapter 1, pp. 13–14), the French ship *Appollon*—sailing to Florida in order to transship cargo into the United States—was seized in Spanish waters and was carried to St. Mary's for collection of the tonnage duty. The French government protested. President Monroe made a vigorous defense of the action to Congress in his annual message of December 3, 1821. "In this case every circumstance which occurred indicated a fixed purpose to violate our revenue laws." (*181*, I, 670) But the government dropped its action, and the captain of the *Appollon* sued the collector of the port for damages. In the Supreme Court Justice Story held the seizure illegal because it had occurred in Spanish waters.

> The laws of no nation can justly extend beyond its own territories, except as regards its own citizens. They can have no force to control the sovereignty or rights of any other nation, within its own jurisdiction. . . . It would be monstrous to suppose that our revenue officers were authorized to enter into foreign ports and territories, for the purpose of seizing vessels which had offended against our laws. . . . It cannot be presumed that Congress would voluntarily justify such a clear violation of the laws of nations.*

During the period in which this issue was contested, the United States recognized neither the British claim nor that of the Buenos Aires government to the Falkland Islands, but itself claimed fishing rights there. The governor appointed by Buenos Aires seized sealskins from two American vessels. The libellant persuaded Captain Duncan of the *Lexington*, a United States ship of war, to destroy the Argentine installation and recover the skins, and he then filed a claim for salvage against the owners of the skins. Justice Smith Thompson of the Supreme Court, sitting on circuit, ruled that salvage should not be awarded because the seizure was illegal.*

In addition to these judicial decisions, numerous rulings of the Departments of Justice, State, and War have forbidden invasion of foreign territory. In 1815 Secretary of State James Monroe said that "no principle is better established than that no government has a right to pursue offenders against its laws, or deserters from its service into the dominions of another." In the same year, during the war with Algiers, an Algerian sloop of war was captured by an American vessel in Spanish waters. Secretary Monroe apologized to Spain, and the vessel was restored to Algiers. (*119*, II, 362)

When an armed force of the Republic of Texas pursued Indians who had committed depredations in Texas into the United States in 1839, Secretary of State John Forsyth instructed the chargé d'affaires to Texas to remonstrate "in strong terms" against "this insult and outrage," to demand satisfactory explanations, and to point out that a repetition "would inevitably lead to collisions between the troops of the two countries which there would be great reason to deplore." (*119*, II, 363)

In 1862 Secretary of State William Seward pointed out to the secretary of the navy that if, as the newspaper reported, an American warship had pursued a British blockade–runner into Canadian waters this was "an inexcusable violation of the Law of Nations, for which acknowledgment and reparation ought to be promptly made." (*119*, II, 363) In 1863 several Confederates who had taken passage on the Union ship *Chesapeake* seized the vessel and sailed her into Canadian waters, where they were obliged to abandon her. A United States ship of war captured her and three prisoners.

The British government demanded the delivery of the vessel, the release of the prisoners on British soil, and an apology and disclaimer by the United States. President Lincoln determined that the United States had violated the law of nations and agreed to these demands.[3]

In 1864 a group of Confederates invaded Vermont from Canada and pillaged the town of Saint Albans. Major General John Adams Dix, who commanded the Department of the East, issued a general order that, if necessary, all such marauders should be pursued into Canada in the future, but three days later he revoked the order because it had been disapproved by the President. (*119*, II, 367–68)

In 1876 a United States naval officer asked permission to seize a quantity of silver that belonged to an American citizen and had been taken by a Mexican official. Acting Secretary of State William Hunter wrote, "The President is not authorized to order or approve an act of war in a country with which we are at peace, except in self–defense." (*119*, VII, 167)

Although the law seems to be well settled both by judicial decisions and by administrative rulings, nevertheless, on many occasions, American forces have made brief forays into foreign territory. Numerous border crossings into Spanish and Mexican territories have occurred, but the executive has never authorized a border crossing into Canada. There have been a large number of naval landings for the protection of citizens abroad, but, as we shall see, most of these were authorized by Congress.

We must also recognize a legal qualification of the general principle of international law on this question. Secretary of State Daniel Webster, in a dispute over a British incursion into the territory of the United States, adopted the position that in a case of extreme urgency, when no alternative course is open, a brief trespass not directed at the sovereign of the territory, and carried out for the sole purpose of averting grave impending injury, is justified at international law by the principle of self–defense.

A serious revolution against Great Britain had broken out in French Canada in 1837, and a small force took the field against the British government in Upper Canada. The members of this force were quickly dispersed, and some fled to the United States. A force of Americans and Canadians assembled in New York State and, under the command of Rensselaer Van Rensselaer of Albany, occupied Navy Island on the Canadian side of the Niagara River. (*181*, III, 1679) Soon they numbered perhaps a thousand men, and they discharged artillery at the Canadian shore. The lieutenant–governor of Upper Canada complained to the governor of New York but received no response. On December 28, 1837, the commander of the Canadian forces urged the New York authorities to prevent supplies from being furnished to the force on Navy Island. The American steamer *Caroline*

[3]H. Wheaton, *Elements of International Law*, ed. R. H. Dana (Boston: Little, Brown and Co., 1866), 437–38n. (note by editor).

was ferrying supplies to Navy Island, and on the night of December 29 the Canadian commander sent a force that seized the vessel in its berth at Schlosser, New York, killed some persons, set fire to the ship, towed it into the river, and abandoned it to the current so that it went over Niagara Falls.

On January 5, 1838, Secretary of State Forsyth complained to the British minister Henry S. Fox of "the extraordinary outrage committed from Her Britannic Majesty's Province of Upper Canada on the persons and property of citizens of the United States within the jurisdiction of the State of New York." (*181*, III, 1676) On February 6, Fox justified the action:

> The piratical character of the steamboat *Caroline* and the necessity of self-defense and self-preservation under which Her Majesty's subjects acted in destroying that vessel would seem to be sufficiently established.
>
> At the time when the event happened the ordinary laws of the United States were not enforced within the frontier district of the State of New York. The authority of the law was overborne publicly by piratical violence. Through such violence Her Majesty's subjects in Upper Canada had already severely suffered, and they were threatened with still further injury and outrage. This extraordinary state of things appears naturally and necessarily to have impelled them to consult their own security by pursuing and destroying the vessel of their piratical enemy wheresoever they might find her. (*181*, III, 1677-78)

President Van Buren was in no position to press the matter, for American bands of rebel sympathizers were making raids into Canada. Moreover, the disputed issue of the Maine boundary was more important. Shortly after taking office in 1841, Secretary of State Webster raised the boundary question with Great Britain and raised also the grievance of the *Caroline*. Fox reiterated the British position, and Webster in reply described the only circumstances in which he considered the plea of self-defense valid at international law.

> Under these circumstances, and under those immediately connected with the transaction itself, it will be for her rules of national law the destruction of the "Caroline" is to be defended. It will be for that government to show a necessity of self-defense, instant, overwhelming, leaving no choice of means, no moment for deliberation. It will be for it to show, also, that the local authorities of Canada, even supposing the necessity of the moment authorized them to enter the territories of the United States at all, did nothing unreasonable or excessive; since the act, justified by the necessity of self-defense, must be limited by that necessity, and kept clearly within it. It must be shown that admonition or remonstrance to the persons on board the "Caroline" was impracticable, or would have been unavailing. It must be shown that daylight could not be waited for; that there could be no attempt at discrimination between the innocent and the guilty; that it would not have been enough to seize and detain the vessel; but that there was a necessity, present and

inevitable, for attacking her in the darkness of night, while moored to the shore, and while unarmed men were asleep on board, killing some and wounding others, and then drawing her into the current above the cataract, setting her on fire, and, careless to know whether there might not be in her the innocent with the guilty, or the living with the dead, committing her to a fate which fills the imagination with horror. A necessity for all this the government of the United States cannot believe to have existed.

All will see that, if such things be allowed to occur, they must lead to bloody and exasperated war. (*233*, VI, 261)

In his first annual message on December 7, 1841, President John Tyler revived the case of the destruction of the *Caroline*. (*181*, III, 1929) He asserted, "This Government can never concede to any foreign government the power, except in a case of the most urgent and extreme necessity, of invading its territory, either to arrest the persons or destroy the property of those who may have violated the municipal laws of such foreign government or have disregarded their obligations arising under the law of nations." He warned, "When border collisions come to receive the sanction or to be made on the authority of either Government general war must be the inevitable result." And he expressed the hope that the British government would renounce the precedent set in the case of the *Caroline*.

In April of 1842 Lord Alexander Ashburton arrived in Washington as a special envoy to resolve differences between Great Britain and the United States, especially the issue of the Maine boundary. On July 27 Secretary of State Webster took up the question of the destruction of the *Caroline* in a letter to Lord Ashburton. On the following day Ashburton replied. (*233*, VI, 292, 295) He was entirely in agreement with Webster's exposition of international law. The inviolability of territory was "the most essential foundation of civilization." But all jurists agreed that the duty of respecting territory might be suspended by a "strong, overpowering necessity." "It must be for the shortest possible period, during the continuance of an admitted overruling necessity, and strictly confined within the narrowest limits imposed by that necessity." He then reviewed the occurrence to show that the attack was justified under Webster's formula. Ashburton concluded that the action was justifiable but admitted that there had been a violation of territory, and he expressed regret that "some explanation and apology for this occurrence was not immediately made." Webster announced he was satisfied with this apology. (*233*, VI, 300) On August 11 President Tyler sent the Webster–Ashburton treaty settling the Maine boundary to the Senate. On the case of the *Caroline* he said that Ashburton's letter "has seemed to me sufficient to warrant forbearance from any future remonstrance against what took place as an aggression on the soil and territory of the country." (*181*, III, 2022)

Thus the two governments agreed that, in such a case of immediate necessity as Webster described, an act of self–defense involving invasion of foreign territory, but not directed at the foreign government, was not an act of war. Of course it does not follow that the President may undertake such action without congressional authorization. The framers of the Constitution assigned to him only the power to respond to sudden attack upon the United States as an act of self-defense. In all other matters the President's right to use the armed forces depends, as we shall see, upon specific congressional authorization. It is under such authorization that United States naval officers have emulated the Canadian commander by making sudden brief incursions into foreign territory for the defense of citizens in cases of dire need.

Webster's formulation of the law of self-defense is not only the American but also the generally accepted view of the international law on the subject. At the Nuremberg trials the defendants argued that the German occupation of Norway in 1940 was a preventive action undertaken to forestall Allied occupation. The International Military Tribunal ruled that "preventive action in foreign territory is justified only in case of 'an instant and overwhelming necessity for self-defense, leaving no choice of means, and no moment of deliberation.' " (119, II, 412) And the Tribunal rejected the German contention that a state may judge for itself the necessity of self-defense; this would legitimize wars of aggression on the pretext of self-defense.

What the Germans had relied on was not really the law of self-defense but the so-called principle of self-preservation. This theory has been used rhetorically by aggressors who justify invasions as averting harm that might otherwise result if the territory were not occupied. Unless self-defense is confined to the narrow limits Webster described, it is not possible to fix any outer boundary. The plea of self-preservation could justify every country in the world in attempting to occupy the entire globe. Self-preservation so viewed cannot be a meaningful legal concept.

It appears, however, that the adoption of the United Nations Charter has reduced the scope of legitimate self-defense by ruling out all anticipatory action. Quincy Wright has said:

> It is true that traditional international law permitted military action in self-defense if there were an instant and overwhelming necessity permitting no moment for deliberation, i.e., if hostile forces were about to attack. It seems clear, however, that the San Francisco Conference, by limiting self-defense to cases of "armed attack," intended to eliminate all preventive or pre-emptive action in order to maintain to the utmost the basic obligation of members of the United Nations to "refrain in their international relations from the threat or use of force." (244, 750, 764-65)

President Richard Nixon's undisclosed bombing of the territory of Cambodia from 1969 until August 15, 1973 (18), when he was forbidden by statute to carry out further acts of war in Indochina,* was clearly a violation of sovereignty and of international law and, since he lacked congressional authorization, of American constitutional law. The military expedition into Cambodia on April 30, 1970, was likewise illegal. On that day Nixon told

December 11, 1941, with Germany; on the same day, with Italy; on June 5, 1942, with Bulgaria; on the same day, with Hungary and with Rumania.* All these resolutions authorized the President to use the army, the navy, and the militia for the prosecution of war.

Since these wars were formally declared by Congress, none of them produced litigation concerning the power to initiate war. In two cases, however, the Presidents' actions made congressional declaration inevitable: the Second World War and the Mexican War. The latter was provoked by then-President James K. Polk.

When Texas was a political subdivision of Mexico, its western boundary was the Nueces River, but the Republic of Texas claimed also the territory between the Nueces and the Rio Grande. On March 1, 1845, Congress passed a joint resolution stating the conditions for the annexation of Texas. "*First*, Said State to be formed, subject to the adjustment by this government of all questions of boundary that may arise with other governments. . . ."* On December 2, 1845, President Polk informed Congress that Texas had acceded to all the terms of the resolution and that nothing remained to be done but to admit Texas. (*181*, II, 2236) On December 29, Congress passed a joint resolution declaring that the people of Texas had adopted a constitution and "assented to and accepted the proposals, conditions, and guarantees" stipulated in the joint resolution of March 1; therefore, Texas was admitted into the Union on an equal footing with the original states.*

In 1848 Henry Clay, adverting to the resolution of March 1, asked in the Senate: "How are disputed boundaries to be settled? Is it not in one of two modes—by treaty or by war? If by treaty, the settlement is made by the President and the Senate; if by war, the war power is exclusively with Congress."* President Polk had at first undertaken negotiation but then attempted to fix the boundary by military action without consulting Congress. Of course he provoked a war.

On October 15, 1845, the Mexican minister for foreign affairs agreed to receive an envoy. Polk gave John Slidell full powers to negotiate both the boundary and an accumulation of claims for injuries inflicted by Mexico upon citizens of the United States. (*181*, III, 2339) The Mexican government refused to receive Slidell, as it was willing to discuss only the boundary and not the claims for indemnification. Nevertheless, Polk kept Slidell in Mexico through the first two months of 1846. On March 1, 1846, on the President's instructions, Slidell again presented his credentials and asked to be officially received to undertake negotiations. On March 12, the Mexican government "insultingly refused," as Polk put it, to receive Slidell, who then returned to the United States. (*181*, III, 2340)

In the meantime, in August 1845, at the request of the Republic of Texas, Polk had sent a strong squadron to the coast of Mexico and a military force under General Zachary Taylor to Corpus Christi, on the west bank of the Nueces River, within the territory that was still subject to negotiation. As Polk later told Congress, this was to repel "any invasion of the Texas territory which might be attempted by the Mexican forces." (*181*, III, 2238–39) On January 13, 1846, while Slidell was still attempting to begin negotiations at the Mexican capital, President Polk ordered General Taylor to advance from Corpus Christi to a position on the Rio Grande opposite the Mexican military post at Matamoros. This order was carried out between March 11 and March 28. Taylor was under orders not to limit himself to defensive operations if attacked but to carry the war over the Rio Grande into Mexico. (*20*, 108)

The Mexican commander at Matamoros ordered General Taylor to withdraw. On April 24 a small American force encountered a Mexican force on the east bank of the Rio Grande; sixteen Americans were killed or injured, and others were taken prisoner. Thereafter, Mexicans crossed the Rio Grande in considerable numbers. Taylor won the battles of Palo Alto and Resaca de la Palma on May 8 and 9, but Polk did not know of these engagements when he sent his war message to Congress on May 11. Referring solely to the collision of April 24, he told Congress that "Mexico has passed the boundary of the United States, has invaded our territory and shed American blood on American soil." (*181*, III, 2292) On May 13 Congress resolved that "by the act of the Republic of Mexico, a state of war exists between that Government and the United States."*

Neither the joint resolution of March 1, 1845, nor the resolution of annexation of December 29, 1845, claimed the territory between the Nueces and the Rio Grande. Consequently Polk was hard–pressed to maintain that this was American soil. In his war message he said that the area was included in a congressional district; this, of course, had been done by Texas and not by Congress. In addition, Polk said that two days after annexing Texas, Congress had made Texas a revenue district and had provided for five surveyors, one of whom was to be stationed at Corpus Christi.* Even if this were a covert repudiation of negotiation and a surreptitious act of annexation, it would be an annexation only of Corpus Christi and not of the entire territory between the Nueces and the Rio Grande. On December 8, 1846, Polk tried to strengthen his case by pointing out that on February 6, 1846, Congress had established certain post roads extending west of the Nueces. (*181*, III, 2334) But it is not by such measures that a nation defines its boundaries.

Polk's actions were deeply resented by the Whigs. On January 3, 1848, John W. Houston of Delaware introduced in the House of Representatives a resolution lauding General Taylor and his force for their victory at Buena Vista and authorizing the presentation of a gold medal to Taylor. Thomas J. Henley of Indiana moved to instruct the Committee on Military Affairs to include the words "engaged as they were in defending the rights and honor of the nation." George Ashmun of Massachusetts, provoked by this endorsement of the war, moved to add the words "in a war unnecessarily and unconstitutionally begun by the President of the United States." Ashmun's amendment carried by a vote 85–81,* and the resolution was dropped. However, on February 8 Alexander H. Stephens of Georgia reintroduced the original Houston resolution, and it was enacted on May 9.*

Abraham Lincoln of Illinois voted for the Ashmun amendment. Apparently his friend William H. Herndon wrote to Lincoln justifying Polk's action in crossing the Nueces as a legitimate preventive measure to forestall a Mexican invasion. Lincoln's reply has become famous.

> Let me first state what I understand to be your position. It is that if it shall become necessary to repel invasion, the President may, without violation of the Constitution, cross the line and invade the territory of another country, and that whether such necessity exists in any given case the President is the sole judge. . . .
>
> Allow the President to invade a neighboring nation whenever he shall deem it necessary to repel an invasion, and you allow him to do so whenever he may choose to say he deems it necessary for such a purpose, and you allow him to make war at his pleasure.
>
> The provision of the Constitution giving the war-making power to Congress was dictated, as I understand it, by the following reasons: Kings had always been involving and impoverishing their people in wars, pretending generally, if not always, that the good of the people was the object. This our convention understood to be the most oppressive of all kingly oppressions, and they resolved to so frame the Constitution that no one man should hold the power of bringing oppression upon us. But your view destroys the whole matter, and places our President where kings have always stood. (102, II, 51–52)

Congress has passed four conditional declarations of war. In 1853 an American naval vessel was on the Paraguayan side of waters allegedly common to Paraguay and Argentina. Paraguay had closed its waters to foreign ships of war, and a Paraguayan fort shelled the *Water Witch*, which returned the fire. In his annual message to Congress on December 8, 1857, President James Buchanan announced his intention to demand redress and asked Congress to authorize him to use "other means in the event of a refusal." (181, IV, 2980) By joint resolution of June 2, 1858, he was authorized to "adopt such measures and use such force as, in his judgment, may be necessary and advisable."* Several ships of war were sent, and the difficulties with Paraguay were adjusted by commissioners, without resorting to violence. (181, IV, 3091)

In 1871 three American steamships were seized by one of the two belligerent factions that were contending for control of the government of Venezuela. One ship was voluntarily returned; the other two were yielded up on demand of the commander of the U.S.S. *Shawmut*. On June 17, 1890, Congress passed a resolution authorizing the President "to promptly obtain indemnity . . . and to secure this end he is authorized to employ such means or exercise such power as may be necessary."* The matter was arbitrated, and an indemnity of $150,000 was awarded to the United States.

In 1886 Spain acknowledged a debt to the heirs of a naturalized American citizen, Antonio Maximo Mora, for property losses during the Ten Years War in Cuba, but no payment was made. On March 2, 1895, Congress passed a "Joint Resolution Calling on the President to take such measures as he may deem necessary to consummate the agreement."* This resolution did not authorize the use of force, so there was no declaration of war pure and simple. But the threat of such a declaration, as always with a conditional declaration of war, was implicit. The State Department collected the sum, according to the *New York Sun*, "by a process closely resembling blackmail." (*241*, 87)

On April 20, 1898, President McKinley signed a joint resolution demanding that Spain withdraw from Cuba and relinquish her authority over the island; the President was directed to use the land and naval forces to carry the resolution into effect.* Spain severed diplomatic relations on April 21, and on April 25 Congress passed an act declaring that a state of war with Spain had existed since April 21.*

On several occasions Congress has authorized limited war—that is, action restricted as to objective or as to instrument. The four Barbary states—Morocco, Tripoli, Algiers, and Tunis—considered themselves at war with all Christian states with which they did not have treaties of peace. They sold treaties of peace and preyed upon the shipping of all states with which they were at war. The larger European powers could easily have destroyed them, but they found it more profitable to pay the Barbary states and keep them in business, for they greatly reduced the competition of smaller powers, such as the Italian states. In 1783 Benjamin Franklin wrote that "it was said to be a maxim among the English merchants that 'if there were no Algiers, it would be worth England's while to build one.' " (*83*, 17)

The Continental Congress ratified a treaty of peace with Morocco in 1787 and with Tunis in 1798. Relations with Morocco were for the most part friendly until 1802, when the emperor of Morocco denounced the treaty and declared war. On November 4, 1803, President Jefferson informed Congress that a Moroccan cruiser had seized an American merchant vessel, but the United States frigate *Philadelphia* had then captured both. He asked Congress "to consider the provisional authorities which may be necessary to restrain the depradations of this power should they be continued." (*181*, I, 352) On December 5 he informed the Congress that the emperor of Morocco had disavowed the action of his cruiser, had agreed to amicable adjustment of all difficulties, and had confirmed the treaty of 1787. (*181*, I, 353)

There were two naval wars with Algiers and one with Tripoli. In 1785 Algerian corsairs seized two American vessels and enslaved their crews; in 1793 they took a number of American vessels. On December 16, 1793, President Washington informed Congress of his efforts "for the ransom of our citizens and establishment of peace with Algiers." (*181*, I, 140) But on March 3, 1794, he reported the lack of progress in the negotiations with Algiers. (*181*, I, 144) On March 27, 1794, Congress passed an act reciting that "the depradations committed by the Algerine corsairs on the commerce of the United States render it necessary that a naval force be provided for its protection," and the act authorized the construction of six frigates.* A treaty of peace with Algiers was ratified by the Senate on March 2, 1796. On March 15, 1796, the President informed Congress that peace had been made but suggested that Congress might not wish to discontinue all naval construction. (*181*, I, 185) On April 20 Congress voted that three frigates should be completed.*

A limited war with France occurred between 1798 and 1801. As a result of French interference with American shipping, Congress suspended commercial intercourse with France, denounced the treaties with France, established a Department of the Navy and a Marine Corps, augmented the navy, and provided for raising an army in case of need.*

Congress enacted a number of statutes that provided for belligerency. An act of May 28, 1798, recited that French vessels had recently captured vessels and property of United States citizens on and near the coast, and it authorized the President to instruct the commanders of United States naval vessels to seize as a prize "any such armed vessel which shall have committed or which shall be found hovering on the coasts of the United States, for the purpose of committing depradations on the vessels belonging to citizens thereof" and also to recapture American vessels taken by the French.* On June 28, 1798, Congress passed further prize legislation for "public armed vessels."* On July 9, 1798, Congress voted that the President might grant commissions to owners of private armed ships to capture armed French vessels and to recapture American vessels.* An act of March 3, 1799, provided that if the President should find that American seamen impressed on the ships of the enemies of France captured by the French were maltreated, he must cause "the most rigorous retaliation" to be inflicted on French prisoners.* The naval war founded on these acts was ended by treaty in 1801.

This episode raised the questions of whether Congress might declare an imperfect war, or only a perfect war, and whether the determination of the scope of imperfect war lay with Congress. The Supreme Court rendered three important decisions.

The first case was *Bas v. Tingy*, decided in 1800.* The commander of the *Ganges*, a vessel of the United States Navy, filed a libel for salvage against the *Eliza*, which he had rescued from the French. The claim was founded on an act of 1799. The owners of the *Eliza* defended on the ground that the United States was not at war, France was not an enemy, and the act was inapplicable. The Supreme Court unanimously held for the libellant. Justice Bushrod Washington wrote the most extended opinion.

> Every contention by force between two nations, in external matters, under the authority of their respective governments, is not only war, but public war. If it be declared in form, it is called solemn, and is of the perfect kind. . . . But hostilities may subsist between two nations, more

confined in its nature and extent; being limited as to places, persons, and things; and this is more properly termed imperfect war; because not solemn, and because those who are authorized to commit hostilities, act under special authority, and can go [no] further than to the extent of their commission. . . . Now, if this be the true definition of war let us see what was the situation of the United States in relation to France. In March, 1799, Congress had raised an army, stopped all intercourse with France; dissolved our treaty, built and equipped ships of war; and commissioned private armed ships; enjoining the former, and authorizing the latter, to defend themselves against the armed ships of France, to attack them on the high seas, to subdue and take them as prize, and to re-capture armed vessels found in their possession. . . . What then is the evidence of legislative will? In fact and law we are at war; an American vessel fighting with a French vessel, to subdue and make her prize, is fighting with an enemy, accurately and technically speaking: and if this be not sufficient evidence of the legislative mind, it is explained in the same law.[1]

Chief Justice John Marshall was not yet on the bench when *Bas v. Tingy* was decided, but he had an opportunity to discuss the war in *Talbot v. Seeman* in 1801.* Upholding the right of a United States ship of war to take a prize, he said:

The whole powers of war being, by the Constitution of the United States, vested in Congress, the acts of that body can alone be resorted to as our guides in this inquiry. It is not denied, nor in the course of the argument has it been denied, that Congress may authorize general hostilities, in which case the general laws of war apply to our situation; or partial war, in which case the laws of war, so far as they actually apply to our situation, must be noticed.*

The third case is *Little v. Barreme*, decided in 1804.* The nonintercourse act of February 9, 1799, authorized the seizure within American waters of any vessels owned or hired by residents of the United States that after March 1 might trade with any French territory. It also authorized the President to instruct the commanders of public armed ships to seize on the high seas any American vessel "bound to or sailing to any port of place within the territory of the French republic, or her dependencies." President John Adams instructed naval commanders to seize American vessels "bound to or from French ports." Captain Little captured a Danish brigantine, the *Flying Fish*, which was bound from the French port of Jérémie to the Danish island of St. Thomas. In the course of the chase, the captain of the *Flying Fish*, apparently in the erroneous belief that he was exposed to capture under American law, threw overboard the ship's log and other papers. He had prepared a false document stating that he had been forced into Jérémie by

[1]Bas v. Tingy, 4 U.S. (4 Dall.) 40–42 (1800). Attorney General Charles Lee said that Congress had established a state of "maritime war." 1 Op. Att'y Gen. 84 (1798); 1 Op. Att'y Gen. 85 (1798).

French ships. Believing that the vessel was American, Captain Little took it into Boston as a prize.

The district court for Massachusetts ordered the vessel and cargo to be restored to the owner but refused to award damages for the unlawful seizure. The actions of the captain of the *Flying Fish* in destroying his papers and in preparing a written excuse were suspicious and constituted "a sufficient excuse for the capture, detention and consequent damages." In a state of war, neutrals owe certain duties; they "shall destroy none of their papers, nor shall carry false papers, under the hazard of being exposed to every inconvenience resulting from capture, examination, and detention; except the eventual condemnation of the property." The district judge continued, "It does not appear to me to be material what is the nature of the war, general, or limited."*

On appeal the circuit court awarded $8,504 damages against Captain Little, and the Supreme Court affirmed. Chief Justice Marshall wrote the opinion of the Court.

> It is by no means clear that the President of the United States, whose high duty it is to "take care that the laws be faithfully executed," and who is commander in chief of the armies and navies of the United States, might not, without any special authority for that purpose, in the then existing state of things, have empowered the officers commanding the armed vessels of the United States, to seize and send into port for adjudication, American vessels which were forfeited by being engaged in this illicit commerce. But when it is observed that the general clause of the first section of the act, which declares that such vessels may be seized, and may be prosecuted in any district where the seizure shall be made, obviously contemplates a seizure within the United States, and that the 5th section gives a special authority to seize on the high seas, and limits that authority to the seizure of vessels bound, or sailing to, a French port, the legislature seems to have prescribed that the manner in which this law shall be carried into execution, was to exclude a seizure of any vessel not bound to a French port. Of consequence, however strong the circumstances may be, which induced Captain Little to suspect the *Flying Fish* to be an American vessel, they could not excuse the detention of her, since he would not have been authorized to detain her had she been really American.[2]

Since the President's instructions collided with the act of Congress, they were illegal and could neither justify the seizure nor excuse Captain Little from damages.

[2]Little v. Barreme, 6 U.S. (2 Cranch) 177–78 (1804). In his concurring opinion in Youngstown Sheet & Tube Co. v. Sawyer, 343 U.S. 579, 662 (1952), Justice Clark treated the first sentence in this quotation as a recognition that the President has a constitutional power concurrent with that of Congress that must, however, give way to congressional legislation on the same topic. "In my view—taught me not only by the decision of Chief Justice Marshall in Little v. Barreme but also by a score of other

The Supreme Court has from the beginning held that contemporaneous legislative interpretations of the Constitution are highly persuasive as to its meaning. Here we have not only legislative but also judicial judgments that Congress may initiate action short of general war, that the initiation both of general war and of action short of general war belongs to Congress, and that it is for Congress to prescribe the dimensions of the war.

In 1802 a limited war began with Tripoli. As noted earlier, in Chapter 2 (pp. 23–25), this was precipitated by a declaration of war by Tripoli. Congress responded by passing on February 6, 1802, an act reciting that "the regency of Tripoli, on the Coast of Barbary, has commenced a predatory warfare against the United States." The act authorized the President "fully to equip, officer, man and employ such of the armed vessels of the United States as may be judged requisite by the President of the United States, for protecting effectually the commerce and seamen thereof on the Atlantic ocean, the Mediterranean and adjoining seas." He might instruct the commanders of the vessels to seize the property of the bey of Tripoli and his subjects, and he might also "cause to be done all such other acts of precaution or hostility as the state of war will justify, and may, in his opinion, require." He might also commission privateers.*

In 1810, President Madison laid claim to West Florida on the theory that Spain had transferred it to France in 1800 and Napoleon had sold it to the United States as part of the Louisiana purchase in 1803. By a secret act of February 12, 1813, Congress authorized the President to occupy all of West Florida, employing such part of the military and naval force as he might deem necessary.* There was a small Spanish garrison only at Mobile, and General James Wilkinson occupied that city without resistance on April 15. Since the congressional authorization was limited to the seizure of territory that the United States had already claimed, this must be considered a limited war.

On November 17, 1812, President Madison sent to Congress the report of the American consul on the "hostile proceedings" of the dey of Algiers. The dey had expelled the consul from the country, following this with "acts

---

pronouncements [not cited] of distinguished members of this bench—the Constitution does grant to the President extensive authority in times of grave and imperative national emergency. . . . I cannot sustain the seizure in question because here, as in Little v. Barreme . . . , Congress had prescribed methods to be followed by the President in meeting the emergency at hand." There is no mention of concurrent power or of emergency in *Little v. Barreme*. It seems obvious that Marshall's reference to "the then existing state of things" was to the other statutes established by Congress for the limited war with France. Marshall said that it was arguable, though far from certain, that in the absence of a congressional prohibition these statutes might have permitted the President to seize an American vessel leaving a French port. Marshall had explicitly stated his views in Talbot v. Seeman, 5 U.S. (1 Cranch) 1, 28 (1801). "The whole power of war being, by the Constitution of the United States, vested in Congress, the acts of that body can alone be resorted to as our guides in this inquiry."

of more overt and direct warfare against the citizens of the United States trading in the Mediterranean." (*181*, I, 506, 539) On February 23, 1815, Madison sent his next message on the subject to Congress.

> The considerations which made it unnecessary and unimportant to commence hostile operations on the part of the United States being now terminated by the peace with Great Britain, which opens the prospect of an active and valuable trade of their citizens within the range of the Algerine cruisers, I recommend to Congress the expedience of an act declaring the existence of a state of war between the United States and the Dey and Regency of Algiers, and of such provisions as may be required for the vigorous prosecution of it to a successful issue. (*181*, I, 539)

On March 3 Congress passed an act copied from the declaration of war against Tripoli in 1802.* With a fleet of ten ships, Commodore Stephen Decatur subdued Algiers and exacted a treaty of peace.

In the twentieth century, before the declarations of general war against Germany and Italy on December 11, 1941, President Franklin D. Roosevelt committed several acts of war, and Congress passed at least one statute, as well as the Lend-Lease Act, instituting a state of limited war against both Germany and Italy. One of the first of these acts of war, at the outbreak of World War II, occurred when the President established a naval patrol for some hundreds of miles into the Atlantic to report the presence of German and later Italian naval vessels. The information was relayed to the British. This made the United States, to a limited extent, a cobelligerent of Great Britain.

In the evacuation of British, French, and Belgian soldiers at Dunkirk between May 29 and June 2, 1940, ten British destroyers were lost and seventy-five damaged; this amounted to nearly half the British destroyer fleet. As early as May 15, five days after taking office, Prime Minister Winston Churchill had asked President Roosevelt for the loan of forty or fifty old destroyers. On July 31, after further losses, he pleaded for fifty or sixty. The United States had previously decommissioned fifty destroyers built during the First World War, and the administration now made an agreement to transfer them to Great Britain in exchange for ninety-nine-year leases on six naval bases on British territory in the western hemisphere. Churchill insisted that two other bases be regarded as gifts. On August 27, 1940, Attorney General Robert H. Jackson advised the President that an act of 1883 authorized the President to sell naval vessels and an act of 1940 authorized him to transfer, exchange, sell, or otherwise dispose of naval vessels and equipment if the chief of naval operations should certify that this materiel was not essential to the defense of the United States. These acts, Jackson said, authorized the destroyer exchange. However, an act of June 15, 1917, forbade sending out of the United States, during a war in which the United States was a neutral, vessels built under an agreement to deliver them to a belligerent nation. This, Jackson said, would preclude delivery to Great Britain of the mosquito boats currently under construction for the United States Navy. Jackson also asserted that the President might accept the naval bases without a treaty if acceptance entailed no legal obligation on the part of the United States. This authority derived both from the President's position as commander in chief and from statute.* The chief of naval operations certified that the destroyers might be spared, and on September 3, 1940, the President announced the exchange.

This was only a stopgap. In his annual message on January 6, 1941, the President asked Congress "for authority and funds sufficient to manufacture sufficient munitions and war supplies of many kinds, to be turned over to those nations which are now in actual war with aggressor nations." He assured Congress that "such aid is not an act of war, even if a dictator should unilaterally proclaim it so to be." (153, 668–69) On March 11, 1941, Congress passed the Lend–Lease Act which provided that the President might authorize the manufacture of "any defense article for the government of any country whose defense the President deems vital to the defense of the United States" and might "transfer title to, exchange, lease, lend, or otherwise dispose of," to any such government, any article manufactured under the act.* The act did not designate the recipients of such aid or the adversaries who threatened the defense of the United States. But those adversaries had been positively identified as Germany and Italy by the President and by Congressmen. At the time the act was passed, Great Britain was the nation chiefly eligible for aid, but when Germany invaded the Soviet Union on June 22, 1941, that country became eligible also. In short, states became beneficiaries of the act not by designation, but by virtue of their adversary relation to the Axis Powers. Secretary of War Henry L. Stimson called it "a declaration of economic war." (207, 360) It was more than that: it was a declaration of limited war.

The Lend–Lease Act provided that "nothing in this Act shall be construed to authorize or to permit the authorization of convoying vessels by vessels of the United States." In April 1941, however, the United States took over the patrol of the Atlantic to the 25th parallel, releasing British ships for other duties. The line was subsequently adjusted to include Iceland on July 7, 1941, when the President informed Congress that by agreement with the government of Iceland he had as commander in chief landed marines to supplement and eventually replace British forces there. In the same message he announced that he had instituted convoys to Iceland and all other "strategic outposts." (154, 255) On September 11 he announced that he had ordered the navy to attack Axis submarines at sight. (154, 391) On November 17, at President Roosevelt's request, Congress authorized the arming of merchant vessels.* On December 11 Germany and Italy declared war on the United States, which responded with general declarations of war on the same day.

Six times Congress has passed what might loosely be called contingent declarations of war, but of the five that actually fell in this category, only one produced war. In 1811 Spain was paralyzed by civil war, and the United States was on the brink of war with Great Britain. It was feared that the British might establish a base in Spanish Florida for the purpose of attacking the United States. On January 15, 1811, Congress authorized the President to employ the army and navy to take possession of and occupy East Florida in case an arrangement should be made with local authorities for delivering up the territory to the United States or in case "any foreign government" should attempt to occupy the territory.* The resolution was secret and was not published until 1818. It was not an ultimatum to Great Britain, for it was not communicated. Primarily authorizing resistance to a British landing, it also authorized an act of war against Spain. However, a companion resolution, also secret, provided that the occupation should be temporary pending negotiation. The resolution can hardly be called a conditional declaration of war; it was contingent legislation for an act of war upon the occurrence of either of two conditions. In 1812 General George Matthews occupied Amelia Island in East Florida, but neither of the conditions in the act had been fulfilled, and congressional pressure forced Madison to withdraw the general. In 1818 President Monroe cited the act to justify an attack upon a group of adventurers on Amelia Island (*181*, I, 593), but the conditions of the act had not been met in this case either.

On January 2, 1819, President Monroe asked his cabinet whether it would be proper to suggest that Congress authorize the President, on certain contingencies, to take possession of parts of Spanish Florida. Secretary of War John Calhoun and Secretary of the Treasury William Crawford opposed the proposal; Secretary of State John Quincy Adams and Attorney General William Wirt favored it. Calhoun said that "Congress ought to pass laws only on existing facts, and not upon speculative anticipations." Wirt cited the act of 1811 as proof that "Congress did legislate upon speculation as well as fact." (*4*, IV, 207) Monroe dropped the idea.

In 1839 the location of the Maine border was in dispute with Great Britain. On March 3 Congress authorized the President

> to resist any attempt on the part of Great Britain to enforce, by arms, her claim to exclusive jurisdiction over that part of Maine which is in dispute between the United States and Great Britain; and for that purpose to employ the naval and military forces of the United States and such portions of the militia as he may deem it advisable to call into service.*

The act further authorized the President, if actual invasion of the United States should occur, or if in his opinion there was imminent danger of invasion before Congress could be convened, to accept the services of volunteers up to the number of fifty thousand and to build or procure vessels on the Great Lakes. The act was to expire sixty days after Congress should reconvene. It authorized the secretary of the treasury to borrow ten million dollars for the execution of its provisions.*

This was not a conditional declaration of war. It did not call on Great Britain for reparations but for inaction. Nor was it, as it has been called, truly a contingent declaration of war. (*14*, 46) By the militia act of 1795 the President was already authorized to call out the militia to repel invasion.* The resolution added an authorization to use the army and the navy, but if, as the framers supposed, the President had constitutional authority to employ the national forces to repel an invasion, the resolution gave him no new combat power. Its legal effect was exhausted by the authorization to raise volunteers and to procure vessels. Perhaps its purpose was not legal but minatory: it may have been intended to emphasize to Great Britain the importance that the United States attached to its territory. On December 2, 1839, President Van Buren informed Congress that the "extraordinary powers vested in me for the defense of the country in an emergency, considered so far probable as to require that the Executive should possess ample means to meet it, have not been exerted." (*181*, III, 1746)

The United Nations Participation Act of 1945, the Formosa Resolution of 1955, and the Middle East Resolution of 1957 all undertook to commit the nation to war in certain contingencies, but none of them produced war.* Only the Tonkin Gulf Resolution of 1964 has had that effect.* The resolution delegated to the President the power to use force, in his discretion, to assist any member of protocol state of the Southeast Asia Collective Defense Treaty Organization in defense of its freedom against any aggressor. This was considered justification of the war in Indochina until 1971, when the resolution was repealed.

Such contingent legislation raises the problem of the delegation of legislative power, a problem that had hardly emerged when Monroe asked his cabinet about contingent congressional authorization in 1819. It will be argued later that under the law of delegation, the power to make war cannot be transferred to the President. At this point, however, we are concerned only with the meaning of the war clause. Does the grant of the power to Congress "to declare war" include the power "to declare future wars," whether by authorizing presidential action or by other means? No, it does not.

A state of war is, according to international law, a legal status. Because it effects a change of legal status, a declaration of war is by joint resolution rather than by statute. One cannot effect a future change of status in the present. One cannot enter into a future state of war in the present, any more than one can enter into a future state of marriage in the present. It is, of course, possible to become engaged, to incur an obligation to enter into a given status or to declare an intention to enter into that status, dependent upon the occurrence of a contingency in the future. But the occurrence of that contingency will not itself bring about a change of legal status. Only the legally operative act, such as a declaration of war, can effect a change of legal status after the contingency has occurred.

To phrase the matter in philosophical terms, a declaration of war is what John L. Austin called a "performative utterance." (9, 232–55) A performative utterance is not reportorial; it is neither true nor false. It is a set of words by which the speaker makes a commitment or works a consequence, such as "I promise" or "I do take this woman to be my lawful wedded wife"—words whose function is to do something rather than merely to say something. Typically, a performative utterance has the subject in the first person and the verb in the present tense, although language affords other equivalent expressions. If the verb were in the past tense, "I promised," the sentence would no longer be performative; it would merely report, truly or falsely, a past event. An utterance with the verb in the future tense, "I shall promise," would not be performative, because one cannot in the present perform in the future; it would merely be a forecast that a performative utterance will be made in the future. To be sure, it is possible to make a performative utterance in the present about a contemplated performative utterance, as "I promise that I will take this woman to be my wife in six months." But at the end of six months there will not be a marriage unless the appropriate performative utterance is made at that time.

The words *"Resolved, by the Senate and House of Representatives . . .* That the state of war between the United States and the Imperial German Government . . . is hereby formally declared" are in effect a performative utterance in the "first person singular present indicative active," as Austin puts it. The words "The Congress shall have power . . . To declare war" authorize such a performative utterance. But they authorize only performative utterances, and only performative utterances by Congress. Only Congress may declare war, and it may declare only present wars, not future wars.

It is, of course, possible to promise in the present to go to war upon the occurrence of a contingency in the future, as explained earlier, but such a promise is not an exercise of the power of Congress to declare war. The treaty may be dishonored, as the United States in 1793 dishonored the treaty of alliance with France of 1778. Or the treaty may be honored after the occurrence of the contingency, but only by a declaration of war in the present tense by the two houses of Congress.

Westel W. Willoughby makes this distinction in his reply to those who argued that subscribing to the Covenant of the League of Nations would invade the war power of Congress.

> An agreement to declare and wage war, and a declaration of war, are distinct and different acts. Thus, the United States may, by a treaty, pledge its faith that it will, under given circumstances, go to war, but the arising of those circumstances cannot operate of themselves, *ipso facto*, to place the United States in a state of war. For that a declaration of a state of war by Congress is necessary, and this is true even when, as in the case of the Covenant of the League of Nations, it is declared that

"Should any member of the League resort to war in disregard of its covenants under Articles 12, 13, or 15, it shall *ipso facto* be deemed to have committed an act of war against all other members of the League of Nations which hereby undertake immediately to subject it to the severance of all trade or financial relations, etc." In any such, or other case the United States would not find itself at war until Congress has so recognized or declared it. (*240*, I, 531–32)

It might be thought that a conditional declaration of war is a declaration of future war, but a moment's reflection will show that this is not true. A conditional declaration of war without a declaration pure and simple does not institute a state of war; for that a declaration pure and simple at a later date is necessary. A conditional declaration coupled with a declaration pure and simple does immediately institute a state of war but suspends hostilities in order to give the adversary an opportunity to comply with an ultimatum.

Although it is legally impossible to declare a future war, it is factually possible to take in the present a decision that will become operative at a future date and will automatically produce a condition of war. Herman Kahn asserts it is technologically possible to create nuclear devices that will be triggered by specified misdeeds of the Soviet Union and will destroy the earth. (*94*, 145–49) The "Doomsday Machine" can be set irrevocably, insuring a future war not only without the will but also even against the will of the President and Congress in office at that time. If, as Thomas Jefferson believed, "the earth belongs to the living," and not to the dead, we have no right to sentence our children or our children's children to war because of our own anxieties or apprehensions. They should be allowed to choose for themselves. This is what the framers intended.

Congressional declarations of war, whether general or limited, pure and simple or conditional, have always been addressed to a known adversary; one cannot declare war against, or be in a state of war with, an unknown adversary. Such declarations have always defined the scope of the hostilities or the acts of war authorized. They have always instituted contemporaneous hostilities. One cannot be in a future state of war. Except for one conditional declaration of war unaccompanied by a declaration pure and simple—a single case in our history—declarations have explicitly authorized the use of the armed forces. In the case of general declarations, the use of the army, the navy, and the militia has been specified; in the case of limited wars, the authorization has often been confined to the use of the navy and privateers. If Congress should declare war without authorizing the use of armed force, the legal state of war would exist, but the President would be able to respond only to attack.

To this account, however, there are the exceptions of four contingent declarations of war that have not produced the legal state of war, and the Tonkin Gulf Resolution, by which Congress purported to authorize the President to enter into a state of war in the future, and the President did so. Surely the framers, who thought that they had, as Jefferson said, "given an effectual check to the Dog of war by transferring the power of letting him loose from the Executive to the Legislative body" (87, XV, 384–98), never intended that Congress should lose its power to control the institution of a state of war. They never supposed that a state of war could arise except as a result of a contemporaneous decision of Congress on the basis of contemporary known facts or as a result of the sudden attack of an enemy.

There are those who believe that the unprecedented magnitude of the evils of modern war is a reason for relaxing the constitutional limits and making it easier to enter into war. They value "flexibility" in foreign policy and favor statutes that would enable the President, like Zeus, to brandish his thunderbolts to counter perceived threats to American security around the world. The framers had a different view of the requirements of flexibility. They authorized conditional declarations of war in order to avoid the necessity of making declarations pure and simple. And on three of the four occasions on which Congress has made conditional declarations of war, the issue has been resolved without recourse to general war.

While the United States may not legally institute a state of war in the absence of a contemporaneous declaration by Congress, it has scarcely been doubted that the President may respond to general war launched against the United States by a foreign enemy. The debates at the Constitutional Convention make it clear that the President was to have power "to repel sudden attacks." (53, I, 21) At the same time, it is clear that Congress was to have the policy–making role of "judging . . . the causes of war" and of thus determining when the United States should initiate hostilities against a foreign nation. (111, II, 6423) In conformity with these general contours of war–making authority, the President's war power was to be limited both by the exigencies of the "sudden attack" giving rise to its use and by the responsibility to defer to the policy–making branch of the government at the earliest possible moment. (226, 1, 9)

Proponents of a broad reading of presidential war power, on the other hand, maintain that The Prize Cases support a more expansive view of the President's emergency power. (66, 442; 194, 202–6) For example, Senator Goldwater asserts, on the authority of the scholarship of Bernard Schwartz, that The Prize Cases, "properly construed," support the view that the President may initiate foreign hostilities without a declaration of war under "the principle of national self-defense." (66, 442)

In The Prize Cases, the Supreme Court sustained in a 5–4 opinion the legality of President Lincoln's Civil War blockade of southern ports prior to the congressional declaration of war.* The Court was closely divided on the question of whether the President's constitutional power included authority to recognize a state of war and to institute a blockade under the law of nations.* Members of the Court agreed that the President may neither declare war nor launch general war against a foreign enemy. In addition, all agreed that the President possesses constitutional power to repel an attack on the United States. Under the broadest reading of the majority opinion, the disagreement in the Court centered on the question of whether the actions of a foreign nation or domestic insurgents might themselves create a state of general war, so that the President might also respond offensively and invoke the prerogatives of a nation at war. This internal debate on the scope of the President's constitutional power does not provide support for a presidential prerogative to intervene in foreign lands whenever he believes that the nation's vital interests are at stake.

The conflicting views among members of the Court reflected different readings of the law of nations which, in turn, led to contrasting views of the municipal law of the United States. In dissent, Justice Nelson argued that only Congress could legally recognize the existence of a state of war under the law of nations. The invasion by the southern states established the existence of war "in a material sense" but could not create a state of war de jure so as to oblige neutrals to respect the belligerent right to blockade.[3] Accordingly, the attempt to exclude neutral nations represented an illegal act of war. At the same time, Justice Nelson did not doubt the President's authority to respond to an "insurrection at home or invasion from abroad," including power to use the armed forces to the extent necessary to deal with the crisis.[4]

Writing for the majority, Justice Grier contended that the material fact of war established a "state of war" for purposes of international law.[5] Although the President lacked authority "to initiate or declare a war," he did have power to acknowledge the state of war brought about by hostile invasion, whether by the armed forces of an internal rebellion or of a foreign state.[6] In addition, Justice Grier emphasized certain special circumstances that

[3]". . . in one sense, no doubt this is war, and may be a war of the most extensive and threatening dimensions and effects, but it is a statement simply of its existence in a material sense, and has no relevancy or weight when the question is what constitutes war in a legal sense, in the sense of the law of nations, and of the Constitution of the United States. . . . [B]efore [war] can exist, in contemplation of the law, it must be recognized or declared by the sovereign power of the state, and which sovereign power by our Constitution is lodged in the Congress of the United States civil war, therefore, under our system of government, can exist only by an Act of Congress. . . ." The Prize Cases, 67 U.S. (2 Black) at 690 (1863) (Nelson, dissenting).

[4]Ibid., 692.

[5]Ibid., 666.

[6]"If a war be made by invasion of a foreign nation, the President is bound to resist force, by force. He does not initiate the war, but is bound to accept the challenge. . . . And whether the hostile party be a foreign invader, or States organized in rebellion, it is nonetheless a war, although the declaration of it be 'unilateral.' " Ibid., 668.

further substantiated the existence of a state of war and helped to legitimate the President's decision to go beyond the mere repelling of the attack and to order acts of war, including a blockade, against the South. These special circumstances included the occupation of United States territory by the rebels, Great Britain's diplomatic recognition of a state of belligerency by the time the blockade had been instituted, and the common understanding that civil wars generally are not publicly proclaimed as are wars against foreign nations.[7]

The Prize Cases may thus be read narrowly as providing support only for the view that the President's statutory power to call out the militia to quell domestic rebellion provided him full authority to recognize the existence of a state of civil war.[8] Even the broadest reading of *The Prize Cases*, however, would still not support the view that the President may wage offensive war whenever he feels America's security would otherwise be threatened. Under either reading, *The Prize Cases* recognize a relatively narrow exception to the general rule that the President may not wage offensive war without a congressional declaration of war. Indeed, the Court's majority affirmed that "Congress alone has the power to declare a national or foreign war" and that the President "has no power to initiate or declare a war either against a foreign nation or a domestic State."[*]

The Supreme Court's ruling on de facto war in *The Prize Cases* was supported by historical precedent and by the statements of leading commentators on the Constitution. The Court had previously held, in cases arising out of the Whiskey Rebellion, that domestic insurgents might create a material state of civil war, or war de facto. In *United States v. Mitchell*, for example, a circuit court convicted a participant in an attack on the home of one General Nevill. The defendant had been indicted "for high treason, by levying war on the United States," and the issue became whether the rebellion constituted "levying war" under Article III of the Constitution.[*] The circuit court concluded that an insurrection for public rather than private

[7]Ibid., 666–67, 669. Justice Grier's opinion refers to the condition existing between the states as a state of war and asserts that it constituted war de facto. The Court thus held in effect that war in fact (war de facto) may itself constitute a legal state of war (war de jure) at international law, if it evidences an intent to be at war. Writers on international law, such as John Bassett Moore, agree with the thesis that war de jure may exist without a formal declaration of war. (*119*, VII, 171) Moore, however, would reserve the term *war de facto* for acts of war that do not create all the rights and obligations of war de jure at international law, although, in another sense, even war de facto is the making of war "in a legal sense." (*118*, V, 195–96)

[8]The court stressed not only that civil wars are not typically heralded by a declaration of war, but also that the Constitution does not empower Congress to declare war "against a State, or any number of States." (2 Black at 668) The distinction between the initiation of civil wars and foreign wars is upheld by leading commentators. See Moore, *119*, VII, 171; Van Alystyne, *226*, 12 n.21.

motives (in this case, to prevent the execution of the act of Congress imposing excise tax), constituted levying war by a "usurpation of the authority of government," a matter of "national concern."[9] The majority's view that the acts of another nation may create a state of war at international law and authorize presidential resistance was not one lacking historical support.

In *United States v. Smith*, for example, Justice Paterson contended that another nation might create "a state of complete and absolute war" either by invading the United States or by means of a formal declaration of war.* In either case, the President would then be in a position "to carry hostilities into the enemy's own country."* Similarly, Madison wrote to Monroe in 1827, "The only case in which the Executive can enter a war, undeclared by Congress, is when a state of war has 'been actually' produced by the conduct of another power, and then it ought to be made known as soon as possible to the Department charged with the war power."[10]

Clearly, there are some line–drawing problems implicit in this approach to defining the scope of the President's constitutional war power. First, as demonstrated elsewhere, it is up to Congress to determine when a mere act of war deserves a military response beyond the necessities of pure self–defense, whether by way of reprisal or of formal, general war. However, the line between hostile acts of war and hostilities that create a state of war may not always be a clear one. It is well known that powerful nations have waged war, and even invaded nations, while categorizing their acts as defensive measures or as reprisals, insisting that the result of their acts was something short of a legal state of war.[11] The less powerful nation, perhaps wishing to avoid wider hostilities, and third party nations preferring to avoid the obligations of neutrals, have frequently joined in the characterization of the hostilities as something less than a state of war.[12] Thus, in practice, the

---

[9]It should be noted that while *The Whiskey Rebellion Cases* lend support to the Court's position in *The Prize Cases,* the issues raised by the treason charges did not require the Mitchell court to address the question of whether the same acts of rebellion would have created a state of war for purposes of the international law questions raised in *The Prize Cases.*

[10]*111,* II, 600. Other courts and commentators have expressed similar views of the power of the President to wage offensive war where a state of war is commenced by a foreign enemy. See, e.g., Dole v. The Merchant's Marine Insurance Company, 51 Me. 465 (1862). (Congress alone may declare war, but war may be initiated by other nations so that it exists without any declaration by Congress.) And see Hamilton, *71,* VIII, 249–52.

[11]See generally Bowett, *20,* 117–20; Brownlie, *23,* 27–28, 38–40, 384–401; Moore, *119,* VII, 153–54; and Schwarzenberger, *196,* 460.

[12]The classic example of the situation where no interested party wished to acknowledge the existence of a state of war involved hostilities between Japan and China in the 1930s. In particular, between 1937 and 1941, Japan engaged in extensive

distinction between acts of war and a state of war instituted without formal declaration is frequently blurred.

Given this confusion, some historical contexts could have provided Presidents with opportunities to confuse an act of war with a state of war and invoke broad powers. For example, in *The Prize Cases*, the Court supported its broad definition of war as a material fact, in part, by relying on the historical precedent of the Mexican War. When Congress declared war against Mexico, it recognized "a state of war as existing *by the Act of* the Republic of Mexico," referring to the battles of Palo Alto and Resaca de la Palma.* Under such an interpretation of international law, the President might have recognized a state of war as having been instituted by Mexico, and he might have waged offensive war without a congressional declaration, even though it is not clear that Mexico had deliberately created a general state of war between the two countries.[13]

It is equally clear that a declaration of war against the United States may not always create an immediate and continuing threat such as to give carte blanche to the President to wage war. In *The Prize Cases*, the Court relied on the statement of Lord Stowell that "a declaration of war by one country only, is not a mere challenge to be accepted or refused at pleasure by the other."* Nevertheless, it generally should be up to Congress to determine the nation's response to a declaration of war. America's war against Tripoli in 1801 provides a historical example of why this should be. As noted previously (*see* Chapter 2, pp. 23–25), President Jefferson had sent a naval squadron to protect American commerce in the Mediterranean. After a naval skirmish with Tripoli, President Jefferson sought authorization from Congress to take necessary steps, including offensive measures, to protect American commerce. Subsequent to this initial encounter, but prior to his request to Congress for additional authority, President Jefferson learned that Tripoli had declared war on the United States. (*201*, 212) With Congress in a position to determine the appropriate American response, and with no more immediate emergency presented by the mere news of the declaration, it would have been unreasonable to assume that President Jefferson was now released from his obligation to seek the will of Congress. Nothing in *The Prize*

---

land and air operations against China, until it "controlled most of China's ports and had invaded thirteen Chinese provinces." (*23*, 387) Yet during that time neither state acknowledged the existence of a state of war. The League of Nations declined to adopt resolutions based on Article 16, which prohibited "resort to war," because it assumed that enforcement would be too costly and believed that recognition of a state of war might inhibit a possible settlement. In addition, the United States preferred not to recognize the conflict as "war" because its neutrality legislation would have worked to the benefit of the Japanese aggressors, while the United States favored China. (*23*, 387–88) See generally the sources cited in note 11.

[13]Indeed, under the particular circumstances of the Mexican War, it may be argued that President Polk illegally maneuvered the United States into war and had thus already usurped the war power of Congress.

Cases, or in the statement of Madison alluded to previously, would relieve the President of the duty to defer to Congress at the earliest moment. Moreover, it is simplistic to assert that declarations of war are not challenges to be accepted or refused; in some contexts, they are little more than that. For example,

> when Bulgaria, Hungary, and Rumania declared war on the United States on December 13, 1941, President Roosevelt ignored the declarations. Only later, as a gesture of friendship to the Soviet Union, did he ask Congress to recognize that the United States was at war with those countries. Such empty declarations still leave open the decision whether to turn the "paper war" into an actual war, and, hence, theoretically remain candidates for congressional, rather than presidential war-making. (*126*, 1781)

If the balance struck by the framers is to be maintained, it is important to acknowledge that the President's power to recognize the existence of a state of war, and to act accordingly, must always be limited by this duty to turn to the policy-making branch at the earliest possible moment. (*226*, 9) Given this limitation, the thesis of *The Prize Cases* is not difficult to sustain. The doctrine there presented has very little to do with the debate in recent years about the roles of the President and Congress in the war powers area. Nothing in *The Prize Cases* suggests that the President might simply wage offensive war in a far-off land without even the pretext of finding that an enemy had instituted a state of war against the United States.[14] There was no claim, for example, that North Vietnam had brought about a state of war against the United States. In fact, the United States strained to call its actions there by any name but war. Whatever the potential difficulties in drawing a firm line between acts of war and the institution of general war by a foreign enemy, clearly the war clause does not grant the President power to respond offensively without prior authorization of Congress to either acts of war or the institution of a state of war against a third country.

Some have argued, perhaps validly, that the traditional distinction between an act of war and a state of war, or war de facto and war de jure, is more confusing than helpful.[15] Several scholars have called for recognition

---

[14]E.V. Rostow, however, contends that the concession that the President may wage war if the United States is attacked by a foreign country implicitly acknowledges that he may wage war whenever he construes a foreign action as "directed *against the security* of the United States." (*189*, 850 n.28) But, as R. Berger observed in response, "It is precisely this difference between an attack on the United States and acts which are deemed by the President to menace 'the security of the United States' upon which the whole debate hinges." (*14*, 49 n.145) It is for Congress to determine when America's security is threatened sufficiently to justify war, unless war is actually thrust upon us.

[15]See Bowett, Brownlie, and Schwarzenberger, cited in note 11. See also Jessup, *91*, 98.

of an intermediate state between war and peace, and a rejection of the traditional dichotomy between the two.[16] Whatever the fate of these eighteenth-century labels, however, it is essential that the basic role of Congress as the policy-making branch for the initiation of war be re-established.

[16]See Schwarzenberger, *196*, 460 (advocating recognition of "status mixtus"); Jessup, *91*, 98 (advocating recognition of "intermediate status"). Compare McDougal and Feliciano, *109*, 9–10 (arguing that the events and decisions involving "inter-state coercion" are more complex than the war/peace dichotomy or the proposed trichotomy recognizing an intermediate state).

Chapter 5

PRESIDENTIAL REFERENCES TO CONGRESS AND REFUSALS TO ACT

In establishing the early and continuing understanding of where the authority resides to use armed force abroad, it is instructive to examine the cases in which Presidents have asked Congress for authority and Congress has failed to authorize hostile action. Most of these cases have not been proposals for general war; they have been proposals for limited war or acts of war. But each time the President has conceded that the subject fell within the authority of Congress, and on many occasions the executive has refused to act because of a lack of congressional authorization.

In 1792 William Blount, governor of the Southwest Territory, wrote to Secretary of War Henry Knox expressing his apprehension of Indian attack and describing his preparations. On October 9 Knox deferred to Congress. "Until their judgments shall be made known it seems necessary to confine all your operations to defensive measures." (26, IV, 195) On November 26 Knox wrote to Blount that the President felt he could not act. "He does not conceive himself authorized to direct offensive operations against the Chickamaugas. If such measures are to be pursued they must result from the decisions of Congress who solely are vested with the powers of War." (26, IV, 220)

On December 7 President Washington sent two of Blount's letters and an extract from a reply by Knox to Congress.

It remains to be considered by Congress whether in the present situation of the United States it be advisable or not to pursue any further or other measures than those which have been already adopted. (*181*, I, 126)

Congress took no action. In 1795 Blount renewed his representations to Secretary of War Timothy Pickering. Pickering addressed a severe letter of rebuke to Blount for his alarmism and especially for his indiscretion in predicting intervention by the United States on behalf of the Indian enemies of the Creeks. (*26*, IV, 389)

In a special message to Congress on December 6, 1805, President Jefferson described the dispute with Spain over the boundary between Louisiana and Florida, and the course of conduct adopted by Spain.

Considering that Congress alone is constitutionally invested with the power of changing our condition from peace to war, I have thought it my duty to await their authority for using force in any degree which could be avoided. I have barely instructed the officers stationed in the neighborhood of the aggressions to protect our citizens from violence, to patrol within the borders actually delivered to us, and not to go out of them but when necessary to repel an inroad or to rescue a citizen, or his property; and the Spanish officers remaining at New Orleans are to depart without further delay. . . .

The present crisis in Europe is favorable for pressing such a settlement, and not a moment should be lost in availing ourselves of it. Should it pass unimproved, our situation would become much more difficult. Formal war is not necessary—it is not probable it will follow; but the protection of our citizens, the spirit and honor of our country require that force should be interposed to a certain degree. It will probably contribute to advance the object of peace.

But the course to be pursued will require the command of means which it belongs to Congress exclusively to yield or to deny. (*181*, I, 377)

Congress took no action.

A treaty for the cession of Florida to the United States by Spain was agreed upon by commissioners for the two states in 1819, but on December 7, 1819, President Monroe complained to Congress that the King of Spain had not yet ratified the treaty. This Monroe considered a grievance.

A treaty concluded in conformity with instructions is obligatory, in good faith, in all its stipulations, according to the true intent and meaning of the parties. Each party is bound to ratify it. (*181*, I, 626)

Monroe therefore proposed, in effect, the seizure of Florida, forcibly putting "the conditions of the treaty into effect in the same manner as if it had been ratified by Spain, claiming on their part all its advantages and yielding to Spain those secured to her." (*181*, I, 626)

But the King of Spain was sending a minister to the United States to ask for explanations on certain points and to explain the delay in the ratification of the treaty. It would be magnanimous to hear him, and nothing would be lost by delay, so Monroe asked for a conditional declaration of war.

> It is submitted, therefore, whether it will not be proper to make the law proposed for carrying the conditions of the treaty into effect, should it be adopted, contingent; to suspend its operation, upon the responsibility of the Executive, in such manner as to afford an opportunity for such friendly explanations as may be desired during the present session of Congress. (*181*, I, 627)

Congress did not act, and on May 9, 1820, Monroe sent another message to Congress, explaining that the United States would be justified in seizing Florida but that he hoped to arrive at a speedy and satisfactory settlement with Spain and advised postponing any decisions. (*181*, I, 641) In 1821 Spain ratified the treaty, and the Senate ratified it for the second time.

In his annual message to Congress on December 7, 1824, President Monroe described the activities of pirates who put out from the Cuban shore, plundered American shipping, and fled again to the safety of Spanish territory.

> It is presumed that it must be attributed to the relaxed and feeble state of the local governments, since it is not doubted, from the high character of the governor of Cuba, who is well known and much respected here, that if he had the power he would promptly suppress it. Whether those robbers should be pursued on the land, the local authorities be made responsible for these atrocities, or any other measure be resorted to to suppress them, is submitted to the consideration of Congress. (*181*, II, 827)

The Senate asked for further information, and Monroe sent a special message on January 13, 1825. He proposed three expedients: "one by pursuit of offenders to the settled as well as the unsettled parts of the island from whence they issue, another by reprisal on the property of the inhabitants, and a third by the blockade of the ports of those islands." Probably, he added, neither Spain nor the local government of Cuba would resent such action. "It is therefore suggested that a power commensurate with either resource be granted to the Executive, to be exercised according to his discretion and as circumstances may imperiously require." (*181*, II, 848) Congress took no action, and the problem was resolved by United States naval commanders who on their own initiative pursued the pirates ashore and destroyed their bases.

President Jackson likewise encountered resistance to similar requests to Congress. In his third annual address, on December 6, 1831, he reported to Congress that an American vessel had been seized "by a band acting, as they pretend, under the authority of the Government of Buenos Ayres." He had added an armed vessel to the squadron protecting American shipping in those waters and was about to make diplomatic inquiries. "In the meantime, I submit the case to the consideration of Congress, to the end that they may clothe the Executive with such authority and means as they may deem necessary for providing a force adequate to the complete protection of our fellow-citizens fishing and trading in those seas." (*181*, II, 1116) Congress ignored the proposals.

In 1831, the French government agreed by treaty to satisfy American claims for French aggressions on American shipping between 1800 and 1817, but in 1834 this still had not been done. In his annual message on December 9 of that year, President Jackson asked for the power to exact reprisals from French shipping and property if the French Chambers failed to vote the money at their next session. The Senate by resolution unanimously rejected this request. (*181*, II, 1325)

On April 29, 1848, President Polk reported to Congress an offer from the governor of the province of Yucatan in Mexico to transfer the "dominion and sovereignty of the peninsula" to the United States in return for assistance against the Indians, who were "waging a war of extermination against the white race." Similar offers had been made to Spain and Great Britain. Polk said that he did not intend to propose the acquisition of sovereignty over the territory, but neither could the United States allow Spain or Great Britain to acquire it.

> I have considered it proper to communicate the information contained in the accompanying correspondence, and I submit it to the wisdom of Congress to adopt such measures as in their judgment may be expedient to prevent Yucatan from becoming a colony of any European power, which in no event could be permitted by the United States. (*181*, IV, 2433)

A bill authorizing the President "to take temporary military occupation of Yucatan, and to employ the army and navy of the United States to assist the people of Yucatan in repelling the incursions of the Indian savages, now overrunning and devastating the country," passed the House but was dropped by the Senate when it was learned that the war in Yucatan had been brought to a close by a treaty between the government of the province and the Indians.*

On February 28, 1854, the American ship *Black Warrior* was seized in Havana, allegedly for violation of harbor restrictions. On March 10 the House of Representatives asked for information. On March 15 President Pierce sent a special message, together with a report from the secretary of state. Pierce said that he had demanded indemnity from Spain.

> In case the measures taken for amicable adjustment of our difficulties with Spain should, unfortunately, fail, I shall not hesitate to use the authority and means which Congress may grant to insure the observance

of our just rights, to obtain redress for injuries received, and to vindicate the honor of our flag.

In anticipation of that contingency, which I earnestly hope may not arise, I suggest to Congress the propriety of adopting such provisional measures as the exigency may seem to demand. (*181*, IV, 2768)

On August 1 Pierce replied to a resolution of inquiry from the Senate that "nothing has arisen since the date of my former message to 'dispense with the suggestions therein contained touching the propriety of provisional measures by Congress.' " (*181*, IV, 2779) But on December 4 he held out the hope of an amicable settlement as a result of a change of ministers in Spain (*181*, IV, 2811), and on December 31, 1855, he reported to Congress that Spain had "disavowed and disapproved the conduct of the officers who illegally seized and detained the steamer *Black Warrior* at Havana" and had paid the indemnity required. (*181*, IV, 2869)

President Buchanan requested and was repeatedly denied special war powers. On December 8, 1857, December 6, 1858, February 18, 1859, and December 19, 1859, he requested authority to use the land and naval forces to protect transit over the Isthmus of Panama if need should arise. (*181*, IV, 2978, 3048, 3071, 3100) On February 18, 1859 (*181*, IV, 3069), and December 19, 1859, he asked for the power to enforce redress in case American ships were confiscated in Latin American harbors. These requests were refused on the ground that compliance would involve the delegation of the war power of Congress. They will therefore be treated at greater length in Chapter 13.

On December 6, 1858, Buchanan reported that hostile Indians in northern Mexico had raided over the border, committing depredations on settlers and arresting the settlement of Arizona. He requested authority to establish military posts in Mexico. (*181*, IV, 3045) Refused, he repeated the proposal in his message of December 19, 1859. In the same message he recommended sending an expeditionary force into Mexico to obtain redress from a rebel government that had killed several American citizens. These requests, too, were rejected by Congress.

On January 31, 1917, the German government announced that on and after February 1 it would use submarines against all ships in designated areas of the high seas. On February 3 President Wilson addressed a joint session of the Congress. He did not expect the German threat to be executed, but if it should be, he would come before Congress again "to ask that authority be given to me to use any means that may be necessary for the protection of our seamen and our people in the prosecution of their peaceful and legitimate errands on the high seas."* On February 28 Wilson returned to Congress. Two American vessels had been sunk. Since Congress was about to adjourn, he asked for authority to practice "*armed* neutrality."

No doubt I already possess that authority without special warrant of law, by the plain implication of my constitutional duties and power, but I prefer, in the present circumstances, not to act upon general implication. I wish to feel that the authority and the power of the Congress are behind me in whatever it may become necessary for me to do.*

On February 27 a bill had been introduced in the Senate which provided that the President might supply American–owned merchant vessels of American registry "with defensive arms, fore and aft, and also with the necessary ammunition and means of making use of them; and that he be, and is hereby, authorized and empowered to employ such other instrumentalities as may, in his judgment and discretion, seem necessary and adequate to protect such vessels. . . ."* A filibuster prevented a vote on the act, and Congress dissolved on March 4. On March 12 President Wilson announced that he would put armed guards on merchant ships without congressional authority. Germany replied that if this occurred the guards would be treated as pirates. On March 21 Wilson summoned Congress to meet in special session on April 2. On that day he confessed that his plan had been futile and asked for a declaration of war, saying, "Armed neutrality . . . is practically certain to draw us into the war without either the rights or the effectiveness of belligerents."*

The arming of merchant vessels without incorporating them into the naval force was of dubious legality at international law. Moreover, an act of Congress of 1819 authorized any merchant vessel of American registry to defend itself against aggression or search by another merchant ship but not against a public armed vessel of a nation in amity with the United States.* And furthermore, no act of Congress authorized the President to assign guns and gun crews to private vessels. It seems clear that Wilson's action was illegal. Moreover, it was impolitic. If he considered the German action intolerable, he should have asked Congress for a conditional declaration of war on February 26. Conceivably this might have caused the Germans to revoke the objectionable policy.

In a number of occasions, the executive authority has refused to employ armed force abroad because Congress had not authorized it, and a certain evidentiary value attaches to the statements made in these cases. In 1793 Governor Edward Telfair of Georgia became agitated at the possibility of attack by the Creek Indians and demanded federal action; he also considered using the state militia independently. Secretary of War Knox wrote to him expressing the President's disapproval and reminding Telfair that only Congress might authorize offensive war. (152, 51) In 1792 and 1795 the secretary of war had sent similar rejections to requests of Governor Blount of the Southwest Territory, who wanted war with the Chickamaugas.

Another case is especially interesting in view of the current contention, which we shall fully examine in Chapter 12, that the President may make an executive commitment and thereby invest himself with the war power. For even the authors of our first and most famous commitment, the Monroe Doctrine, did not attribute the war power to the President with that declaration. In his seventh annual message on December 2, 1823, President James Monroe told the Congress and the world:

> With the existing colonies or dependencies of any European power we have not interfered and shall not interfere. But with the Governments who have declared their independence and maintained it, and whose independence we have, on great consideration and on just principles, acknowledged, we could not view any interposition for the purpose of oppressing them, or controlling in any other manner their destiny, by any European power in any other light than as the manifestation of an unfriendly disposition toward the United States. (*181*, II, 787)

On July 1, 1824, José María Salazar, the minister of Colombia to the United States, told Secretary of State Adams he had authentic information that France was about to inform his government that she would recognize the independence of Colombia only if it instituted a king, Simón Bolívar or another. The threat of French aggression was implicit. Adams asked Salazar to present his views in writing, and on July 2 the minister wrote Adams a communication which expressed the satisfaction of his government with the announcement of the Monroe Doctrine and inquired "in what manner the Government of the United States intends to resist on its part any interference of the Holy Alliance for the purpose of subjugating the new Republics or interfering in their political forms?" (*183*, 89)

Adams took the matter to the President, and on July 7 he summarized in his diary the cabinet discussion on Salazar's note. "Hope that France and the Holy Allies will not resort to force against [Colombia]. If they should, the power to determine our resistance is in Congress." (*183*, 90) But apparently this was a tentative disposition of the question, for on August 2 President Monroe wrote to Madison describing the problem and commenting, "The Executive has no right to compromit the nation in any question of war, nor ought we to presume that the people of Columbia [*sic*] will hesitate as to the answer to be given to any proposition which touches so vitally their liberties." (*119*, VI, 446) On August 6 Adams replied to Salazar that "by the Constitution of the United States, the ultimate decision of this question belongs to the Legislative Department of the Government." (*183*, 91) In any case, the French threat was empty, for nothing more transpired.

The negotiations in 1844 for the annexation of the Republic of Texas provoked a bewildering variety of statements. In order to induce the Texas government to send a special envoy to Washington to negotiate a treaty of annexation, on his own authority General W. S. Murphy, the United States chargé d'affaires in Texas, assured the Texas secretary of state that during the negotiations the United States would "assume the attitude of a defensive ally of Texas against Mexico"; would maintain a naval force in the Gulf of Mexico, dragoons on the Texas border, and infantry in southern ports of the United States; and would guarantee the independence of Texas in case the negotiations should fail. On March 11 the acting secretary of state of the

United States transmitted President Tyler's repudiation of these assurances.

> The employment of the army or navy against a foreign Power, with which the United States are at peace, is not within the competency of the President; and whilst he is not indisposed, as a measure of prudent precaution, and as preliminary to the proposed negotiation, to concentrate in the Gulf of Mexico, and on the Southern borders of the United States, a naval and military force to be directed to the defence of the inhabitants and territory of Texas at a proper time, he cannot permit the authorities of that Government or yourself to labor under the misapprehension that he has power to employ them at the period indicated by your stipulations.[1]

On April 12 General Murphy reported this disclaimer to the Texan government, but on the same day the treaty was signed in Washington. On April 22 Tyler submitted it to the Senate. On May 15 Tyler, replying to an inquiry from the Senate, stated that because Mexico had threatened to declare war if a treaty of annexation should be ratified, he had concentrated a squadron of vessels in the Gulf and had stationed a military force on the border of Texas. The commander of the squadron had been "directed to cause his ships to perform all the duties of a fleet of observation and to apprise the Executive of any indication of a hostile design upon Texas on the part of any nation pending the deliberations of the Senate upon the treaty, with a view that the same should promptly be submitted to Congress for its mature deliberation." (181, III, 2170) But on May 31, in reply to another inquiry, he misstated his message of May 15. He alleged that he had then "adverted to the duty which in my judgment, the signature of the treaty for the annexation of Texas had imposed upon me, to repel any invasion of that country by a foreign power while the treaty was under consideration by the Senate." (181, III, 2174) On June 8 the Senate rejected the treaty by a vote of 16 yeas to 35 nays. On June 10 Tyler sent the treaty to the House of Representatives with the suggestion that Texas be annexed by joint resolution. This was eventually accomplished on December 29, 1845.

Similar acknowledgements of congressional authority followed. In 1848 Secretary of State Buchanan wrote to the commissioner to Hawaii of a proposal to collect claims by force and therein acknowledged that "the President could not employ the naval force of the United States to enforce [their] payment without the authority of an act of Congress. The war-making power alone can authorize such a measure." (119, VII, 163) In 1851 Secretary of State Webster rejected a proposal that the United States participate in a dispute between France and Hawaii.

---

[1]*Senate Doc. No.* 349, 28th Cong., 1st Sess., 10 (1844). Murphy's assurances are from a letter by the Texan Secretary of State Anson Jones to Murphy of February 14, 1844 (p. 4). On the same day Murphy assured Jones of full compliance "as far, therefore, as my power and authority go."

In the first place, I have to say that the war-making power in this Government rests entirely with Congress; and that the President can authorize belligerent operations only in the cases expressly provided for by the Constitution and the laws. By these no power is given to the Executive to oppose an attack by one independent nation on the possessions of another. (*119*, VII, 163)

And in 1857 Secretary of State Lewis Cass wrote to the British foreign secretary, explaining the American refusal to join in the Anglo-French expedition against Peking.

This proposition, looking to a participation by the United States in the existing hostilities against China, makes it proper to remind your lordship that, under the Constitution of the United States, the executive branch of this Government is not the war-making power. The exercise of that great attribute of sovereignty is vested in Congress, and the President has no authority to order aggressive hostilities to be undertaken.

Our naval officers have the right—it is their duty, indeed—to employ the forces under their command, not only in self-defense, but for the protection of the persons and property of our citizens when exposed to acts of lawless outrage, and this they have done both in China and elsewhere, and will do again when necessary. But military expeditions into the Chinese territory cannot be undertaken without the authority of the National Legislature. (*119*, VII, 164)

Congress, as we have seen, rejected President Buchanan's four requests for power to police the Isthmus of Panama. In 1860 the American Atlantic & Pacific Steamship Canal Company asked for executive action to enforce certain claims against Nicaragua. On March 3 Secretary of State Cass wrote to the secretary of the Canal Company:

The employment of the national force, under such circumstances, for the invasion of Nicaragua is an act of war, and however just it may be, it is a measure which Congress alone possesses the constitutional power to adopt. The President has in three [*sic*] separate messages brought to the attention of that body this subject of the employment of force for the protection of our citizens. . . . But these appeals to Congress have produced no result. . . .

Cases may occur where the circumstances may justify the employ-ment of our naval or military forces, without special legislative provision, for the protection of our citizens from outrage, but it is not necessary to examine the extent or limit of this right, because the principle is inapplicable in your case, where you demand a forcible interposition with the Nicaraguan Government, in order to give effect to the contract to which you refer. (*119*, VII, 165–66)

In 1861 President Buchanan introduced a variation on this theme: he refused to make an agreement to limit Congress in dealing with the rebellion.

In a message to Congress on January 28, 1861, he reported a series of resolutions passed by the legislature of Virginia with a view to resolving the issue between North and South. Virginia proposed that a conference of states be held in Washington and that in the meantime the states that had seceded and the President should agree to abstain from all acts of violence. Buchanan applauded the plan, but said he could not make the agreement proposed.

> However strong may be my desire to enter into such an agreement, I am convinced that I do not possess the power. Congress, and Congress alone, under the war-making power, can exercise the discretion of agreeing to abstain "from any and all acts calculated to produce a collision of arms" between this and any other government. It would therefore be a usurpation for the Executive to attempt to restrain their hands by an agreement in regard to matters over which he has no constitutional control. If he were thus to act, they might pass laws which he should be bound to obey, though in conflict with his agreement.
> Under existing circumstances, my present actual power is confined within narrow limits. It is my duty at all times to defend and protect the public property within the seceding States so far as this may be practicable, and especially to employ all constitutional means to protect the property of the United States and to preserve the public peace at this seat of the Federal Government. (181, V, 3193)

We have already seen that when in 1876 a United States naval officer asked permission to seize a quantity of silver that belonged to a United States citizen and had been taken by a Mexican official, Acting Secretary of State Hunter rejected the request, saying, "The President is not authorized to order or approve an act of war in a country with which we are at peace, except in self-defense." (119, VII, 167) Julio R. Santo, a naturalized citizen of the United States of Ecuadorean origin, was imprisoned in Ecuador in 1881 on account of alleged participation in a political uprising. The U.S.S. Wachusett was dispatched to Ecuador, but Secretary of State Thomas Bayard wrote in 1885 to the consul-general at Guayaquil that its mission was one of peace and goodwill, to achieve a mutually honorable solution.

> The purpose of her presence is not to be deemed minatory; and resort to force is not competently within the scope of her commander's agency. If all form of redress, thus temperately but earnestly solicited, be unhappily denied, it is the constitutional prerogative of Congress to decide and declare what further action should be taken. (119, VII, 109)

Finally, in 1911 the ambassador to Mexico informed President Taft that "President Diaz was on a volcano of popular uprising . . . in which case he feared that the 40,000 or more American residents in Mexico might be assailed, and that the very large American investments might be injured or destroyed." Accordingly, President Taft assembled troops in Texas and California, and ships at Galveston and San Diego, and instructed the chief of staff:

It seems my duty as Commander in Chief to place troops in sufficient number where, if Congress shall direct that they enter Mexico to save American lives and property, an effective movement may be promptly made. . . .

The assumption by the press that I contemplate intervention on Mexican soil to protect American lives or property is of course gratuitous, because I seriously doubt whether I have such authority under any circumstances, and if I had I would not exercise it without express congressional approval. Indeed, as you know, I have already declined, without Mexican consent, to order a troop of Cavalry to protect the breakwater we are constructing just across the border in Mexico at the mouth of the Colorado River to save the Imperial Valley, although the insurrectos had scattered the Mexican troops and were taking our horses and supplies and frightening our workmen away. My determined purpose, however, is to be in a position so that when danger to American lives and property in Mexico threatens and the existing Government is rendered helpless by the insurrection, I can promptly execute congressional orders to protect them, with effect. (*84*, III, 2447–48)

Through the early twentieth century, then, the executive—both the various Presidents and many of their cabinet members—has recognized, both publicly and privately, the jurisdiction of Congress in acts of war. Both by requesting permission to act and by refusing to act without the necessary legislative fiat, Presidents have acknowledged this understanding of the separation of powers. Before discussing the delegation of this power to the President, and the abuses of the war-making power by modern executives, it will be necessary to discuss the President's military powers.

Chapter 6

THE GOVERNMENT
OF THE ARMED FORCES

Article I, Section 8 of the Constitution provides:

> The Congress shall have power . . .
> To declare war, grant letters of marque and reprisal, and make rules concerning captures on land and water;
> To raise and support armies, but no appropriation of money to that use shall be for a longer term than two years;
> To provide and maintain a navy;
> To make rules for the government and regulation of the land and naval forces;
> To provide for calling forth the militia to execute the laws of the Union, suppress insurrection and repel invasion;
> To provide for organizing, arming and disciplining, the militia, and for governing such part of them as may be employed in the service of the United States, reserving to the states respectively, the appointment of the officers, and the authority of training the militia according to the discipline prescribed by Congress. . . .

On the other hand, Article II, Section 2 begins:

> The President shall be Commander in chief of the army and navy of the United States, and of the militia of the several states, when called into the actual service of the United States. . . .

Although the commander in chief clause does not purport to invade the legislative powers of Congress recited in Article I, some commentators have insisted that it gives the President a "co-ordinate war power" under which he may constitutionally exercise some or all of the powers assigned to Congress in Article I without the concurrence of Congress. (*159, 461*)

The purpose of this chapter is to describe the extent of the power held by Congress over the armed forces. It will be shown that the armed forces exist only by virtue of acts of Congress; that the authority of the President over the armed forces, so far as it exists, is conferred by Congress under its power "to make rules for the government and regulation of the land and naval forces"; that Congress may assign the control of the armed forces to officers other than the President; that aside from the constitutional power of the President to use the forces placed under his control to repel a sudden attack, the armed forces may be used only to pursue legislatively authorized goals and only when Congress has prescribed their use in the pursuit of those goals. The power remaining for the President as commander in chief is the subject of the next chapter.

In 1789 Congress adopted the Army of the Confederation and enacted the Articles of War for its government. By subsequent acts Congress has provided for enlarging and reducing the army, the navy, and the air force, and for organizing the militia and reserve forces. Without congressional action there can be no armed forces for the President to command. In 1870, in *United States v. Hosmer,* the Supreme Court ruled that President Lincoln's action in enlisting volunteers at the outbreak of the Civil War was illegal but had been ratified by the act of Congress of August 6, 1861.*

When Congress enacted the Articles of War in 1789, it required in Section 3 that all commissioned and noncommissioned officers and privates of the army swear "to observe and obey the orders of the President of the United States, and the orders of the officers appointed over me."* This has been retained in all the revisions of the military code to this day. In 1792 the Articles of War were made applicable to the militia when called into the service of the United States.*

The oath of obedience to the President and to superior officers constrains the President in assigning commands to military units, for the statute assigns command to the officer of highest rank, or the senior officer if there are two or more of equal rank. In order to relax this restraint on President Lincoln, on December 21, 1861, Congress provided:

> That the President of the United States shall have the authority to select any officer from the grades of captain or commander in the navy and assign him to the command of a squadron with the rank and title of a "flag officer"; and any officer thus assigned shall have the same authority and receive the same obedience from the commanders of ships in his squadron holding commissions of an older date than his that he would be entitled to receive were his commission the oldest; and to receive, when so employed, the pay to which he would have been entitled if he were on the active list of the navy.*

On April 4, 1862, Congress provided for the army that "whenever military operations may require the presence of two or more officers of the same grade in the same field or department, the President may assign the command of the forces in such field or department without regard to seniority of rank."* On January 2, 1868, Congress provided that when different commands of the armed forces serve together, the officer of highest rank is to command unless the President directs otherwise.*

The history of the office of commanding general illustrates the principle. In 1821 Congress reduced the number of major generals from two to one, and the junior of the two, Andrew Jackson, resigned rather than accept demotion. Secretary of War Calhoun then instituted the office of "commanding general" by army regulation and appointed Major General Jacob Brown to the post. The office was recognized in appropriation acts and in two other statutes,* but Congress enacted no legislation concerning the command powers of the commanding general. Throughout the nineteenth century, except perhaps for a part of the Civil War period, it was understood that the Articles of War required that the officer of highest rank hold the post of commanding general. From 1821 to 1828 this officer was Major General Jacob Brown; from 1828 to 1841, Major General Alexander Macomb; and from 1841 to 1861, Major General Winfield Scott, who in 1855 was made a brevet lieutenant general under a joint resolution authorizing the President and the Senate to make such an appointment in order to acknowledge eminent services of the major general in the war with Mexico.*

At the outbreak of the Mexican War, President Polk had not wanted Scott to win credit in the war, for Scott was a Whig. Polk therefore told Congress that it was necessary to provide for "the appointment of a general officer to take command of all our military forces in the field." (181, IV, 2358) He intended to appoint Senator Thomas Hart Benton of Missouri to this position, but the bill to create a lieutenant generalship failed in the Senate. Polk allowed Scott to take command of the southern campaign. Scott stripped General Zachary Taylor in northern Mexico of most of his troops, took Veracruz, and in a few months took Mexico City. In the meantime, there was no practicing commanding general.

Winfield Scott was nearly seventy-five years old when the Civil War broke out. On May 3, 1861, without statutory authority, President Lincoln announced an increase of the regular army by 22,714 officers and men, and on May 14 he appointed George B. McClellan and John C. Frémont major generals. McClellan had been made major general of volunteers on April 23; Frémont was appointed from civilian life. Lincoln nominated them to the Senate on July 16, naming McClellan first; their appointments would be approved August 3. On July 29 Congress enacted that four major generals should be added to the regular army,* and on August 6 Congress ratified Lincoln's actions of calling out the militia and augmenting the armed forces.* On August 19 Lincoln nominated Henry W. Halleck to the office of major general; Halleck was confirmed on February 3, 1862. The order of seniority was then Scott, McClellan, Frémont, and Halleck.

McClellan, in command of the Army of the Potomac, elbowed the aged Scott aside; Scott resigned on October 31, 1861. On November 1 Lincoln wrote to McClellan, "I have designated you to command the whole army." There is nothing peculiar about this appointment, but it is perplexing that opinion at the time attributed the designation to McClellan's merits rather than to his seniority. As a commanding general McClellan proved to be a great disappointment, and on March 11, 1862, the President issued his War Order No. 3: "Maj.-Gen. McClellan having personally taken the field at the head of the Army of the Potomac, until otherwise ordered he is relieved from the command of the other military departments, he retaining command of the Department of the Potomac."

John C. Frémont stood next in seniority, but he was unacceptable, so for some months Lincoln and Secretary of War Edwin M. Stanton undertook to conduct the war. On June 26, 1862, Lincoln announced the formation of the Army of Virginia and ordered Frémont to bring his Army Corps to serve under John Pope, a major general in the volunteers whom Lincoln elevated to brigadier general in the regular army. He made the nomination to the Senate on July 11. Of course, a major general could not serve under a brigadier general, and in any case Frémont had had friction with Pope; Frémont asked to be relieved of his command "for personal reasons." He was never given another command. On July 23 Halleck was appointed commanding general. There could be no question of his giving orders to Frémont, who though still in the service was in effect retired, but McClellan still commanded the Army of the Potomac. McClellan had been insubordinate to his senior, Scott, and certainly would have yielded nothing to his junior, Halleck. McClellan was removed from his command on November 5, 1862, and was never offered another. Because of Halleck's unwillingness to accept responsibility, Lincoln and Stanton continued to make the major decisions until 1864. On February 29, 1864, Congress authorized the President to appoint a lieutenant general from the officers of the army "not below the rank of major-general, most distinguished for courage, skill, and ability, who, being commissioned as lieutenant-general, may be authorized, under the direction, and during the pleasure of the President, to command the armies of the United States."* The office was designed for Ulysses S. Grant, and on March 9 Lincoln appointed him lieutenant general and commanding general. In 1866 the rank of general of the army was created, to be filled by appointment by the President with the approval of the Senate from among those holding a general's commission.* The office was intended for Grant, and he was appointed. Grant had four successors as commanding general before the office was abolished in 1903. In each case the incumbent was also the officer of highest rank in the army.

By enacting the Articles of War, Congress had made it necessary that the commanding general be superior in rank to all his subordinates, but

Congress might alter this. In 1903 Congress created the office of chief of staff. The chief of staff was to have supervision, under the direction of the President or the secretary of war, of all troops of the line and of all staff departments; he was "to be detailed by the President from officers of the Army at large not below the grade of brigadier general."* In 1915 Congress enacted, "There shall be a Chief of Naval Operations, who shall be an officer on the active list of the navy, appointed by the President with the advice and consent of the Senate, from among the officers of the navy not below the grade of captain, for a period of four years, who shall, under the direction of the Secretary of the Navy, be charged with the operations of the fleet."* In 1947 Congress created the office of chief of staff of the air force; the act for the navy was copied except that the chief of staff was to be appointed "from among the officers of general rank who are assigned to or commissioned in the Air Force."*

Clearly, the military superior to whom members of the armed forces owe obedience, owes his command to an act of Congress. Does the duty of obedience to the President derive from the same statute, or does it derive from the commander in chief clause of the Constitution?

Prima vista, one is likely to adopt the latter view. In 1853 Attorney General Caleb Cushing advised the President, "No act of Congress, no act even of the President himself, can, by constitutional possibility, authorize or create any military officer not subordinate to the President."* At that time the statutes permitted the President to give orders directly to military units. During the Civil War the President, the secretary of war, and the commanding general all gave orders independently. On one occasion the secretary of state, in a telegram over the President's name, ordered a vessel on one mission, and the secretary of the navy ordered it on another. (*114*, 94–98)

But in the course of our history Congress has limited, in three different ways, the President's power to issue commands to the armed forces. As a result, Congress made it impossible for the President to convey an order except through the medium of a designated subordinate. If the subordinate was recalcitrant, the President could not reach the lower echelons by a personal order; unless he could replace his immediate subordinate with a more obedient one, the President was helpless. Attorney General John Y. Mason stated the rule in 1846 when he told the President that he could not overrule a decision made by the secretary of war under a statute that did not provide for an appeal to the President. "He has the power of removal, but not the power of correcting, by his own official act, the errors of judgment of incompetent or unfaithful subordinates."*

The first act cutting the President off from the army was the Command of the Army Act of 1867.* In that year Congress divided the southern states into military districts put under military rule. Feeling that some of the commanders had shown too much deference to the governments installed in these states by Lincoln and Johnson, Congress declared on July 19, 1867, that these were "not legal State governments" and that if they continued they were to be "subject in all respects to the military commanders of the respective districts, and to the paramount authority of Congress."* The commanding general of a district might remove any officer of a state government and substitute an officer or soldier of the army, subject to the disapproval of the general of the army. The general of the army was to have the same power of removal and appointment. The congressional program of reconstruction was to be put into effect by the military. Thus the army was given its orders directly by Congress. To insure the exclusion of the President, on March 2, 1867, Congress had passed a rider to an appropriation act which came to be called the Command of the Army Act. It provided that "all orders and instructions issued by the President or Secretary of War shall be issued through the General of the army"—that is, through General Grant—and it forbade the removal of the general without the consent of the Senate. The ninth article of impeachment of Andrew Johnson alleged that on February 22, 1868, the President had called to him William H. Emory, a brevet major general who commanded the troops in the department of Washington, and had argued that the Command of the Army Act was un-constitutional. According to the ninth article, the President hoped to persuade Emory to receive orders from the President that would prevent Stanton from holding the office of secretary of war, despite the tenure guaranteed him by the Tenure of Office Act. Yet no proof of this allegation was offered at the trial of Johnson. The Command of the Army Act was repealed at the request of President Grant in 1870.*

In 1947 Congress enacted the National Security Act.* This act, together with related legislation, produced a result rather like that of the Command of the Army Act. Each of the three military forces was placed under a chief of staff; the chiefs of staff were subordinated to the secretary of the army or the navy or the air force; these positions were made responsible to the secretary of defense, who alone can give orders to the armed forces. On August 23, 1974, Secretary of Defense James Schlesinger revealed that during the days immediately preceding President Nixon's resignation, Schlesinger and the Joint Chiefs of Staff had taken precautions to insure that no orders from the White House reached the forces except through the "constitutional and legislated chain of command." (Salt Lake Tribune, Aug. 24)

Congress also limited the President's access to the National Guard. The Militia Act of 1795 authorized the President to call forth the militia for certain purposes, and to that end he might issue his orders "to such officer or officers of the militia as he shall think proper."* According to the Supreme Court, this language authorized the President to make requisition either from the governors or from the officers of the state militia.* As it happened, the second course was never employed. But in 1908 Congress changed the law. It provided for calling out the National Guard in case of invasion or danger of invasion, in case of rebellion or danger of rebellion against the authority of the United States, and whenever the President might be unable to execute the laws of the United States with the regular forces. "Orders for these purposes shall be issued through the governors of the States, the territories, Puerto Rico, and the Canal Zone, and, in the District of Columbia, through the commanding general of the National Guard of the District of Columbia."* If, before 1908, the President had issued an order to a state adjutant-general calling forth the National Guard, and if his order had been disobeyed, the officer could have been court-martialed. After 1908, the President could no longer issue an order to an adjutant-general in the cases recited in the statute; he could address only the governor. No sanction for noncompliance by a governor has ever been enacted, nor may the President substitute himself for the governor and call forth the militia in a state. At the outbreak of the Civil War not only the governors of the seceding states, but also those of Missouri and Kentucky rejected President Lincoln's call for militia. Delaware supplied one regiment, and the governor of Maryland extorted a promise that his militia would not be used outside Maryland and the District of Columbia.

The position of a governor under this law resembles his position under Article IV of the Constitution. The interstate rendition clause of this article imposes on a governor the duty to surrender a fugitive charged with crime upon the request of the governor of the state from which he fled; an act of 1793 declared that upon appropriate demand "it shall be the duty of the executive authority of the state" to cause a fugitive to be arrested and delivered up.* But in 1861, in *Kentucky v. Denison*, the Supreme Court interpreted the duty as merely moral. "The act does not provide any means to compel the performance of this duty, nor inflict any punishment for neglect or refusal on the part of the executive of the state; nor is there any clause or provision in the Constitution which arms the government of the United States with this power."* Congress has not subsequently made available any legal process against a governor in this case. *Kentucky v. Denison* is sound as a matter of statutory construction; the dictum that the Constitution would not permit Congress to establish compulsory process seems doubtful. One supposes that Congress might impose a sanction upon a governor who refused to call up the state militia, but Congress has not done so. As in *Kentucky v. Denison*, the performance of the duty "is left to depend on the fidelity of the state executive."

Thus Congress has controlled the President in giving orders to the armed forces. In addition, Congress has given its own orders directly. It has not only prescribed the organization of the armed forces and regulated the conduct of their personnel, as by the Articles of War and the Uniform Code of Military Justice, but also imposed tasks to be performed, without using the President as an intermediary. In addition, Congress has subjected officers and men directly to the orders of civilian authorities other than the President—judges, commissioners of the federal courts, marshals, customs officers, the secretaries of state, treasury, navy, and interior, ministers to foreign countries, and governors of states. In 1916 Congress provided that officers and enlisted men should be detached from the navy and the Marine Corps to serve the republic of Haiti.*

On a number of these topics, judicial decisions and opinions of attorney generals have upheld the power of Congress. In 1861 Attorney General Edward Bates advised President Lincoln that he could not create a bureau to deal with the militia because such action was legislative in nature.* In 1862 Bates advised the secretary of the navy that the President as commander in chief had no power to fix the relative ranks of line and staff officers in the navy without the authorization of Congress, the single institution empowered to make rules and regulations for the government of the land and naval forces.*

Attorney General Henry Stanbery ruled that an act of 1865, which gave an officer dismissed by the President a right to a trial by court-martial if he made oath that he had been wrongfully dismissed, was a valid exercise of the power of Congress to make rules and regulations for the government of the land and naval forces.* In 1866 Congress enacted that no officer in the military or naval service was to be dismissed in peacetime except pursuant to the sentence of a court-martial or in commutation of such a sentence. When a cadet engineer was discharged because there was no vacancy for him to fill, the Supreme Court upheld the statute and ruled that he was entitled to his salary.* In *United States v. Symonds*, in 1887, the Supreme Court held that the secretary of the navy, acting alone or by direction of the President, had no power to order that a lieutenant who was in fact performing sea duty should be paid at the rate fixed for shore service.* In 1949, a navy regulation that extended court-martial jurisdiction beyond the term of enlistment in which the offense had occurred was held invalid by the Supreme Court as the regulation conflicted with the governing statute.*

The power of the President and his secretaries to make regulations of a legislative character depends solely on statute. In 1813 Congress provided for provisional rules concerning the duties of specified officers that were to be continued or rejected by Congress; in 1816 Congress approved them.* Sitting on circuit in 1823, Chief Justice Marshall said, "A legislative recognition of the actually existing regulations of the Army must be understood as giving to those regulations the sanction of the law. . . ."*

In 1853 President Pierce issued a "System of Orders and Instructions" for the navy. Attorney General Cushing replied to an inquiry from the secretary of the navy as to the legality of these rules.

> On the letter and theory of the Constitution the President has no separate legislative powers. The Constitution has carefully distinguished the two powers, the executive or administrative, and legislative, one from the other. The President, whether as Executive of the United States, or as commander-in-chief of the Army and Navy, has no legislative power of himself alone, except in his peculiar relation to, and conjunction with,

the two Houses of Congress. But the "System of Orders and Instructions" is, in my judgment, an act in its nature essentially and emphatically legislative, not executive, and, therefore, can have no legality, unless or until sanctioned by Congress, either by previous authorization, or by subsequent enactment, neither of which grounds of legality does it possess. . . .

In the views thus presented, it is not intended to say that the President, as commander-in-chief of the land and naval forces, has not some power to issue directions and orders. So has a commander in command of a squadron, or a general in the field. But such orders and directions, when issued by the President, must be within the range of purely executive or administrative action.*

The practice was for Congress to adopt by statute such rules of the secretary of the navy as it wished to give the force of law. But in 1862 it enacted:

That the orders, regulations, and instructions heretofore issued by the Secretary of the Navy be, and they are hereby, recognized as the regulations of the Navy Department, subject, however, to such alterations as the Secretary of the Navy may adopt, with the approbation of the President of the United States.*

In 1886 the Supreme Court attributed the validity of the navy regulations to this authorization by Congress.*

Officers who obey unauthorized commands of the President are themselves liable for damages. When Captain Little seized a vessel during the limited war with France in obedience to an order of the President that exceeded the statutory authorization, he was held in damages.* When Secretary of State Seward caused a civilian to be arrested in New York during the Civil War and was sued for false imprisonment, the state Supreme Court ruled that the secretary's action could not be justified under the President's power as commander in chief.* After the conviction of a civilian in Indiana by a military commission had been held unconstitutional by the Supreme Court in *Ex parte Milligan*,* Milligan sued General Alvin P. Hovey, who had arrested him, and the officers who had sat on the commission, and he recovered damages.* In 1877 two army officers, who in obedience to superior orders destroyed a trader's whiskey, were held liable because the statute permitted such destruction only in Indian territory.*

Nor may the President assign to a member of the armed forces a duty not imposed on him under statutory authority. In *United States v. Ripley*,* in 1833, and in *Gratiot v. United States*,* in 1841, the Supreme Court held that when an officer is employed in the performance of nonstatutory duties, it must be by contract that gives the officer extra compensation—and of course the power to make such contracts requires legal authorization. In 1953 the Supreme Court held that when a statute provides for conscription of persons—such as doctors—because of their professional skills, they must be assigned to duty "within the categories which rendered them liable to induction."* When President Theodore Roosevelt took the marines from naval ships and stationed them on shore, Congress attached a clause to the naval appropriation act which provided that no part of the appropriation for the Marine Corps could be expended unless marine officers and enlisted men served on board naval vessels. Attorney General George Wickersham upheld this clause.* In 1913 Attorney General James McReynolds, subsequently a Supreme Court justice, ruled that a navy regulation, which permitted staff officers of the Marine Corps to be detached from headquarters and given other duties, contravened the governing statutes and was therefore illegal.* In 1923 Attorney General Harry Daugherty advised the President that he should not use the navy to enforce the National Prohibition Act because there was no statute authorizing the employment of the navy for this purpose, rejecting the suggestion that the President possessed such power "by virtue of his combined constitutional powers, as Commander in Chief of the Army, Navy, and Militia, when in the service of the United States, and the duty that rests upon him to see that the laws are enforced."*

These decisions do not preclude the possibility that the President as commander in chief may have nonstatutory powers that we have not mentioned; this is the subject of the next chapter. But they do seem to establish that the President's relation to the armed forces is created and controlled by statute. The same propositions can be established by the constitutional law of usage. This stems from *Stuart v. Laird*, which in 1803 initiated the proposition that when a Congress contemporaneous with the framing of the Constitution (the latest date recognized as contemporaneous is 1806) has enacted one or more statutes that amount to a legislative interpretation of an ambiguous provision of the Constitution, and this interpretation is sustained by long acquiescence or by the enactment of later statutes of the same tenor, the legislative interpretation is, in one formulation, "entitled to great weight,"* in another, "almost conclusive,"* in another, "conclusive,"* in *Stuart v. Laird*, "too strong and obstinate to be shaken or controlled."*

Without conceding that the provisions of Article I of the Constitution quoted at the beginning of this chapter are in any way ambiguous, it can be demonstrated that the exposition of them offered above is fully supported by contemporaneous legislative interpretations and that a multitude of statutes passed concerning the armed forces would be profitless, but it is pertinent to cite enough to show that the constitutional law of usage establishes two points. First, with the exception of repelling sudden attacks, the President may not use the armed forces to accomplish any purpose unless Congress has authorized the use of the forces for that purpose. And second, statutes passed before and after 1806 have put the control of detachments of the armed forces under officers and agencies other than the President.

President Washington, however, made a false start. Because Great Britain was interfering with American shipping, on March 26, 1794, Congress imposed a thirty–day embargo on all vessels in the ports of the United States except those permitted to leave "under the immediate direction of the President" and provided further "that the President of the United States be authorized to give such instructions to the revenue officers of the United States, as shall appear best adapted for carrying the said resolution into full effect."* Two days later Washington informed Congress that he had requested the governors of the states to use the militia if necessary to detain vessels. "This power is conceived to be incidental to an embargo." (*181*, I, 144) Neither house protested, but Washington was clearly wrong. In the militia act of 1792 Congress had specified the purposes for which the President might call out the militia—enforcing an embargo was not one of them. *Expressio unius exclusio alterius.* Moreover, Congress had provided that the revenue officers should execute the law.

Since calling forth the militia requires an express act of Congress, it is hard to see how this could be authorized by implication. But one must admit that a statute may, by implication, authorize other military action. When Congress authorized the President to procure or build nineteen vessels to protect the commerce of the United States in 1803, it surely intended that he put them to that use.* But since 1878 there has not been, and cannot be, any implied power to use the army. The Posse Comitatus Act, which was passed in that year, makes it a criminal offense to use the army to execute the laws unless that use is expressly authorized by the Constitution or by statute.

Four classes of statutes are relevant to the determination of the issue of presidential and congressional control of the use of the armed forces: congressional authorizations of war; congressional authorizations of the use of the militia and the army in times of invasion, insurrection, or domestic disorder; congressional instructions that the President or another official, or an officer of the army or navy, use military personnel to perform a particular duty; and congressional prohibitions on the use of the military for a particular purpose or in a particular place.

As we have already seen, a declaration of war always specifies the force the President is to use; his authority to use whatever force—the army, the navy, or the militia—is derived from the joint resolution. In 1798 and 1799 Congress authorized the use of the navy against France. This contempora-neous interpretation was adopted in later declarations of limited war and was upheld by the Supreme Court, which ruled that the power to initiate limited, as well as general, wars belonged to Congress and that the President could not go further in hostilities than authorized by Congress.

Our second category of statutes consists of general prospective authorizations for the use of the militia and the armed forces. Limited acts were passed to carry on the Indian war in the Northwest Territory, but the first general act was 1 Stat. 264 (1792). This act provided that if the United States should be invaded by any foreign nation or by an Indian tribe the President might call forth militia from the state or states most convenient to the place of danger to repel the invasion. In case of insurrection in any state against its government, the President, on the application of the legislature of the state, or of the governor if the legislature could not be convened, might call forth militia from any other state or states to suppress the insurrection. Furthermore, if the execution of the laws of the United States should be obstructed in any state by a combination too powerful to be suppressed by judicial proceedings or by the United States marshal, and if this fact should be certified to the President by a federal judge, the President might employ militia to enforce the laws. But before using the militia to suppress insurrection against a state government or to prevent obstruction of the execution of federal laws in any state, the President must by proclamation "command such insurgents to disperse, and retire peaceably to their respective abodes, within a limited time." By 1 Stat. 424 (1795), the statute was repealed and reenacted, but the requirement of judicial notification was dropped.

By 2 Stat. 443 (1807), Congress provided that in all cases in which the President was authorized to call forth the militia for the suppression of insurrection or obstruction to the laws of the United States or any state or territory, he might employ for the same purpose such part of the land or naval forces as he judged necessary. However, he must first issue a proclamation calling upon the insurgents to disperse.

The essential features of the acts of 1795 and 1807 persist to this day.* The most common use of these acts has been in labor disputes, either at the requests of the governors of states or at the allegations that the execution of federal laws is being obstructed. In either case, it is necessary for the President to issue a proclamation calling upon the insurgents to disperse. When President Cleveland, over the protest of Governor John Altgeld of Illinois, sent troops to Chicago in 1894 to break the Pullman strike on the pretext, quite unfounded, that the execution of federal laws was being obstructed, he forgot to issue the proclamation. The governor of Oregon in a tart telegram reminded him of his duty, and Cleveland issued the proclamation five days late.

The third category of statutes, those that impose specified tasks on the armed forces aside from wars and the suppression of riot and insurrection, can conveniently be divided into two classes: the statutes that authorize the President to employ the armed forces to carry out one or another stated function; and those that impose the duty of action directly upon inferior military officers or instruct inferior officers to perform a function at the command of a civil officer other than the President or the secretaries in the Defense Department. Representative statutes of these types can be found in Appendix B.

We should also take into account statutes forbidding the use of the armed forces, sometimes under heavy penalty to the executive. By 12 Stat. 354 (1862), Congress established "an additional Article of War." It prohibited all officers and persons in the military or naval service of the United States to employ any of the forces under their command to return fugitive slaves, and it provided that any officer found guilty by court-martial of violating this article should be dismissed from the service. Then on July 17, by 12 Stat. 591 (1862), Congress provided that no fugitive slave escaping from any state or territory should be delivered up unless the claimant made oath that he was the owner and that he had not in any way given aid and comfort to the rebellion, "and no person engaged in the military or naval service of the United States shall, under any pretence whatever, assume to decide on the validity of the claim of any person, or surrender up any such person to the claimant, on pain of being dismissed from the service."

On February 25, by 13 Stat. 437 (1865), Congress forbade all officers to bring troops or armed men to an election place—"unless such force be necessary to repel armed enemies of the United States or to keep the peace at the polls"—or otherwise to interfere with the election, under heavy penalty. The reenactment in 35 Stat. 1092 (1909) omitted the words "or to keep the peace at the polls" and softened the penalty. This act was provoked by the allegation that provost-marshals had used troops in Maryland and Delaware to secure the election of Republicans.

The so-called Posse Comitatus Act, 20 Stat. 30 (1878), a rider to an appropriation bill, forbade the use of any part of the army "as a posse comitatus, or otherwise, for the purpose of executing the laws, except in such cases and under such circumstances as such employment of said force may be expressly authorized by the Constitution or by act of Congress." Violation of the act was to be punished by a fine not exceeding ten thousand dollars and imprisonment not exceeding two years. This act ended an abuse that had begun in 1856.

On February 15, 1851, a mob attacked the United States marshal and his deputy marshals in the United States courthouse in Boston and rescued a fugitive slave who was being held under the Fugitive Slave Act. On February 18 President Millard Fillmore issued a proclamation denouncing this action, exhorting all citizens and all civil and military officers and personnel to assist in the enforcement of the law and commanding the United States district attorney and all other persons concerned with the execution of the laws to have the offenders arrested and tried. (181, IV, 2645) On the same day the Senate by resolution asked the President for information on the episode and for his opinion as to whether additional legislation was necessary to insure more vigorous execution of the laws. To the latter question he replied by reciting the commander in chief clause, adding:

> From which it appears that the Army and Navy are by the Constitution placed under the control of the Executive; and probably no legislation of Congress could add to or diminish the power thus given by increasing or diminishing or abolishing altogether the Army and Navy. Not so with the militia. The President can not call the militia into service, even to

execute the laws or repel invasions, but by the authority of acts of Congress passed for that purpose. (*181*, IV, 2640)

Therefore, Fillmore noted, the requirement of the Militia Act of 1795 that the President issue a proclamation before using the militia to execute the laws should be repealed, for the proclamation "would often defeat the whole object by giving such notice to persons intended to be arrested that they would be enabled to fly or secrete themselves." The act of 1807, requiring a proclamation before the army or navy was used to execute the laws, contravened, probably inadvertently, the constitutional authority of the President.

> For greater certainty, however, it may well be that Congress should modify or explain this act in regard to its provisions for the employment of the Army and Navy of the United States, as well as that in regard to calling forth the militia. It is supposed not to be doubtful that all citizens, whether enrolled in the militia or not, may be summoned as members of the *posse comitatus*, either by the marshal or a commissioner according to law, and that it is their duty to obey such summons. But perhaps it may be doubted whether the marshal or a commissioner can summon as the *posse comitatus* an organized militia force, acting under its own appropriate officers, without the consent of such officers. This point may deserve the consideration of Congress. (*181*, IV, 2641)

Thus Fillmore made the extraordinary assertion that he had the constitutional right to use the army and navy as a national police force. He asked Congress to confirm this, and also to give him the militia, organized under its officers, as an additional police force.

Congress did nothing of the sort. But in 1854 the question came up again. A marshal in Chicago employed twelve policemen and a party of militiamen to prevent the rescue of a fugitive slave in Chicago and made a claim for their subsistence and per diem compensation. Attorney General Cushing ruled that the claim was valid.

> The law having made it the official duty of the marshals to obey and execute all such warrants and precepts to them respectively directed, and, after the arrest, to keep the person arrested safely, the same law has given to the marshal the power and authority to call to his aid a sufficient force, the whole power of his district, if necessary, or a sufficiency thereof—a competent *posse comitatus*—to guard against threatened rescue. . . .
>
> These considerations apply as well to the military as to the civil force employed; for the *posse comitatus* comprises every person in the district or county above the age of fifteen years, (Watson's Sheriff, p. 60) whatever be their occupation, whether civilians or not; and including the military of all denominations, militia, soldiers, marines, all of whom are alike bound to obey the commands of a sheriff or marshal. The fact that they are organized as military bodies, under the immediate command of their own officers, does not in any wise affect their legal character. They are still the posse comitatus.*

The argument is unsound. If the first act providing for a posse comitatus, the Judiciary Act of 1789, had been susceptible to this interpretation, it was amended by the act of 1807, which placed stringent limitations on the use of the army to execute the laws.

On January 24, 1856, President Pierce said in a message to Congress that if the Free Staters of Kansas should engage in organized resistance to the proslavery government that had supposedly been instituted under an act of Congress, this would be "treasonable insurrection."

> In such an event the path of duty for the Executive is plain. The Constitution requiring him to take care that the laws of the United States be faithfully executed, if they be opposed in the Territory of Kansas he may, and should, place at the disposal of the marshal any public force of the United States which happens to be within the jurisdiction, to be used as a portion of the *posse comitatus*; and if that do not suffice to maintain order, then he may call forth the militia of one or more States for that object, or employ for the same object any part of the land or naval force of the United States. (*181*, IV, 2891)

On February 11, 1856, employing the act of 1807, Pierce issued a proclamation against "unlawful combinations against the constituted authority of the Territory of Kansas or of the United States" and threatened to use the army and the local militia to suppress them. The Republicans in the House of Representatives included a provision in the army appropriation bill forbidding the use of any part of the military force of the United States to enforce enactments of "the alleged Legislative Assembly of the Territory of Kansas," but they were obliged to abandon it. The bill passed in a special session on August 30 without this section. On September 11, 1856, the new territorial governor, John W. Geary, issued a proclamation reciting that a force of the regular army "sufficient to secure the execution of the laws" had been placed at his disposal; therefore, the militia called out by his predecessor was disbanded, and all other bodies of armed men were ordered to disband or leave the territory. Geary gave direct orders to the military force and also ordered them to assist the marshal as a posse.

On December 8, 1857, President Buchanan told Congress in his first annual message that he had appointed a new governor and other federal officials for the Utah Territory and had "sent with them a military force for their protection and to aid as a *posse comitatus* in case of need in the execution of the laws." (*181*, IV, 2986)

During Reconstruction, the occupying forces in the South were used to police and also to serve as posses to United States marshals. In 1877 the House attached a rider to the army appropriation bill forbidding the use of the funds to support either of two rival governments in Louisiana "until such government shall have been duly recognized by Congress." The bill went to conference three times, but eventually the Democratic House surrendered to the Republican Senate, and the bill was passed without the rider on

November 21, 1877. However, in 1878 the Posse Comitatus Act, 20 Stat. 151, 152, was passed as a step in the abandonment of the effort at Reconstruction. Thereafter, it was a criminal offense to use the army "as a posse comitatus or otherwise" to execute the laws without express authorization. A terser version of the act, 70A Stat. 626, which extends the prohibition to the air force, was enacted on August 10, 1956, but Alaska was exempted from the scope of the act. Then 73 Stat. 144 (1959) extended the act to Alaska. The prohibition has never been applied to the navy, but this does not mean that the navy may be used to execute the laws without express authorization. It means that the penal sanctions do not attach if this misuse occurs. There has never been a prosecution under the act, but several court decisions and opinions of attorney generals have assumed that the act is valid.[1] Doubt was expressed by Attorney General Herbert Brownell, Jr., in an opinion on November 7, 1957, when he assured President Eisenhower that his use of troops to execute the laws in Little Rock, Arkansas, was proper because it had been done under the current version of the act of 1807, and the requisite proclamation had been issued. The action did not violate the Posse Comitatus Act because the act of 1807 expressly authorized the use of the army. He added gratuitously, "There are in any event grave doubts as to the authority of Congress to limit the constitutional powers of the President to enforce the laws and preserve the peace under circumstances which he deems appropriate."* To be sure, Fillmore and Taft shared his doubts, but such doubts should be dispelled by the evidence reviewed above—judicial opinions, opinions of attorney generals, and the long legislative practice whose function under the law of usage is to resolve doubt.[2]

[1]The act was held constitutional in Wrynn v. United States, 200 F. Supp. 457, 465 (D.C.D.N.Y. 1961). Its validity was assumed in Jones v. United States Secretary of Defense, 346 F. Supp. 97, 100 (D.C.D. Minn. 1972); Burris v. State, 473 S.W. 2d 19, 22 (Tex. Crim. App. 1971); Hubert v. State, 504 P. 2d 1245, 1246 (Okl. Cr. 1972); Hildebrandt v. State, 507 P. 2d 1323 (Okl. Cr. 1973); Lee v. State, 513 P. 2d 125, 126 (Okl. Cr. 1973); 16 Op. Att'y Gen. 162 (1878); 17 Op. Att'y Gen. 71 (1881); 17 Op. Att'y Gen. 242 (1881); 19 Op. Att'y Gen. 293 (1889); 19 Op. Att'y Gen. 368 (1889).

[2]Taft thought that the Posse Comitatus Act limited marshals but not the President. "By statute, Congress has forbidden the United States marshals to call the army as a *posse comitatus*, but that is not the use of the army by direction of the President under his power as Commander in Chief. Congress may refuse to vote the appropriation for an army, or might repeal the law organizing the army but it cannot provide an army of which the President must be Commander-in-Chief, and then in the law of its creation limit him in the use of the army to enforce any of the laws of the United States in accordance with his constitutional duty." (*212*, 599, 611-12) Actually the act was not addressed to marshals but to all officers, including the President. It had been provoked by actions of the President, and it forbade the use of the army to execute the laws without specific authorization "as a posse comitatus or otherwise." Taft's opinion conflicts with the judicial opinions reported here and with our whole legislative history.

The Selective Training and Service Act of 1940, 54 Stat. 885 (1940), provided that no man inducted under the act should be employed outside the western hemisphere except in the territories and possessions of the United States.

The Department of Defense Appropriation Act of 1970* forbade the use of any of the funds appropriated to finance the introduction of American ground combat troops into Laos or Thailand; this prohibition was repeated in the acts for 1971, 1972, and 1973.* The 1971 Act also provided:

Nothing [above] shall be construed as authorizing the use of any such funds to support Vietnamese or other free world forces in actions designed to provide military support and assistance to the Government of Cambodia or Laos: *Provided further*, That nothing contained in this section shall be construed to prohibit support of actions required to insure the safe and orderly withdrawal of U.S. Forces from Southeast Asia, or to aid in the release of Americans held as prisoners of war.*

This was copied into subsequent appropriation acts, and the Special Foreign Assistance Act of 1971 forbade the use of the funds appropriated to support any United States ground combat troops or advisers in Cambodia.*

In amending the Selective Service Act of 1967 by 85 Stat. 348, 360 (1971), Congress declared that it was "the sense of Congress that the United States terminate at the earliest practicable date all military operations of the United States in Indochina" and described a series of steps the President should take toward this end. When this proved ineffective, Congress incorporated a stronger statement in the National Procurement Authorization Act.

It is hereby declared to be the policy of the United States to terminate at the earliest practicable date all military operations of the United States in Indochina, and to provide for the prompt and orderly withdrawal of all United States military forces at a date certain, subject to the release of all American prisoners of war held by the Government of North Vietnam and forces allied with such Government and an accounting for Americans missing in action who have been held by or known to such Government or such forces.*

Congress spelled out the steps it requested the President take to implement this policy: establish a final date for withdrawal of all military forces, contingent upon the release of all prisoners; negotiate an immediate cease-fire; and negotiate an agreement for phased and rapid withdrawals of military forces in exchange for a corresponding series of prisoner releases. Upon signing the bill, President Nixon made a formal statement that the policy announced by Congress "does not represent the policies of this Administration" and that he intended to ignore the congressional policy.*

Finally, in the so-called Eagleton amendment to a supplementary appropriation bill, 87 Stat. 130, passed on July 1, 1973, Congress enacted:

> Notwithstanding any other provision of law, on or after August 15, 1973, no funds herein or heretofore appropriated may be obligated or expended to finance directly or indirectly combat activities by United States military forces in and over or from the shores of North Vietnam, South Vietnam, Laos or Cambodia.

Thus, in the end, Congress prevailed on the Indochina war.

As a final example of legislative restriction on executive war power, there is 90 Stat. 771, 776 (1976), providing:

> Notwithstanding any other provision of law, no assistance of any kind may be provided for the purpose, or which would have the effect, of promoting or augmenting, directly or indirectly, the capacity of any nation, group, organization, movement or individual to conduct military or paramilitary operations in Angola unless and until the Congress directly authorizes such assistance by law enacted after the date of enactment of this section.

With the reservations noted in the next chapter, it seems clear that the composition, structure, use, and actions of the armed forces are entirely determined by acts of Congress. This is not to say that Presidents have not usurped power. This has happened frequently; some of the cases are reported in Chapters 8–10. But executive usage cannot establish constitutional power. Only legislative usage dating from the earliest history of the Republic can do this. And the legislative usage clearly confirms the exclusiveness of congressional power over the armed forces.

Chapter 7

THE COMMANDER
IN CHIEF CLAUSE

The President shall be commander in chief of the army and navy of the
United States, and of the militia of the several states, when called into
the actual service of the United States.

U.S. Constitution, Art. II, Sec. 2.

The office of commander in chief has never carried the power of war
and peace nor was it invented by the framers of the Constitution. It was
a century and a half old when the Constitution was adopted. Charles I
introduced the term into English law in 1639. To meet the Scots in the
First Bishops War he raised an army and appointed the Earl of Arundel
commander in chief. He instructed the Earl to "withstand all Invasions,
Tumults, Seditious Conspiracies" and authorized him to execute "the law
martial" in the performance of his duties. (30, I, 425-29) With the outbreak
of the Civil War, both King and Parliament appointed regional commanders
in chief, and in 1645 the Parliament appointed Sir Thomas Fairfax
commander in chief of all its forces, "subject to such orders and directions
as he shall receive from both Houses or from the Committee of Both
Kingdoms." Oliver Cromwell succeeded to this office and title, but he
preferred the title of captain general, and later he became lord protector.
There continued to be subordinate commanders in chief, and each fleet was
put under a commander in chief. When the cabinet system developed in the
eighteenth century, the several commanders in chief of armies were subject to the secretary of war. The Duke of Wellington complained that "the

commander in chief cannot move a Corporal's Guard from one station to another, without a Route countersigned by the Secretary of War. This is the fundamental principle of the constitution of the British Army." (30, II, 761) Parallel to this military history, the practice developed of entitling the governor of a crown colony as commander in chief. In a number of suits against such officers it has been established that a commander in chief is subject to civil law and is personally liable in tort for making jurisdiction over civilians.*

A number of commanders in chief were appointed for North America during the eighteenth century. General Thomas Gage was commander in chief from 1763 to 1776. He was the instrument through whom George III, according to the Declaration of Independence, "affected to render the Military independent of and superior to the Civil Power." The memory of his quartering of troops with civilians prompted the adoption of the Third Amendment of the Constitution. In addition, there was usually a commander in chief of the militia of each colony, whether royal, proprietary, or chartered. The constitutions adopted during the Revolution made the state governor the commander in chief, or captain general and commander in chief, of the state militia.

On June 15, 1775, the Continental Congress unanimously chose George Washington as "general." (92, II, 91) His commission, approved on June 17, appointed him "General and Commander in chief, of the army of the United Colonies." (92, II, 96) It instructed him to maintain strict discipline and to follow the Articles of War, which were to be enacted to govern the forces, "and punctually to observe and follow such orders and directions, from time to time, as you shall receive from this. or a future Congress of these United Colonies, or committee of Congress." On June 30 the Congress would adopt the Articles of War. (92, II, 111–12)

On June 20 the Congress ordered General Washington to repair to Massachusetts Bay and take command of the army of the United Colonies. His orders concluded:

> And whereas all particulars cannot be foreseen, nor positive instructions for such emergencies so before hand given but that many things must be left to your prudent and discreet management, as occurrences may arise upon the place, or from time to time fall out, you are therefore upon all such accidents or any occasions that may happen, to use your best circumspection and (advising with your council of war) to order and dispose of the said Army under your command as may be most advantageous for the obtaining the end for which these forces have been raised, making it your special care in discharge of the great trust committed unto you, that the liberties of America receive no detriment. (92, II, 101)

The Congress did not hesitate to issue directions to the commander in chief on matters large and small. On October 5, 1775, the commander in chief was ordered to intercept two British vessels. (92, III, 276) On November

10, 1775, he was "directed in case he should judge it practicable and expedient" to send a force into Nova Scotia. (*92*, III, 178) On June 17, 1776, he was ordered to send General Gates to take command in Canada (*92*, V, 448) and to send to Canada "such small brass or iron field pieces as he can spaire." (*92*, V, 451) The Congress also issued orders directly to Washington's subordinates without consulting him. On June 27, 1775, General Philip John Schuyler was sent to Ticonderoga and Crown Point; if it were practicable, he was to invade Canada. (*92*, II, 109) On July 17, 1775, General David Wooster was ordered to send one thousand men to Albany. (*92*, II, 186) On June 14, 1776, Schuyler was ordered to fortify Fort Stanwix. (*92*, V, 442) On December 11, 1776, General Israel Putnam was ordered to send harassing parties into New Jersey. (*92*, VI, 1023)

The failure of the Continental Congress to vote adequate supplies for the army has caused some commentators to assert that the Constitutional Convention thought the powers of the commander in chief inadequate and intended to give the President greater power than that possessed by General Washington. (*189*, 833, 840–41) If this were so, it is strange that to describe the authority of the President, the framers used the very title the commentators consider to have carried insufficient authority during the Revolution; furthermore, the framers did not specify any of the new powers that the commentators believe were intended to be given to the commander in chief by the new Constitution. In particular, it is strange that the framers did not give the President the power to raise supplies for the army, since this was the respect in which the Continental Congress failed Washington.

In historical usage the title of commander in chief has been a generic term referring to the highest officer in a particular chain of command. It may therefore be applied to a military officer at a level lower than the President and has been so used throughout our history. Major General Anthony Wayne, who commanded the army in the Northwest Territory from 1792 to 1796, was called "commander in chief," and his tombstone bears that title. (*8*, 80) On May 28, 1798, Congress passed "An Act authorizing the President of the United States to raise a Provisional Army." The act provided that the President might appoint, with the consent of the Senate, "a commander of the army which may be raised by virtue of this act, and who being commissioned as lieutenant–general may be authorized to command the armies of the United States."* On July 2 President Adams nominated Washington "Lieutenant–General and Commander in Chief of all the armies raised, or to be raised, in the United States," and on the following day the Senate unanimously approved. On July 18 Hamilton was nominated to the post of inspector general, with the rank of major general, under the same act; he was confirmed the next day.[1] On March 3, 1799, Congress enacted:

[1]The names of two other major generals, Charles C. Pinckney and Henry Knox, followed Hamilton's in the list, but President Adams wished Knox to be second in

> That a commander of the army of the United States shall be appointed
> and commissioned by the style of General of the Armies of the United
> States, and the present office and title of Lieutenant–General shall be
> abolished.*

This seems to be a congressional appointment of Washington to the post
of general of the armies. After Washington's death on December 14, 1799,
Major General Hamilton became the senior officer, but Adams did not
designate him commander in chief. On June 15, 1800, President Adams, as
he was authorized to do by the original act, dissolved the provisional army,
which in any case had not materialized, and Hamilton lost his post. Brigadier
General James Wilkinson, who had succeeded to the command of Anthony
Wayne in the West, was once again the officer of highest rank. In 1806 and
1807 he signed affidavits as "Brigadier General and commander in chief of
the Army of the United States."* An Act for the Government of the Navy
of the United States, passed on March 2, 1799, contemplated that each fleet,
squadron, or detached vessel should have a commander in chief, and this
usage is still followed.* In 1815 the Supreme Court of New York spoke of
the officer in command of a military detachment at Burlington, Vermont,
as "commander in chief of a division of the army."* After the office of
commanding general was created in 1821, the commanding general was
sometimes called commander in chief, sometimes general in chief. The
orders for the funeral procession for President William Henry Harrison in
1841 spoke of "the General Commanding in Chief the Army of the United
States," meaning Major General Macomb. (181, III, 1881) On June 8, 1846,
President Polk called Macomb's successor, Scott, commander in chief of the
army. (181, III, 2298) On November 1, 1861, Secretary of the Treasury
Salmon P. Chase wrote to Colonel T. M. Key: "Let us thank God and take
courage. McClellan will be Commander in Chief from today." (124, 224)
McClellan spoke of his predecessor, Scott, as commander in chief and of
himself by the same title. (124, 194, 222)

By the Constitution, of course, the President has been commander in chief
of these commanders in chief. There was no debate of the commander in
chief clause in the Constitutional Convention. Pinckney of South Carolina,
in the plan he presented to the Convention on May 29, 1787, introduced
the title of President and proposed, "He shall, by Virtue of his Office, be
Commander in chief of the Land Forces of U.S. and Admiral of their Navy."
(53, III, 606) The South Carolina constitution of 1776 provided for a
"president and commander–in–chief," and that of 1778 provided for a
"governor and commander–in–chief." (217, III, 3243, 3249) The Virginia
plan, which was presented to the Convention on the same day, contained

---

command to Washington; he yielded reluctantly to Washington's insistence on
Hamilton. For the dispute see 64, II, 86–104; 231, XI, 280–88, 300–314, 530–48; and
3, VII, 589n.

no such provision. (53, I, 20ff.) The plan presented to the Convention by William Paterson for New Jersey on June 15 provided for a plural executive and read: "That the Executives besides their general authority to execute the federal acts ought to appoint all federal officers not otherwise provided for, & to direct all military operations; provided that none of the persons composing the federal Executive shall at any time take command of any troops, so as personally to conduct any enterprise as General, or in other capacity." (53, I, 244) The proviso was intended to prevent a military coup. It does not appear that Hamilton proposed the title commander in chief in the plan he read to the Convention on June 18. The version taken down by Madison instead contained the words: "to have the direction of war when authorized or begun."[2] When a committee of detail was created to assemble a constitution, the Pinckney plan, the Paterson plan, and the resolutions previously adopted by the convention were referred to it. In the report of the committee, the commander in chief clause was introduced, although not precisely in its final form. It seems clear that the clause derived from Pinckney's draft.

Even the most apprehensive members of the Convention did not fear the legal powers conferred by the commander in chief clause. But they did share the concern expressed in the New Jersey plan: an executive who took personal command of troops might use them illegally to overthrow the republic. Luther Martin reported to the Maryland legislature:

> Objections were made to that part of this article by which the President is appointed commander-in-chief of the army and navy of the United States, and of the militia of the several states; and it was wished to be so far restrained, that he could not command in person; but this could not be obtained. (49, I, 378)

The same misgivings were expressed in the ratifying conventions. George Mason, who had been a delegate to the Constitutional Convention, said in the Virginia ratifying convention:

> He admitted the propriety of his being commander-in-chief, so far as to give orders and have a general superintendency; but he thought it would be dangerous to let him command in person, without any restraint, as he might make a bad use of it. He was, then, clearly of opinion that

[2]34, 292. The version in the Hamilton papers (70, IV, 208) reads, "The Governor . . . to be the Commander in Chief of the land and naval forces and of the Militia of the United States—to have the direction of war, when authorised or begun." Robert Yates of New York and David Brearly of New Jersey appear to have made verbatim copies of the paper from which Hamilton read; they both omit the commander in chief clause and read "to have the entire direction of war when authorized or begun." See also 214, 983, 987. The notes of George Read of Delaware (214, 985), and of John Lansing and Robert Yates of New York (70, IV, 208), also lack the commander in chief clause. The plan in the Hamilton papers appears to be a slightly expanded version of that read to the convention; presumably the additions were made subsequently.

the consent of a majority of both houses of Congress should be required before he could take command in person. (*49*, III, 496)

Patrick Henry predicted that "the President, in the field, at the head of his army, can prescribe the terms on which he shall reign master, so far that it will puzzle any American ever to get his neck from under the galling yoke." (*49*, III, 59) Monroe feared that a President might escape punishment because he commanded the army. (*49*, III, 220)

In defense of the commander in chief clause it was said that the clause was familiar and innocuous. In the North Carolina ratifying convention, James Iredell, who became an associate justice of the Supreme Court, gave this reassurance:

> I believe most of the governors of the different states have powers similar to those of the President. In almost every country, the executive has command of the military forces. From the nature of the thing, the command of armies ought to be delegated to one person only. The secrecy, despatch, and decision, which are necessary in military operations, can only be expected from one person. The President, therefore, is to command the military forces of the United States, and this power I think a proper one; at the same time it will be found to be sufficiently guarded. A very material difference may be observed between this power, and the authority of the king of Great Britain under similar circumstances. The king of Great Britain is not only the commander-in-chief of the land and naval forces, but has power, in time of war, to raise fleets and armies. He also has the power to declare war. The President has not the power of declaring war by his own authority, nor that of raising fleets and armies. These powers are vested in other hands. The power of declaring war is expressly given to Congress, that is, to the two branches of the legislature. . . . They have also expressly delegated to them the powers of raising and supporting armies, and of providing and maintaining a navy. (*49*, IV, 107–8)

And Richard Spaight, who had been a delegate to the Convention, said that Congress could control the commander in chief because it alone had the power to raise and support armies. (*49*, IV, 114)

Hamilton had already written in No. 69 of the *Federalist Papers*:

> . . . the President is to be commander-in-chief of the army and navy of the United States. In this respect his authority would be nominally the same with that of the King of Great Britain, but in substance much inferior to it. It would amount to nothing more than the supreme command and direction of the military and naval forces, as first General and Admiral of the confederacy; while that of the British kings extends to the *declaring* of war and to the *raising* of fleets and armies,—all which, by the Constitution under consideration, would appertain to the Legislature. (*34*, 465)

The Supreme Court has never held that the clause conferred any other powers than those of a military commander, "the commander in chief of the *army* and *navy* of the United States, and of the *militia*. . . ." In 1847 goods were shipped to Philadelphia from Tampico, which was under American military occupation during the Mexican War. The collector of the port of Philadelphia collected duties; the shipper sued to recover the amount. Chief Justice Taney ruled for the Court that Tampico was a foreign port and the collection of duties was proper. To be sure, the United States might annex territory.

> But this can be done only by the treaty–making power or the legislative authority, and is not a part of the power conferred upon the President by the declaration of war. His duty and his power are purely military. . . . The power of the President under which Tampico and the State of Tampaulitos were conquered and held in subjection was simply that of a military commander prosecuting a war waged against a public enemy by authority of his government.*

In *United States v. Sweeny* in 1895, Justice Henry Brown for the Court said of the commander in chief clause that its object was to vest in the President "such supreme and undivided command as would be necessary to the prosecution of a successful war."* In 1919 Senator George Sutherland, later Associate Justice Sutherland, wrote: "Generally speaking, the war powers of the President under the Constitution are simply those that belong to any Commander-in-Chief of the military forces of a nation at war. The Constitution confers no war powers upon the President as such." (*211*, 73)

In 1949, in *Hirota v. MacArthur*, the Supreme Court held that it had no authority to review convictions of Japanese war criminals by an international military tribunal.* Justice William O. Douglas concurred. He insisted that review was not precluded by the fact that the tribunal was international, but by the fact that the decision to participate in the trial was a political decision within the realm of judgment assigned to the President. Douglas said that the power of the President as commander in chief "is vastly greater than that of troop commander. He not only has full power to repel and defeat the enemy; he has the power to occupy the conquered territory . . . and to punish the enemies who violated the law of war."* But these are the powers of any troop commander at the common law of war; the President, like any troop commander, must act within the limits of the law of war and of municipal law.

The Supreme Court has never attributed to the President as commander in chief any other powers than those conferred by the common law of war. But there is a serious constitutional question. Did the Constitution permanently incorporate the common law of war of 1789, or did it give the President a nonstatutory authority which can be altered by statute or by treaty or by the evolution of the customary common law of war?

In the former case, which might be called the constitutional theory, the President's power as commander in chief cannot be limited by statute or treaty. In that case such a treaty as the Hague Convention of 1907, which limited the powers of the commander in chief in the conduct of war in a large number of ways, is invalid because it encroaches on the President's constitutional authority.* The second theory, which might be called the nonstatutory theory, does not entail this unfortunate rigidity. The common law of war is a branch of international law. Since the earliest days of our Republic it has been settled that international law is incorporated in our municipal law but also that it can be deprived of its status as part of our municipal law by statute or treaty.* In this theory, the President's power is like that of the courts. By virtue of their judicial power the courts administer international law, including the common law of war, but when this law is displaced by a statute or a treaty it becomes the duty of the courts to administer this superseding municipal law.* Similarly, the President possesses the authority of a commander in chief as prescribed in the common law of war, but this authority can be increased or diminished by act of Congress or by treaty.

There is a body of opinion in favor of the constitutional theory on one topic—the movement of troops and the direction of campaigns. In a minority opinion for four justices in *Ex parte Milligan* in 1866, Chief Justice Salmon Chase included a much-quoted dictum, "Congress cannot direct the conduct of campaigns. . . ."* The other statements on the problem are extrajudicial.[3] Taft wrote in 1915:

> When we come to the power of the President as Commander in Chief, it seems perfectly clear that Congress could not order battles to be fought on a certain plan, and could not direct parts of the Army to be moved from one part of the country to another. (*212, 599, 610*)

[3]There is another dictum which the reader might consider. After the surrender of Germany in 1945 a group of Germans in China continued to transmit military information about American movements to the Japanese. They were captured and convicted, before a military commission, of offenses against the law of war; they sought release by habeas corpus from the district court of the District of Columbia. On certiorari Justice Jackson argued that an enemy alien outside the territorial jurisdiction of the United States had no right of access to American courts (the law of war originally barred resident enemy aliens as well). He then noted that eight clauses of the Constitution confer war powers on the Congress and that the President is commander in chief. These provisions authorized the United States to set up military commissions on foreign soil. Then he added, inconsistently, since he had just passed on the issue, "Certainly it is not the function of the Judiciary to entertain litigation—even by a citizen—which challenges the legality, the wisdom, or the propriety of the Commander-in-Chief in sending our armed forces abroad or to any particular region." If the trial were illegal, only China had a right to complain, and China had expressly consented. "The issue tendered by '(b)' involves a challenge to conduct of diplomatic and foreign affairs, for which the President is exclusively responsible." And he cited United States v. Curtiss-Wright Export Corp., 299 U.S. 304 (1936), which had held the issue justiciable, and Chicago & Southern Air Lines v. Waterman Steamship Corp., 333 U.S. 123 (1948).

The decision does not suggest that Congress might not have modified the common law of war and given the enemy aliens access to the courts. To the complaint

In 1917 Charles Evans Hughes told the American Bar Association:

> There is no limitation upon the authority of Congress to create an army and it is for the President as Commander-in-Chief to direct the campaigns of that army wherever he may think they should be carried on. . . . (*81*, 7)

Congress, he said, might pass whatever legislation was necessary to prosecute the war with vigor and success, and "this power is to be exercised without impairment of the authority committed to the President as Commander-in-Chief to direct military operations." Westel W. Willoughby thought that the President might send troops outside the United States in time of war "when the military exigencies of the war so require," and his action "can probably not be controlled or limited by Congress." (*240*, III, 1567) Willoughby thought the President might also send troops abroad in time of peace, even though Elihu Root thought otherwise.

But Congress has often directed or limited the movement of troops. In 1794 Congress authorized the stationing of up to 2,500 militiamen in the four western counties of Pennsylvania.* In 1836 Congress appropriated fifty thousand dollars for the removal of Fort Gibson from Indian territory and its relocation at or near the border of Arkansas.* As a matter of fact, Congress has often irritated the military departments by requiring the use of one or another fort or navy yard. In 1940 Congress provided that no military

---

that Articles 60 and 63 of the Geneva Convention had been violated, Jackson replied that this was not true; the concession of the validity of the treaty seems to adopt the nonstatutory theory. Johnson v. Eisentrager, 339 U.S. 763, 789 (1950). Three justices dissented from the disposition of the case.

Chicago & Southern Airlines v. Waterman Steamship Corp., cited above, was also decided by Justice Jackson. By the Civil Aeronautics Act, decisions of the Civil Aeronautics Board on air routes were subject to approval, denial, or alteration by the President but were then reviewable by a court of appeals, except that orders granting certificates of convenience and necessity to foreign carriers approved by the President were exempt from judicial review. The court of appeals of the Fifth Circuit interpreted the statute to permit it to review an order for a foreign route because it was granted to a citizen carrier. The Supreme Court reversed, holding that all orders dealing with foreign routes were exempt from review, whether granted to a citizen carrier or an alien carrier. It rested this interpretation of the statute on considerations of policy. Four other justices concurred in Justice Jackson's opinion. "The President, both as Commander-in-Chief and as the Nation's organ for foreign affairs, has available intelligence services whose reports neither are nor ought to be published to the world. . . . But even if courts could require full disclosure, the very nature of executive decisions as to foreign policy is political, not judicial. Such decisions are wholly confided by our Constitution to the political departments of the government, Executive and Legislative." Here Jackson seems to be saying that the licensing of foreign carriers requires statutory authorization but that the Constitution forbids judicial review of the executive decision. Perhaps Jackson meant to suggest that the matter was not justiciable for want of standards, as in Federal Radio Commission v. General Electric Co., 281 U.S. 464 (1930).

selectee should be stationed outside the western hemisphere.* Beginning in 1969, Congress enacted restrictions on the use of American troops in Indochina;* in 1973 it terminated employment there altogether.* It is not for want of constitutional power that Congress has not controlled the movement of troops more frequently; it is because the problems of military management do not often lend themselves to legislative decision. On July 11, 1861, Senator Lyman Trumbull was unable to persuade the Republican caucus to support his resolution instructing General Scott to take Richmond before July 20, 1861. (*114*, 186-87)

More persuasive, however, are the legislative precedents that establish constitutional law by usage. As the preceding chapter showed, Congresses contemporaneous with the adoption of the Constitution passed six acts placing contingents of the armed forces under the command of persons other than the commander in chief or any military officer. Since legislation of this sort continues to this day, we must conclude that, if the matter were ever in doubt, usage has since established that the commander in chief has no power of which he cannot be stripped by statute except that of resisting sudden attack upon the United States.

On a few occasions the Supreme Court has confronted the problem. *Brown v. United States*, in 1814, involved a libel to confiscate a quantity of British-owned lumber in the United States during the War of 1812. Chief Justice Marshall held that the executive, "in executing the laws of war," could not confiscate such enemy property. In dictum he conceded that Congress might authorize the confiscation, as is of course the case. Justice Story dissented on the ground that under the common law of war the executive might effect such a seizure unless Congress had forbidden the action.

> By the constitution, the executive is charged with the faithful execution of the laws; and the language of the act declaring war authorizes him to carry it into effect. In what manner, and to what extent, shall he carry it into effect? What are the legitimate objects of the warfare which he is to wage? There is no act of the legislature defining the powers, objects or mode of warfare. By what rule, then, must he be governed? I think the only rational answer is by the law of nations as applied to a state of war. . . . If any such acts are disapproved by the legislature, it is in their power to narrow and limit the extent to which the rights of war shall be exercised; but until such limit is assigned, the executive must have all the rights of modern warfare vested in him, to be exercised in his sound discretion, or he can have none.*

In *United States v. Eliason*, in 1842, the Supreme Court held that an officer assigned a function under an army regulation was obliged to perform it without additional recompense.* Since, as we saw in the *Ripley* and *Gratiot* cases in the preceding chapter, the President cannot impose duties on officers beyond their statutory obligation, what *United States v. Eliason* means is that the President may impose duties within the statutory responsibility assigned to the officer.

Ex parte Vallandigham, decided in 1864, raised the issue obliquely.* Clement Laird Vallandigham was tried and convicted by a military commission for speaking against the war; he sought review by writ of certiorari. The Supreme Court held that it might exercise appellate jurisdiction only over courts that possessed the judicial power of the United States, and this was not true of military tribunals. Their jurisdiction was of two kinds. "First, that which is conferred and defined by statute; second that which is derived from the common law of war." Vallandigham should have employed the writ of habeas corpus, as Milligan did two years later.*

In *Swaim v. United States*, in 1897, the Supreme Court held that the President, as commander in chief, might validly convene a court-martial without statutory authorization.* Existing acts of Congress were intended to supply an alternative, but not an exclusive, course. The Court quoted with approval the report of a Senate committee that the commander in chief of any army possessed this power "in the absence of legislation expressly prohibitive." Since it will yield to statute, it is clear that the power of the commander in chief is conferred by the common law of war and not by the Constitution.

In 1925 Attorney General John G. Sargent replied to an inquiry from the secretary of the interior as to whether it would be illegal to attach a fringe to a United States flag. "The presence, therefore, of a fringe on military colors and standards does not violate any existing Act of Congress. Its use or disuse is a matter of practical policy, to be determined, in the absence of statute, by the Commander in Chief."*

Finally, Chief Justice Harlan Fiske Stone thus defined the power of the commander in chief:

> The Constitution thus invests the President with power to wage war which Congress has declared, and to carry into effect all laws passed by Congress for the conduct of war and for the government and regulation of the Armed Forces, and all laws defining and punishing offenses against the law of nations, including those which pertain to the conduct of war.*

Most of the decisions that describe the nonstatutory authority of the commander in chief arose from events in the Civil War. By the common law of war, a military commander has certain powers with regard to property.* In case of actual necessity, a military commander in the field may appropriate friendly property in order to put it to beneficial use, without compensating the owner; however, if he acts without reasonable grounds to believe that there is a pressing emergency, the commander is personally liable in damages.* Thus, only "an immediate and impending danger from the public enemy, or an urgent necessity for the public service can justify the taking of private property to prevent it from falling into the hands of the enemy, or for the purpose of converting it to the use of the public."*

If, however, the property is taken for use in a genuine emergency, the commander has acted lawfully, and the United States is liable for the value of the property under the eminent domain clause. On several occasions during the Civil War, an assistant quartermaster commandeered steamboats for a brief period. The court of claims found that there had been "imperative military necessity" and awarded compensation; the Supreme Court affirmed this in *United States v. Russell.*[4] Yet this rule of immediate necessity confines only the military and not Congress. Congress has provided for the taking of private property in time of war and the payment of just compensation. All that is needed to justify the action is that the taking bear a relation to a legitimate objective.*

A commander may occupy, but may not annex, territory.* He may confiscate enemy property only out of military necessity, never for gain.* He may institute martial law in the conquered territory and may try the conquered by court–martial.* Indeed, as long as the military government persists, he may try by court–martial American civilians who accompany the armed forces.* The military commander may impose import duties in the conquered territory.* He may institute a provisional government and may enact law to be administered by the provisional government.* He may establish courts that have conclusive judgments.* Apparently the provisional government has legal standing until Congress replaces it.*

On the other hand, the power of the commander in chief does not extend beyond the military necessity.* A prize court is not necessary for a successful occupation of enemy territory; therefore, if a commander attempts to establish a prize court, its judgments are void.*

In domestic territory, a military commander may exercise the powers of civil government only in a theater of war or in conquered rebellious territory. In December 1806, General Wilkinson, in pretended fear that Aaron Burr was about to attack New Orleans with six or seven thousand men, established what amounted to a military dictatorship in the city. John Adair, whom Wilkinson arrested, subsequently sued him in a superior court of Mississippi for false imprisonment and recovered $2,500. (*107*, 250) Congress ultimately appropriated $3,000 to pay the judgment, costs, and interest.*

---

[4]"Extraordinary and unforeseen occasion[s] arise, however, beyond all doubt, in cases of extreme necessity in time of war or of immediate and impending public danger, in which private property may be impressed into the public service, or may be seized, or appropriated to the public use, or may even be destroyed without the consent of the owner. Unquestionably, such extreme cases may arise, as where the property taken is imperatively necessary in time of war to construct defenses for the preservation of a military post at the moment of an impending attack by the enemy, or for food or medicine for a sick and famishing army utterly destitute and without other means of such supplies, or to transport troops, munitions of war or clothing . . . where the necessity for such reinforcement or supplies is extreme and imperative . . . provided it appears that other means of transportation could not be obtained, and that the transports impressed were imperatively required for such an immediate use." United States v. Russell, 80 U.S. (13 Wall.) 623, 627–28 (1871)

On December 15, 1814, General Jackson declared martial law in New Orleans. On January 8, 1815, he defeated the British, and on the twenty-seventh day they reembarked and sailed away, but Jackson continued to maintain martial law. When a newspaper published a letter complaining of this, Jackson extorted the author's name from the publisher and imprisoned the offender. On March 5 the federal district judge, Dominick A. Hall, issued a writ of habeas corpus; Jackson locked him up. The federal district attorney applied for a writ of habeas corpus to a state court judge; Jackson arrested them both. On March 11 he expelled Judge Hall from the city. But when official word of the treaty of peace reached Jackson on March 13 he ended martial law. Judge Hall returned, and on March 31 he fined Jackson one thousand dollars for contempt. Thirty years later, on February 14, 1844, Congress repaid this sum to Jackson with six percent interest.* Jackson, who considered his actions fully warranted, regarded this as a tardy vindication. The Supreme Court of Louisiana, opening its March term in 1815, had held Jackson's declaration of martial law illegal and no obstacle to its sitting but had upheld an act of the state legislature of December 18, 1814, closing the courts until May 1.*

During the same war the Supreme Court of New York ruled that three arrests of civilians by the military were illegal. An attachment against the commanding general responsible for an arrest was issued in *Matter of Stacy*,* and damage suits against the officers responsible for the detention were upheld in *Smith v. Shaw** and *McConnel v. Hampton*.* These decisions were commended by the United States Supreme Court in *Ex parte Milligan*.*

The Case of the Floyd Acceptances held that the President might not supply the army without statutory authority.* Russell, Waddell, and Majors had contracts to provide supplies and transportation to the United States Army in Utah. To raise money in advance of the contract date of payment they drew bills of exchange on Secretary of War John Floyd, and he accepted them. They negotiated these and paid off the first five million dollars on the bills as they received payments from the United States, but they failed to retire the last one million dollars. The holders of this paper then sued the United States in the court of claims, lost, and appealed to the Supreme Court. Justice Miller ruled that the secretary of war had no authority to accept bills of exchange, and indeed the practice was forbidden by statute. The plaintiffs argued what was perfectly true: actions of the secretary of war were imputable to the President. (*114*, 37) But Miller announced, "We have no officers in this government from the President down to the most subordinate agent, who does not hold office under the law, with prescribed duties and limited authority." Justice Nelson wrote a dissenting opinion in which Justice Clifford joined. They would have upheld the acceptances on the theory that the act authorizing the secretary of war to make contracts implicitly authorized the acceptances in order to escape the dire consequences of the majority opinion.

The Army and Navy must be fed, and clothed, and cared for at all times and places, and especially when in distant service. The Army in Mexico or Utah are not to be disbanded and left to take care of themselves, because the appropriation by Congress, for the service, has been exhausted, or no law can be found on the statute book authorizing a contract for supplies. (*114*, 685)

It is well settled that only Congress may suspend the privilege of the writ of habeas corpus. During his dictatorship in New Orleans, General Wilkinson arrested a number of suspected conspirators involved in the alleged treasonable plans of Burr and sent several to Washington. On January 22, in response to an inquiry from the House, President Jefferson endorsed Wilkinson's charges against Burr but asserted that there was now no serious danger. Nevertheless, on January 23 the Senate passed a bill to suspend the privilege of the writ of habeas corpus for three months, then the House overwhelmingly rejected the bill on first reading on January 26.* Justus Erich Bollman and James Swartwout arrived under custody and were committed by the circuit court for the District of Columbia on January 27. They applied to the Supreme Court for a writ of habeas corpus. The case was argued for several days. On February 13 Chief Justice Marshall ruled:

> If any time the public safety should require the suspension of the powers vested by this act in the courts of the United States, it is for the legislature to say so.
> That question depends on political considerations. on which the legislature is to decide. Until the legislature will be expressed, this Court can only see its duty, and must obey the laws.*

On February 21 the chief justice delivered the opinion of the Court: the government's evidence, if accepted as true, did not support the charge of treason, and the prisoners were released.

At the outbreak of the Civil War President Lincoln claimed the authority to suspend the privilege of the writ of habeas corpus and delegated it widely. John Merryman was one of a number of citizens of Maryland arrested and detained by General George Cadwalader in Fort McHenry on the charge of treason. On May 25, 1861, Merryman and several others were transferred to the civil authorities (*229*, II, 226), but it appears that no one knew this for at least three days. On May 26 a petition for a writ of habeas corpus was presented to Taney, chief justice of the Supreme Court, sitting on circuit. Taney ordered that the writ should issue, directed to Cadwalader. Unaware that he no longer held the petitioner, Cadwalader made return that there were serious charges against Merryman and that he had suspended the privilege of the writ under authorization by the President. He asked Taney to postpone action until he could receive instructions from the President. On May 27 Taney ordered an attachment of Cadwalader issue, to be returned at noon of the following day. On May 28 the marshal made return to the writ of attachment that he had not been allowed to enter the gate of Fort

McHenry. Taney observed that the marshal had the right to summon a posse comitatus to assist him, but in view of the superior force arrayed against him he excused the marshal from doing anything more. Taney wrote an opinion which was filed in the office of the circuit court, with a copy to the President. Only Congress might suspend the privilege of the writ, not the President.

> The short term for which he is elected, and the narrow limits to which his power is confined, show the jealousy and apprehension of future danger which the framers of the constitution felt in relation to that department of the government and how carefully they withheld from it many of the powers belonging to the executive branch of the English government which were considered as dangerous to the liberty of the subject; and conferred (and that in clear and specific terms) those powers only which were deemed essential to secure the successful operation of the government. . . .*

On the President's power to see that the laws are faithfully executed, Taney said:

> He is not authorized to execute them himself, or through agents or officers, civil or military, appointed by himself, but he is to take care that they be faithfully carried into execution, as they are expounded and adjudged by the co-ordinate branch of the government to which that duty is assigned by the constitution. It is thus made his duty to come in aid of the judicial authority, if it shall be resisted by a force too strong to be overcome without the assistance of the executive arm; but in exercising this power he acts in subordination to judicial authority, assisting it to execute its process and enforce its judgments.
>
> With such provisions in the constitution, expressed in language too clear to be misunderstood by any one, I can see no ground whatever for supposing that the president, in any emergency, or any state of things, can authorize the suspension of the privileges of the writ of habeas corpus, or the arrest of a citizen, except in aid of the judicial power. He certainly does not faithfully execute the laws, if he takes upon himself legislative power, by suspending the writ of habeas corpus, and the judicial power also, by arresting and imprisoning a person without due process of law.
>
> Nor can any argument be drawn from the nature of sovereignty, or the necessity of government, for self-defense in times of tumult and danger. The government of the United States is one of delegated and limited powers. . . .*

Taney concluded by saying that Cadwalader might have misunderstood his orders, and therefore he was sending the proceedings in the case, together with his opinion, to the President, whose duty it was to take care that the laws be faithfully executed. In the meantime, however, Merryman had either been released or was in the custody of the judicial authorities. He was not indicted.

On July 5, 1861, Attorney General Edward Bates delivered an opinion that the President might suspend the privileges of persons arrested during great and dangerous rebellions, "for he is especially charged with the public safety; and he is the sole judge of the emergency which requires his prompt action."* But every court that passed on executive suspension of the privilege of the writ held the action unconstitutional.* Congress was therefore obliged to pass an act authorizing the suspension of the writ "in certain cases" until a grand jury had had an opportunity to indict; this power was to last as long as the rebellion.* Presidential suspensions under this act were upheld.*

Ex parte Milligan was decided in 1866.* Milligan was a civilian in Indiana, arrested by General Hovey and convicted by a military commission. The Supreme Court held that he should be released by habeas corpus. Justice David Davis for the majority ruled that the commission did not possess the judicial power of the United States, because the Constitution vested that in the courts. It could not be justified "on the mandate of the President," for his duty was "to execute, not to make, the laws." There remained only "the laws and usages of war," and these "can never be applied to citizens in states which have upheld the authority of the government, and where the courts are open and their process unobstructed."*

In a concurring opinion for four justices, Chief Justice Chase made what appears to be the only conscious judicial choice of the theory that the power of the commander in chief is defined by the Constitution and is therefore immutable. Chase said: "Congress cannot direct the conduct of campaigns," adding, "nor can the President, or any commander under him, without the sanction of Congress, institute tribunals for the trial and punishment of offenses, unless in cases of a controlling necessity, which justifies what it compels, or at least insures acts of indemnity from the justice of the legislature."* Since there was no such desperate emergency in the present case, Chase and his three colleagues concurred in the outcome.

Kurtz v. Moffitt was a habeas corpus action by a deserter from the army against two police officers who had arrested him.* Their defense was that an army regulation provided a reward should be paid to "any person" who should deliver a deserter to an officer of the army. The Supreme Court, through Justice Horace Gray, construed the regulation instead as not authorizing arrest by nonmilitary personnel.

> Upon full consideration of the question, and examination of the statutes, army regulations, and other authorities, . . . we are of opinion that by the existing law a peace officer or private citizen has no authority as such, and without the order and direction of a military officer, to arrest or detain a deserter from the army of the United States. Whether it is expedient for the public welfare and the good of the army that such an authority should be conferred is a matter for the determination of congress.*

In 1906 President Theodore Roosevelt made one of his flamboyant gestures. Between sixteen and twenty members of three companies of black soldiers were involved in a race riot in Brownsville, Texas. Being unable to discover the culprits, the President ordered the dishonorable discharge, without trial, of 168 men. One soldier sued for his salary in the district court. The United States defended on the merits, and also because the court lacked statutory jurisdiction. The plaintiff demurred. The court sustained the plaintiff's demurrer on the merits but dismissed the suit on jurisdictional grounds. The Supreme Court held that it lacked the power to review by writ of error.* But on January 9, 1974, the Department of the Army announced that it would pay twenty-five thousand dollars to the last survivor of the group discharged, Dorsie W. Willis. (*New York Times*, Jan. 11) Yet this action of Roosevelt's is often cited as evidence of the President's constitutional authority.

Let us summarize what we have established in these two chapters concerning the commander in chief: He is commander of the forces affirmatively placed at his command by act of Congress. The duties of these are imposed by act of Congress. In addition, he possesses the authority of a commander in chief at the common law of war. This is concerned with the conduct of war declared by Congress, the performance of other duties prescribed by Congress, the treatment of the enemy and enemy property, the government of conquered territory, the government of domestic territory in a war zone, and related topics. But the common law of war is subject to alteration by statute and by treaty, and the Constitution sets limits to the common law of war as it does to statute and to treaty. The commander in chief has no powers outside the boundaries of these propositions.

Chapter 8
INDIAN WARS
AND BORDER CROSSINGS

    The American Indian tribes did not fit well into a legal order European in origin. The tribes were not sovereign, but they had some of the attributes of political entities. In 1831, in *Cherokee Nation v. Georgia*, Chief Justice Marshall said that the tribes domiciled in the United States were "domestic dependent nations" in "a state of pupilage" rather than foreign states.* But for our purposes it is important that they were able to make treaties with, and war against, the United States. The treaties were ratified by the Senate. The legislative, executive, and judicial branches of the national government invariably called the conflicts "wars."

    Six hundred sixty-six treaties were made with Indian tribes.* In 1778 the United States made a treaty of "perpetual peace and friendship" and alliance with the Delaware Indians. (95, II, 3) Between 1784 and 1786 the United States made treaties with the tribes domiciled within its territory with which it had been at war during the Revolution, granting them peace and promising them favor and protection or friendship and protection. The tribes acknowledged that they were under the protection of the United States and renounced the protection of any foreign sovereign. (95, II, 5–17) In 1795, after the battle of Fallen Timbers, Major-General Anthony Wayne negotiated a treaty with the hostile tribes of the Northwest Territory "to put an end to a destructive war." (95, II, 39) Between 1814 and 1817 peace treaties were negotiated between the United States and Indian tribes that had supported the British during the War of 1812. (95, II, 105–40) Occasionally

thereafter treaties of peace were negotiated at the conclusion of Indian wars.[1]
After 1825 it became common to require an Indian tribe to admit in the treaty
"that they reside in the United States, acknowledge their [the United States]
supremacy, and claim their protection." (95, II 225)

In 1862 Congress provided, "Whenever the tribal organization of any
Indian tribe is in actual hostility to the United States, the President is
authorized, by proclamation, . . . to declare all treaties with such tribes
abrogated by such tribes. . . ."* In 1871, in an act making appropriations
for payments due to many Indian tribes by treaty, Congress included the
prohibition, "No Indian nation or tribe shall be acknowledged or recognized
as an independent nation, tribe or power with whom the United States may
contract by treaty."* Thereafter, the treaty–making procedure was substituted with the practice of authorizing by statute both the appointment of
commissioners to make an agreement and the enactment of legislation based
on the report of the commissioners.* The Indian tribes retained some kind
of corporate existence. In 1885 the Supreme Court upheld the legislative
power of Congress over the tribes. Because the United States had previously
dealt with the tribes by treaty, because the states in which they lived were
hostile to the Indians, and because no other authority could pass legislation
applicable to all tribes, the Court said that it fell to Congress to legislate for
the Indian tribes.*

Yet these ideas were not very firmly held. After his victory over Custer
on the Little Big Horn in 1876, Sitting Bull fled with his warriors to Canada.
The Canadian authorities insisted that they were American Indians and the
United States should persuade them to return. The United States took the
position that they were now British Indians and the Canadians should keep
them at home. (119, II, 437–38)

An act passed in 1891 made the United States liable to suit in the court
of claims on past or future claims "for property of citizens of the United States
taken or destroyed by Indians belonging to any band, tribe, or nation, in
amity with the United States, without just cause or provocation on the part
of the owner or agent in charge, and not returned or paid for."* The court
of claims and the Supreme Court were therefore called upon to decide
whether given associations of Indians had been at war with the United States
when individual Indians took or destroyed property. In 1886 Geronimo's
band of less than a hundred men, women, and children had negotiated a
surrender to General Nelson Miles as prisoners of war, and the court of claims

---

[1]July 18, 1825 (95, II, 237); July 30, 1825 (95, II, 239); July 30, 1825 (95, II, 242);
Sept. 21, 1832 (95, II, 349). The treaties of Oct. 21, 1867, with the Kiowa and the
Comanche tribes (95, II, 977), of Oct. 28, 1867, with the Cheyenne and the Arapaho
(95, II, 984), and of April 29, 1868, with the Sioux and the Arapaho (95, II, 998), all
began, "From this day forward all wars between the parties to this agreement shall
cease."

ruled, "It was therefore, from a legal point of view, a case of a war by the minority of the minority of a subdivision of a tribe."*

The colonial charters of Connecticut, Rhode Island, Pennsylvania, and Maryland authorized them to make defensive, but not offensive, wars. Article VI of the Articles of Confederation provided, "No state shall engage in war unless it be invaded or menaced with invasion by some Indian tribe." The framers of the Constitution provided that no state should, without the consent of Congress, "engage in war, unless actually invaded, or in such imminent danger as will not admit delay." The problem the framers had in mind was war with Indians. (53, III, 548)

The Northwest Ordinance, which was enacted in 1787 for the government of the Northwest Territory, stipulated:

> The utmost good faith shall always be observed toward the Indians; their land and liberty shall never be taken from them without their consent; and in their property, rights and liberty, they never shall be invaded or disturbed, unless in just and lawful wars authorized by Congress. . . . (217, II, 961)

The Ordinance was reaffirmed under the Constitution by the first Congress of the United States.* It was incorporated by reference in the acts creating the Southwest Territory, the Mississippi Territory, the Indiana Territory, the Illinois Territory, and the Michigan Territory.*

The United States never declared war on an Indian tribe. In theory, all the Indian wars were responses to sudden attacks. The first Indian war under the Constitution, however, was a response specifically authorized by Congress.

The constitutional government had inherited from the Confederation an intermittent war in the Northwest Territory. On September 16, 1789, the President informed Congress of the existence of "reciprocal hostilities of the Wabash Indians and the people inhabiting the frontiers bordering the river Ohio" and suggested the "expediency of making some temporary provision for calling forth the militia for the purposes stated in the Constitution." (181, I, 53) On September 29 Congress adopted the army of the Confederation and authorized the President to call the militia into service "for the purpose of protecting the inhabitants of the frontiers of the United States from the hostile incursions of the Indians."* On April 30, 1790, Congress authorized the enlargement of the army to 1,216 enlisted men and, in order to aid them "in protecting the inhabitants of the frontiers of the United States," renewed the President's authority to call out the militia.* On December 8, 1790, in his second annual message to Congress, President Washington reported that "frequent incursions have been made on our frontier settlements by certain banditti of Indians from the northwest side of the Ohio."

> These aggravated provocations rendered it essential to the safety of the Western settlements that the aggressors should be made sensible that

the Government of the Union is not less capable of punishing their crimes than it is disposed to respect their rights and reward their attachments. As this object could not be effected by defensive measures, it became necessary to put in force the act which empowers the President to call out the militia for the protection of the frontiers, and I have accordingly authorized an expedition in which the regular troops in that quarter are combined with such drafts of militia as were deemed sufficient. (*181*, I, 74)

Both houses commended the President's action. (*181*, I, 78)

The expedition had already departed and returned. Brigadier General Josiah Harmar, under orders of Secretary of War Knox to "extirpate utterly, if possible," the banditti (*235*, 20), had set out on September 30 and had returned to Fort Washington on the Little Miami after suffering heavy losses. On March 3, 1791, to make "further provision for protection of the frontiers," Congress again augmented the army.* At the order of Knox, on August 7, 1791, Major General Arthur St. Clair set out from Fort Washington. He too suffered severe losses and retreated in great disorder. He resigned his commission in 1792, and Major General Wayne replaced him. Wayne won the battle of Fallen Timbers in 1794 and in 1795 negotiated treaties of peace which were approved by the Senate.

In this case President Washington had acted with the approval of Congress; on later occasions he refused to act without it. As we have seen, when Governor Blount of the Southwest Territory asked for an expedition against the Chickamaugas, Secretary Knox replied on November 26, 1792, that only Congress might declare war. (*26*, IV, 195) On December 7 the President sent this correspondence to Congress for consideration. (*181*, I, 126) Congress did not act. In 1795 Secretary of War Pickering again rebuffed Blount. (*26*, IV, 389) In 1793 Secretary Knox cautioned the governor of Georgia, who wished to use the Georgia militia against the Creeks, that only Congress might declare war. (*152*, 47)

Nevertheless, the initiation of offensive war against Indian tribes was not uncommon. In 1811 Tecumseh was attempting to organize a confederation of all the Indians on the western frontier. On November 7, 1811, President Madison reported to Congress that Major General William Henry Harrison, governor of the Indiana Territory, had marched to the northwestern frontier. This was occasioned by "several murders and depradations committed by Indians, but more especially by the menacing preparations and aspect of a combination of them on the Wabash, under the influence and direction of a fanatic of the Shawanese tribe." (*181*, I, 478) The expedition burned Prophet's Town on the Tippecanoe Creek. On December 11 Madison reported this to Congress as a considerable victory. It was of course insignificant, and did not prevent Tecumseh from perfecting the alliance of tribes that assisted the British in the War of 1812.

On no occasion, after an Indian war had been initiated, did any President refer the issue to Congress for a declaration of war, as the Constitution contemplated. In the case of a protracted war, such as the Second Seminole War, the President reported to Congress on its progress. (*181*, III, 1718, 1834, 2007) The formless and intermittent character of Indian warfare, and its peculiar status as a rebellion of a dependent nation within the territory of the United States, no doubt encouraged the informality with which Indian wars were treated. As Chief Justice Marshall said in *Cherokee Nation v. Georgia*, "The condition of the Indians in relation to the United States is perhaps unlike that of any other two people in existence."*

The total number of Indian wars is incalculable. Before the Civil War they were often fought by the state or territorial militia; the United States reimbursed the government that supplied the troops.* After the Civil War most of the collisions were between the United States cavalry and Indians in the Great Plains. Between 1865 and 1898 the army fought 943 engagements with Indians. (*46*, 148–49)

Indian wars inevitably led to border crossings. Behind the first group of violations of a frontier, however, lay ulterior motives: the appetites for Spanish Florida of President Madison and Secretary of State Monroe, of President Monroe and Secretary of State Adams, and of Major General Jackson.

In the latter half of 1810, a group of Americans declared West Florida an independent state, seized Baton Rouge, and asked for annexation to the United States. President Madison ignored them. Instead, on October 27, 1810, he issued a proclamation based on the implausible argument that the Spanish cession of Louisiana to France in 1800 included all of Florida west of the River Perdido and that France had sold this whole territory to the United States in 1803. The proclamation ordered the governor of the Orleans Territory to take possession of Florida between the Mississippi and the Perdido. (*181*, I, 465) The Spanish governor of West Florida, Juan Vicente Folch, was in no position to resist either the rebels or the United States. On December 2, 1810, he wrote to the secretary of state:

. . . I have decided on delivering this province to the United States under an equitable capitulation, provided I do not receive succor from Havana or Vera Cruz, during the present month, or that his Excellency the Marquis of Someruelos, (on whom I depend,) should not have opened directly a negotiation on this point.*

On January 3, 1811, President Madison sent to Congress, "in confidence," Governor Folch's letter, and he also made a proposal concerning East Florida.

I recommend to their consideration also the expediency of authorizing the Executive to take temporary possession of the said Territory, in pursuance of arrangements which may be desired by the Spanish authorities; and for making provision for the government of the same during such possession.

The wisdom of Congress will at the same time, determine how far it is expedient to provide for the event of a subversion of the Spanish authorities within the Territory in question, and an apprehended occupancy thereof by any other foreign power. (*181*, I, 473)

The reference to a foreign power was to Great Britain. Since Spain was under the control of France, it was feared that the British in their war with Napoleon might occupy Florida. Congress responded by passing, on January 15, 1811, a secret act authorizing the President to take temporary possession of any part of Florida east of the Perdido if an arrangement should be made with the "local authority of the said territory," or if any foreign government should attempt to occupy the territory or any part of it.* The act was not published until 1818.

General George Matthews and Colonel John McKee were appointed commissioners to receive the surrender of Governor Folch or any other local authority and to occupy East Florida if a foreign force should appear to be about to take the country. Matthews seized Amelia Island in East Florida and generated a revolutionary government of American citizens to cede East Florida to him. But this was too blatant for Congress, and Madison recalled Matthews and McKee.

On February 12, 1813, Congress passed a secret act authorizing the President to "occupy and hold all that tract of land called West Florida, which lies west of the river Perdido, not now in possession of the United States," and for this purpose "to employ such parts of the military and naval force of the United States as he may deem necessary."* General Wilkinson occupied Mobile, the only Spanish post in the area, on April 15, 1813.

On June 18, 1812, Congress had declared war on Great Britain. In May of 1813 a British fleet occupied Amelia Island, which lay in Spanish waters at the mouth of St. Mary's River, the boundary between Florida and Georgia. In 1814 the British established a base at Pensacola, but Major General Jackson, acting without superior orders, expelled them.

In 1817 a group of adventurers, led first by one Gregor MacGregor purportedly acting for several Latin American states, and then by Louis Aury, took possession of Amelia Island. Aury announced that he was annexing the island to the Mexican Republic. In his first annual message, on December 2, 1817, President Monroe suggested that the occupiers had no sponsorship from any Latin American country and complained that the island had been made "a channel for the illicit introduction of slaves from Africa into the United States, an asylum for fugitive slaves from the neighboring States, and a port for smuggling of every kind." (*181*, I, 583) On January 13, 1818, Monroe announced to Congress that "the establishment at Amelia Island has been suppressed, and without the effusion of blood." (*181*, I, 592)

Monroe rested his action on rather doubtful ground, the secret act of 1811. The act provided for American intervention at the request of a local authority, but there had been no such request; or, alternatively, if a foreign government occupied a part of Florida, but Monroe himself denied that Aury represented a foreign government. Nevertheless he told Congress:

> The path of duty was plain from the commencement, but it was painful to enter upon it while the obligation could be resisted. The law of 1811, lately published, and which it is therefore proper now to mention, was considered applicable to the case from the moment that the proclamation of the chief of the enterprise was seen, and its obligation was daily increased by other considerations of high importance already mentioned, which were deemed sufficiently strong in themselves to dictate the course which has been pursued. (*181*, I, 593)

Of greater moment was the invasion of Florida in 1818 by Major General Jackson. In 1816, during fighting between Seminoles and Georgians, Brigadier General Edmund Gaines was authorized by the secretary of war to pursue fleeing Indians into Florida, but he was ordered to avoid hostilities with the Spanish. In 1817 the command was transferred to Jackson with the same orders. He was given a force of 1,800 men and was authorized to call upon the governors of adjoining states for militia if he should think this necessary. Instead, he raised one thousand volunteers in West Tennessee and appointed officers. General Gaines, also without orders, raised an army of 1,600 Creek Indians and appointed their officers, with a brigadier general at their head. On March 10, 1818, Jackson and Gaines entered Florida.

On March 25 President Monroe offered a justification of the invasion to Congress. In 1795 Spain had agreed by treaty to restrain Indians in her territory from committing hostilities against the United States, but "her very small and incompetent force in Florida" had been unable to do so.

> When the authority of Spain ceased to exist there, the United States have a right to pursue their enemy on a principle of self-defense. . . . Orders have been given to the general in command not to enter Florida unless it be in pursuit of the enemy, and in that case to respect the Spanish authority wherever it is maintained. . . . (*181*, I, 601)

Jackson had a different view of his mission. On January 6, 1818, he had written confidentially to President Monroe, offering to take all Florida from Spain in sixty days. In a posthumously published account, he asserted that he had received authorization to do this from Monroe through an intermediary, Congressman John Rhea, but in 1819 he had destroyed Rhea's letter at Rhea's request in order to spare Monroe embarrassment. (*63*, 240–43) However this may be, he encountered virtually no resistance from Indians; he did take the Spanish forts of St. Marks and Barrancas and occupied Pensacola. He court-martialed and executed two British subjects, Alexander Arbuthnot and Robert C. Armbrister. These actions caused a great stir. The Senate created a select committee to inquire into the conduct of the "Seminole war," and on February 24, 1819, the committee made a report condemning Jackson and Gaines. No law existed that allowed even the

President to enlist volunteers. Only the President and the Senate might appoint officers of the regular army; the appointment of officers of the militia belonged to the states. The generals' orders had forbidden them to confront the Spanish. The treatment of Arbuthnot and Armbrister had been unnecessarily severe. The committee opined that Spain's violation of the treaty of 1795 was justification for war but said that "General Jackson had no power to declare or make the war; that neither he, nor even the President of the United States had any discretion or power to judge, what was, or was not, cause of war; this, the Constitution had wisely lodged in Congress."*

The House also created a select committee, which recommended the censure of Jackson because of his execution of Arbuthnot and Armbrister.* But neither house condemned Jackson. Secretary of State Adams believed that this demonstration of the impotence of the Spanish might persuade them to cede Florida. No doubt it did prompt the Spanish minister to sign the treaty of cession on February 22, 1819. The King of Spain did not ratify the treaty until 1821.

By the treaty, both parties renounced all claims to indemnities for recent events in the Floridas, with the proviso: "The United States will cause satisfaction to be made for the injuries, if any, which by process of law, shall be established to have been suffered by the Spanish officers, and individual Spanish inhabitants, by the late operations of the American army in Florida."* On March 3, 1823, Congress provided for the payment of such claims by the secretary of the treasury on the advice of the territorial judges in Florida.* The secretary of the treasury ruled that the act applied only to claims for injuries inflicted in 1818. In 1834 Congress extended liability to claims for losses suffered in 1812 and 1813.*

In the next group of border crossings, Indians were pursued into the United States by Texans, and into Texas by Americans. But it was the Mexican border that was most frequently violated. Mexico and the United States blamed each other for permitting their Indians to carry out raids across the border. With the westward migration after the Civil War, increased pressure was put on the Plains Indians, and they often raided on both sides of the border. From June 1, 1877, to February 24, 1880, American forces were under orders to pursue invaders into Mexico if necessary; Mexico protested. From 1882 to 1886, and from 1890 to 1896, each state waived objection to the other's pursuit of Indians over the border. (119, II, 4245)

Pursuit of hostile Indians gravitated almost unnoticed into pursuit of rustlers and other bandits. In the twentieth century the most famous border crossing occurred. After the raid on Columbus, New Mexico, by the Mexican revolutionary leader Francisco Villa on March 9, 1916, President Wilson, without consulting Congress, sent a large force into Mexico in pursuit; the force remained there from March 16, 1916, to February 5, 1917. It came into collision with the forces of President Venustiano Carranza, who denounced the invasion as a hostile act. On February 18, 1917, the secretary of war instructed General Pershing to pursue any future invaders not more than sixty miles into Mexico and to remain not more than three days. (29, 343) Several such pursuits occurred. On June 15, 1919, Villa attacked Juárez, across the Rio Grande from El Paso. In response, American troops surged into Mexico, shattering Villa's army.

The American conduct toward Canada has been very different. As we have seen, on the one occasion when an American captain crossed the Canadian border, he was discharged from the service. In 1867 the American minister in London was instructed to request permission for United States troops to pursue hostile Indians over the Canadian border in an uninhabited stretch of territory east of the Rockies. He was told to admit that the United States did "not claim as a right that its armed forces shall in any case cross the frontier." (119, II, 437) The request was refused. In 1883 Secretary of State Frederick Frelinghuysen proposed to the British minister in Washington the negotiation of an agreement, similar to that with Mexico, which would allow the United States and Canada reciprocal rights to pursue Indians over the border. The Canadian government refused but proposed an enlargement of existing extradition treaties so that an Indian charged under oath with felony or serious outrage against property would be surrendered for trial in the country in which the offense had occurred. (119, II, 440)

It is certain that many of the Indian wars were not defensive; they were provoked by whites. Moreover, many of them lasted long enough for the President to consult Congress. As for the border crossings, probably not many could be brought within the stringent definition of self-defense laid down by Webster in the case of the *Caroline*. In any case, the President's use of troops, except for repelling invasion, requires statutory authorization, and only Monroe, in his expulsion of the smugglers from Amelia Island in 1818, made even a specious claim of such authorization.

The Constitution was perhaps not perfectly suited to the circumstances of nineteenth-century America. The status of the Indian tribes was anomalous; unpoliced frontiers compounded the problem. But the legal irregularities appear to have occurred only when it was a case of the strong confronting the weak. The contrast between our treatment of Mexico and our respect for Canada is striking.

Certainly Congress never adopted an adequate Indian policy. It was not obliged to do so; the executive spared it that necessity by the use of force. But force cannot supply a constructive solution to social problems. It did not do so in the case of the American Indians.

Chapter 9
LISTS OF WARS

Not until 1950 was it asserted by any officer or organ of the United States government that the President had a constitutional right to initiate war. But since that date the State Department has made the claim at least twice (*10*, 173; *113*, 474), and officials in the State Department and the Department of Justice have flirted with it.[1] Senator Goldwater and a few academic commentators have supported it with varying degrees of vehemence.[2]

The central reliance of all these arguments is on the allegation—which, as we shall see, is entirely unsupported by fact—that in the course of our history the President has very frequently exercised the power to make war without congressional authorization—and that he has done so on one or two hundred occasions. If these executive precedents do exist, some explanation would be needed to account for their transformation into law. The argument most frequently offered is that of Henry P. Monaghan that "history has legitimated the practice of presidential war-making." (*115*, 19)

Is it the case that governmental power can be acquired by usage? Justice Felix Frankfurter said for a unanimous Court, "Illegality cannot attain legitimacy through practice."* In an opinion for eight justices in *Powell v.*

[1]Undersecretary of State Nicholas Katzenbach, *U.S. Commitments to Foreign Powers*, Hearings before the Senate Committee on Foreign Relations, 90th Cong., 1st Sess. (1967), 126; Assistant Attorney General William H. Rehnquist (*165*, 163); Secretary of State William P. Rogers (*185*, 1194); Solicitor General Erwin N. Griswold, 117 Cong. Rec., 28977.

[2]Henry P. Monaghan (*115*, 19); Leonard G. Ratner (*159*, 461); Eberhard P. Deutsch (42, 27); Eugene V. Rostow (*189*, 833); Terry Emerson (*51*, 53).

McCormack, Chief Justice Earl Warren said, "That an unconstitutional action has been taken before surely does not render that action any less unconstitutional at a later date."*

But this does not mean that usage plays no part in our legal order. In certain circumstances the Supreme Court has accepted a congressional interpretation of the Constitution. In two sets of cases, an executive or administrative interpretation of a statute may acquire legal standing. A review of the law on these topics will make it clear that presidential war making has not been legitimized by history.

Stuart v. Laird was decided in 1803.* In that case the appellant challenged the jurisdiction of the circuit court that had decided against him, on the ground that that court had been illegally constituted. In conformity with the Judiciary Act of 1789 a Supreme Court justice—Marshall, as it happened —had sat on the circuit court. But Marshall had never been appointed a circuit judge. Subsequent decisions have held on the merits that Congress may assign a judge other duties than those of the office to which he was appointed, but in this case the Court resolved the question principally by resort to usage. Counsel for the appellee argued that "it is most probable that the members of the first congress, many of them having been members of the convention which formed the constitution, best knew its meaning and true construction. But if they were mistaken, yet the acquiescence of the judges and of the people under that construction, has given it a sanction which ought not now to be questioned."* Justice Paterson adopted this argument.

> To this objection, which is of recent date, it is sufficient to observe, that practice and acquiescence under it for a period of several years, commencing with the organization of the judicial system, affords an irresistable [*sic*] answer, and has indeed fixed the construction. It is a contemporary exposition of the most forcible nature. This practical exposition is too strong and obstinate to be shaken or controlled. Of course, the question is at rest, and ought not to be disturbed.*

It is possible to invoke *Stuart v. Laird* only when the meaning of a clause of the Constitution is doubtful and extraneous aid in interpretation is needed. The rule was given more precise expression in later cases. Justice Miller put it thus: "The construction placed upon the Constitution by the first act of 1790, and the act of 1802, by the men who were members of the convention which framed it, is of itself entitled to very great weight, and when it is remembered that the rights thus established have not been disputed during a period of nearly a century, it is almost conclusive."* Frequently, however, the Court has asserted that the question is not doubtful, and usage has been adduced merely as confirmatory evidence.[3]

---

[3]The Judiciary Act of 1789 was cited as evidence of the intent of the framers in order to support the decisions of the Supreme Court in 1816 (Martin v. Hunter's

All the conditions of *Stuart v. Laird*—ambiguity, contemporaneous congressional interpretation, and reiteration of the interpretation or acquiescence—must be met. In 1969, in *Powell v. McCormack*, the Court was confronted with the argument that the fact that the individual houses of Congress had repeatedly excluded members for reasons other than lack of the constitutional qualifications, established that they had a right to do so. The Court found the precedents not conclusive, and not grounded on a contemporaneous interpretation, since, "what evidence we have of Congress' early understanding confirms our conclusion that the House is without power to exclude any member-elect who meets the Constitution's requirements for membership."*

The doctrine of *Stuart v. Laird* applies only to congressional interpretations of the Constitution. The members of an early Congress, "many of them having been members of the convention which formed the constitution, best

---

Lessee, 14 U.S. [1 Wheat.] 305, 351, see also Houston v. Moore, 18 U.S. [5 Wheat.] 1, 26 [1820]), in 1821 (Cohens v. Virginia, 19 U.S. [6 Wheat.] 264, 420), and in 1884 (Ames v. Kansas, 111 U.S. 449, 469). In 1819, in McCulloch v. Maryland, 17 U.S. (4 Wheat.) 316, 401, Chief Justice Marshall attached weight to the fact that the first Congress had created the first bank of the United States. In 1842 Justice Story said that the constitutionality of the fugitive slave law of 1793 was clear, but if it were doubtful, then long acquiescence in the contemporaneous congressional construction would have removed the doubt. (Prigg v. Pennsylvania, 41 U.S. [16 Pet.] 539) In 1851 the Court followed an act of 1789 as an interpretation of the commerce clause. (Cooley v. the Board of Wardens, 53 U.S. [12 How.] 299) In 1883, acts of 1790 and 1802, together with acquiescence in this interpretation, were said to illuminate the copyright clause of the Constitution. (Burrow-Giles Lithographic Co. v. Sarony, 111 U.S. 53, 57 [1884]) In 1885 an act of 1797 that authorized the secretary of the treasury to remit certain fines and forfeitures was upheld on the authority of *Stuart v. Laird* against the argument that the act invaded the pardoning power of the President. (The *Laura*, 114 U.S. 411) In 1890 the Court held that Congress might make an appraiser's valuation of imported goods final. "The uniform course of legislation and practice, in regard both to the mode of selection of the merchant appraiser or as to the conclusive effect of the appraisal, are entitled to great weight. Stuart v. Laird. . . ." (Auffmordt v. Hedden, 137 U.S. 310, 329) The first such act had been passed in 1789. In 1892 (Field v. Clark, 143 U.S. 649, 691), and again in 1936 (United States v. Curtiss-Wright Export Corp., 299 U.S. 304, 329), the Court cited a series of statutes, beginning with an act of 1792, authorizing the President to invoke contingent legislation in the field of foreign trade as evidence supporting further legislation of this sort. In 1937 it upheld a congressional tax challenged under the general welfare clause on the ground that "Congress, from the beginning of its history, has accepted and legislated upon that view of the broad meaning of the term." (Cincinnati Soap Co. v. United States, 301 U.S. 308, 314) In 1942 an act of 1806 allowing the trial of spies by court-martial was cited as supporting a similar provision in the Articles of War. (*Ex parte* Quirin, 317 U.S. 1, 41) In 1903 (Downes v. Bidwell, 182 U.S. 244, 286), in the strange opinion of which Mr. Dooley said, "Mr. Justice Brown wrote the opinion of the court, eight Justices dissenting," Brown made a confused appeal to the principle of *Stuart v. Laird*. In 1927 the Court held that the individual houses of Congress might investigate and compel testimony, citing an act of 1798. (McGrain v. Daughtery, 273 U.S. 135, 174)

knew its meaning and true construction." An action by a single chief
executive, either Washington or Madison, who had been a member of the
Convention, is not the institutional decision demanded by *Stuart v. Laird*,
although it may well deserve consideration along with other evidence.

Nevertheless, there is one Supreme Court decision that attempts to
establish executive power by executive usage. In 1925, in *Ex parte Grossman*,
Chief Justice William Howard Taft held that the President's pardoning power
extended to pardoning for criminal contempt and supported his argument
by the fact that twenty-seven such pardons had been granted since 1840.*
"Such long practice under the pardoning power and acquiescence in it
strongly sustains the construction it is based on. Stuart v. Laird. . . ."⁴ But
Stuart v. Laird justifies only congressional interpretations of ambiguous
provisions of the Constitution and requires that those be passed by a
Congress containing a number of the framers: the latest statute upheld on
the authority of *Stuart v. Laird* was passed in 1806.

It is well established that the executive cannot gain power by long-
continued usurpation. In *Youngstown Sheet & Tube Co. v. Sawyer*, in 1952,
the Court held that the President had no inherent power to seize industrial
property, although the opinion included an appendix that listed eighty-three
such seizures since the beginning of the Civil War, for fourteen of which no
statutory authority was claimed.* In *United States v. United States District Court*,
in 1972, the Supreme Court unanimously held that the authorization of a
large number of warrantless wiretaps by a long and uninterrupted series of
Presidents did not legalize the practice.* In *United States v. Nixon*, in 1974,
a unanimous Court held that the President had no "absolute, unqualified
privilege" to withhold information from the courts, although his predecessors
had frequently claimed and exercised "executive privilege."* In *Train v. City
of New York*,* in 1975, the Court unanimously held that the President had
no right to refuse to spend money appropriated by Congress, although this
had very frequently been done, and the practice extended back, by one
argument, to 1803.* *Ex parte Grossman* can be defended, if at all, not on the
ground of executive usage but only on Taft's other argument, that the
framers intended the President to possess the pardoning power of the King
of England, which included the power to pardon for criminal contempts.

On two other occasions the rule of *Stuart v. Laird* has been abused.
Purportedly relying on the principle of that case, the Supreme Court has twice
supported a decision upholding state action by citing state statutes roughly
contemporaneous with the adoption of the Constitution and initiating a

---

⁴Observe that antiquity accompanied by acquiescence is entirely irrelevant to the
constitutionality of an act not based on an interpretation supplied by a statute passed
in the generation of the framers. The act declared invalid by Chief Justice Taft himself,
in Myers v. United States, 272 U.S. 52 (1924), was fifty years old; that declared invalid
in Reichart v. Felfs, 73 U.S. (6 Wall.) 160 (1868), had been passed in 1812; nine others
ranged from fifteen to thirty-seven years in age when declared invalid.

policy frequently followed by later state statutes.* Of course the state legislatures that passed the first statutes contained few, if any, framers of the Constitution, and there is no reason to impute to them knowledge of the "meaning and true construction" of the Constitution. Since the argument purported to rest on the rationale of *Stuart v. Laird* and offered no other rationale, and the cases fail to meet the tests of *Stuart v. Laird*, this feature of the decisions must be considered plainly wrong.

A good deal of indecision marked the positions of the several justices in the *Steel Seizure Case.** In the opinion of the Court, Justice Hugo Black reported that the government had undertaken to justify the unauthorized seizure of steel plants by appealing to an "inherent power" of the President, "power 'supported by the Constitution, by historical precedent, and by court decisions.' "* To this Black replied:

> The President's power, if any, to issue the order must stem either from an act of Congress or from the Constitution itself. There is no statute that expressly authorizes the President to take possession of property as he did here. Nor is there any act of Congress to which our attention has been directed from which such a power can fairly be implied. . . .
>
> The order cannot properly be sustained as an exercise of the President's military power as Commander-in-Chief of the Armed Forces. . . .
>
> Nor can the seizure order be sustained because of the several constitutional provisions that grant executive power to the President. . . .
>
> It is said that other Presidents without congressional authority have taken possession of private business enterprises in order to settle labor disputes. But even if this be true, Congress has not thereby lost its exclusive constitutional authority to make laws necessary and proper to carry out the powers vested by the Constitution "in the Government of the United States, or in any Department or Officer thereof."*

In a separate opinion, Justice Frankfurter asserted that "a systematic, unbroken executive practice, long pursued to the knowledge of the Congress and never before questioned, engaged in by Presidents who have sworn to uphold the Constitution, making as it were such exercise of power part of the structure of our government, may be treated as a gloss on 'executive power' vested in the President by §1 of Art. II."* And he cited *United States v. Midwest Oil Co.*, which is discussed below. But that case treated congressional acquiescence as statutory authorization, not as a gloss on the Constitution. One hopes that Frankfurter meant no more than was held in *Midwest Oil*. Could he have supposed that power could be lost by Congress by disuse and acquired by the President by usage? In any case, Frankfurter reduced the number of unauthorized seizures to three and concluded that this number was too small to amount to "the kind of executive construction of the Constitution revealed in the Midwest case."

Three of the justices who held the President's action illegal considered it unnecessary to discuss the question of usage. A fourth, Justice Robert H.

Jackson, said of the seizure that the claim—"practice of prior Presidents has authorized it"—was unfounded.*

The three dissenting justices, in an opinion by Chief Justice Vinson, raised the argument on executive usage to the highest point it has ever attained. Vinson said:

> A review of executive action demonstrates that our Presidents have on many occasions exhibited the leadership contemplated by the Framers. . . . With or without statutory authorization, Presidents have at such times dealt with national emergencies by acting promptly and resolutely to enforce legislative programs, at least to save those programs until Congress could act. Congress and the courts have responded to such executive initiative with consistent approval.*

He illustrated this emergency power by rehearsing an extraordinary melange of episodes from American history, some of which did not involve emergencies of any kind, some of which involved unquestionably legal action, and most of which were not concerned with the saving of congressional programs. Vinson's contention does not bear the slightest resemblance to *Stuart v. Laird*. He not only adduces no contemporaneous congressional interpretation of the Constitution, but also cites no contemporaneous executive interpretation: not one of the executive actions he adduces before the Civil War was legally doubtful. Whereas the rule of *Stuart v. Laird* is used to remove doubt about the meaning of a single ambiguous phrase in the Constitution, Vinson would sweep away the whole document by subjecting perfectly unambiguous phrases to an overriding presidential emergency power. This is a perfect formula for dictatorship.

Executive usage finds its proper role not in the interpretation of the Constitution but in the interpretation of statutes. There are two relevant rules. In 1827, in *Edwards' Lessee v. Darby*, Justice Robert Trimble held, "In the construction of a doubtful and ambiguous law, the contemporaneous construction of those who were called upon to act under the law, and were appointed to carry its provisions into effect, is entitled to very great respect."* This language has been echoed in a multitude of cases.* Of course, a court, before invoking *Edwards' Lessee v. Darby*, must satisfy itself that the executive interpretation is a defensible construction of a doubtful act. If the meaning of the act is clear, an erroneous administrative interpretation, like an erroneous judicial interpretation, will be rejected.* In the absence of judicial construction of the statute, an administrative agency may change its interpretation, but it has been said that this cannot be done retroactively.* And the new interpretation, like the old, is subject to judicial scrutiny.

In the second case, an administrative agency adopts an indefensible interpretation of a statute. It is possible for Congress to ratify and adopt the administrative interpretation. In 1832, in *United States v. Arrendondo*, Justice Henry Baldwin said:

Where Congress have, by confirming the reports of commissioners or other tribunals, sanctioned the rules and principles on which they were founded, it is a legislative affirmance of the construction put by these tribunals on the laws conferring the authority and prescribing the rules by which it should be exercised; or which is to all intents and purposes of the same effect in law. It is a legislative ratification of an act done without previous authority, and this subsequent recognition and adoption is of the same force as if done by pre-existing power and relates back to the act done.*

The most frequent occasion for the invocation of this rule is in the interpretation of a statute that reenacts an earlier statute to which an erroneous administrative interpretation has been attached. If Congress reenacts the statute with knowledge of the administrative interpretation, it is often said to incorporate that interpretation and to give statutory standing to what was previously unlawful.* This tradition has produced one singular decision. Through the nineteenth century, Congress passed several statutes making public lands available for private occupation, but on some hundreds of occasions, without authorization in the relevant statute, the President withdrew a part of the land from the right of entry. In 1915, in *United States v. Midwest Oil Co.*, the Court upheld a 1909 withdrawal by President Taft of certain lands from the appropriation of oil rights offered to the public by an act passed in 1897.* Without doing extreme violence to the precedents, the Court might have argued that the act of 1897, passed as it was with the knowledge of earlier executive withdrawals, silently adopted the practice. But the Court used looser language. The "long-continued practice, known to and acquiesced in by Congress," had gained the "implied consent of Congress."* It is of course unwarranted to hold that an executive abuse gains legal standing if Congress does not correct it. In a closely parallel case the Supreme Court held that a well-established, well-known, and long-contin-ued practice of granting suspended sentences did not justify the federal courts in doing this when the statute did not authorize it.* We may suppose that the Supreme Court really upheld the withdrawal in *Midwest Oil* because it wished to prevent giving away oil that the navy needed. However that may be, the case is one of statutory interpretation. It does not hold that the President possesses a constitutional power to defy statutes, and one can only admire the imaginations of those authors who cite the case as a justification for presidential wars.

It will be observed, then, that executive usage cannot affect the interpretation of the Constitution. The only decision looking in this direction is *Ex parte Grossman*, and this case did not purport to break new ground; it is a misapplication of *Stuart v. Laird*. Executive usage plays a role in our legal system only in the interpretation of doubtful statutes and in implied congressional adoption of executive interpretation by the reenactment of a statute. There is reason for the rule. If the President were able, by a series of usurpations, to give constitutional status to his own claims, he could upset the balance of the Constitution and concentrate all power in his own hands. Neither the courts nor Congress would have the right to restrain him. But executive construction or misconstruction of statutes can be corrected by Congress; there is not the same danger of a perversion of the legal order.

Suppose, however, that the law were otherwise, that the President might, by initiating a series of wars, acquire a constitutional power to initiate war. This power could be acquired only under a claim of right. But our Presidents have never claimed the right to initiate war or to undertake acts of war. They have always offered more temperate, if less ingenuous, justifications for their actions—they have alleged that they were merely executing treaties or acts of Congress or rules of international law. Washington, Jefferson, Madison, Monroe, Jackson, Tyler, Buchanan, Lincoln, and Taft have all been quoted as denying that the President has the power to begin war or to carry out acts of war. Adams (*4*, IV, 207) and Grant (*181*, VI, 4022) also conceded that only Congress might undertake acts of hostility.

Nevertheless subordinate officials of the Truman, Johnson, and Nixon administrations have frequently claimed for the President a right to initiate war, and a few politicians and publicists have supported them. The argument ignores the settled law on usage. It contends that on a very large number of occasions Presidents have committed acts of war or engaged in war without legal authorization and that the occurrence of these events establishes the legality of such past and future wars.

The argument derives not from legal sources, but from a literary tradition which needs examination. It all begins with *The Right to Protect Citizens in Foreign Countries*, a monograph published in 1912 by J. Reuben Clark, Jr., the solicitor of the State Department. Clark was concerned not with municipal law, but with international law. He contended that a temporary incursion into foreign territory for the sole purpose of protecting citizens was not intervention, which was usually considered illegal at international law, but nonpolitical "interposition," which, he asserted, was not unlawful. He compiled a list of forty-five episodes, all but two of which (interventions in Samoa and Cuba) were, he said, mere interpositions and therefore justified at international law. He raised the question whether at municipal law the President had the right of interposition, and he suggested that the action might be justified as an exercise of executive power, but this opinion was "with no thought or pretense of more than a cursory consideration. It is entirely possible that a more detailed and careful study would lead to other or modified conclusions." (*28*, 48) His tentative argument ran thus. Citizens are entitled to protection at international law. International law is part of the law of the United States, and the President may therefore execute international law. The most obvious weakness in this argument is the fact that citizens of the United States have no rights whatever at international law. Foreign states owe duties to the United States and not to its citizens. The vindication of the rights of the United States at international law has been entrusted by the Constitution to Congress and not to the President.

In 1928 Milton Offutt published *The Protection of Citizens Abroad by the Armed Forces of the United States.* Offutt discarded Clark's misgivings and adopted his argument: In the execution of the laws, the President might execute international law by protecting citizens abroad. Offutt listed seventy–five military actions abroad, the latest in 1926. In 1934 the State Department published a third edition of Clark's monograph and added to Clark's appendix, listing foreign actions cases or clusters of cases under the names of eleven countries. Most of these were naval landings for the protection of citizens. In the same year Captain Harry Alanson Ellsworth of the Marine Corps prepared a study called *One Hundred Eighty Landings of United States Marines, 1800–1934.* This was published in mimeographed form; it was reproduced by the Headquarters of the Marine Corps in 1964 and 1974. Most of the landings could find arguable justification under statute as naval landings for the protection of citizens.

On July 10, 1941, a revolution in legal theory occurred. Defending in the Senate President Roosevelt's unauthorized action in sending troops to Iceland, Senator Tom Connally argued that the President, not as chief executive but as commander in chief, might send forces wherever he wished. To support this contention he cited eighty–five cases of the commitment of forces abroad.* These were simply the cases in Clark's appendix and in the 1934 supplemental list.

In 1945, James Grafton Rogers, a former assistant secretary of state, published *World Policing and the Constitution.* He itemized 149 cases or clusters of cases between 1798 and 1941 under the heading "A Chronological List of Military Operations of the United States Abroad." Unaware of the congressional authorization of landings for the protection of citizens (described in the next chapter), he said that in not more than one or two dozen of these cases had Congress authorized "the employment of men and guns." He added that in the great majority of the 149 cases there was no collision of hostile forces and no bloodshed.

In 1950, in order to justify President Truman's entry into the Korean War, the State Department made the logical extension of Senator Connally's reinterpretation of the commander in chief clause. If the commander in chief may send forces into foreign countries, this may well entail war; therefore, the President may send forces abroad to initiate war. The memorandum asserted:

> In many instances, of course, the Armed Forces have been used to protect specific American lives and property. In other cases, however, United States forces have been used in the broad interests of American foreign policy and their use could be characterized as participation in international police action. (*10*, 174)

In support of this assertion, Senator Connally's list of eighty–five episodes was reproduced. However, the State Department did not wish to rely solely on this argument. It also referred to the President's executive power, his power as commander in chief, his power to conduct the foreign relations of the United States, and the United Nations Charter.

In 1956 the Library of Congress prepared for John W. McCormack, the majority leader of the House of Representatives, a list of actions undertaken by the President under the title *The Powers of the President as Commander in Chief of the Army and Navy of the United States.** A majority of the cases were domestic actions authorized by statute.

In 1966, something more than a year after President Johnson's massive commitment of troops in Vietnam, the State Department produced a memorandum to justify this action. It asserted that the President as commander in chief has "the power to deploy American forces abroad and commit them to military operations when the President deems such action necessary to maintain the security and defense of the United States." (*113*, 474, 485) In addition, it appealed to the grant of executive power, the President's "prime responsibility for the conduct of foreign relations," the Southeast Asia Collective Defense Treaty, and the Tonkin Gulf Resolution. Moreover, it asserted:

> Since the Constitution was adopted there have been at least 125 instances in which the President has ordered the armed forces to take action or maintain positions abroad without obtaining prior congres-sional authorization, starting with the "undeclared war" with France. (*113*)

We should reiterate that, as the Supreme Court three times asserted, the war with France (1798–1800) was a limited war initiated by acts of Congress and defined in all its dimensions by acts of Congress. The 125 cases appear to be James Grafton Rogers's 149 cases minus—given the more generous definition—the one or two dozen congressionally authorized cases. Then the memorandum added the Korean War and President Eisenhower's landing of marines in Lebanon in 1957 as further evidence.

In 1967 the State Department published a study called *Armed Actions Taken by the United States Without a Declaration of War, 1789–1967*. The prefatory statement asserted:

> The President, who is designated in the Constitution as "Commander in Chief of the Armed Forces," has full control over the use of these forces. On his own authority he may, and frequently has, committed them to armed action to protect the national interest beyond the borders of the United States. (7)

The study listed 137 cases, derived from Rogers's list of 149 cases with some dropped and others subdivided.

In 1970 the Library of Congress prepared for the Subcommittee on National Security Policy and Scientific Developments of the House Committee on Foreign Affairs a list of "Instances of Use of United States Armed Forces Abroad, 1789–1970." (*80*, 50–57) The list is a conflation of the Rogers list and the 1967 State Department list; it runs to 165 cases.

On August 3, 1971, Senator Goldwater inserted in the *Congressional Record* a speech by Solicitor General Erwin N. Griswold which, without giving a list, asserted:

> Indeed, if the record is closely examined, one can count one hundred sixty-one separate instances in which this nation was engaged in hostilities against a foreign power, between 1798 and 1945, including the Civil War; and only six of these involved a formal declaration of war.*

On April 26, 1971, Goldwater had inserted in the *Congressional Record* a list of what he called "153 military actions taken by the United States abroad without a declaration of war." This too was a combination of the Rogers list and the 1967 State Department list. On August 28 the senator characterized these 153 hostile operations as 150 "wars." On December 18 he asserted that by continuing study he had learned that there had been "at least 192 military actions undertaken by U.S. forces without a declaration of war, eighty-one of which involved actual combat or ultimatums tantamount to the use of force." The senator's efforts culminated in the publication in 1973 of a list compiled by his legal assistant, Terry Emerson, of "199 U.S. military hostilities abroad without a declaration of war, 1798-1972," which, according to Emerson, justified Monaghan's assertion that "history has legitimated the practice of presidential war-making."*

The lists are not accurately characterized by their compilers. For the purpose of analysis, the latest official list, that prepared by the State Department in 1967, is used here. The proportions of cases remain fairly constant through all the lists. Sometimes a case might fall under more than one heading, but it is placed here under what appears to be the most appropriate title. The cases in the State Department list can be categorized thus:

1. Actions for which congressional authorization was claimed	7
2. Naval self-defense	1
3. Enforcement of law against piracy, no trespass	1
4. Enforcement of law against piracy, technical trespass	7
5. Landings to protect citizens before 1862	13
6. Landings to protect citizens, 1865-1967	56
7. Invasion of foreign or disputed territory, no combat	10
8. Invasion of foreign or disputed territory, combat	10
9. Reprisals against aborigines	9
10. Other reprisals not authorized by statute	4
11. Minatory demonstrations without combat	6
12. Intervention in Panama	1
13. Protracted occupation of Caribbean states	6
14. Actions anticipating World War II	1
15. Bombing of Laos	1
16. Korean and Vietnamese Wars	2
17. Miscellaneous	2
Total	137

The first category in the list contains three of the limited wars declared by Congress; it includes one of the four conditional declarations of war. It includes two forays into Spanish Florida, purportedly undertaken under statutory authorization, and Woodrow Wilson's seizure of Veracruz on April 21, 1914, said to have been ratified by the joint resolution of April 22, 1914.

A number of the other cases can be justified in terms other than presidential initiative. As for category 2, naval vessels have the right of self–defense at international and municipal law. Category 3 is merely obedience to statute. Although his naval commanders did not share his views, President Monroe took the position that the landings in category 4 required statutory authorization. We have no contemporary discussion of the thirteen landings in category 5. As we shall see, some of the fifty–six landings in category 6 enjoyed statutory authorization. The invasion of foreign territory in categories 7 and 8 was illegal, but if the United States claimed the territory, the President's action in sending troops was not an act of war. Reprisals, as we have seen, are acts of war, and today naval regulations forbid officers to undertake them. The minatory demonstrations at sea in category 11 were intended to make other states nervous but were not acts of war. Theodore Roosevelt's intervention in Panama was naked aggression, and the United States paid twenty–five million dollars as compensation to Colombia.*

Category 13 represents merely an aspect of the involvement of the American executive in the Caribbean area. American forces actually occupied and administered three Caribbean countries: Cuba from 1906 to 1909, Haiti from 1915 to 1934, and the Dominican Republic from 1916 to 1924. On other occasions, forces of marines were permanently stationed in a Caribbean country in order to influence local politics; the longest such interventions were those in Nicaragua from 1912 to 1925 and from 1926 to 1933. In addition, the customshouses of sovereign states were occupied now and again, with or without authorization by treaty, and their finances were administered by the United States for extended periods. On occasion, at the instance of the United States, Latin American countries agreed to put their import duties in the hands of a representative of foreign bankers in case of default on a loan. But in no case was the executive action said to be grounded on a presidential war–making power.

The treaty power was involved in the occupation of Cuba, Haiti, and the Dominican Republic. The so–called Platt Amendment was included in the 1903 treaty with Cuba. One of its terms read:

> . . . the Government of Cuba consents that the United States may exercise the right to intervene for the preservation of Cuban indepen-dence, the maintenance of a government adequate for the protection of life, property, and individual liberty, and for discharging the obligations with respect to Cuba imposed by the treaty of Paris on the United States, now to be assumed and undertaken by the Government of Cuba.*

With this provision the United States placed Cuba under military administration from 1906 to 1909. On July 26, 1915, at a time of great disorder in Haiti, American marines landed at Port-au-Prince. A government acceptable to the United States was instituted; the United States concluded a treaty with this government on September 15.* On November 29 a modus vivendi was signed, putting the treaty into effect provisionally. The treaty was approved by the United States Senate on February 28, 1916. Under this agreement the financial affairs of Haiti were placed in the hands of a general receiver and a customs adviser nominated by the President of the United States to the President of Haiti; the Haitian constabulary was put under the command of American officers nominated by the one President to the other. The treaty contained a clause like that in the Platt Amendment:

> . . . should the necessity arise, the United States will lend an efficient aid for the preservation of Haitian Independence and the maintenance of a government adequate for the protection of life, property, and individual liberty.*

In 1916 Congress authorized the President to detach naval and marine officers and enlisted men to serve in the Haitian constabulary.* In 1933 an executive agreement for withdrawal of forces in 1934 was concluded, but the agreement provided for the continuance of American financial control until outstanding bonds were retired. (122, 307-8) In the Dominican Republic, the United States was less fortunate. The country was occupied in 1916, but it was impossible to find a pliant native government—the nation was controlled directly by an American military governor until a subordinate native government was installed in 1922. In 1924 the occupation forces were withdrawn. A Convention of Ratification was signed on June 12, 1924, and was ratified by the United States on January 21, 1925.* It recited that "the Dominican Republic has always maintained its right to self-government, and the disoccupation of its territory and the integrity of its sovereignty and independence." The Dominican Republic had never delegated authority to any foreign power to legislate for it, but it understood that "the internal interests of the Republic" required the ratification of many of the acts of the Military Government; the treaty then recited the orders and regulations that it ratified. No word in the treaty endorsed the American occupation.

In other cases, no legal pretext for intervention existed except for the protection of American citizens. But in any case, the use of military force to execute a treaty or to protect citizens requires congressional authorization.

In at least one case, no legal theory whatever was available to justify the action. After the seizure of Port-au-Prince in Haiti in 1915, Secretary of State Robert Lansing wrote to President Wilson that he was "not at all sure what we ought to do or what we legally can do." Wilson replied that he too feared that "we have not the legal authority to do what we apparently ought to do but that the United States must send sufficient troops to subordinate local governments and completely control the country." Lansing suggested that a humanitarian excuse be offered. It could be alleged that the marines had occupied Haitian ports to relieve the famine induced by their landing: guerrillas in the interior had blocked the roads to the occupied cities and thus had interrupted the movement of food. (*193*, 67, 70)

One hardly knows what to make of Secretary Lansing's declaration of May 15, 1917. A rebellion broke out in Cuba in February of 1917 against President Mario García Menocal, who had stolen the election of 1916. With the consent of President Menocal the United States landed marines. On April 6, 1917, the United States declared war on Germany, and on April 7 Cuba declared war. Secretary Lansing's warning of May 15 read:

> In the present war, in order to insure victory, Cuba, as well as the United States, has two great obligations, one military and the other economic. Therefore, as the Allied Powers and the United States must depend to a large extent upon the sugar production of Cuba, all disturbances which interfere with this production must be considered as hostile acts, and the United States Government is forced to issue this warning that unless all those in arms against the Government of Cuba return to their allegiance it may become necessary for the United States to regard them as its enemies and to deal with them accordingly. (*122*, 42–43)

The marines were withdrawn in 1922.

There were several motives for the American interventions. One was to prevent the occupation of the customshouses of a debtor nation by a European state whose citizens had unsatisfied claims against the debtor. It was feared that such an action might pose a military threat to the Panama Canal. Secretary of the Navy Josephus Daniels alleged that the seizure of Haiti and the Dominican Republic in 1915 was intended to prevent Germany from establishing submarine bases in those countries. (*37*, 178) This unrealistic fear cannot have been a major consideration. In the particular case of Haiti, it was also considered desirable to strike from the Haitian constitution the provision forbidding foreigners to own land if they had not resided in the Republic for five years; this was done in 1918. In many cases, the principal motives were obtaining reimbursement for American creditors of delinquent debtor nations and securing for American banking houses the opportunity of making further loans. None of the major operations had the protection of the lives of American citizens as an object. The claim of a right to protect the property of citizens was extended to include the maintenance of a political system in which American-owned enterprises enjoyed a permanent right to continue their operations. This was an avowed ground for President Coolidge's intervention in Nicaragua in 1926.* The conduct of the United States toward the small republics to the south bears a striking resemblance to the American policy since 1950 in Asia; the latter is a projection of the former into a considerably less manageable environment. In neither case was Congress made an active participant in formulating the policy. The policy could not have survived debate if it had not always been presented as a *fait accompli*.

Unaccountably, one of the most striking examples of presidential initiative is omitted from all the lists. The Banque Nationale of Haiti was privately owned; the National City Bank of New York was a large minority stockholder. In 1914 the Banque held a trust fund of $500,000 in gold belonging to the government of Haiti, set aside for the redemption of an issue of paper money. A New Yorker named Henry R. Wehrhane, a vice-president of the Banque Nationale, asked the State Department to transport the gold to New York, and he cabled the Banque Nationale to surrender the gold. Two naval vessels were sent to Port-au-Prince; a detachment of marines landed, went to the Banque, received Haiti's gold, and spirited it away. Secretary of State William Jennings Bryan indignantly rejected the Haitian ambassador's suggestion that there was anything irregular about this bold theft. (*144*, 365–82)

As for category 14, illegal presidential acts of war, as well as a congressional declaration of limited war in the form of the Lend–Lease Act, occurred before the Second World War, as we have already seen. No one would allege that presidential bombing of Laos was authorized by the Constitution or by statute. President Truman's entry into the Korean War was defended by the State Department as authorized by treaty—that is, by the United Nations Charter—and by the executive precedents we have been considering. (*10*, 174) The Vietnam War was alleged to be authorized by the Southeast Asia Collective Defense Treaty, the Tonkin Gulf Resolution, and the executive precedents. (*113*)

Relatively few of the 137 cases in the 1967 State Department list were ordered by the President. Many of them were trivial actions undertaken by a naval officer in a distant port on his own responsibility. One supposes that some of these cases were never reported to the President. But some were sufficiently important to be noticed and reproved. The State Department list recognizes only two such cases: the repudiation of General Matthews's activities in Florida in 1812 and of General John Sedgwick's action in attacking the Mexican town of Matamoros in 1866. But there were others. The list reports General David Porter's reprisal in Puerto Rico in 1824, without mentioning that Porter was court-martialed and suspended six months for this action, causing him to resign. (*130*, 14–15) The list reports Captain Silas Duncan's landing in the Falkland Islands in 1832 (*130*, 20–22), without noticing that a circuit court held his action illegal.* Commodore Matthew Perry's expedition to Japan in 1852 is listed, but there is no mention of Secretary of State Webster's warning to him: "He will bear in mind that as the President has no power to declare war his mission is necessarily of a pacific character, and he will not resort to force unless in self-defence." (*192*, 54)

The list reports the arrest of the filibusterer William Walker in Nicaragua by Commodore Hiram Paulding for violation of the Neutrality Act, noting that the action was "tacitly disavowed" by the State Department. This leaves a false impression. After the arrest Paulding wrote to his wife: "I have taken strong measures in forcing him from neutral territory. It may make me President or may cost me my commission." (197, 39) Walker gave his parole and returned by mail steamer to Washington, where Secretary of State Cass said that the executive had no power to detain him; Walker was released. The Senate and the House demanded information about the arrest. President Buchanan reported to the Senate on January 7, 1858. He observed that Paulding had committed "a grave error" and that he disapproved of this conduct; however, he asserted that Paulding had acted "from pure and patriotic motives and in the sincere conviction that he was promoting the interests and vindicating the honor of his country." (181, IV, 2997-98) This extenuation provoked bitter criticism in Congress of Buchanan himself.

The list mentions a series of marine landings in Colombia between April and November 1902. It fails to say that when these forces were used to prevent the transportation of Colombian troops on the Panama Railroad in September and October, Colombia protested, and Secretary of State John Hay expressed regret, saying that there had been "no intention to infringe sovereignty or wound dignity of Colombia." (79, 44-45) The list reports that in 1912 a small force of marines landed in Honduras at the request of the American vice-consul in order to prevent the seizure of an American-owned railroad by the government of Honduras. It neglects to add that the government of Honduras protested and that two days later the Navy Department ordered the marines withdrawn. The commander of the *Petrel* complied and informed the local authorities that he had "received instructions from my government not to forcibly resist seizure of the railroad by the authorities of Honduras." (142, 1353)

Indeed, as we have already seen, it is illegal for the President, or anyone but Congress, to authorize the intrusion of a public force into foreign territory. No one has undertaken to collect a list of the cases in which this rule has been enforced against overzealous officers. If this were done, it might be of quite respectable length. A number of cases are reviewed elsewhere; let us add a few more. In 1808 President Jefferson took a very serious view of an attack by one army and several navy officers upon Spanish territory. He referred the case to the two services for disciplinary action and brought the question before the cabinet. (89, XII, 167) In 1845 Captain Philip Voorhees of the frigate *Congress* was court-martialed and suspended three years for breach of neutrality during a struggle between two Latin American countries. (119, I, 178-82) A case that would certainly be found in all the lists if it weren't for its outcome was the American participation in the revolution in Hawaii in 1893. At the request of the American minister, American forces landed, ostensibly for the protection of citizens but actually to intimidate the supporters of Queen Lydia Liliuokalani. The revolutionaries then announced the annexation of Hawaii to the United States, but President Cleveland, when he learned the truth, repudiated the whole transaction. (*181*, VIII, 5892)

One cannot be sure, but the number of cases in which Presidents have personally made the decisions, unconstitutionally, to engage in war or in acts of war probably lies between one and two dozen. And in all those cases the Presidents have made false claims of authorization, either by statute or by treaty or by international law. They have not relied on their powers as commander in chief or as chief executive.

In the case of executive wars, none of the conditions for the establishment of constitutional power by usage is present. The Constitution is not ambiguous. No contemporaneous congressional interpretation attributes a power of initiating war to the President. The early Presidents, and indeed everyone in the country until the year 1950, denied that the President possessed such a power. There is no sustained body of usage to support such a claim. It can only be audacity or desperation that leads the champions of recent presidential usurpations to state that "history had legitimated the practice of presidential war-making."

Chapter 10
NAVAL LANDINGS

In dictum, in *Murray v. The Charming Betsy,* Chief Justice Marshall said:

> The American citizen who goes into a foreign country, although he owes
> local and temporary allegiance to that country, is yet, if he performs no
> other act changing his condition, entitled to the protection of his own
> government; and if, without the violation of any municipal law, he should
> be oppressed unjustly, he would have a right to claim that protection,
> and the interposition of the American government in his favor would
> be considered as a justifiable interposition.*

Two later Supreme Court dicta also speak of protection abroad as a right
of United States citizenship.*

A citizen may be threatened abroad in two ways. In the case put by Chief
Justice Marshall above, a foreign government treats the American oppres-
sively. If the United States should exert force for his protection, the action
would be an act of war. Our wars with the Barbary states were authorized
by Congress precisely for the protection and rescue of citizens from foreign
governments. In 1827 Secretary of State Clay advised that the navy should
not use force to liberate American seamen imprisoned in a foreign port. "The
employment of force is justifiable in resisting aggressions before they are
complete. But when they are consummated, the intervention of the authority
of government becomes necessary if redress is refused by the aggressor."
(*119*, VII, 163) In 1868 Congress enacted that if a citizen should be "unjustly
deprived of his liberty by or under the authority of any foreign government,"
the President should attempt to obtain his release by means "not amounting
to acts of war."* This act is still in force.

In the second case, citizens of the United States may be threatened by politically unorganized aborigines or by the private action of riotous or rebellious citizens in a foreign state, or they may be imperiled during a civil war. Invasion of territory without the consent of the local sovereign is an act of war and may lead to protracted war, as during the Boxer Rebellion. But there is an exception: if the intervention is not directed at the local sovereign, and if there is "a necessity of self-defense, instant, overwhelming, leaving no choice of means, no moment for deliberation"—to use Webster's language in the case of the *Caroline*—the action is not an act of war at international law.

Although an interposition in this exceptional case would not be an act of war, it would still require statutory authorization. The protection of the rights of citizens is a responsibility of Congress and not of the President. In *Prigg v. Pennsylvania*, in 1842, the Court held that the fugitive slave clause of the Constitution was self-executing, so that the owner of a slave might recapture him without governmental intervention, but that governmental intervention must be authorized by Congress.*

This does not exactly agree with the existing case law concerning the specific question. The destruction of Greytown by Captain Hollins is always cited as evidence of a constitutional right of the President to protect citizens.* However, it was in fact an unauthorized act of reprisal and consequently an unauthorized act of war.

And there is a distortion of fact in the famous case of *In re Neagle*.* In 1853, Martin Koszta, a Hungarian subject who had declared his intention of acquiring American citizenship but had not yet done so, was arrested in Smyrna and carried aboard the Austrian vessel *Hussar*. Captain Duncan Ingraham of the American sloop of war *St. Louis* learned of this, trained his guns on the *Hussar*, and demanded the release of Koszta. After a period of stalemate, the two commanders accepted the arbitration of the French consul awarding Koszta to Ingraham. In the ensuing correspondence with the Austro-Hungarian government, Secretary of State William Marcy conceded that Koszta was not a citizen but asserted that at international law the United States had the right to protect a domiciled alien.* In his annual message to Congress on December 5, 1853, President Pierce justified the action as the defense of a citizen (*181*, V, 210), and Congress eventually voted Captain Ingraham a gold medal.* Thirty-seven years after the event, the Supreme Court in *In re Neagle* fixed upon the Koszta case as evidence of a right of the President to enforce not only acts of Congress and treaties but also "the rights, duties and obligations growing out of the Constitution itself."* Yet Captain Ingraham had acted not under, but against the instructions of the President and the secretary of the navy. It seems clear that his action was illegal when undertaken but was later ratified by the congressional commendation and gold medal.

The first sustained discussion of the problem is the monograph of the solicitor of the State Department, J. Reuben Clark, Jr., *The Right to Protect*

Citizens in Foreign Countries by Landing Forces. Clark distinguished between "an intervention by one power in the local political affairs of another power," as for the purpose of preserving or installing a particular form of government, and "interposition upon behalf of citizens." (28, 24) "The sole motive for this nonpolitical intervention or interposition is the protection of citizens or subjects either from the acts of the government itself or from the acts of persons or bodies of persons resident within the jurisdiction of a government which finds itself unable to afford the requisite protection." (28, 25) Clark rehearsed forty-five cases of American actions, most of them purportedly landings for the protection of citizens, and suggested that forty-three of them constituted interpositions rather than interventions. They were therefore warranted at international law, and Clark argued that the President might enforce international law without an authorizing statute. But he concluded with the warning that these opinions were tentative and might not survive a more careful study.

Indeed they will not. A "nonpolitical" interposition for the protection of citizens "from the acts of the government itself" may have been fully justified at the international law of Clark's day, but it was clearly an act of war and violation of an act of Congress. Interposition for the protection of citizens from rioters was also an act of war unless it met the conditions of extreme urgency described in the case of the *Caroline*. And even if it met those conditions, it would be legal only if there were a statute authorizing the action.

Initially, however, the executive made naval landings without statutory authority. From 1819 to 1825 pirates put out from Spanish islands in the Caribbean, plundered American shipping, and fled to the safety of shore. When Commodore David Porter was appointed to the command of the West Indian squadron in 1823, Secretary of the Navy Smith Thompson exceeded his own authority by giving Porter permission to pursue pirates ashore, under specified conditions.

> In regard to pirates, there is no neutral party; they being the enemies of the human race, all nations are parties against them, and may be considered as allies. The object and intention of our government is to respect the feelings, as well as the rights of others, both in substance and in form, in all the measures which may be adopted to accomplish the end in view. Should, therefore, the crews of any vessels which you have engaged in acts of piracy, or which you have just cause to suspect of being of that character, retreat into the ports, harbors, or settled parts of the islands, you may enter, in pursuit of them, such ports, harbors, and settled parts of the country, for the purpose of aiding the local authorities, or people, as the case may be, as to seize and bring the offenders to justice, previously giving notice that this is your sole object. Where the government exists, and is felt, you will in all instances respect the local authorities, and only act in aid of and co-operation with them; it being the exclusive purpose of the United States to suppress piracy; an object

in which all nations are equally interested; and in the accomplishment of which, the Spanish authorities and people will, it is presumed, cordially co-operate with you. (*6*, II, 652)

But President Monroe believed that such action needed congressional sanction. On December 7, 1824, in his annual message to Congress, he raised the problem of piracy in the Caribbean and said, "Whether those robbers should be pursued on the land, the local authorities be made responsible for these atrocities, or any other measure be resorted to suppress them, is submitted to the consideration of Congress." (*181*, II, 827) Congress did not act, but Porter suppressed the pirates.

Landings in pursuit of pirates could seldom meet the conditions laid down by Webster in the case of the *Caroline*. Landings for the protection of citizens from a mob in a foreign country, however, might be demanded by an instant and overwhelming necessity for interposition. There were thirteen such landings between 1833, when the first occurred, and 1862. The practice was authorized under statute in 1862 or, more accurately, by a regulation pursuant to statute in 1865.

In 1862 Congress authorized the secretary of the navy to make regulations, subject to the approbation of the President.* These regu-lations had the force of law.* In 1865 the secretary issued *Regulations for the Government of the United States Navy*. Article 310 instructed the commander in chief of a fleet, squadron, or vessel.

> On arriving within the limits of his station on foreign service, he is to place himself in communication with the diplomatic agents of the United States thereabouts, and is to afford them, on his own responsibility, such aid and co-operation in all matters for the benefit of the government as they may require, and as he may judge to be expedient and proper. (*161*, 196)

This should be read together with Article 467 of the 1863 edition of *The United States Consul's Manual: A Practical Guide for Consular Officers*, which provided:

> Consular officers will refrain from requesting, except through the medium of the Department of State, the presence of United States vessels at the ports in their respective consular districts, unless for the protection of the lives and property of American citizens which might be endangered by delay; in such a case the consular officer will present to the com-mander of the vessel a statement of the facts, who will act upon his own responsibility, subject to the general or special orders he may have received from the Navy Department. (*224*, 196)

The upshot of these two provisions is that a senior naval officer, by virtue of regulations prescribed by the secretary of the navy under authorization by Congress, should, on his own responsibility and on his own evaluation of the situation, act "for the protection of the lives and property of American citizens which might be endangered by delay."

The protection of citizens by naval landings was granted at the request of consular agents on twenty-six occasions during the period between 1865 and the present. During this same period, forces were landed on fifteen other occasions to protect consular property, and though no evidence survives that the landings were a result of a request by a consular officer, one would suspect that this was indeed the case.

In 1868, *Consular Regulations: A Practical Guide for Consular Officers* (*33*) was issued. Article 535 of this edition reproduced verbatim Article 467 of the 1863 edition of *The United States Consul's Manual*. In 1870 the Navy Department issued a new series of *Regulations for the Government of the United States Navy*. (*162*) The "Duties of the Commander-in-Chief" had undergone serious revision. The articles replacing Article 310 of the 1865 Regulations in the 1870 edition provided:

> 52. He will preserve, so far as in him lies, the best feeling and the most cordial relations with the ministers and consuls of the United States on foreign stations, and will extend to them every official courtesy. He will also duly consider such information as they may have to give him relating to the interests of the United States, but he will not receive orders from such sources, and he will be responsible to the Secretary to the Navy, in the first place, for his acts.

> 53. He will not take upon himself the power of inflicting punishment upon the people of any civilized nation with whom we have treaties, for any violation, alleged or otherwise of such treaties or of international law.

> 54. In the absence of a diplomatic representative of the United States, he will enter into correspondence on matters of this kind with the authorities of the nation which may be supposed to have been the aggressor, and will take the earliest opportunity to communicate all the information in his possession to the government of the United States.

This is an admonition to the naval commander not to treat information from ministers and consuls regarding the interests of the United States as an obligation or order to act. The commander is responsible to the secretary of the navy for his acts, not to ministers and consuls on foreign stations. His prerogative to act remains, but he is warned that this prerogative derives from the secretary of the navy and not the State Department. The addition of this admonition to the commander in chief in the 1870 *Naval Regulations* is puzzling. The language of the 1865 Regulation does say "as they may require," possibly lending itself to the interpretation that "aid and co-operation" is to be afforded "as they may *order*"; however, no instances of this interpretation are known. Events between 1865 and 1870 hardly justify this stern warning to naval commanders not to receive orders from ministers and consuls of the United States on foreign stations. Only one landing to protect citizens was requested by a consul in this period; that was in 1865, when the consul at Panama asked for a force from the U.S.S. *St.*

Marys to protect the lives and property of American residents during a revolution. A possible explanation might lie in Article 53 of the *1870 Regulations*. No provision forbidding reprisals by naval commanders appears in the 1865 edition of the *Naval Regulations*. However, during the period between 1865 and 1870, two instances of reprisal ordered by a naval commander occurred. Curiously enough, both were ordered by the same officer, Rear Admiral Henry H. Bell. (*130*, 48–50) The first occurred in 1866 in China and the second in 1867 on the island of Formosa. In the second instance, approximately 180 officers and men were landed under the command of Admiral Bell to punish natives of Formosa who allegedly had murdered the crew of the American barque *Rover* when it had been wrecked on the southeastern part of the island. The first case requires a closer examination. The American consul at Newchwang, China, Francis P. Knight, was assaulted by forces under one of the many war lords who roamed the territory during this period harassing foreigners. Rear Admiral Bell, commanding the Asiatic Squadron, ordered Commander Robert Townsend, aboard the U.S.S. *Wachusett*, to Newchwang to insure that the leader and the men involved in the assault were properly punished. Commander Townsend verified that the men who had participated in the incident were being brought to justice by the Chinese authorities; however, when it appeared that the leader was not going to be arrested, Commander Townsend sent a sizable force ashore to arrest this man and insure that he was eventually convicted. Though no evidence exists that any orders were given by the consular officers or received by naval officers to execute a landing to avenge the injury to the American Consul at Newchwang, this is the only case during this period in which questionable conduct occurred involving both naval and consular officers. In any event, Article 53 of the 1870 edition of *Regulations* included a specific prohibition on acts of reprisal and corrected this omission from the 1865 edition.

Whatever the reason for the change in the naval regulations, in 1874 the *Regulations Prescribed for the Use of the Consular Service of the United States* (*164*, 15–16) reflected the same change in policy. Consular officers were warned that "the Navy is an independent branch of the service, not subject to the orders of this Department." Article 56 of the 1874 regulations in its entirety read:

> 56. They are also reminded that the Navy is an independent branch of the service, not subject to the orders of this Department, and that its officers have fixed duties prescribed for them; they will therefore be careful to ask for the presence of a naval force at their ports only when public exigencies absolutely require it, and will give the officers in command in full the reasons for the request, and leave with them the responsibility of action.

In 1876 the Navy again revised its regulations; however, the provisions covering the duties of the commander in chief with regard to ministers and

consuls of the United States on foreign stations remained virtually
unchanged. Regulations for the Consular Service were revised in 1881, 1888,
and 1896, and these too continued the provisions of Article 56 of the 1874
edition of the regulations.

The 1893 edition of the *Regulations for the Government of the United States
Navy* (*163*, 67) contained a striking clarification of the problem. Under the
heading "A Commander-in-Chief," three articles read:

> 284. On occasions where injury to the United States or to citizens thereof
> is committed or threatened, in violation of the principles of international
> law or treaty rights, he shall consult with the diplomatic representative
> or consul of the United States, and take such steps as the gravity of the
> case demands, reporting immediately to the Secretary of the Navy all
> the facts. The responsibility for any action taken by a naval force,
> however, rests wholly upon the commanding officer thereof.

> 285. The use of force against a foreign and friendly state, or against
> anyone within the territories thereof, is illegal. The right of self-preserva-
> tion, however, is a right which belongs to states as well as to individuals,
> and in the case of states it includes the protection of the state, its honor,
> and its possessions, and the lives and property of its citizens against
> arbitrary violence, actual or impending, whereby that state or its citizens
> may suffer irreparable injury. The conditions calling for the application
> of the right of self-preservation cannot be defined beforehand, but must
> be left to the sound judgment of responsible officers, who are to perform
> their duties in this respect with all possible care and forbearance. In no
> case shall force be exercised in time of peace otherwise than an
> application of the right of self-preservation as above defined. It can never
> be exercised with a view to inflicting punishments for acts already
> committed. It must be used only as a last resort, and then only to the
> extent which is absolutely necessary to accomplish the end required.

> 286. Whenever in the application of the above mentioned principles it
> shall become necessary to land an armed force in foreign territory on
> occasions of political disturbance where the local authorities are unable
> to give adequate protection to life and property, the assent of such
> authorities or of some one of them, shall first be obtained, if it can be
> done without prejudice to the interests involved.

Here is general authorization, carefully safeguarded as to circumstances,
to naval commanders to land forces to protect the lives and property of
citizens under the right of self-preservation. The exercise of this authority
is "left to the sound judgment of responsible officers" to discern when a
landing is necessitated by "the right of self-preservation [that] cannot be
defined beforehand." The assent of local authorities is desirable but not
necessary when it cannot be obtained "without prejudice to the interests
involved." The codes promulgated in 1896, 1905, 1920, and 1948 have

contained substantially similar provisions.

The question is bound to arise as to whether the act of 1862 authorizing the secretary of the navy to make regulations with no restriction in subject is an unconstitutional delegation of power. But the delegation must be interpreted, if possible, in such a way as to save its constitutionality. The President was given a similarly broad power in 1926 under a statute that read, "The Secretary of State may grant and issue passports . . . under such rules as the President shall designate and prescribe. . . ." In 1958, in *Kent v. Dulles*, the Supreme Court held that the delegation must be interpreted as limited to the topics on which restrictive rules had been made in the past: the denial of passports for lack of citizenship or because they were sought in order to escape prosecution for crime or to advance criminal schemes.* Since there had been thirteen naval landings to rescue citizens before 1862, it seems fair to assume that this action was one of those Congress intended to authorize when it passed the act of 1862.

Indeed, restrictive interpretation of an overly broad statute, when this is possible, is standard practice. When Congress has passed regulatory statutes that in language exceed its delegated powers, the Court has if possible limited their meaning to the constitutionally permissible area.*

Between 1865 and 1874 five more landings to protect citizens occurred. In 1874, when Congress passed the *Revised Statutes*, it reenacted the 1862 statute, presumably with knowledge of the administrative interpretation of the statute.* When Congress thus reenacts a statute, it adopts the established administrative interpretation. Consequently, whatever meaning and status the act of 1862 may have had, the *Revised Statutes* confirmed the practice of making naval landings for the protection of the citizens in case of emergency.

Since the enactment of the *Revised Statutes* in 1874, more than seventy landings purportedly for the protection of citizens have been carried out. But there is reason to doubt that all of these actually met the conditions of the navy regulations. The regulations place the power of decision and the responsibility on the local commander in chief, but in the days of cable and, later, wireless or radio communications, the decision came to be taken by the President. He is not authorized by the regulations to make such a decision, but the naval officer is in no position to defy him. Inevitably the motives for intervention changed. Instead of the appraisal by a naval officer of the immediate circumstances, the President made the appraisal, almost inevitably in terms of large political and economic interests rather than the security of the citizens involved. Parker T. Moon has evaluated our interventions in the Caribbean thus:

> The killing of Americans in Caribbean countries is rarer than in Chicago, and usually happens after we have intervened, not before. There had been no butchery of Americans in Haiti in 1915 when our marines were landed; the official documents show that the State Department was

concerned about the National Bank, the railway, and customs collection. In the Dominican Republic in 1916 the motive was not protection of lives, but increase of American control. To justify our most recent intervention (1926–29) in Nicaragua, the State Department issued a pamphlet in the Appendix of which is found a long list of appeals by American concerns which feared injury to their property or business interest in Nicaragua but it does not appear that any Americans were killed until the landing of the marines had been ordered. Even if this question of American lives were as real as Mr. Hughes implied, it would not necessarily call for armed intervention. When Americans are killed in foreign countries outside the Caribbean we do not customarily land marines.

There is more substance in the problem of protecting "property," under which term all sorts of business interests, concessions sometimes of doubtful character, and even expectations of profit seem to be included. The announced policy of recent administrations has been to protect not only American but also European property in the Caribbean. . . . (*117*, 186–87)

Other instances also show clear abuse of the navy regulations. In 1874 there was a dispute over the succession to the throne of Hawaii. At the request of the Hawaiian minister of foreign affairs, relayed by the United States minister to Hawaii, Commander George Belknap landed 150 men and a gatling gun, took possession of the courthouse, and insured the installation of King David Kalakaua. This action for the protection of the rights of American citizens was undertaken against an American citizen, the dowager Queen Emma, who was the other claimant to the throne.*

President Lyndon Johnson's invasion of the Dominican Republic is the most striking act of illegality. Juan Bosch had been elected President of the Republic in December 1962 by fifty-eight percent of the vote in that country's first free election. He was not favored by Washington and was overthrown by a military coup within a few months. On April 24, 1965, a portion of the army rebelled against the ruling military junta and called upon President Bosch to return. By April 28 the junta was hard-pressed, and leader Colonel Pedro Bartolome Benoit asked for American assistance on the ground that their defeat would be a victory for communism. He was told that "the United States would not intervene *unless he said that he could not protect American citizens present in the Dominican Republic.*" (*62*, 89) He amended his plea, and on the same day President Johnson announced:

The United States government has been informed that American lives are in danger. These authorities are no longer able to guarantee their safety and they have reported that the assistance of military personnel is now needed for that purpose. I have ordered the Secretary of Defense to put the necessary American troops ashore in order to give protection to hundreds of Americans who are still in the Dominican Republic and to escort them safely back to this country. (*206*, 234)

To rescue those hundreds of Americans, 21,000 troops were landed and 9,000 more deployed on naval vessels off the shore. The troops were not withdrawn when the citizens were evacuated; they remained to insure that Bosch did not return and that his faction capitulated.

Before intervening, President Johnson informed congressional leaders that "United States Marines would be landed in Santo Domingo that night for the sole purpose of protecting the lives of Americans and other foreigners." However, as Senator William J. Fulbright wrote:

> Four months later, after an exhaustive review of the Dominican crisis by the Senate Foreign Relations Commission in closed sessions, it was clear beyond reasonable doubt that although saving American lives may have been a factor in the decision to intervene on April 28, the major reason was a determination on the part of the United States government to defeat the rebel, or constitutionalist, forces whose victory at that time was imminent. (62, 49)

It will be observed that the President and not a naval officer decided to intervene and that the intervention was not for the protection of citizens but for the protection of a foreign military dictatorship. A similarly egregious modern example of intervention under false pretenses occurred when American troops invaded Grenada. President Ronald Reagan insisted the invasion was necessary both to protect American citizens and to restore democracy in Grenada, but the nature of the invasion and the circumstances surrounding it belie any conclusion other than that the administration decided to intervene in Grenada in order to mitigate a perceived communist threat. This matter will be dealt with fully in Chapter 16.

There is, to be sure, the circuit court precedent of *Durand v. Hollins*, which claims a constitutional power for the President to protect citizens.* But even if one accepts this eccentric decision, still the President does not have authority to undertake acts of war on the pretext of protecting citizens or for the purpose of restoring democracy wherever it is threatened. Indeed, in *The Prize Cases*, Justice Nelson, who wrote the decision in *Durand v. Hollins*, denied that President Lincoln might treat the rebellion as a war without statutory authorization.

Chapter 11

THE PRESIDENT
AS UNIVERSAL PROVIDENCE

Article II, Section 1 of the Constitution reads, "The executive power shall be vested in the President of the United States of America." Sections 2 and 3 detail a number of functions of the President, including the charge that "he shall care that the laws be faithfully executed."

Madison said: "The natural province of the executive magistrate is to execute the laws, as that of the legislature is to make laws. All his acts, therefore, properly executive, must presuppose the existence of the laws to be executed." (*111*, I, 614–15) This is what John Dickinson meant when he said in the Constitutional Convention, "The Executive is merely ministerial."[1]

This is not to say that all the duties of the President are ministerial in the ordinary sense of the word. On July 27, 1789, Congress created a Department of Foreign Affairs headed by a secretary who was to carry on diplomatic correspondence; he was to "conduct the business of the said department in such manner as the President of the United States shall from time to time order or instruct."* On September 15, 1789, Congress changed the name to Department of State and added to the secretary's responsibilities the custody of the records of the United States.* In 1803 William Marbury sued the secretary in his capacity of custodian of records in order to obtain a commission as justice of the peace for the District of Columbia; the

---

[1] *53*, I, 108–9. Roger Sherman of Connecticut said that "he considered the Executive magistracy as nothing more than an institution for carrying the will of the Legislature into effect." (*53*, I, 65) This characterization was never disputed during the Convention.

commission had been duly signed by President Adams before he left office.* Chief Justice Marshall ruled that in the field of diplomatic correspondence the President had an allowable range of discretion, and this discretion was not subject to judicial review. When Congress created subordinates, like the secretary of state, to assist the President in such matters, they were subject to "the will of the President" and were similarly immune. "In such cases, their acts are his acts; and whatever opinion may be entertained of the manner which executive discretion may be used, still there exists, and can exist, no power to control that discretion. The subjects are political. They respect the nation, not individual rights, and being entrusted to the executive, the decision of the executive is conclusive." This is a circumlocutory way of saying that the President's decision on topics entrusted to him by law for decision is lawful.

But the situation created by the second statute governing the secretary was quite different. Congress had charged him with custody of the records, and Marshall said: "When the legislature proceeds to impose on that officer other duties; when he is directed peremptorily to perform certain acts; when the rights of individuals are dependent on the performance of those acts; he is so far the officer of the law; is amenable to the law for his conduct; and cannot at his discretion sport away the vested rights of others." Under these circumstances, the President could not lawfully forbid the secretary to perform his legal duty and was therefore presumed not to have done so. Marbury was entitled to his commission.

The President's authority to carry on diplomatic correspondence is not an exercise of constitutionally conferred power. In his capacity of executive, the President's powers and duties are dependent on legislation. Congress has sometimes given him directions with great particularity. For example, as a consequence of the disclosure of corruption in the Teapot Dome oil leases, Congress passed a joint resolution by which the President was "authorized and directed to cause suit to be instituted and prosecuted for the annulment and cancellation of the said leases and contract" and was also "authorized and directed to appoint, by and with the advice and consent of the Senate, special counsel who shall have charge and control of such litigation, anything in the statutes touching the powers of the Attorney General of the Department of Justice to the contrary notwithstanding."*

Congress very frequently—indeed, usually—confers powers and duties directly on subordinate executive officers; once again, the directions have sometimes been highly particularized. In 1840 Congress resolved that the secretary of the navy should be "authorized and instructed" to transport Horatio Greenough's statue of George Washington from Florence, Italy, to Washington, D.C. In 1841 Congress altered its earlier decision that the statue be placed in the center of the rotunda of the Capitol and charged the secretary with placing it in such part of the rotunda as he deemed best.*

Only Congress may create subordinate executive offices.* Only Congress may abolish them. When President Nixon ordered the dismantling of the

Office of Economic Opportunity, District Judge William B. Jones enjoined the acting director from obeying. He said of the claim that Nixon was exercising executive power, "If the power sought here were found valid, no barrier would remain to the executive ignoring any and all Congressional authorization."[2]

We have seen that the duties of military officers are governed by statute and cannot be altered by the commander in chief. Similarly the President may not authorize a civil officer to perform duties assigned by statute to another. President Monroe ordered the collector and surveyor of customs of New York to seize a vessel under the Neutrality Act of 1794. But that statute allowed him to act only through the land and naval forces; therefore, the Supreme Court held the collector and surveyor liable in damages for the illegal seizure of the vessel.* In 1918, President Wilson seized the railroads under a statute that provided that they be operated by the secretary of war, but he gave the practical direction of the railroads to the secretary of the treasury. A district court suggested that this was illegal; however, it did not find it necessary to decide the question.*

It goes without saying that obedience to a presidential order that violates a statute exposes an officer to liability for damages inflicted. Captain George Little of the United States frigate *Boston* seized a vessel in 1799 during the war with France in obedience to an order of President Adams but in contravention of an act of Congress; he was held liable for $8,504 in damages.* Acting under the instructions of the secretary of the treasury, which were imputable to the President, the collector of the port of New York detained syrup, demanding a bond in excess of that fixed by statute; he was

---

[2]Local 2677, American Federation of Government Employees v. Philipps, 358 F. Supp. 60, 77 (D.C.D.C. 1973). Nor may this result be achieved by indirection. In 1889 an inspector general of the Treasury Department recommended that the office of inspector of foreign steam vessels be abolished because it was a sinecure, and the secretary proposed this to Congress, but Congress did not act. Glavey was an inspector of domestic steamships in New Orleans; in 1891 the secretary appointed him also to the post of inspector of foreign steam vessels by a letter which read, "You are hereby appointed to service in connection with your appointment as local inspector of hulls of steam vessels, as a special inspector of foreign steam vessels, without additional compensation." Three years later Glavey was removed from both positions. He sued for the statutory salary attached to the office of inspector of foreign steam vessels for the past three years. The Supreme Court held that it would be contrary to public policy to allow an officer to contract away his salary. "It would lead to the grossest abuses if a candidate and the executive officer who selects him may combine together so as to exclude from consideration the whole class of men who are willing to take the office on the salary Congress has fixed, but will not come for less. . . . In this way the subject of salaries for public officers would be under the control of the executive department of the government. Public policy forbids the recognition of any such power as belonging to the head of an executive department." Glavey v. United States, 182 U.S. 595, 601 (1901), quoting Miller v. United States, 103 F. 413, 415–16 (Cir. Ct. S.D.N.Y. 1900).

held liable for loss resulting from the deterioration of the syrup.* Two army officers, acting under superior orders, destroyed whiskey on land to which the Indian title had been extinguished; they were held liable because the statute permitted destruction only in the Indian territory.* Acting under the instructions of the secretary of treasury, the secretary of state, and the President, the collector of the port of New York detained a vessel that had complied with all the statutory requirements for clearance to sail; he was held liable for the loss suffered.*

Furthermore, while executive officers are held to obedience to statute regardless of the instructions of the President, a subordinate officer may even be authorized by Congress to initiate legally binding orders to the President himself. In 1974, the attorney general, under his statutorily conferred rule-making power, authorized a special prosecutor to investigate offenses arising out of the 1972 presidential election; to investigate allegations involving the President, the White House staff, and presidential appointees; and to contest the assertion of executive privilege. In *United States v. Nixon*, a unanimous Court of eight justices, in an opinion by Chief Justice Warren Burger, held that the special prosecutor might cause a *subpoena duces tecum* to be issued to the President for the production of evidence.*

In many cases, Congress charges the secretary of a department with a function and does not specify the subordinate he is to employ; it allows him to delegate the task in his discretion. Where Congress has charged a subordinate with the performance of a function, however, the power to act lies with that officer and not with the President. Attorney General Wirt advised President Monroe that if the laws

> require a particular officer by name to perform a duty, not only is that officer bound to perform it, but no other officer can perform it without a violation of the law; and were the President to perform it, he would not only not be taking care that the laws were faithfully executed, but he would be violating them himself. The constitution assigns to Congress the power of designating the duties of particular officers: the President is only required to take care that they execute them faithfully.*

Consequently, attorneys general have ruled that the President may not overrule or correct the decision of auditors and comptrollers in the Treasury Department* or of the Commissioner of Pensions;* furthermore, the President may not prevent a recalcitrant district attorney from prosecuting a suit except by removing him.* And, aside from a possible constitutional power to remove officers whom he himself appoints,* the President has only statutory power to remove subordinate officers. He has no power to remove officers appointed by the secretaries of departments.* When Secretary of the Treasury William Duane refused to withdraw the deposits of the United States from the Bank of the United States, President Jackson was obliged to remove Duane and appoint Roger Taney to succeed him. In 1973, when

President Nixon wished to discharge Archibald Cox, the special prosecutor for the Watergate affair, he was obliged to request the resignation of the attorney general and to remove his deputy in order to bring up in succession an acting attorney general who would dismiss Cox.

Nor may the President forbid an officer to perform a duty imposed upon him by Congress. When Postmaster General Amos Kendall, on President Jackson's orders, refused to pay a debt of the United States, Taney, this time as chief justice of the Supreme Court, said, "To contend that the obligation imposed on the President to see the laws faithfully executed implies a power to forbid their execution, is a novel construction of the Constitution, and entirely inadmissible."* When President Nixon ordered the impoundment of funds Congress had ordered to be spent, nineteen inferior courts and ultimately the Supreme Court enjoined his subordinates to obey the law.*

Indeed, the very idea of the rule of law is the proposition that the executive is subject to law. At the time of the Revolution and in the early days of the Republic, it was thought that republican government differed from the monarchies of Europe precisely in this respect. This idea still dominates our jurisprudence. But in recent years some publicists have argued that the grant of executive power to the President carries with it a right to adopt initiatives that can only be called legislative. Those who advance this argument use language so cloudy as to render the idea unfit to solve any concrete problem. Nevertheless, the term *executive power*, like the term *commander in chief*, is cast into discussion in the expectation that it will emanate an aura of authority that will silence criticism. For example, Solicitor General Griswold has said:

> Specifically, the Constitution provides explicitly that "The Executive power shall be vested in a President of the United States of America." Obviously this means something; and it is not merely a passive grant. The grant of Executive power is broad and general. It is made more concrete by the further provision that "The President shall be Commander-in-Chief of the Army and Navy of the United States," and the provision that "he shall take care that the laws be faithfully exercised." Our President is not, and never has been thought to be, from the time of Washington on to the present, a mere automaton, doing what he is told; nor is he a mere moderator, standing by to carry out the directives of other officers and branches of the government. Of course, the President acts under the law. He is subject to numerous checks and balances. He can be widely controlled by Congress, through the appropriation power and otherwise and like all other officers, he is subject to impeachment. But as President, he has great powers—great Executive power because he is the Chief Executive—and we would not want to have it otherwise. Any political organism needs a spokesman, someone with the capacity to lead, and marshal its forces, someone to meet emergencies, someone with the capacity to act, someone to speak, and in proper situations, to make decisions. That is what we mean by

Executive power; and the Constitution expressly grants "The Executive power" to the President.*

This rhetoric is straight out of the dissenting opinion of Chief Justice Vinson in the *Steel Seizure Case*, which denied that the framers created "an automaton impotent to exercise the powers of Government at a time when the survival of the Republic itself may be at stake." Rather, Vinson asserted, they established "an office of power and independence."* Vinson used this notion to justify unauthorized executive seizure of property. Griswold used it to justify the executive initiation of war.

Griswold did not discuss the Posse Comitatus Act, which forbids the use of the armed forces to execute any law unless the Constitution or an act of Congress expressly authorizes such use for that purpose. But obviously Griswold believes that the President's executive power is something more than the power to execute the laws. He has "the capacity to act," "to make decisions," and "to meet emergencies." No Supreme Court decision has ever adopted this theory; to do so would be to scuttle our whole constitutional system. But champions of executive usurpation insist that there are three such decisions. None of them purports to justify executive war making, but it is necessary to examine them in order to establish the true dimensions of executive power.

In re Neagle was decided in 1890.* The attorney general, whose actions were imputable to the President, authorized the United States marshal in San Francisco to give special protection to Justice Stephen Field when he went to California to sit on circuit because of threats made against him by two disappointed litigants, David S. Terry and his wife. Deputy Marshal David Neagle was assigned to accompany Field, and when they encountered Terry in a railroad station, Neagle shot him. A justice of the peace issued a warrant for the arrest of Neagle and Field, but only Neagle was taken. A petition for a writ of habeas corpus was presented on his behalf to the United States circuit judge. The sheriff produced Neagle but demurred to the petition, so that the only evidence considered was the affidavits in support of the petition. These established justifiable homicide. But the writ could not issue unless Neagle was "in custody for an act done or omitted in pursuance of a law of the United States." It was therefore necessary to show that Neagle had been performing a duty imposed by national law when he shot Terry; otherwise Neagle, and perhaps Field, would have to stand trial for murder in a California court. Justice Miller said, in effect, that national law required Justice Field to go on circuit and that this further implied a law that Field might be protected while performing this national function. Statutes were not the only laws; federal laws might arise in connection with federal legal relations without explicit enactment.

But if the obligation to protect Supreme Court justices on circuit was a law of the United States, why should a deputy marshal need the President's authorization to execute it? Executing this law would fall within his appointed duties; in fact, a command of the President that he not execute it would be void. Yet Justice Miller rested his entire argument concerning executive power on the special instructions of the attorney general. "The correspondence . . . is sufficient, we think, to warrant the marshal in taking the steps which he did take, in making the provisions which he did make, for the protection and defense of Mr. Justice Field."* This seems to imply that the executive created the law that Neagle executed.

But Miller went on to argue that there was also statutory authorization for the homicide. A federal act gave a United States marshal the same authority as a sheriff in the state in which he acted. A sheriff might keep the peace, and "there is a peace of the United States" that a marshal may enforce. This is not persuasive. The sheriff kept the peace of California by enforcing California laws; a marshal would keep the peace of the United States by enforcing federal laws.[3] The upshot of the decision was that the guilt of Neagle could not be canvassed in either a state or a federal court after this *ex parte* proceeding in the federal circuit court. Justice Lucius Lamar wrote a vigorous dissenting opinion in which Chief Justice Melville Fuller joined. The President was not authorized to make laws; that would be invading the domain of Congress. Nor did the "peace of the United States" include the enforcement of the laws of California.

More frequently than is wholesome, the Supreme Court oversteps the limits in hard cases and makes bad law. No doubt the other justices wished an esteemed colleague to be protected; they can hardly have failed to put themselves in his place. Moreover, the spectacle of either Field or his bodyguard being on trial for murder in a California court would have been scandalous and would have had disturbing implications for federalism.

In any case, it will be observed that *In re Neagle* rests on no allegation of emergency. Nor does it attribute any legislative power to the President. It asserts that the President merely executed a law which arose by implication from the legal structure created by Congress and that the marshal executed a law which Justice Miller derived by misreading a federal statute. In no way does the decision support Griswold's theory of executive power.

In re Debs is another such case.* The Pullman strike of 1894 was aimed at all trains drawing Pullman cars. Eager for a showdown with the American Railway Union, the railroads operating out of Chicago attached Pullman cars to as many trains as possible, and these too were struck. There was a certain amount of violence. The grave episode in Chicago was provoked by the action of President Cleveland in sending troops to Chicago over the violent protest of Governor John Peter Altgeld. Attorney General Richard Olney, who in

---

[3]The federal statute read, "The marshals and their deputies shall have, in each State, the same powers, in executing the laws of the United States, as the sheriffs and their deputies may have, in executing the laws thereof." *Revised Statutes*, §147 (1874).

private practice had been a prominent railroad lawyer, sought an injunction in the federal circuit court against Eugene V. Debs and other leaders of the union. The circuit court awarded the injunction on the theory that the Sherman Act was being violated,* and for defiance of the injunction the defendants were committed for contempt. Unwilling to review this decision on the merits (and indeed it seems clear that the defendants were not attempting to secure unto themselves "the entire control of the interstate, industrial, and commercial business in which the population of Chicago and of the other communities along the lines of said roads" were engaged, as the complaint alleged), the Supreme Court denied the petition for a writ of error. It did, however, review and then affirm the denial of a petition for a writ of habeas corpus. In this action the Court said that it ignored the Sherman Act question, not because it differed from the circuit court, but simply because "we prefer to rest our judgment on the broader ground which has been discussed in this opinion, believing it of importance that the principles underlying it should be fully stated and affirmed."

The Court rested on two broad grounds. Justice David Brewer argued at length what no one would deny—that "the nation" and "the national government" had the power to protect interstate commerce and the mails from obstruction. He pointed out that Congress had regulated the railroads, indicating that it approved of railroads and that it had established a post office and had a possessory right in the mails. The attorney general had standing to institute a suit to protect these interests. But Brewer referred to no act of Congress that forbade private obstruction of interstate rail traffic or of the mail. In his lengthy argument about equity, he ignored the critical maxim: "Equity follows the law." Would the strike have afforded ground for a damage suit by the railroads against the workers for failing to operate trains, or by the federal government for failure to move the mails? Certainly not as a matter of national law. Brewer's argument was in effect that the President may create a law, governing interstate commerce and the mails, that is enforceable in an injunction proceeding but nowhere else.

If the President may seek to promote the flow of interstate commerce and the movement of the mail without statutory authorization merely because Congress has the power and inclination to promote the flow of interstate commerce and to carry mail, he may choose one means as well as another. Cleveland might have sought an injunction against the railroads forbidding them to haul Pullman cars; this would have concluded the whole matter expeditiously and without violence. Commerce and the mails would have moved. But the President does not have the range of commission to inhibit private action, even though the private action injures an interest for which Congress in some other connection has shown esteem.

Like Justice Miller in the *Neagle* case, Justice Brewer supplemented his argument about executive power with an unpersuasive claim that, after all, there was legislative authority for the injunction. He contended that since the obstruction of highways is a nuisance, the government may enjoin such an action.* Justice John Harlan, in a much later case, reduced *Debs* to this simple proposition and pointed out that the law of nuisance is state law.* But the President's executive power is a power to execute national laws; he may execute state laws only when the state legislature, or the governor if the legislature cannot be convened, requests protection against domestic violence. This request was notoriously absent in the *Debs* case. And the protection the Constitution contemplates is, of course, physical intervention, not an injunction. Unfortunately, a nonlegal ingredient in the *Debs* case, hysteria, was the true basis for the decision. The Pullman strike appeared to the well-to-do to be the harbinger of red revolution. The judiciary was swept away in the general panic.

In re Debs attributes no substantive power to the President. It gives him standing to sue, but the injunction is to issue from the courts, which in this case exercise the supposed executive power of inventing a law. It is the judiciary and not the President that gratuitously protects interstate commerce and the mails.

The third case commonly cited to support the idea of an innovative executive power is *United States v. Midwest Oil Co.*, decided in 1915.* Yet it held nothing of the sort. An act of 1897 allowed private persons, upon the payment of a nominal fee, to make locations on public lands containing or thought to contain oil. In 1909 the secretary of the interior warned President Taft that the publicly owned supply of oil would soon be exhausted and the United States would be obliged to repurchase what had been its own oil for the navy at great cost. Two days later the President by proclamation withdrew described areas in California and Wyoming from private appropriation, and in 1910 Congress passed prospective legislation authorizing the President to make withdrawals of public lands from occupancy. After the issuance of the proclamation and before the passage of the act, the defendant's assignors filed a location certificate on land withdrawn by the proclamation. The United States filed a bill in equity to recover the land and to obtain an accounting for oil already extracted. It is true that the government did claim a constitutional power for the President, but Justice Lamar, writing the opinion for the Court, rested his decision entirely on statutory grounds. The practice of making withdrawals went back to the early days of the nation. At least 252 executive orders of this sort had been issued. Congress had been fully aware of the practice and had tacitly approved it. "Its silence was acquiescence. Its acquiescence was equivalent to consent to continue the practice until the power was revoked by some subsequent action by Congress."*

This is not the best formulation of the argument. Today, if it wished to uphold the action, the Court would say that in passing the statute in question in 1897, Congress had acted with full knowledge of past administrative construction of the law and had tacitly adopted this construction. Three justices, finding no statutory authorization for the President's action, dissented. The majority opinion contained no suggestion that the President had constitutional power to make the withdrawal. The majority held that Taft had acted under "an implied grant of power" by Congress.[4]

A very able district court opinion on the question of inherent power should be noticed. Without statutory authority, the attorney general brought suit to enjoin the Western Union Telegraph Co. from landing a cable from Barbados at Miami.* District Judge Augustus N. Hand said that this could be done only if there were enabling legislation. He distinguished *Neagle* and *Debs* by saying that in those cases the President was enforcing federal laws, as the Supreme Court had said in each case. In *Midwest Oil*, congressional knowledge of the long-continued executive practice implied consent. Judge Hand observed:

> The implications of the power contended for by the government are very great. If the President has the right, without any legislative sanction, to prevent the landing of cables, why has he not a right to prevent the importation of opium on the ground that it is a deleterious drug, or the importation of silk or steel because such importation may tend to reduce wages in this country and injure the national welfare? In the same way, why does not the President, in the absence of any act of Congress, have the right to refuse to admit foreigners to our shores, and to deport those aliens whose presence he regards as a public menace?*

In short, the three cases that are supposed to expand executive power do not do so. Furthermore, we should notice that two subsequent decisions—the *Steel Seizure Case* and the *Pentagon Papers Case*, both of them concerned with emergencies—expressly repudiated the proposition for which these three cases have been said to stand.

In 1952, during the Korean war, a strike interrupted the production of steel. On April 8 President Truman, acting "by virtue of the authority vested in me by the Constitution and laws of the United States, and as President of the United States and Commander in Chief of the armed forces of the United States," ordered the secretary of commerce to take possession of the plants in order to maintain production. Despite the reference to the laws of the United States, Truman acted without statutory authority. On April 18 the President held a press conference for the members of the American Society of Newspaper Editors. The *New York Times* reported on the conference, repeating a question asked the President:

> If it is proper under your inherent powers to seize the steel mills, can you, in your opinion, seize the newspapers and the radio stations?
>
> Mr. Truman replied that under similar circumstances the President had to do whatever he believed was best for the country.

---

[4]United States v. Midwest Oil Co., 236 U.S. 478 (1915). At 478 the Court attributed the validity of the withdrawal to the "implied consent of Congress." See also 17 Op. Att'y Gen. 160, 163 (1881).

The President refused to elaborate. But White House sources said the President's point was that he had power in an emergency, to take over "any portion of the business community acting to jeopardize all the people." (*New York Times*, April 18, 1952)[5]

When the suit of *Youngstown Sheet & Tube Co.* for an injunction against the secretary of commerce reached the Supreme Court, only two other justices concurred in Chief Justice Vinson's dissenting opinion upholding the President's action. Vinson pointed out that Congress had adopted a number of policies: the Truman Doctrine, the Marshall Plan, and the Mutual Security Act of 1951; it had made large appropriations for defense and had renewed the draft; the Senate had approved the United Nations Charter, the North Atlantic Treaty, and other security treaties; the President had engaged in war in Korea. "The President has the duty to execute the foregoing legislative programs. Their successful execution depends upon continued production of steel and stabilized prices for steel."* Consequently he might seize and operate the steel mills. The argument resembles that of *Neagle* and *Debs*. Since the opinion in *Midwest Oil* gave him no help, Vinson quoted extensively from the government's brief in that case; the brief did indeed advance a theory of inherent executive power. What Chief Justice Vinson did was to invent a second necessary and proper clause. According to the Constitution, Congress may pass all laws necessary and proper for carrying into effect its delegated powers; according to Vinson, the President may pass all laws necessary and proper for carrying into effect policies endorsed by Congress. Vinson attempted to disguise the magnitude of this claim by saying that President Truman had acted in an emergency and had then referred the question to Congress. But Congress, which alone had the power to pass emergency legislation, had not acted and did not act. What Vinson called an emergency was simply the failure of Congress to share President Truman's opinion as to the need for, and the propriety of, plant seizure.

The six justices who constituted a majority rejected Vinson's theory. Justice Black wrote:

> Nor can the seizure order be sustained because of the several constitutional provisions that grant executive power to the President. In the framework of our Constitution, the President's power to see that the laws are faithfully executed refutes the idea that he is to be a lawmaker. The Constitution limits his functions in the lawmaking process to the recommending of laws he thinks wise and the vetoing of law he thinks bad. And the Constitution is neither silent nor equivocal about who shall make laws which the President is to execute.*

Justice Frankfurter argued strongly for the separation of powers, on political as well as legal grounds, and announced his adhesion to the

---

[5]See also *Public Papers of the Presidents: Harry S. Truman, 1952–53* (Washington, D.C.: Government Printing Office, 1966), p. 273.

formulation of Justice Holmes. "The duty of the President to see that the laws be executed is a duty that does not go beyond the laws or require him to achieve more than Congress sees fit to leave within his power."* But history writes a gloss on legal terms. In *Midwest Oil*, a long–continued executive practice had been recognized as law. This is an irrelevant citation, for *Midwest Oil* rested on the theory of congressional consent and not on a theory of inherent presidential power. But Frankfurter found no tacit congressional consent for the practice of plant seizure on executive initiative. Such seizures had been rare. Occasionally Congress had explicitly authorized seizures, and when it did so it had carefully limited executive action. In passing the Taft–Hartley Act for labor disputes, Congress had considered and rejected plant seizure; this was in effect a statutory prohibition on plant seizure.

Justice Douglas believed that there had been an emergency, but "the fact that it was necessary that measures be taken to keep steel in production does not mean that the President, rather than Congress, had the constitutional authority to act."* Justice Jackson said:

> The Solicitor General lastly grounds support of the seizure upon nebulous, inherent powers never expressly granted but said to have accrued to the office from the customs and claims of preceding administrations. The plea is for a resulting power to deal with a crisis or emergency according to the necessities of the case, the unarticulated assumption being that necessity knows no law.*

But the framers had not granted emergency powers to the executive. They may have suspected that emergency powers tend to kindle emergencies. Justice Jackson saw a suggestion in recent history that control over emergency powers must be elsewhere than in the executive in order to safeguard free government, and he therefore rejected the inherent powers formula.*

Justice Harold Burton argued that the Constitution conferred the right to deal with national emergency strikes upon Congress. Congress had established two procedures for dealing with such emergencies, but neither provided for seizure. Congress had reserved to itself the power to authorize seizure in particular cases.

> This brings us to a further crucial question. Does the President, in such a situation, have inherent constitutional power to seize private property which makes congressional action in relation thereto unnecessary? We find no such power available to him under the present circumstances. The present situation is not comparable to that of an imminent invasion or threatened attack. We do not face the issue of what might be the President's constitutional power to meet such catastrophic situations. Nor is it claimed that the current seizure is in the nature of a military command addressed by the President, as Commander–in–Chief, to a mobilized nation waging, or imminently threatened with, total war.*

This passage raises the possibility that in the context of modern war the rule of "imperative military necessity" in *Mitchell v. Harmony** and *United States v. Russell** may apply nationwide. Yet Justice Burton took no position on the question.

Justice Tom Clark concurred in the *Steel Seizure Case* on a theory shared by no other justice. He argued that Congress had power to deal with emergencies, but in the absence of legislation "the President's independent power to act depends upon the gravity of the situation confronting this nation."* It was unnecessary for him to determine the gravity of the present situation, for Congress had exercised its power. At best, the President might claim a concurrent power, and Congress had preempted the field.

New York Times Company v. United States involved suits for injunctions initiated by the Department of Justice to restrain the *Times* and the *Washington Post* from publishing classified documents, the so-called Pentagon Papers.* Principal interest in the case attached to the First Amendment question, but the first issue to be resolved was that of the inherent power of the President. No act of Congress forbade the publication of the papers, and indeed Congress had twice refused to authorize censorship, but the executive sought to enjoin publication on the ground that it would work serious damage to national interests. The case thus presents much the same problem as *Debs*. Six justices denied the right of the government to maintain the suit. The three dissenters thought it premature to resolve any of the issues raised by the case.

In oral argument, Solicitor General Griswold asserted that "there are other parts of the Constitution that grant power and responsibilities to the Executive and . . . the First Amendment was not intended to make it impossible for the Executive to function or to protect the security of the United States."* Justice Black replied:

> The Government does not even attempt to rely on any act of Congress. Instead it makes the bold and dangerously far-reaching contention that the courts should take it upon themselves to "make" a law abridging freedom of the press in the name of equity, presidential power and national security, even when the representatives of the people in Congress had adhered to the command of the First Amendment and refused to make such a law. . . . To find that the President has "inherent power" to halt the publication of news by resort to the courts would wipe out the First Amendment and destroy the fundamental liberty and security of the very people the Government hopes to make "secure."*

Justice Douglas concurred in this opinion and wrote one of his own in which Justice Black concurred; he pointed out that no statute barred publication of the material sought to be used by the newspapers.

Justice Potter Stewart wrote an opinion in which Justice Byron White joined. The executive had the right and the constitutional duty, "as a matter of sovereign prerogative and not as a matter of law as the courts know law," to protect its secrets by making executive regulations governing its own personnel. If a crime defined by Congress should be committed, a prosecution could be instituted. If Congress should pass a law authorizing the executive to institute civil proceedings, the courts could pass on the constitutionality and applicability of the law.

> But in the cases before us we are asked neither to construe specific regulations nor to apply scientific laws. We are asked, instead, to perform a function that the Constitution gave to the Executive, not the Judiciary. We are asked, quite simply, to prevent the publication of material that the Executive Branch insists should not, in the national interest, be published. I am convinced that the Executive is correct with respect to some of the documents involved. But I cannot say that disclosure of any of them will surely result in direct, immediate, and irreparable damage to our Nation or its people. That being so, there can under the First Amendment be but one judicial resolution of the issues before us. I join the judgment of the Court.*

The test of "direct, immediate, and irreparable damage" might overcome the obstacle of the First Amendment, but one cannot see how it could authorize the courts to act without a law to enforce.

Justice White wrote an opinion in which Justice Stewart joined.

> At least in the absence of legislation by Congress, based on its own investigations and findings, I am quite unable to agree that the inherent powers of the Executive and the courts reach so far as to authorize remedies having such sweeping potential for inhibiting publications by the press. Much of the difficulty inheres in the "grave and irreparable danger" standard suggested by the United States. . . . To sustain the Government in these cases would start the courts down a long road and hazardous road that I am not willing to travel at least without congressional guidance and control. . . .
>
> It is thus clear that Congress has addressed itself to the problems of protecting the security of the country and the national defense from unauthorized disclosure of potentially damaging information. Cf. Youngstown Sheet and Tube Co. v. Sawyer. . . . It has not, however, authorized the injunctive remedy against threated publication.*

Justice Thurgood Marshall concurred. There was no doubt as to the power of the President to discipline employees who disclose information, or as to his power to attempt to prevent leaks, in the interest of national security.

> The problem here is whether in this particular case the Executive Branch has authority to invoke the equity jurisdiction of the courts to protect what it believes to be the national interest. See *In re* Debs. . . . The Government argues that in addition to the inherent power of a government to protect itself, the President's power to conduct foreign affairs and his position as Commander-in-Chief give him authority to impose censorship on the press to protect his ability to deal effectively

with foreign nations and to conduct the military affairs of the country. Of course, it is beyond cavil that the President has broad powers by virtue of his primary responsibility for the conduct of our foreign affairs and his position as Commander–in–Chief. . . . And in some situations it may be that under whatever inherent powers the Government may have, as well as the implicit authority derived from the President's mandate to conduct foreign affairs and to act as Commander–in–Chief there is a basis for the invocation of the equity jurisdiction of this Court as an aid to prevent the publication of material damaging to "national security," however that term may be defined.

It would, however, be utterly inconsistent with the concept of separation of power for this Court to use its power of contempt to prevent behavior that Congress has specifically declined to prohibit. . . . The Constitution provides that Congress shall make laws, the President execute laws, and courts interpret law. See Youngstown Sheet & Tube Co v. Sawyer. . . . It did not provide for government by injunction in which the courts and the Executive can "make law" without regard to the action of Congress.*

Justice Harlan wrote a dissenting opinion in which Chief Justice Burger and Justice Harry Blackmun concurred. They did not differ from the majority on the merits, for the cases had been disposed of so hastily that there had been no time to consider the merits; they felt that the cases should be remanded for further consideration. There were seven unresolved questions, the first of these being: "Whether the Attorney General is authorized to bring these suits in the name of the United States. Compare *In re* Debs . . . with Youngstown Sheet & Tube Co. v. Sawyer. . . ."*

For the sake of completeness, however, we should recognize the two decisions the Supreme Court has purported identify two inherent powers of the President. In *Myers v. United States*, in 1924, Chief Justice Taft held for a majority of six justices that the Constitution, when it instructs the President to see that the laws are faithfully executed, impliedly grants him the exclusive right to remove civilian officers whom he appoints, since this enables the President to execute the laws through the officers.* Therefore, an act of Congress requiring senatorial approval of the removal of postmasters was unconstitutional. This opinion has largely lost its strength, and in any case it has no bearing on military matters. Taft himself, only two years earlier, had followed a well–settled line of decision holding that Congress might give to the President and the Senate jointly the power to remove military officers.*

In 1950, in United States *ex rel. Knauff v. Shaughnessy*, Justice Sherman Minton announced for six justices that the President had an inherent power to exclude aliens, this time not to invalidate an act of Congress but to uphold an act authorizing the President to exclude aliens without a hearing.* If the President really had such an inherent power, there would have been no need for the act of Congress, but one cannot believe that Minton would have upheld an exclusion unauthorized by Congress.

Such decisions do not enlarge executive power. But there are unhappy intimations in some of the cases we have reviewed. In the *Steel Seizure Case*, Justice Clark thought that the President might in some circumstances have concurrent power with Congress. In the *New York Times*, Justice Marshall relied in part on the fact that Congress had considered and rejected censorship. This suggests that there are situations in which the President may legislate if Congress has not affirmatively preempted the field or closed the door by considering and rejecting a given course of action. Such a position lends itself to Theodore Roosevelt's "stewardship theory."

> I declined to adopt this view that what was imperatively necessary for the Nation could not be done by the President, unless he could find some specific authorization to do it. . . . I did not usurp power but I did greatly broaden the use of executive power. In other words, I acted for the common well being of all our people whenever and in whatever measure was necessary, unless prevented by direct constitutional or legislative prohibition. (*213*, 144)

William Howard Taft summed up this view, and the whole theory of inherent executive power, quite accurately.

> The mainspring of such a view is that the Executive is charged with responsibility for the welfare of all the people in a general way, that he is to play the part of a Universal Providence and set all things right, and that anything that in his judgment will help the people he ought to do, unless he is expressly forbidden to do it. (*213*, 144)

Chapter 12
POWER IN
FOREIGN RELATIONS

Articles I and II of the Constitution reveal the intent of the framers to give Congress the dominant hand in the establishment of basic policy regarding foreign relations. Indeed, it has been observed that a stranger reading the Constitution would obtain little idea of the vast authority actually exercised by the President today.[1] But the constitutional text and the accounts of the Philadelphia Convention also make it clear that the framers envisioned a foreign affairs partnership between the two political branches. The treaty power, viewed (inaccurately as it turned out) as the major means by which our foreign relations were to be conducted (75, 129), rests with the Senate and the President. Moreover, the ambiguities and potential overlaps of authority in the constitutional grants of power (75, 32), as well as the theory of mixed powers articulated by some of the framers (34, 332; 201, 58), provide additional evidence of the framers anticipation: a foreign policy system emerging out of cooperation and conflict would be slow to take major steps, would lack consensus between the political branches.[2] Finally, as we shall see, the constitutional text does not address all the issues that can be raised about authority in foreign affairs, indicating—or perhaps simply dictat-

[1]Henkin, 75. For a comparison of the textual grants of power to the President and Congress, see Firmage, 57, 79.

[2]42, 276. Justice Jackson observed that "[w]hile the Constitution diffuses power the better to secure liberty, it also contemplates that practice will integrate the dispersed powers into a workable government. It enjoins upon its branches separateness but interdependence, autonomy but reciprocity." Youngstown Sheet & Tube Co. v. Sawyer, 343 U.S. 579, 635 (1952) (concurring opinion).

ing—that custom and practice would also play a role in the development of the allocation of power in foreign relations.

Thus, while some powers to act in foreign affairs are expressly granted, some may be implied from textual grants of power, and still others, seemingly without any basis in the Constitution, have been "created" as a result of decades of custom and practice in the political branches. The outcome of this process, as noted above, is that the President almost certainly exercises greater authority over the conduct of foreign affairs than was contemplated by the framers of the Constitution. It should be acknowledged, however, that this acquisition of power by the executive proceeded at a rapid pace from the earliest days of the Republic and was aided and abetted by a Congress that recognized the natural advantages held by the executive branch.[3] Nevertheless, in those areas where Congress has been granted clear authority, it has been given the final and authoritative word. Moreover, to recognize that Presidents have on occasion robbed Congress and overstepped constitutional bounds in the process of check, balance, and accommodation previously described, is not to say that the precedents necessarily legitimate such acts. The secrecy with which some executive acts have been accomplished indicates that even the actors recognized the disparity between their acts and their legal authority.

Power in foreign relations is divided between the branches of the national government and is possessed largely by the political branches; however, the war power, meaning the power to decide on war and to authorize its initiation, resides in Congress. The executive, under the commander-in-chief powers, performs vital functions. But the decision for or against war resides with Congress. (106, 668) In the Constitution, the powers of Congress to "provide for the common defense," to "raise and support armies," to "provide and maintain a navy," to "regulate commerce with foreign nations," to "define and punish piracies and felonies committed on the high seas, and offenses against the law of nations," to "grant letters of marque and reprisal," to "make rules concerning captures on land and water," to "make rules for the government and regulation of land and naval forces," to "provide for organizing, arming, and disciplining the militia, and for governing such part of them as may be employed in the service of the United States," to "provide for calling forth the militia to execute the laws of the union," to "suppress insurrections and repeal invasions," to "make all laws which shall be necessary and proper for carrying into execution the foregoing powers," and, most important, to "declare war"—all leave the executive war powers to be exercised largely within parameters determined by Congress.

---

[3]For summaries of the growth of presidential power over foreign affairs during the first several administrations, see Sofaer, 201, 127–29, 137–38, 164–66, 224–27, 254–64.

The textual grant of power to Congress to "declare war" provides, with only one qualification, the exclusive power to initiate war.[4] The sole qualification upon this exclusive power to initiate war is the presidential prerogative to use military force to repel sudden attack upon the United States. (226, 6) In the Constitutional Convention, Madison and Gerry made joint motion to change the power of Congress from the power to *make* war (the original wording of the clause proposed by the Committee of Detail), to the power to *declare* war, for the purpose of "leaving to the Executive the power to repel sudden attacks." (53, II, 318–19)

The legislative branch was purposely given the war power as a check upon the impulsive use of military force by the executive. Madison noted that "the executive is the department of power most distinguished by its propensity to war: hence it is the practice of all states, in proportion as they are free, to disarm this propensity of its influence." (111, I, 611, 643)

As commander in chief, the President, under the original understanding of the Constitution, had substantial—but not unlimited—power to direct a war once it had been initiated by Congress. Hamilton, the influential advocate of a powerful presidency, asserted that the President's power "would amount to nothing more than the supreme command and direction of the military and naval forces," explaining that the President lacked the British crown's authority to declare war and raise armies. (34, 465) The President, possessing no power to initiate or wage war other than the power to repel sudden attacks, has been limited by Congress in his exercise of the powers of commander in chief. He may not raise armies without congressional authorization, nor may he violate the laws of war as determined by Congress. (242, 639 ff.)

While the constitutional ideal would place Congress in the driver's seat as the policymaker determining whether to go to war, it has been plausibly argued that the spirit of congressional preeminence was violated quite early in the nation's history.[5] Nevertheless, there were few gross departures from the constitutional norm in the nineteenth century, and there were no open assertions of the view that the President possessed an independent power to initiate war whenever he considered the security of the nation imperiled.

---

[4]James Wilson, recognized as a proponent of a "strong executive," acknowledged that the power to "declare war" was "vested in the legislature at large." (49, II, 528) Congress possesses all war-making powers of the United States. Those powers not specifically falling within the "declare war" provision most assuredly were residual in the "grant letters of marque and reprisal" clause. (106, 672, 696; Chapter 2, supra)

[5]For accounts of military initiatives by early Presidents, see Sofaer, 201, 209–13 (broad authorization of the use of force against Barbary powers by Jefferson); Javits, 85, 36–52 (departures from spirit of original understanding by Jefferson); Sofaer, 201, 303 (covert intervention in East Florida, 1811–1813); and Sofaer, 201, 337–41 (occupation of Amelia Island under President Monroe).

We have shown elsewhere that the "executive wars" cited as precedents for the Vietnam war are, in the main, distinguishable as minor events, often involving the landing of forces to protect American civilians abroad under the authority of Congress. The first precedent for a presidential assertion of the power to initiate war is the Korean War. In that regard, it must simply be affirmed that violation by a President of a clear and exclusive textual grant of authority to Congress must not be taken to legitimate similar subsequent violations.

During the Vietnam era, proponents of executive war making sought to justify, on several grounds, presidential deployment of armed forces without congressional approval. Some maintained that the President's power as commander in chief gave him preeminent powers. (67, 463; 189, 833) Others insisted that Congress, while possessing the primary power to initiate and conduct war, could delegate that power by resolution, treaty, or appropriation act. (226) These arguments are treated in other chapters. It was also asserted that the President may initiate war because of an "inherent power," derived from the executive power or from extra–constitutional sources. (67, 473) While the notion of inherent presidential war power is treated elsewhere in this work, the theoretical arguments relating to the source of power in foreign relations are summarized here.

Proponents of inherent presidential power consistently rely upon the famous 1936 dictum of Justice George Sutherland in United States v. Curtiss–Wright Export Corp. According to Justice Sutherland, power to conduct foreign policy was somehow transferred directly from the British crown to the federal government and does not inhere in the federal government through grant from the Constitution. Consequently, this sovereign power to conduct foreign policy is possessed by the President and is not restricted by the Constitution.* Sutherland's theory is vulnerable on several counts. First, scholars challenging his use of history have demonstrated that "[f]ederal power in foreign affairs rests on explicit and implicit constitutional grants and derives from the ordinary constitutive authority." (105, 29–30) Moreover, Supreme Court cases, decided since Curtiss–Wright, uniformly support the view that power in foreign affairs is rooted in and bounded by the Constitution. In the Steel Seizure Case, Justice Black, writing for the Court, denied any notion of extra–constitutional "executive power."* While the concurring justices emphasized that the President had violated principles of separation of powers by ignoring implicit congressional prohibitions of the challenged conduct,[6] none of them provided any support to Sutherland's

[6]Justices Frankfurter, Douglas, Jackson, Burton, and Clark relied on a congressional refusal to grant the President authority to seize major industries during a national emergency. See Firmage, 57, 88. The concurring opinions are found respectively at 343 U.S. at 593, 629, 634, 655, and 660.

theory that the President possesses independent power as sovereign.[7] More recently, in *Reid v. Covert*, the Supreme Court ruled against the assertion that foreign affairs power may be outside, and hence not limited by, the constitutional prohibitions of due process.*

Equally important, even if some implied grants of power in foreign relations stem in part from the nation's attributes as sovereign, no part of Sutherland's theory would account for those powers being vested in the President. (75, 27) As we shall see, there is little textual or historical support for the view that the President was to be the sole, or even dominant, policymaker in foreign relations.

The distinction must be made between the power of Congress to decide for or against war, a power held uniquely by that body, and the power to determine and conduct foreign policy generally, a far broader power shared by the political branches. The latter power includes the former and may, at times, greatly influence the likelihood of the beginning of war. But the decision for war, so far as it can be distinguished from the general conduct of foreign policy, belongs to Congress.

Some authors have attempted to bolster the claim for a presidential war power by relying on the contention that the President is the "sole organ" of American foreign policy. According to this argument, the President's broad responsibility for America's foreign policy justified his acting in the nation's interest by intervening in Vietnam. (185, 1206–7) A brief review of the history of the sole organ doctrine is therefore warranted.

John Marshall, speaking in the House of Representatives in defense of controversial action taken by President Adams, first described the President as "the sole organ of the nation in its external relations, and its sole representative with foreign nations."* President Adams had given written instructions to a federal judge that a British deserter held in custody by a United States circuit court should be turned over to British authorities in accordance with extradition provisions of the Jay Treaty.[8] In response to inaccurate charges that the President had actually delivered up an American citizen who had been impressed into British service, Marshall gave a speech outlining the facts of the case and the various legal arguments in support of the President's acts.[9] At no time during Marshall's speech did he assert

---

[7]Justice Frankfurter posited that power to act in foreign relations might be obtained by custom or usage, particularly in areas of initial ambiguity, but the opinions generally support the view that Congress is ultimately in command of those areas delegated to it by the Constitution. Justice Jackson pointedly referred to Sutherland's *Curtiss–Wright* theories as dictum. Youngstown Sheet & Tube Co. v. Sawyer, 343 U.S. 635–36, n. 2 (1952).

[8]For an account of the incident, see Moore, *118*, II, 453–54.

[9]Ibid., 453.

that the President's exclusive power to communicate with other nations on behalf of the United States involved power to make foreign policy.[10]

It was Justice Sutherland who first attempted to read substantive power into the phrase. In *United States v. Curtiss–Wright Export Corp.*, Sutherland used Marshall's "sole organ" language to bolster his argument that the traditional prohibition against the delegation of legislative power to the President does not apply in the area of foreign affairs.* In a relatively brief discussion, Sutherland moved from the accepted proposition that "the President alone has the power to speak or listen as a representative of the nation" to finding justification for the challenged delegation of authority in part in "the very delicate, plenary and exclusive power of the President as the sole organ of the federal government in the field of international relations."* The second formulation was the consequence of a subtle shift of position in which Sutherland somehow found that the President's exclusive power to conduct the negotiation of treaties implies both that congressional "participation in the exercise of the power [over external affairs] is significantly limited" by the Constitution and that the President thereby possesses an independent power to make foreign policy, particularly where "congressional legisla-tion is to be made effective through negotiation and inquiry within the international field."

Just as Sutherland's theory of extra–constitutional power has been repudiated by the Supreme Court, his statements concerning the delegation doctrine and the President's authority as sole organ have been severely qualified. While a number of additional authorities are cited in a separate chapter on the delegation doctrine, two judicial statements bear repetition here. First, Justice Jackson, concurring in the *Steel Seizure Case*, reduced *Curtiss–Wright* to the holding that it would be unwise to require Congress "to lay down narrowly definite standards by which the President is to be governed."* Chief Justice Warren later observed that *Curtiss–Wright* does not mean that Congress "can grant the Executive totally unrestricted freedom of choice."* It is clear then that the sole organ language has been limited in its effect to a statement that the nature of the conduct of foreign relations,

---

[10]Tucker v. Alexandroff, 183 U.S. 424 (1902), involved facts similar to those surrounding John Marshall's defense of President Adams's actions. In dicta, the Court discussed various times when the President had granted immunity from territorial jurisdiction to foreign troops passing through the territory of the United States. Justice Brown, speaking for the Court, stated, "While no act of Congress authorizes the executive department to permit the introduction of foreign troops, the power to give such permission without legislative assent was probably assumed to exist from the authority of the President as commander–in–chief of the military and naval forces of the United States." (Id. at 435) Justice Gray, writing for four dissenters, observed, "It is not necessary in this case to consider the full extent of the power of the President in such matters." (Id. at 459) Significantly, neither opinion suggested that the President's authority to permit foreign troops to cross the borders of the United States was derived from a general power to make foreign policy.

and the President's power over communications with foreign nations, ought to be taken into account in determining whether Congress, in granting the President contingent power, has provided sufficient statutory guidelines for presidential action. In short, *Curtiss–Wright* has been read as dealing with constitutional limits on the power of Congress, and its dictum on "sole organ" has been abandoned.

Viewed in this light, the sole organ doctrine is not novel constitutional theory. Other early statesmen had agreed with Marshall that the President held exclusive power to communicate officially with other nations (*34*, 506; *88*, VI, 451), and this power has been continually recognized to the present.[11] It is also true that the President's control of the foreign affairs bureaucracy, his recognized power to negotiate treaties and otherwise communicate officially with other nations, and his authority to grant or withhold diplomatic recognition of other states, necessarily undermine the traditional claim that the President merely conducts foreign relations while Congress alone formulates foreign policy.[12] Indeed, it has been correctly observed that "a President could not conduct foreign relations without thereby making foreign policy." (*75*, 47) More important, Presidents do in fact formulate American foreign policy, and that fact is not likely to go away.

But to acknowledge that the President makes foreign policy is a far cry from the assertion that he is the *sole* foreign policymaker. (*220*, 164) Set against the "sole organ" doctrine is what has been described as the "foreign affairs power" of Congress. (*75*, 74) It has been observed that "[n]o one knows the reaches" of this power—a power that, when combined with the generous grants of power to Congress specified in Article I, has enabled Congress to enact legislation covering a wide variety of subjects relating to the nation's foreign affairs. (*75*, 76)

Beginning with the debate between "Helvidius" (Madison) and "Pacificus" (Hamilton), recurring discussions have disputed whether Congress or the President should be dominant in determining "the condition of the nation" or in formulating American foreign policy. (*75*, 81) As part of this dialogue, Congress has frequently asserted its right to declare national policy in foreign affairs—whether by proclaiming American neutrality in times of war, repudiating treaties or directing Presidents to terminate treaties, recognizing the independence of nations formerly dominated by external powers, or directing Presidents to send delegates to international

[11]*75*, 45–46. The recognition by Congress of the President's monopoly over external communications is illustrated by enactments, the first of which was in 1789, that make it a crime for any person to correspond with a foreign nation with intent to influence its conduct in relation to controversies within the United States. See C. Warren, "Memorandum on the History and Scope of the Laws Prohibiting Correspondence with a Foreign Government," *Senate Doc. No.* 6966, 64th Cong., 2d Sess. (1917).

[12]This was apparently Madison's view when writing as "Helvidius." (*75*, 47, n. 24)

conferences and outlining the objectives to be sought and the limits of the delegates' authority.(75) In 1864, the House of Representatives resolved:

> Congress has a constitutional right to an authoritative voice in declaring and prescribing the foreign policy of the United States, as well in the recognition of new Powers as in other matters; and it is the constitutional duty of the executive department to respect that policy, not less in diplomatic negotiations than in the use of national forces when authorized by law; and the propriety of any declaration of foreign policy by Congress is sufficiently proved by the vote which pronounces it. . . .*

The "Helvidius" position has received other strong endorsements historically. In a famous 1906 debate with Senator John Spooner, Senator Augustus Bacon contended that "Congress and not the President is supreme under the Constitution in the control of foreign affairs."* More recently, Senator Fulbright has maintained that, while we must acknowledge the inevitable overlap between shaping foreign policy and conducting foreign relations, Congress must no longer default on its duty "to participate actively in determining policy objectives and in the making of significant decisions."*

Most significant, the Supreme Court has lent strength to the contention that Congress is the sovereign voice in determining the law and policy of the nation in its external relations. In 1889, in the *Chinese Exclusion Case*, the Supreme Court upheld the power of Congress to exclude aliens, despite the lack of any express constitutional grant of such power, on the ground that Congress could employ the "powers which belong to independent nations."* Since then, the Court has frequently referred to these inherent powers of sovereignty sustaining congressional enactments and has suggested that these powers are held by the legislative branch. In *Perez v. Brownell*, the Court upheld a statute imposing loss of nationality to an American citizen for voting in a political election of a foreign state, using this reasoning:

> Although there is in the Constitution no specific grant to Congress of power to enact legislation for the effective regulation of foreign affairs, there can be no doubt of the existence of this power in the law–making order of the Nation.*

Other judicial statements lend strength to the concept of sovereign power over foreign relations and provide additional support for the view that such sovereignty resides in Congress.*

On the other hand, the President has no power to change the law or even the applicability of comity in foreign affairs. In 1972, in *First National City Bank v. Banco Nacional de Cuba*, the Bank, in a suit by the nationalized Banco Nacional de Cuba for a sum owed, undertook to set off the value of its property nationalized in Cuba.* The legal adviser of the State Department advised the Court that, in the view of the executive, the act of state doctrine should not be applied in this case, and the courts might therefore examine the validity of the nationalization of First National Bank's counterclaim. Only three justices joined in the opinion that the executive might suspend the act of state doctrine, quoting the "sole organ" passage from Marshall. Justice Douglas concurred on the ground that case law required the setoff; he denied that the executive might make the Court "a mere errand boy for the Executive Branch which chooses to pick some people's chestnuts from the fire, but not others."* Justice Lewis Powell concurred because he had misgivings about the act of state doctrine. "I think the courts have a duty to determine and apply the applicable law."* Four justices dissented in an opinion by Justice William Brennan: the act of state doctrine was applicable. Otherwise, "the fate of the individual claimant would be subject to the political considerations of the Executive Branch. Since those considerations change as surely as administrations change, similarly situated litigants would not be likely to obtain even-handed treatment."*

There is, of course, no point in denying that the President is the dominant policymaker in foreign affairs today. At the same time, the historical dialogue has not ended, and Congress continues to display an intent and an ability to gain a stronger hand in formulating American policy. In 1976, Congress created the International Security Assistance and Arms Export Control Act and the Foreign Assistance and Related Programs Appropriations Act.* By these two acts, Congress has undertaken to direct the conduct of foreign policy around the globe. The first act also contains several specific admonitions to the President. For example, it states:

> The Congress views the large-scale and continuing Soviet intervention in Angola, including active sponsorship and support of the Cuban armed forces in Angola, as being completely inconsistent with any reasonably defined policy of detente. . . . Such intervention should be taken explicitly into account in United States foreign policy planning and negotiations.*

In addition, the act directed the President "to enter into negotiations with the Soviet Union intended to achieve an agreement limiting the deployment of naval, air and land forces of the Soviet Union and the United States in the Indian Ocean and littoral countries" and to "use his good offices" to secure the end of civil strife in Lebanon and the continuation of good relations with that country. We have already seen that congressional enactments such as those are part of an established tradition in this country, a tradition that belies the presumption that the President is the sole policymaker in American foreign relations.* And the substantial and explicit textual base in the Constitution, upon which the foreign affairs power of Congress is based, provides that branch with a forceful position whenever its powers are pitted against those of the executive before the courts. (57, 87–88)

But apart from this broad debate over dominance in foreign relations generally, which may admit of conflicting answers to be resolved over time, it is doubtful whether the "sole organ" theory is particularly relevant to the narrower question of the nation's decision to go to war. On this question, the Constitution is clear. The leading commentators, statesmen, and Supreme Court justices have recognized that Congress is the only branch empowered by the Constitution to initiate war. The President may have power to affect the decision for war by his course of conduct in foreign relations generally, and in his control of information and negotiation, but he is not the primary policymaker when it comes time to determine if the nation's interests would be served by war. As we shall see, this fact implies that the President should be cautious even in the exercise of his most clearly recognized constitutional powers, lest he effectively rob Congress of its policymaking role, most particularly its exclusive power to decide for or against war.

The question of the President's power to initiate war can be approached in another way. Retorsion is the practice of peaceful retaliation on a foreign state. Congress has often passed acts of retorsion; in 1817, 1818, and 1820, Congress closed our ports to British shipping because the British navigation acts had restricted trade, allowing only British vessels to carry to British colonies in the Western Hemisphere.* During this same historical period, decisions by Justice Story on circuit and by the Supreme Court both held that the executive has no inherent power to interrupt foreign commerce; this power belongs to Congress.* If the President's authority over foreign affairs does not include the peaceful practice of retorsion, it can hardly justify the initiation of war.

It remains true that the President has dominated even the decision to initiate war in recent decades. But this course of events represents a departure from the balance actually struck by the framers; it is not a simple manuever within the gray areas or spheres of apparently overlapping authority. For these reasons, congressional action during the last decade takes on particular significance. Congress not only repented of the blank check it handed the executive in the Tonkin Gulf Resolution by repealing the Resolution in 1971,* but also took a series of steps to end the Vietnam War as well as to reassert congressional authority over war. Beginning in 1970, Congress enacted the Fulbright proviso,* prohibiting the use of funds for military support of Cambodia, attached a similar prohibition to every subsequent military appropriation act,* prohibited the construing of any American assistance to Cambodia as an American commitment to Cambodian defense,* and prohibited the use of any appropriated funds for military operations in Cambodia.* Finally, and most important, Congress passed through joint resolution (over presidential veto) the War Powers Resolution of 1973.[13]

---

[13]50 U.S.C. §§1541–43 (Supp. 1973). See *128*, 83. Section 1541(a) of the Resolution states:

It is the purpose of this joint resolution to fulfill the intent of the framers of the Constitution of the United States and insure that the collective judgment of both the Congress and the President will apply to the introduction of United States

The Resolution interprets presidential power to introduce American forces into hostilities as being limited to the power to respond to attack or to act pursuant to authorization by congressional statute or declaration of war. Presidential consultation with Congress is required "in every possible instance" before the introduction of American forces into hostilities or situations in which imminent involvement in hostilities is likely. The President must report to Congress the "circumstances necessitating the introduction" and the "constitutional and legislative authority" for the introduction. Within sixty days of the submission of such a report, the President must terminate the use of American armed forces, unless Congress "has declared war or has enacted a specific authorization for such use," has extended the sixty-day period, or has been unable to meet because of armed attack upon the country.[14] Far from being an unwarranted infringement on inherent presidential power, as some have claimed (52, 187; 189, 833), the sixty-day provision is arguably an unconstitutional delegation of congressional war power to the President. (204, 834–35, 845) The provision is the result of political compromises which were essential to assure the votes required to pass the Resolution. (204, 833) Notwithstanding the sixty-day provision, the President must remove American forces from hostilities outside the "United States, its possessions and territories" if there has been no declaration of war or statutory authorization for the use of the armed forces in hostilities and if "Congress so directs by concurrent resolution. . . ."*

Of significance for judicial interpretation of the exercise of the war power, the Resolution stipulates that congressional authorization for the introduction of American armed forces into "hostilities or into situations where the involvement in hostilities" may not be "inferred from any provision of law," including "any appropriation Act, unless such provision specifically authorizes" such introduction. Nor shall such an inference be drawn from "any treaty" unless it is "implemented by legislation specifically authorizing the introduction" of military forces into hostilities or into situations likely to result in hostilities.* These provisions were drafted to prevent a recurrence of judicial rulings like those near the end of the Vietnam conflict, which sustained the constitutionality of the war on the ground that Congress had ratified executive war making by means of military appropriations, extensions of the draft, and other supportive legislative acts.*

In the future, it may be that Congress will remedy what it considers to be gross presidential abuse of power in the conduct of foreign relations by

---

Armed Forces into hostilities, or into situations where imminent involvement in hostilities is clearly indicated by the circumstances, and to the continued use of such forces in hostilities or in such situations.

[14]Ibid., §§1541–44.

necessarily using the impeachment power weapon. The framers clearly held the view that misuse of power, including power exercised in the conduct of foreign relations, was itself a ground for removal of the President. (*56*, 693; *58*, 1028 & n.14) Indeed, serious encroachment by the executive upon the constitutional prerogatives of another branch of government was one of the major evils to be protected against by the impeachment clause. The impeachment provision was seen by the framers as the therapeutic corrective by which the proper balance and check between the branches could be reestablished following abuse by one branch at the expense of the other.

As was noted earlier, the treaty-making power is allocated between the executive and legislative branches, reflecting the intent of the framers for a partnership in the conduct of foreign relations. But while the Constitution provides that the President "shall have Power, by and with the Advice and Consent of the Senate, to make treaties, provided two-thirds of the senators present concur," the Constitution does not indicate how the President is to "make" treaties or how the Senate is to give its advice and consent to presidential action. This lack of specificity on how the treaty power was to be exercised is probably the result of the fact that the framers simply assumed that the international customs and practices of their time would be the model for treaty making under the Constitution. (*75*, 140) This assumption is supported by the fact that the treaty-making process received but little consideration in the Constitutional Convention. (*75*, 373 n.4)

As a consequence of the lack of constitutional guidelines on how the treaty power is to be exercised, the treaty-making process has evolved as a matter of custom. For the most part, the President exclusively has exercised the power to negotiate treaties,[15] and it is now commonly accepted that neither the Senate nor the Congress as a whole has the authority to enter into the negotiating process.[16] In addition to the President's power to "make treaties," the President's constitutional power to "receive Ambassadors and other public Ministers" is customarily cited as a basis for this exclusive executive power of negotiation. (*123*, 232)

Once a treaty has been negotiated, it is submitted by the President to

[15]It is sometimes asserted that presidential consultation with the Senate was abandoned by President Washington after his well-known unsuccessful attempt at personally consulting with the Senate on the terms of a treaty. But Washington continued to ask for the advice of the Senate in writing before negotiations were opened and during their course. (*36*, 68)

[16]*123*, 232. But see Berger, *13*, 4–33, on the original understanding that the Senate was to be a partner in the entire treaty-making process. Congress historically has, on occasion, instructed the President to enter into negotiations and has otherwise attempted to be involved in pre-ratification decision making. In June of 1846, for example, the Senate advised the President to negotiate a treaty with Great Britain over the Oregon border. (*181*, IV, 452)

the Senate. The Senate does not formally advise the President on the treaty[17] but rather exercises its "advice and consent" power by either accepting or rejecting the treaty as submitted or by amending it in some form. (75, 131–36) Once the Senate has approved a treaty, the President may then "make" the treaty by formally concluding it with the nation(s) with which he negotiated it. The President, however, is free not to conclude a treaty that the Senate has approved, as when the Senate approves a treaty in amended form. (75, 134, 136)

There is no definition of a treaty in the Constitution, apparently because the framers saw no need to define what was well known to them in international law. (75, 140) The status of treaties in national law, however, was specified in the supremacy clause: "All Treaties made, or which shall be made, under the authority of the United States, shall be the supreme Law of the Land. . . ." Thus the Supreme Court has regarded treaties as being legally equivalent to the laws of Congress.* The traditional rule is that an act of Congress will therefore supersede a prior treaty obligation, while a treaty will likewise supersede a previously enacted statute. (220, 168; 202, 180)

The Constitution makes no mention of the termination of treaties. This omission leaves open questions as to the circumstances under which treaties may be terminated and, more important, whether the power to terminate treaty obligations is vested in the Senate or in the executive.

Constitutional silence on the matter notwithstanding, there are several means whereby the United States may terminate its treaty obligations. Under international law, a nation has the right to terminate a treaty in response to another nation's breach of an important term of the treaty or in response to a fundamental change in the circumstances. (75, 168) Also, the United States sometimes has the right to terminate a treaty under the treaty's own terms, provided that the United States gives notice to the other nation(s) affected. (75, 167–68) Finally, as a sovereign state the United States has the *power*—but not the right—to abrogate a treaty "and abide the international consequences" of that act. (75, 168)

Assuming that the United States has the right to terminate or abrogate treaties, the Constitution does not specify whether the President may act alone or must obtain the consent of the Senate in making the decision. There is logic in the argument that if the President must obtain the Senate's consent to conclude a treaty, he should also obtain its consent to terminate the treaty.[18] But it has also been argued that perhaps "the framers were

---

[17]For an account of President George Washington's ill-fated attempt at personally consulting with the Senate on the terms of a treaty, see 65, I, 391–96.

[18]For support of this view, see "The Amiable Isabella," 19 U.S. (6 Wheat.) 1, 75 (1821) (Story, J.) (*dictum*); Techt v. Hughes, 229 N.Y. 222, 243, 128 N.E. 185, 192 (1920), *cert. denied*, 254 U.S. 643 (1920) (*dictum*); John Jay, *31*, 437; Rosenfeld, *188*, 658–65.

concerned only to check the President in 'entangling' the United States" and that since " 'disentangling' is less risky and may have to be done quickly, and is often done piecemeal, or *ad hoc*, by various means or acts," senatorial approval of the President's decision to terminate a treaty should not be required.[19] Apart from these theoretical arguments, the President has demonstrated an effective power to terminate treaties, and the Senate has not successfully challenged his right to do so. The first historical example of unilateral abrogation by a President came in 1864 under President Lincoln. Lincoln's notice to Great Britain of withdrawal from the Rush–Bagot Agreement of 1817 was subsequently ratified by Congress. (*129*, 7) It has been in the twentieth century, however, that the President has consistently and effectively asserted the right to terminate treaties. Presidents Taft, Wilson (*200*, V, 317–20), Roosevelt, Truman, and Eisenhower (*129*, 18–30) invoked the power unilaterally to terminate or abrogate American treaties; more recent Presidents have followed their precedents. (*129*, 31–35) The larger number of modern scholars agree that the President has the effective power unilaterally to terminate treaties and that Congress is unlikely to be successful in any attempt to reassert its claim to a share in that power.[20]

The Constitution also fails to address directly the question of whether Congress or the President has the power to end war, or "to make peace." While it is undisputed that a formal treaty of peace may only be concluded by the President after approval by the Senate, it is not clear from the Constitution whether either the President or Congress may unilaterally terminate hostilities. While the President, as commander in chief, has the effective power to end the deployment of troops engaged in conflict, it is also arguable that the power of Congress to declare war "is the power to decide for *war or peace*, and should imply the power to *unmake war* as well as to make it." (*129*, 67) This potential conflict between the President and Congress is addressed to a limited extent by the War Powers Resolution. Under its terms, the President must remove American forces from hostilities, in the absence of statutory authorization or a declaration of war, if "Congress so directs by concurrent resolution."* This provision reflects congressional

---

[19]*75*, 169. This position has also received support in judicial dicta. Charlton v. Kelly, 229 U.S. 447, 474–76 (1913); Terlinder v. Ames, 184 U.S. 270, 285–88 (1902).

[20]See, e.g., Henkin, *75*, 169–70; Nelson, *125*, 907; Tribe, *220*, 165–66; McDougal, *108*, 336; American Law Institute, *Restatement of the Foreign Relations Law of the United States (Revised), Tent. Draft No. 1* (Philadelphia: ALI, 1980), §352.

The conclusion of modern scholars was essentially confirmed by the result reached in Goldwater v. Carter, 100 S. Ct. 533 (1979). In *Goldwater*, the Court dismissed Senator Goldwater's challenge to President Carter's unilateral termination of a mutual defense treaty with Taiwan. Three of the justices would have set the case for oral argument, and Justice Powell indicated that he would have reached the merits under different circumstances. Four justices concluded that the case presented a political question. The only justice who discussed the merits, Justice Brennan, concluded that the President has authority unilaterally to terminate treaties. At the

commitment to its own power over war and its belief that the President has no independent war power that would allow him legally to keep forces in conflict against the will of Congress. The provision leaves unanswered, however, the more difficult question on the scope of the President's power as commander in chief once war has been authorized by Congress. In theory, it seems that Congress should have the final decision as to whether American forces should be withdrawn from conflict, but it also seems likely that the decision will in practice be a cooperative one, requiring good faith and respect for coordinate branches by both sides.

Although the Constitution expressly grants the President only the power to "make treaties," since the first days of the Republic Presidents have entered into other forms of international agreements. (*220*, 168) Generally denominated "executive agreements," these international agreements are actually of two types: presidential agreements, made solely on the basis of the constitutional authority of the President, and congressional–executive agreements, entered into by the President under the authorization of Congress. (*123*, 222) Because executive agreements (the term will be used for both presidential agreements and congressional–executive agreements) are not expressly provided for in the Constitution, Presidents have traditionally entered into them without adhering to the constitutional requirements that govern the making of treaties—particularly the approval of two-thirds of the Senate. (*123*, 223)

Because authority to conclude them is not expressly granted in the Constitution, the validity of executive agreements as law of the land has been questioned. (*220*, 170) It seems, however, that the framers did contemplate that the national government would enter into international agreements other than treaties. The Constitution provides that a state may not enter into a "Treaty Alliance or Confederation" and that "No State shall, without the consent of Congress . . . enter into any Agreement or Compact with . . . a foreign power." The Constitution thus distinguishes treaties, which the states are absolutely prohibited from entering into, from other agreements, which may be entered into by the states with the consent of Congress. It is doubtful that the framers contemplated allowing the states, but not the national government, to conclude agreements other than treaties with other nations. (*220*, 170 n.19)

The Supreme Court has also recognized the President's power to conclude international agreements other than treaties. In *United States v. Belmont*, a case involving the validity of an executive agreement entered into pursuant to the establishment of diplomatic relations with the Soviet Union, the Court concluded that President Roosevelt had the authority to conclude such an

---

least, the case suggests the hurdles that any challenge to presidential action in this area must overcome.

agreement by virtue of his authority as "sole organ" of the national government in foreign affairs.* In addition, Sutherland relied on examples of prior agreements that had been concluded without the advice and consent of the Senate.* In general, these agreements created no general rule of conduct, as a treaty might do, and affected no private right adversely.

Because the "sole organ" rationale is properly disregarded as a justification for the practice of entering into international agreements without Senate approval, scholars have sought to justify the practice on other grounds. One theory posits that the authority to enter into such agreements falls within a "zone of twilight" between presidential and congressional powers. This "zone of twilight," according to the theory, "may be occupied by Congress at will." The failure of Congress to fill this gray area, however, leaves a void which the President may fill. Presidential authority to enter into executive agreements has also been justified as a concomitant of his powers as commander in chief and chief executive. (*123*, 235)

A recurring issue in this area is whether a given international agreement should be embodied in treaty form or in the form of an executive agreement. *United States v. Belmont* has been interpreted by some as intimating that the permissible scope of executive agreements is virtually coextensive with that of treaties. Since so much attention has centered on the case, it requires extended discussion.

It has long been the task of the chief executive of a nation, under the rules of international law, to seek the satisfaction of the claims of its nationals against a foreign state by diplomatic negotiation. In 1918 the Soviet Union confiscated the property of Russian corporations abroad and also national-ized without compensation the property of American nationals within the Soviet Union. A Russian corporation had a sum of money on deposit in the Belmont Bank in New York in 1918. In 1933 President Roosevelt made an agreement by which he recognized the Soviet government. The Soviet government transferred its claims of property in the United States, including the deposit in the Belmont Bank, to the United States, and the Soviet government recognized the claims of American citizens affected by the confiscation. It was agreed that after the rival claims had been computed, whichever government had gained an advantage would pay the surplus to the other. Thus the American creditors would at last gain satisfaction. The Belmont Bank refused to pay the deposit to the United States, alleging that it was founded on confiscation and that the public policy of New York did not recognize claims resulting from confiscation. In *United States v. Belmont* in 1937, the Supreme Court, in an opinion by Justice Sutherland, held that the recognition validated the Russian confiscation under the act of state doctrine, and the executive agreement transferred the Soviet claim to the United States. On the use of the executive agreement, Sutherland said:

> But an international compact, as this was, is not always a treaty which requires the consent of the Senate. There are many such compacts, of

which a protocol, a modus vivendi, a postal convention, and agreements
like that now under consideration are illustrations. See 5 Moore, *Int. Law
Digest*, 210–11.*

Moore uses the term *protocol* to signify the adjustment of inconsiderable
claims of citizens and also to describe agreements as to the purpose and scope
of future negotiations. A modus vivendi is a provisional agreement pending
formal legal action. Moore speaks of postal conventions as agreements made
by the postmaster general with the advice and consent of the President under
the authority of an act of Congress of 1872. By "agreements like that now
under consideration" Sutherland must have referred to numerous agreements detailed by Moore to obtain the satisfaction of the claims or guarantee
of the rights of American citizens. In short, the Belmont case introduced
no new principle. Since the recognition and the assignment of the Soviet
claim were valid at national law, the public policy of no state could stand
against them.

Indeed, the proposition that the President may make valid executive
agreements on a broader scale would alter the original constitutional
understanding; it would mean that a President could commit the United
States to a de facto treaty concerning the most vital interests of the country
without the necessity of obtaining the Senate's consent. (*220*, 171) Practical
politics involving power relations between the political branches usually
dictate that the President respect the constitutional intent calling for
two-thirds Senate approval of fundamental international agreements. In
practice, the executive branch has made some attempt to institutionalize
guidelines for determining whether an agreement should be concluded in
the form of a treaty or of an executive agreement. The Department of State
has issued guidelines which departmental officials are instructed to consider
when deciding the form in which an agreement should be concluded. (*123*,
238) Among the relevant considerations are the preference of Congress
regarding the agreement, whether the agreement will require subsequent
congressional legislation to become effective, past American practice with
respect to agreements of the same type, and general international practice
with regard to the same type of agreements.

Foreign affairs powers are also exercised by the government when it
sends ambassadors and other diplomats to foreign nations and when it
receives other countries' diplomatic representatives. The President and the
Senate share the constitutional power to appoint diplomatic officials. Article
II, Section 2 of the Constitution provides, "[The President] shall nominate,
and by and with the Advice and Consent of the Senate, shall appoint
Ambassadors, other public Ministers and Consuls . . . and all other Officers
of the United States, whose Appointments are not herein otherwise provided
for, and which shall be established by law."

Thus the President has the power to appoint ambassadors and consuls,
subject to the approval of the Senate. The power to appoint lesser diplomatic

officers without the consent of the Senate has been invested by Congress in the President and the secretary of state by laws such as the Foreign Service Act. Such congressional delegation of the appointment power has been upheld by the Supreme Court on the constitutional language that the appointment of some officers of the government was to "be established by Law."*

The President has also been able to appoint special ambassadors and envoys without obtaining Senate confirmation, since the temporary diplomatic assignments have not been considered "offices" under the Constitution. In *United States v. Hartwell*, the Supreme Court determined that the definition of "office" necessarily included the concepts of tenure and duration.*

The President has the exclusive power to "receive Ambassadors and other public Ministers" of foreign nations. Because this grant of power gives the President the right to decline to receive a nation's ambassador, it has been used as a de facto power to recognize or refuse to recognize foreign governments. (32, 541–44) The power to receive foreign diplomats, of course, also includes the power to expel them from the United States at will.

Congress has a powerful textual mandate in the Constitution for the establishment of our basic policy in foreign relations. Congress also possesses the nation's war powers, or those powers which determine our decision to go to war.

Constitutional framers seemed clearly to envision a collaborative relationship between Congress and the President in the establishment and the conduct of American foreign policy.

Although the President is not the "sole organ" of American foreign policy, it is clear that he possesses great power in foreign relations. The President has effective control of critical functions such as the intelligence–gathering capacity, recognition of states, negotiation with foreign governments, deployment of military forces, and dispersal of information relating to foreign relations and bearing upon the decision for war or peace. The executive inevitably has had a significant impact on whether this nation will actually be involved in war. Thus, a significant question is whether the President may constitutionally exercise his enumerated foreign affairs powers in a manner that might provoke war or be treated as an act of war by another state.

One answer that has considerable support holds that the President must refrain from deliberately acting in a way that would practically wrest the war–making decision from Congress. In particular, congressional leaders and Presidents have spoken of the duty of the President to refrain from exercising his recognition power in a way that would impinge on the war power of Congress. And others have contended that neither the President, nor even the President acting with the Senate, could negotiate and ratify treaties that would necessarily lead to war with foreign nations. This general approach has been carried to the extreme of arguing that the President is required to remain essentially passive in dealing with foreign states at war with each other, lest he cause hostilities from one or the other. According to this view, the President could not unilaterally declare American neutrality because such an affirmative act could provoke war.

Undoubtedly, the President should consult Congress before taking steps that would clearly commit the nation to potential hostilities. Thus the President should refrain from recognizing belligerents claiming power within a nation with which we have enjoyed diplomatic relations. It is questionable, however, whether the President should be shackled by the restrictive view that he must avoid all affirmative acts that could conceivably lead to war. Indeed Professor Abraham D. Sofaer has aptly pointed out that the failure to act in some circumstances—for example by the refusal to assert the nation's neutrality—might be as likely to bring us into war as any act of conviction. Even Madison, an early advocate of the restrictive approach to presidential actions impinging on the decision to involve the United States in war, acknowledged that some settings provide the President with the dilemma of taking action that will avoid war with one power while risking hostilities with another.[21]

In general, the President should, as a matter of sound policy and constitutional statesmanship, consult with Congress at the earliest possible moment and avoid steering the nation into situations that make the decision for war a mere *fait accompli*. On the other hand, the ambiguity and doubt that plague this as well as other areas of constitutional interpretation is supportive of the model of separation of powers, previously alluded to, which sees the framers as intending to set the branches in tension with each other, rather than clearly to separate and delineate power. Cooperation between the political branches in the establishment and conduct of foreign policy is assumed. But this approach to separation of powers, which is traced to the writings of Madison, also regards conflict, controversy, and ambiguity as an inherent part of the checks and balances by which we maintain liberty. (*34*, 349)

---

[21]President Washington, for example, refused to negotiate treaties with Denmark and Sweden in 1794 because of the possibility of provoking war with Great Britain. Sofaer concludes that this reflected not only his policy of avoiding war, but also "his respect for, if not complete agreement with, the view that Congress should be consulted before any action is taken that could cause war." (*201*, 101) Congressman John Page of Virginia contended that the United States could not enter a treaty of alliance with a nation that was at war because it might "provoke another to make war on the United States." In 1793, Madison wrote to Jefferson to object to Washington's famous proclamation of neutrality. He objected that such a pronouncement "could not properly go beyond a declaration of the fact that the U.S. were at war or peace, and an injunction of a suitable conduct on the Citizens." (*201*, 111) Madison's view gave the President no power to make judgments or agreements that might involve war or peace, for he possessed "no other discretion than to convene and give information to the legislature on occasions that demand it." (*201*, 115) "As he [Madison] recognized, refusing (as a part of neutral policy) to enforce a treaty term to avoid war with one nation might lead to war with its adversary." (*201*, 115)

Chapter 13

THE DELEGATION
OF THE WAR POWER

The constitutional distribution of powers among the several organs of the national government and between the national government and the states was the result of careful deliberation by the Constitutional Convention. Congress may not alter this distribution by legislative act. It follows that Congress may not transfer to the executive, the judiciary, or private citizens the functions for which Congress itself has been made responsible. This would be tantamount to amendment of the Constitution by statute.

Nevertheless, almost from the beginning of our history Congress has authorized the executive and the judiciary to engage in subsidiary rule making. This is not an unconstitutional delegation of legislative power if certain obvious conditions are met. In 1935 Chief Justice Charles Evans Hughes gave the classic statement of these conditions in *Schechter Poultry Corporation v. United States.*

> The Congress is not permitted to abdicate or to transfer to others the essential legislative functions with which it is vested. We have repeatedly recognized the necessity of adapting legislation to complex conditions involving a host of details with which the national Legislature cannot deal directly. We pointed out in the Panama Refining Case that the Constitution has never been regarded as denying to Congress the necessary resources of flexibility and practicality, which will enable it to perform its function in laying down policies and establishing standards, while leaving to selected instrumentalities the making of subordinate rules within prescribed limits and the determination of facts to which the policy as declared by the Legislature is to apply. But we said that the

constant recognition of the necessity and validity of such provisions, and the wide range of administrative authority which has been developed by means of them, cannot be allowed to obscure the limitations of the authority to delegate, if our constitutional system is to be maintained.*

The practice of rule making under delegated power was first discussed by Chief Justice Marshall in *Wayman v. Southard.* Congress had authorized the federal courts to make rules of practice. Marshall recognized that delegation would be improper in some areas but asserted that it was possible on minor topics.

> It will not be contended that Congress can delegate to the courts, or to any other tribunals, powers which are strictly and exclusively legislative. But Congress may certainly delegate to others, powers which the legislature may rightfully exercise itself. . . .
>   The line has not been exactly drawn which separates these important subjects, which must be entirely regulated by the legislature itself, from those of less interest, in which a general provision may be made, and power given to those who are to act under such general provisions to fill up the details.*

No later decision has identified the powers that are "strictly and exclusively legislative" and therefore will support no delegation whatever. However, the framers believed that certain political powers must be exercised only by Congress if republican government were to survive. Presumably these could not be delegated to the President. Distrust of the executive, prompted and supported by all history, caused them to vest the power of initiating war exclusively in the Congress. Hamilton, in the *Federalist*, and supporters of the Constitution, in the state conventions, argued that the system was safe precisely because the President would never be able to exercise this power.

In addition to the political considerations that led the framers to deny the power to initiate war to the President, the philosophy that governs the delegation of power by Congress precludes legislation authorizing the President to begin a war. As we noted in Chapter 4 (pp. 65–67), it is impossible for Congress to enact governing standards for launching future wars. There is a world of difference between a delegation in the field of foreign or interstate commerce and the authorization of a future war. In the first case, Congress directs the President to establish a rule of conduct for citizens within a legal order which is shaped and controlled by Congress itself. Under these circumstances, Congress can foretell the consequences of the delegation and is genuinely determining the policy to be applied. In the second case, the President is authorized to initiate a war in a future international environment in which significant details, perhaps even major outlines, change from month to month or even from day to day. The posture of international affairs in the future cannot be known to Congress at the time the resolution is passed. But appropriate international conditions are precisely the standards that must be specified if Congress is to give meaningful direction to an executive initiation of war. If Congress authorizes or mandates a war without regard to the entire complex of international relations, it is not determining policy for the future, it is casting dice.

There remains, however, a wide range of powers of "less interest" in which it is possible to delegate the authority to make rules in conformity with standards enacted by Congress. In his famous address to the American Bar Association on "War Powers and the Constitution," Hughes recognized the necessity and the propriety of subsidiary rule making by the executive after Congress had declared war.

> War demands the highest degree of efficient organization, and Congress in the nature of things cannot prescribe many important details as it legislates for the purpose of meeting the exigencies of war. . . . The principles governing the delegation of powers are clear, and while they are of the utmost importance when properly applied, they are not such as to make the appropriate exercise of legislative power impracticable. . . . Congress cannot be permitted to abandon to others its proper legislative functions; but in time of war, when legislation must be adapted to many situations of the utmost complexity, which must be dealt with effectively and promptly, there is special need for flexibility and for every resource of practicality; and of course whether the limits of permissible delegation are in any case overstepped always remains a judicial question.*

Congress has also delegated its powers in another way, by passing contingent legislation that is to come into effect only when the President or another officer finds that a stipulated set of facts exists. In 1813, in *The Brig Aurora*, the Supreme Court upheld an act providing for the revival of the embargo against Great Britain should the President find that France had ceased to violate the rights of American shipping.* Like administrative rule making, contingent legislation has become a very important part of our legal system. But here too Congress must perform the legislative function. In 1935, in *Panama Refining Co. v. Ryan*, Chief Justice Hughes held invalid a section of the National Industrial Recovery Act of 1933 that authorized the President to forbid the interstate transportation of petroleum by state law in the state of production.

> Section 9(c) is brief and unambiguous. It does not attempt to control the production of petroleum and petroleum products within a state. It does not seek to lay down rules for the guidance of state legislators or state offices. It leaves to the states and to their constituted authorities the determination of what production shall be permitted. It does not qualify the President's authority by reference to the basis or extent of the state's limitation of production. Section 9(c) does not state whether or in what circumstances or under what conditions the President is to prohibit the transportation of the amount of petroleum or petroleum

products produced in areas of the state's permission. It establishes no criterion to govern the President's course. It does not require any finding by the President as a condition of his action. The Congress in section 9(c) thus declares no policy as to the transportation of the excess production. So far as this section is concerned, it gives the President an unlimited authority to determine the policy and to lay down the prohibition, or not to lay it down, as he may see fit.*

That is to say, where contingent legislation is possible, Congress must specify the conditions under which the President is to invoke it. Delegation of power by contingent legislation is then governed by the same rules as delegation of the rule-making power, and indeed this is what Chief Justice Hughes said in the *Schechter Poultry Co.* case. It follows that Congress may not pass contingent legislation on topics "strictly and exclusively legislative." If the power to initiate war is exclusively legislative, Congress may not authorize the President to go to war upon the occurrence of specified facts in the future. This principle was recognized early in our history.

In 1831 the payment by France of outstanding claims for injuries to American shipping during the Napoleonic wars was agreed upon by treaty, but Louis Philippe was unable to persuade his legislature to vote the money. In his annual message to Congress on December 1, 1834, President Jackson said, "I recommend that a law be passed, authorizing reprisals upon French property, in case provision shall not be made for the payment of the debt at the approaching session of the French Chambers." (*181*, II, 1325) On the same day Representative Nathaniel H. Claiborne complained in the House:

> If this power be conferred upon him, it will be virtually conferring upon the President unconstitutional power—a power to declare war. . . . Gentlemen have read history to little effect, if they are ready to clothe a single individual with the power of making war.*

On January 5, 1835, Albert Gallatin wrote to Edward Everett:

> In every case, particularly when hostilities are contemplated, or appear probable, no government should commit itself as to what it will do under certain future contingencies. It should prepare itself for every contingency—launch ships, raise men and money, and reserve its final decision for the time when it becomes necessary to decide and simultaneously to act. The proposed transfer by Congress of its constitutional powers to the Executive, in a case which necessarily embraces the question of war or no war, appears to me a most extraordinary proposal, and entirely inconsistent with the letter and spirit of our Constitution, which vests in Congress the power to declare war and grant letters of marque and reprisal. (*119*, VII, 127–28)

On January 6, 1835, Henry Clay presented for the Senate Committee on Foreign Relations a report describing the nature of reprisals and the constitutional duty of Congress to retain its authority, rather than delegating it to the executive. On the basis of this report, the Senate unanimously rejected Jackson's request. The matter was finally adjusted by negotiation in 1836.

In his first annual message on December 8, 1857, President Buchanan described the interest of the United States in "the freedom and security of all the communications across the isthmus" of Panama and the danger that these communications might be interrupted either by invasions of American filibusters—these were the days of William Walker—"or by wars between the independent States of Central America." He also recited the irrelevant circumstance of the American guarantee of the neutrality and sovereignty of New Granada or Colombia. "Under these circumstances I recommend to Congress the passage of an act authorizing the President, in case of necessity, to employ the land and naval forces to carry into effect this guaranty of neutrality and protection. I also recommend similar legislation for the security of any other route across the Isthmus in which we may acquire an interest by treaty." (181, IV, 2978) No action was taken, and Buchanan renewed his request in his message of December 6, 1858. The routes over the Isthmus were "of incalculable importance" to the United States; they were a highway in which Nicaragua and Costa Rica had "little interest when compared with the vast interests of the rest of the world. Whilst their rights of sovereignty ought to be respected, it is the duty of other nations to require that this important passage shall not be interrupted by the civil wars and revolutionary outbreaks which have so frequently occurred in that region." Again he requested authorization to use military force if necessary to protect the trade route and "the lives and property of American citizens." (181, IV, 3047-48) The Senate Committee on Foreign Relations reported a bill, but no action was taken. On February 18, 1859, President Buchanan sent a special message repeating his request. In addition to interruption of peaceful transit over the isthmus, the continual revolutions produced successive confiscations of American property in Central American harbors.

> If the President orders a vessel of war to any of those ports to demand prompt redress for outrages committed, the offending parties are well aware that in case of refusal the commander can do no more than remonstrate. He can resort to no hostile act. . . . The remedy for this state of affairs can only be supplied by Congress, since the Constitution has confided to that body alone the power to make war. Without the authority of Congress the Executive cannot lawfully direct any force, however near it may be to the scene of the difficulty, to enter the territory of Mexico, Nicaragua, or New Granada for the purpose of defending the persons and property of American citizens, even though they may be violently assailed whilst passing in peaceful transit over the Tehuantepec, Nicaragua, or Panama routes. He cannot, without transcending his constitutional power, direct a gun to be fired into a port or land a seaman or marine to protect the lives of our countrymen on shore or to obtain redress for a recent outrage on their property. . . .

I therefore earnestly recommend to Congress, on whom the responsibility exclusively rests, to pass a law before their adjournment conferring on the President the power to protect the lives and property of American citizens in the cases which I have indicated, under such restrictions and conditions as they may deem advisable. (*181*, IV, 3070–71)

Senator Seward made a speech directly challenging the message, as an appeal to Congress to surrender the power to make war.* Neither house acted on the President's proposal.

In his third annual message, on December 19, 1859, Buchanan made a last futile request. He asked for a law to permit him to police the isthmus and also "to employ the naval force to protect American merchant vessels, their crews and cargoes, against violent and lawless seizure and confiscation in the ports of Mexico and the Spanish American States when these countries may be in a revolutionary condition." He argued that such a law would not involve an unconstitutional delegation of the war power.

It will not be denied that the general "power to declare war" is without limitation and embraces within itself not only what writers on the law of nations term a public or perfect war, but also an imperfect war, and, in short, every species of hostility, however confined or limited. Without the authority of Congress the President cannot fire a hostile gun in any case except to repel the attacks of an enemy. It will not be doubted that under this power Congress could, if they thought proper, authorize the President to employ the force at his command to seize a vessel belonging to an American citizen which had been illegally and unjustly captured in a foreign port and restore it to its owner. But can Congress only act after the fact, after the mischief has been done? Have they no power to confer upon the President the authority in advance to furnish instant redress should such a case afterwards occur? Must they wait until the mischief has been done, and can they apply the remedy only when it is too late? To confer this authority to meet future cases under circumstances strictly specified is as clearly within the war–declaring power as such an authority conferred upon the President by act of Congress after the many exigencies must arise imperatively requiring that Congress should authorize the President to act promptly on certain conditions which may or may not afterwards arise. (*181*, IV, 3100–101)

And Buchanan appealed to the precedent of the *Water Witch*. To obtain redress for the shelling of the *Water Witch* and the satisfaction of certain outstanding claims of American citizens against Paraguay, Congress had on June 2, 1858, by joint resolution authorized the President "to adopt such measures and use such force as in his judgment may be necessary and advisable in the event of a refusal of just satisfaction by the Government of Paraguay."

"Just satisfaction" for what? For "the attack on the United States steamer *Water Witch*" and "other matters referred to in the annual message of the President." Here the power is expressly granted upon the condition that the Government of Paraguay shall refuse to render this "just satisfaction." In this and other similar cases Congress have conferred upon the President power in advance to employ the Army and Navy upon the happening of contingent future events; and this most certainly is embraced within the power to declare war. (*181*, IV, 3101)

What was involved in the case of the *Water Witch* was not contingent legislation; it was what Vattel called a conditional declaration of war. This is an ultimatum that affords the enemy an opportunity to make restitution or compensation for a wrong before a declaration of war pure and simple is announced. Contingent legislation contemplates action upon an evaluation by the President of circumstances that have not yet occurred; a conditional declaration of war results from a congressional evaluation of past events. A contingent delegation to the President would leave the decision for war or peace in the future to the President; in a conditional declaration of war, Congress has already decided for war, but offers the enemy an opportunity to avert it by yielding up the fruits of war.

In the case of the *Water Witch*, the occasion for war was in the past. Congress had determined that the shelling of the *Water Witch* was a *casus belli* and that the use of force against Paraguay was feasible and in accord with the national interest under existing circumstances. But in his request for power to police the isthmus routes and foreign harbors, Buchanan was asking that the President be authorized to determine, on some future occasion, whether events as yet unknown constituted a *casus belli* and whether under these future conditions it was desirable or prudent to use force. He was asking Congress to grant him the power of decision for war or peace.

The vice would not be cured but aggravated in a postdated declaration of war that eliminated presidential discretion and made war perfectly automatic upon the occurrence of stated events in the future. Clay had considered it a peculiarly unfortunate feature of Jackson's proposal for reprisal on French shipping that the President might interpret the legislation as mandatory. He might feel obliged to go to war when stated events occurred, regardless of the circumstances. According to Clay, the Constitution requires that Congress itself appraise the immediate circumstances before the nation voluntarily enters into a state of war. Therefore, Congress could not authorize war with France without hearing France's reasons for the failure to pay the claims and without considering "the actual posture of things as they may then exist," including the contemporary state of international politics and in particular, no doubt, the attitude of Great Britain. Clay's argument went beyond the rule against the delegation of legislative power. He argued, in effect, that Congress itself cannot make a declaration of a future war dependent upon the occurrence of stipulated facts, because war is an enterprise in which all the contemporary circumstances must be weighed.

This is eminently reasonable. If Congress were allowed to declare a future war upon the occurrence of specified conditions, those conditions might arise in the context of other unforeseen circumstances in which the war would work a mortal injury to national interests and national security; yet the President would be legally obliged to go to war. Surely it would be better to give the President the choice of war or peace. But even a presidential choice is not necessary. Rather, Congress should assume its full constitutional responsibility to monitor circumstances that might meet its conditions for war. Then, if occasion for a war should arise, Congress will be able at that time to evaluate all the circumstances and itself choose war or peace. As we have seen, the words *to declare war* contemplate such a contemporary decision and implicitly exclude the declaration or authorization of future wars.

Only once, in the secret resolution of 1811, has Congress passed a declaration of war contingent upon the occurrence of specified future events. In recent years, however, it has passed no less than four laws purporting to give the President the option of making war on future occasions.[1] These are clearly unconstitutional delegations of the war power.

Article 43 of the United Nations Charter provides for agreements between the Security Council and member states by which the latter promise to supply armed forces for military action ordered by the Security Council to maintain or restore international peace and security. The United Nations Participation Act, passed by Congress in 1945, authorized the President to negotiate such an agreement with the Security Council.* If it should be confirmed by Congress by act or joint resolution, "The President shall not be deemed to require the authorization of the Congress to make available to the Security Council on its call an order to take action under Article 42 of said Charter and pursuant to such special agreement or agreements the armed forces, facilities, or assistance provided for therein." The act does not say that the President must make the force available. It seems to assume that he may do so or fail to do so as he thinks best. If he chooses to do so, he need not seek the approval of Congress. This is indisputably a delegation of the power to make war.

When President Truman entered the Korean War in 1950, he claimed that he was acting under the authority of a vote of the Security Council of the United Nations. But no agreement for the supply of troops had been made with the Security Council, and of course no such agreement had been approved by Congress.

Secretary of State Dulles was responsible for two other delegations. In 1955 President Eisenhower requested what has come to be known as the Formosa Resolution. After cursory hearings and limited debate, Congress

---

[1]The so-called Cuba Resolution, 76 Stat. 697 (1962), to which President Kennedy appealed when he blockaded Cuba, and the so-called Berlin Resolution, 76 Stat. 1429 (1962), are not considered here because neither purported to authorize the President to do anything whatever.

resolved, "The President of the United States be and he hereby is authorized to employ the Armed Forces of the United States as he deems necessary for the specific purpose of securing and protecting Formosa and the Pescadores against armed attack."* Dulles was also responsible for the passage of the Middle East Resolution of March 9, 1957. The resolution recited the determination of the United States to preserve "the independence and integrity of the nations of the Middle East" and provided that "if the President determines the necessity thereof," armed forces might be employed to protect them.*

The Tonkin Gulf Resolution of August 10, 1964, was the fourth delegation of the war power and the most important, for it was made the principal justification for President Johnson's commitment, beginning on February 7, 1965, of more than a half million troops to Vietnam in the first open and acknowledged American participation in the war.* On several occasions during the spring and summer of 1964, South Vietnamese vessels had attacked islands and coastal areas of North Vietnam. On August 2 and August 4, according to the Johnson administration, North Vietnamese patrol boats attacked two American destroyers in the Gulf of Tonkin. The administration asserted that the presence of these vessels at the time of a South Vietnamese attack on North Vietnam was pure coincidence. They were not convoying the attacking vessels but were quite independently carrying out their duty of patrolling the high seas.* The American destroyers suffered no hits and were reported to have sunk at least three North Vietnamese patrol boats.

On August 4 President Johnson ordered air attacks on North Victnamese naval installations by way of reprisal, and on August 5 he sent a message to the Senate. The message recited: "Our purpose is peace . . . the United States intends no rashness, and seeks no wider war." But he requested the passage of a resolution similar to the Formosa Resolution "to give convincing evidence to the aggressive Communist nations, and to the world as a whole, that our policy in Southeast Asia will be carried forward—and that the peace and security of the area will be preserved."* Senator Fulbright promptly introduced the Tonkin Gulf Resolution. The process of congressional enactment was completed on August 10.

The resolution recited that North Vietnamese vessels had deliberately and repeatedly attacked United States naval vessels in international waters as a part of a campaign of aggression that the Communist regime in North Vietnam was waging against its neighbors and the nations joined with them in defense of their freedom. Continuing, the resolution noted that the United States desired only that the peoples of southeast Asia "should be left in peace to work out their own destinies in their own way," adding that "the United States is, therefore, prepared, as the President determines, to take all necessary steps, including the use of armed force, to assist any member or protocol state of the Southeast Asia Collective Defense Treaty requesting assistance in defense of its freedom." The member and protocol states were

Cambodia, Laos, "the free territory of Vietnam," Australia, New Zealand, Pakistan, the Philippines, Thailand, Great Britain, and France. The words of the resolution appear to have been carefully chosen for their ambiguity, but they certainly bear the interpretation put upon them by the Johnson administration: the President might, if he deemed it wise, employ any means he wished, including the use of armed force, if any of these states alleged that its freedom needed defense. If, for example, the Tonkin Gulf Resolution had had legal status, and if it had still been in effect in December 1971, when Indian troops entered Bangladesh, President Nixon would have had the right to intervene on the side of Pakistan if requested.

Suppose we waive the objection that the war power is legislative and nondelegable and that only Congress, by joint resolution, may initiate war. Suppose we waive the objection that a declaration of war cannot be postdated but must be simultaneous with the initiation of the war. Suppose we treat the initiation of war as one of those matters of "less interest" on which Congress may delegate power to the President. It still remains true that in the United Nations Participation Act, the Formosa Resolution, the Middle East Resolution, and the Tonkin Gulf Resolution, Congress did not fix standards to govern the President. It cannot be said that these legislations meet the test applied in the dozens of cases in which delegations have been held valid. "He was the mere agent of the law-making department to ascertain and declare the event upon which its expressed will was to take effect."* In each of these resolutions, as in *Panama Refining Co. v. Ryan*,* the President was given the option of acting or not acting as he thought best. As Justice Benjamin Cardozo said in *Schechter Poultry Corporation v. United States*, this is "delegation unconfined and vagrant."*

But Assistant Attorney General William H. Rehnquist undertook to vindicate the Tonkin Gulf Resolution.

> It has been suggested that there may be a question of unlawful delegation of powers here, and that Congress is not free to give a blank check to the President. Whatever may be the answer to that abstract question in the domestic field, I think it is plain from *United States v. Curtiss–Wright Export Corp.*, which was decided only a year after *Schechter Poultry Corp. v. United States*, that the principle of unlawful delegation of powers does not apply in the field of external affairs. (*165, 171–72*)

There have been dozens of delegation decisions before and after the *Curtiss–Wright* case, many of them dealing with external affairs, and in all of them the traditional doctrine, that formulated by Chief Justice Hughes in the *Panama Refining* and *Schechter* cases, has been affirmed. Of the four federal statutes held invalid as attempted delegations of legislative power, one dealt with a matter of "less interest" under the war power, a regulation of prices.* We must therefore inquire whether *Curtiss–Wright* will bear the weight Rehnquist and others have put on it.

Justice Sutherland's opinion in *Curtiss–Wright* is certainly peculiar. In 1934 Congress passed a joint resolution authorizing the President, after consultation with specified parties, to forbid the sale of arms to the participants in the Gran Chaco War "if the President finds that the prohibition . . . may contribute to the reestablishment of peace between those countries." Sutherland's opinion asserted, though in the end it did not hold, that there were no constitutional limits on the delegation of legislative power to the President in the field of foreign affairs. The argument is distributed over three levels.

The first level is that of interstate succession. At the time of the Revolution, British sovereignty over the colonies was divided into two parts. Sovereignty in foreign affairs was inherited by the Confederation, and the several states had no share in it.[2] The states inherited sovereignty in their internal affairs. In 1789 the Constitution redistributed the sovereignty of the states, but the national government inherited directly from the Confederation the status of "sole possessor of external sovereignty" ("save in so far as the Constitution in express terms qualified its exercise"!)* Since this status did not come from the Constitution, it was not limited by Article I, Section 1, which forbids the delegation of legislative power.

This is a strange argument. What was involved in the *Curtiss–Wright* case was an act necessary and proper to effectuate an embargo on exports. But

[2]In United States v. Curtiss–Wright, at 299 U.S. 316, Justice Sutherland said that at the Declaration of Independence "the powers of external sovereignty passed from the Crown not to the colonies severally, but to the colonies in their collective and corporate capacity as the United States of America. See Penhallow v. Doane, 3 U.S. (3 Dall.) 54, 80, 81. . . ." Justice Paterson's opinion in *Penhallow v. Doane,* to which Sutherland appealed, said that Congress had exercised the war power after 1776, not by inheritance from the British crown, but "with the approbation of the people" (Id. at 80) and because the several states had bound themselves. (Id. at 82) Justice Blair said the states had delegated to Congress not necessarily the general war power, but the power to wage war with Great Britain; it is hard to regard this as an inheritance from the British crown. (Id. at 110) Justice Cushing said that the states had been sovereign save for such powers as they had delegated to Congress for carrying on the war. (Id. at 117)

In Ware v. Hilton, 3 U.S. (3 Dall.) 199, 224 (1796), Justice Chase said: "In *June* 1776, the Convention of *Virginia formally* declared, that Virginia was a free sovereign, and independent state: and on the 4th of *July,* 1776, following, the *United States,* in Congress assembled, declared the *Thirteen United Colonies* free and independent states; and that as *such,* they had full power to levy war, conclude peace, &c. I consider this as a declaration, not that the *United Colonies jointly,* in a *collective* capacity, were independent states, &c., but that *each* of them, had a right to govern itself by its own authority, and its own laws, without any control from any other power on earth." Justice Chase agreed with Justice Paterson that before the adoption of the Articles, the powers of Congress "were derived from *the people* they represented, expressly given through the medium of their State Conventions, or State Legislatures; or that after they were exercised they were impliedly ratified by the acquiescence and obedience of the people." (Id. at 231)

this power could not have been inherited from the Continental Congress, for the Continental Congress had no power to restrain exports. Article IX of the Articles of Confederation merely confirmed the earlier practice which assigned this power to the states.

> The United States in Congress assembled shall have the sole and exclusive right and power of . . . entering into treaties and alliances, provided that no treaty of commerce shall be made whereby the legislative power of the respective states shall be restrained from imposing such imposts and duties on foreigners as their own people are subjected to, and from prohibiting the exportation or importation of any species of goods or commodites, whatsoever. . . . (*214*, 31)

It is notorious that one of the motives for adopting the national Constitution was to confer on the Confederation a power it had not previously possessed, that of regulating foreign and interstate commerce. Beyond this, Sutherland's idea of divided sovereignty is untenable for the reason he himself gives, "A political society cannot endure without a supreme will somewhere."[*]

Even if the idea of extraconstitutional power in *Curtiss–Wright* were intellectually defensible, it has been repudiated by the Supreme Court. In 1957, in Reid v. Covert, Justice Black held: "The United States is entirely a creature of the Constitution. Its power and authority have no other source. It can only act in accordance with all the limitations imposed by the Constitution."[*] Although Justice Black wrote for only four justices, the opinions of the two concurring justices and the two dissenting justices implied agreement with this general proposition. Three years later, in *Kinsella v. United States ex rel. Singleton*, Justice Charles E. Whittaker and Justice Stewart announced their adhesion to the proposition stated by Black in *Reid v. Covert*.[*]

At the next level of the argument in *Curtiss–Wright*, Justice Sutherland abandons the theory of extraconstitutional power and attempts to argue that in foreign affairs the Constitution permits a delegation of legislative power to the President. He believes that one establishes this if he splices together the congressional power over foreign commerce and the fact that "the President is the sole organ of government in its external relations, and its sole representative with foreign nations." The inaccuracy of the "sole organ" theory has already been demonstrated. We might note in passing that it was precisely the division of powers between Congress and the other organs of government that gave rise to the rule against delegation; this feature of our government could hardly support legislation that obliterates the division.

Sutherland's first argument denied the relevance of the Constitution in foreign affairs; his second argument purported to rest on the Constitution, but gave it an unconventional reading; and his third argument relied on a well-established constitutional principle dating from *Stuart v. Laird*, decided in 1803.[*] Since Sutherland appealed to the formulation of the rule by the first Justice Harlan in *Field v. Clark*,[*] it is worthwhile to quote what Justice Harlan actually held on the delegation issue.

That Congress cannot delegate legislative power to the President is a principle universally recognized as vital to the integrity and mainte-nance of the system of government ordained by the constitution. . . . Legislative power was exercised when congress declared that the suspension should take effect upon a named contingency. What the president was required to do was simply in execution of the act of congress. It was not the making of law. He was the mere agent of the law-making department to ascertain and declare the event upon which its expressed will was to take effect.*

Of course this is not the passage Justice Sutherland quoted from *Field v. Clark.* The rule of *Stuart v. Laird* is the proposition that a contemporaneous congressional interpretation of the Constitution that has enjoyed long acquiescence fixes the meaning of the Constitution in a doubtful case. *Field v. Clark* involved the invocation of congressionally fixed tariff duties on certain imports by the President when he should find that the exporting nation charged "reciprocally unequal and unreasonable" duties on products from the United States. When this delegation was challenged, Justice Harlan cited a list of statutes, beginning with an act of 1794, which, he said, established "that, in the judgment of the legislative branch of the government, it is often desirable, if not essential, for the protection of the interests of our people against the unfriendly or discriminating regulations established by foreign governments, to invest the president with large discretion in matters arising out of the execution of statutes relating to trade and commerce with other nations." And he announced the rule quoted from *Field v. Clark* by Justice Sutherland.

. . . the practical construction of the constitution, as given by so many acts of congress, and embracing almost the entire period of our national existence, should not be overruled, unless upon a conviction that such legislation was clearly incompatible with the supreme law of the land. *Stuart v. Laird.* . . .*

But Sutherland altered the moral. Whereas in *Field v. Clark* Justice Harlan had said that these precedents supported delegations "for the protection of the interests of our people against the unfriendly and discriminatory regulations established by foreign governments," Justice Sutherland said that the precedents were acts of Congress "authorizing actions by the President in respect of subjects affecting foreign relations, which either leave the exercise of the power to his unrestricted judgment, or provide a standard far more general than that which has always been considered requisite with regard to domestic affairs."* And Sutherland concluded:

The uniform, long-continued and undisputed legislative practice just disclosed rests upon an admissible view of the Constitution which, even if the practice found far less support in principle than we think it does, we should not feel at liberty at this late day to disturb. . . .

It is enough to summarize by saying that, both upon principle and in accordance with precedent, we conclude there is sufficient warrant for the broad discretion vested in the President to determine whether the enforcement of the statute will have a beneficial effect upon the reestablishment of peace in the affected countries. . . .*

But even if one accepts Sutherland's broad view of the precedents, these were all, like the joint resolution in *Curtiss–Wright*, exercises of the power over foreign commerce. One supposes that Justice Sutherland himself would have recoiled from an act delegating to the President the power to make war in his "unrestricted judgment." No such statute was included in his list of precedents; no such statute could be validated by appeal to *Stuart v. Laird*.

Sutherland's second and third arguments, whether sound or unsound, acknowledge the supremacy of the Constitution and thus repudiate the historical excursion we have called the first argument. This was recognized in *Youngstown Sheet and Tube Co. v. Sawyer*. Concurring in the decision that presidential seizure of factories was unconstitutional, Justice Jackson observed that much of Sutherland's opinion in *Curtiss–Wright* was dictum and that the holding on delegation was merely a passage Sutherland had quoted from the opinion that in foreign affairs it was unwise to require Congress "to lay down narrowly definite standards by which the President is to be governed."* In *Zemel v. Rusk*, Chief Justice Warren quoted the *Curtiss–Wright* case but went on to observe, "This does not mean that simply because a statute deals with foreign relations, it can grant the Executive totally unrestricted freedom of choice."*

Many subsequent Supreme Court decisions have cited *Curtiss–Wright*, but rarely has delegation been at issue in those decisions. For example, in *United States ex rel. Knauff v. Shaughnessy,** Justice Minton, who wrote the opinion, held that Congress might authorize the executive to exclude aliens without a hearing.* He cited the *Curtiss–Wright* case, but he also cited *Fong Yue Ting v. United States* which had already established that aliens might be excluded or expelled arbitrarily.* The *Shaughnessy* case went off on the law of alienage rather than on the law of delegation. In the Supreme Court decisions since 1936 that did involve delegation of legislative power in foreign affairs, the Court applied the orthodox doctrine of *Panama Refining Co. v. Ryan* and *Schechter Poultry Corp. v. United States*. If there ever were a distinct *Curtiss–Wright* rule, it has been *sub silentio* overruled.

There have been two decisions on delegations under the commerce clause—the problem of the *Curtiss–Wright* case—and like the *Curtiss–Wright* case these two cases had political overtones. In 1926 Congress provided, "The Secretary of State may grant and issue passports . . . under such rules as the President shall designate and prescribe." In 1952 the President approved a rule introduced by the secretary of state that would make the issuance of a passport conditional upon the satisfaction of tests as to political belief and affiliation. In 1958, in *Kent v. Dulles*, in order to save the statute, the Court held that Congress had intended to authorize the President to impose restrictions only within the two categories into which inquiry was made before 1926: questions of citizenship and allegiance; and seeking a passport to escape the law or otherwise engage in illegal conduct. When Congress delegates power over passports, "the standards must be adequate to pass scrutiny by the accepted tests. Panama Refining Co. v. Ryan. . . ."* The secretary's rule was held invalid.

Seven years later, however, in 1965, the Court discovered that there had been a third administrative practice before 1926 that Congress had in mind when it delegated the rule-making power in that year. Congress had intended to authorize rules imposing area restrictions on the issuance of passports. Chief Justice Warren quoted a passage from the *Curtiss–Wright* case but went on to say:

> This does not mean that simply because a statute deals with foreign relations, it can grant the Executive totally unrestricted freedom of choice. However, the 1926 Act contains no such grant. We have held, Kent v. Dulles supra, and reaffirm today, that the 1926 Act must take its content from history: it authorizes only those passport refusals and restrictions "which it could fairly be argued were adopted by Congress in the light of prior administrative practice." Kent v. Dulles. . . . So limited, the Act does not constitute an invalid delegation.*

Justice Black dissented. He thought the act void on its face and ignored the argument that it could be saved by limiting it to established administrative practice.

> For Congress to attempt to delegate such an undefined law-making power to the Secretary, the President, or both, makes applicable to this 1926 Act what Mr. Justice Cardozo said about the National Industrial Recovery Act: "This is delegation running riot. No such plenitude of power is susceptible of transfer." A.L.A. Schechter Poultry Corp. v. United States. . . . See also Panama Ref. Co. v. Ryan. . . .*

Six times since 1936 the Supreme Court has passed on the question of the validity of delegations in matters "of less interest" under the war power. Each time it has sustained the act, but each time it has invoked the traditional tests of *Panama Refining* and *Schechter*. On no occasion has it mentioned *Curtiss–Wright*.

In *Hirabayashi v. United States*, in 1943, the Court upheld the congressional authorization of a curfew for persons of Japanese ancestry in wartime. Chief Justice Stone held that Congress might grant this power without holding hearings to determine the danger.

> The Constitution as a continuing operating charter of government does not demand the impossible or the impractical. The essentials of the legislative function are preserved when Congress authorizes a statutory command to become operative, upon ascertainment of a basic conclusion of fact by a designated representative of the Government. Cf. The Aurora,

7 Cranch 382. . . ; United States v. Chemical Foundation, 227 U.S.1. . . . The present statute . . . satisfied those requirements.*

The first case cited by Stone involved foreign commerce, the second the confiscation of enemy property under the war power; both affirmed the orthodox doctrine on delegation.

In 1944, in *Yakus v. United States,* the Court upheld the administrative fixing of prices under the Emergency Price Control Act. After citing several cases that state the established rule on delegation, Chief Justice Stone observed:

> Only if we could say that there is an absence of standards for the guidance of the Administrator's action, so that it would be impossible in a proper proceeding to ascertain whether the will of Congress has been obeyed, would we be justified in overriding its choice of means for effecting its declared purpose of preventing inflation.*

In the same year, in *Bowles v. Willingham*, the Court upheld another feature of the same act. Mr. Justice Douglas wrote:

> There is no grant of unbridled discretion as appellee argues. Congress has not told the Administrator to fix rents whenever and wherever he might like and at whatever levels he pleases. . . . Congress has here specified the basic conclusions of fact upon the ascertainment of which by the Administrator its statutory command is to become effective.*

And he cited several recent cases that stated the established rule against delegation.

In 1948, in *Woods v. Cloyd W. Miller Co.*, the Court upheld another act passed under the war power, the Housing and Rent Act of 1947. Justice Douglas wrote:

> The powers thus delegated are far less extensive than those sustained in Bowles v. Willingham. . . . The standards prescribed pass muster under our decisions. See Bowles v. Willingham . . . and cases cited.*

In the same year, in *Lichter v. United States*, the Court upheld the Renegotiation Act of 1942. Holding that the act contained sufficiently definite standards to guide the administrator, Justice Burton wrote, "This action of Congress came within the scope of its discretion as described by Chief Justice Hughes in Panama Ref. Co. v. Ryan. . . ." *

As in *Kent v. Dulles*, in *Oestereich v. Selective Service System Local Board No. 11*, in 1968, restrictive interpretation was given to an act of Congress, in this case an act passed under the power to raise armies, in order to avoid the constitutional issue of delegation.* The Selective Service Act granted a deferment to students preparing for the ministry, but in 1967 Congress provided for the induction of "delinquents." James J. Oestereich had been given the statutory deferment but was reclassified as a delinquent by his local Board, acting under a Selective Service System regulation, because he returned his registration certificate in protest against the Vietnam War.

Justice Douglas for the Court held the reclassification illegal. "Even if Congress had authorized the Boards to revoke statutory exemptions by means of delinquency classifications, serious questions would arise if Congress were silent and did not prescribe standards to govern the Boards' actions." In concluding that the statute must not be interpreted as precluding preinduction judicial review, he relied in part on the proposition that "the statutory delinquency concept" was not "sufficiently buttressed by legislative standards."

In *United States v. Robel* the majority of the Court held that the Subversive Activities Control Act, which made it unlawful for any member of an organization listed by the Subversive Activities Control Board to accept employment in what was designated a "defense facility" by the secretary of defense, was void on its face for overbreadth; therefore, they did not reach the question of delegation.* Justice Brennan concurred on the ground that the act contained "no meaningful standard by which the Secretary is to govern his designations."

The present state of the law was recognized in two district court decisions on the war power in 1968. Both courts ruled that the statute allowing the President to call up the ready reserve for twenty-four months was not an unconstitutional delegation of legislative power because Congress had fixed adequate standards. The first cited the *Schechter* and *Panama Refining* cases as controlling authorities; the second, *Lichter v. United States.**

On the other hand, the courts of appeals of two circuits honored the "blank checks," to use the language of Assistant Attorney General Rehnquist, by which Congress acquiesced in the Vietnam War. They did so even after the repeal of the Tonkin Gulf Resolution. In 1971 the court of appeals for the second circuit simply pronounced an *ipse dixit*.

> The Congress and the Executive have taken mutual and joint action in the prosecution and support of military actions in Southeast Asia. . . . The Tonkin Gulf Resolution . . . was passed at the request of President Johnson. . . . Congress has ratified the executive's initiative by appropriating billions of dollars to carry out military operations in Southeast Asia and by extending the Military Selective Service Act with full knowledge that persons conscripted under that act had been, and would continue to be, sent to Vietnam. . . .
>
> There is, therefore, no lack of clear evidence to support a conclusion that there was an abundance of continuing mutual participation in the prosecuting of the war. Both branches collaborated in the endeavor, and neither could long maintain such a war without the concurrence and cooperation of the others.*

This is a very fair account of what occurred. The Vietnam War was a cooperative action. The President determined whether there should be war, who the enemies should be from time to time, and eventually, whether there should be no war. Congress contributed men and money for the President to use against whatever Indochinese he chose if he should decide to make war; Congress left him free to discontinue war at will. In short, Congress abdicated. The court of appeals upheld this cooperative action without considering that the war power is not delegable, without even mentioning the constitutional tests of delegable action, without considering the law of ratification by appropriation, and without giving to the repeal of the Tonkin Gulf Resolution its natural effect—the repeal of all earlier legislation authorizing war in Indochina.

The court of appeals for the first circuit, on the other hand, did glance obliquely at the problem of delegation.

> . . . in a situation of prolonged but undeclared hostilities, where the executive continues to act not only in the absence of any conflicting Congressional claim of authority but with steady Congressional support, the Constitution has not been breached. The war in Vietnam is the produce of the jointly supportive action of the two branches to whom the congeries of the war powers have been committed. Because the branches are not in opposition, there is no need of determining boundaries. Should either branch be opposed to the continuance of hostilities, however, and present the issue in clear terms, a court might well take a different view. This question we do not face.*

This seems to say that the prohibition on the delegation of legislative power ("the jointly supportive action of the two branches"), which is directed against Congress, can be invoked only by Congress. This was not the holding in *Schechter Poultry Corporation v. United States* or *Panama Refining Co. v. Ryan*. In the view of this court of appeals, the powers of Congress are proprietary perquisites of Congress, and if they are exercised by another, with the consent of Congress, no legal injury is done. But the framers did not entrust the war power to Congress for the benefit of congressmen; they did so for the benefit of the citizenry. They believed that a decision for war should be taken by a broadly representative group after debate and deliberation; for that body to shirk its responsibility and transfer the power of decision to a single man was to acquiesce in tyranny.

If these two circuit court cases were rightly decided, the present state of the law is paradoxical. The two courts of appeals have held that when it is a matter of initiating war, Congress need make no decision as to the adversary or the character or the scope of hostilities; it may give the President a free hand to carry out his undisclosed or unformulated purposes by merely satisfying his demands for men and money. He may choose war or peace. He may send troops and bombers to South Vietnam, North Vietnam, Cambodia, Laos, and Thailand at will; or he may withdraw them at will. But in matters of "less interest" under the war power, such as price fixing or renegotiation of contracts, the uniform line of decision in the Supreme Court is that Congress must determine the policy and leave to the President the power only to "fill up the details."

But Congress appears not to have learned the lesson of the Indochina War. After giving the President a blank check to embark on war and spending years in a struggle to extricate the country from the consequent war, Congress then enacted the War Powers Resolution of 1973, the recited purpose of which was to fulfill "the intent of the framers of the Constitution of the United States and to insure that the collective judgment of both the Congress and the President will apply to the introduction of United States Armed Forces into hostilities" but which actually endorsed future delegations of power. According to Section 8, entitled "Interpretation of Joint Resolution," the President may engage in hostilities if an act of Congress has authorized this, or if a treaty should be ratified and should be implemented by legislation authorizing the use of the armed forces. Clearly this section contemplates that Congress shall make advance authorizations in general terms and that the President shall have the power, although not the duty, of engaging in hostilities under such statutes. Section 8 also holds that the President and the Senate may make treaties promising to engage in hostilities in the future and that Congress may contemporaneously authorize the President to invoke the treaty and plunge the country into war at any time during the life of the treaty. This hardly fulfills the intent of the framers. The War Powers Resolution considers it proper for the President to engage in war if at an earlier date, perhaps at a very much earlier date, Congress—necessarily acting in total ignorance of the future problem, of the future circumstances, and even of the future antagonist—has issued a blank check.

Other sections of the War Powers Resolution raise similar constitutional issues. For example, Section 4(a) (1) allows the President to use military force without congressional authorization so long as he "reports" to Congress within forty-eight hours of the deployment. Section 5(b) allows this unauthorized deployment to continue for up to ninety days unless Congress acts to terminate it. Opponents of the resolution argued that these provisions grant "a legal basis for the President's broad claims of inherent power to initiate war" that he did not previously have under the Constitution. These opponents preferred a Senate proposal that sought to reaffirm the proper role of Congress, limiting the circumstances under which the President could deploy the armed forces to those recognized by constitutional law. Instead, these limitations appear in the precatory "Purpose and Policy" section of the resolution and have no legal effect on the President's power to commence war.

Section 3 of the resolution, entitled "Consultation," is full of ambiguities that permit the President to usurp further the power of Congress. This section requires the President to "consult" with Congress "in every possible instance" before involving the United States troops in "hostilities," actual or imminent. To "consult" supposedly means more than to inform; it is said to require advice, opinion, and, when appropriate, approval. "Every possible instance" is intended to exclude only such dire circumstances as a hostile missile attack. And "hostilities" is meant to encompass any state of confrontation, whether or not shots have been fired. But those vague guidelines do not pass the constitutional tests of specificity required for any delegation by Congress.

Far from attacking the War Powers Resolution as an unconstitutional delegation of the war power of Congress, the most strident critics have attacked it as an unconstitutional infringement on the President's war power—a reflection, perhaps, of how heavily the "constitutional 'balance' of authority over warmaking has swung . . . to the President in modern times." President Nixon vetoed the resolution with indignation; President Ford challenged its constitutionality; and President Reagan has refused to concede that congressional authorization is required for his various military excursions, although he has feigned compliance with the resolution.

The most debated provision has been Section 5(c), which allows Congress, by concurrent resolution, to require the President to remove troops engaged in the hostilities abroad. A concurrent resolution does not require the President's signature, nor is it subject to his veto. The power of Congress to have the last word—the so-called legislative veto—has often been challenged and finally was held unconstitutional in *Immigration and Naturalization Service v. Chadha*.* The reasoning of that decision apparently invalidates Section 5(c) of the War Powers Resolution. The Senate subsequently sought to bring that section within constitutional limits by providing that any congressional action requiring the President to withdraw United States forces engaged in hostilities abroad must follow certain priority procedures that do not constitute a legislative veto.

Whether Congress is willing and able to reassert its proper constitutional role in deciding when to use the war powers remains to be seen. Its attempt to do so in the War Powers Resolution seems, at least in part, to have failed. The resolution is an overbroad delegation of the war power of Congress that essentially writes the President a blank check. Unfortunately, court challenges to such flagrantly unconstitutional delegations of the war power encounter substantial practical roadblocks. Both supporters and opponents of the War Powers Resolution agree that its constitutionality is not likely to be adjudicated. Those difficulties, however, should not obscure the clear status of the law: the Supreme Court has never held that Congress may delegate the power to initiate war to the President. Even the dictum in the *Curtiss–Wright* case said nothing of the sort. And the dictum in *Curtiss–Wright* has neither paternity nor progeny.

The rule against the delegation of legislative power is our only legal guarantee of the continuance of republican government. The Roman republic perished through delegation, and Ulpian wrote its epitaph, "What pleases the prince has the force of law, since by a royal law established concerning his sovereignty the people confers all its sovereignty and power upon him."[3]

[3]*Justinian's Digest*, 1, 4, 1.

Chapter 14

RATIFICATION
AND DELEGATION
BY APPROPRIATION

When the President undertakes an action that may lawfully be initiated only by Congress, Congress may, unless there is some constitutional obstacle to retroactive legislation, lend the necessary legislative authority to such action by ratification. An illustration is the act of August 6, 1861, in which Congress provided:

> That all the acts, proclamations and orders of the President of the United States after the fourth of March, eighteen hundred and sixty-one, respecting the army and navy of the United States, and calling out or relating to the militia or volunteers from the States, are hereby approved and in all respects legalized and made valid, to the same intent and with the same effect as if they had been issued and done under the previous express authority and direction of the Congress of the United States.*

Taft considered President Wilson's occupation of Veracruz an act of war and illegitimate since it had occurred before Congress gave the necessary authority, but he said that the resolution passed on the following day was "full and immediate ratification." (*213*, 96)

It is possible to ratify an unauthorized action by passing an appropriation act. In 1905 a circuit court held that President McKinley's intervention in China at the time of the Boxer Rebellion was war and was ratified by Congress when it voted wartime pay to the troops in China.* Ratification may have a prospective, as well as retroactive, effect. If the executive action introduces a change of status, upon ratification the new status is authorized for the future. The Supreme Court has decided five cases in which such a change was alleged to have been approved by the enactment of an appropriation act.

When an appropriation has been held to ratify and adopt an executive initiative, that initiative has been plainly identified in the appropriation act. In *Isbrandtsen–Moller Co. v. United States*, in 1937, the Court held that an executive order by which the President abolished the Shipping Board and transferred its functions to the Department of Commerce had been ratified by three successive appropriation acts "all of which made appropriations to the Department of Commerce for salaries and expenses to carry out the provisions of the shipping act as amended and refer to the executive order."* *Brooks v. Dewar*, decided in 1941, involved a practice introduced by the secretary of the interior, contrary to statute.* Instead of issuing term permits for the use of public grazing lands based on the individual values of the permits, as the law required, the secretary had made a practice of issuing temporary licenses at a uniform fee. Congress, with full knowledge of this practice, had repeatedly appropriated twenty–five percent of the revenue from the licenses for the improvement of the range. The Court held that this was ratification. In *Fleming v. Mohawk Co.*, in 1947, the Court held that when the President had consolidated agencies and Congress had appropriated funds for the new administrative creation this was "confirmation and ratification of the action by the Chief Executive."*

In two cases the Court has held that appropriation sustaining an unauthorized executive action did not imply legislative ratification. Without statutory authority, during World War II, the Relocation Authority adopted the policy of detaining citizens of Japanese origin, whose loyalty had been satisfactorily established, in relocation centers if they would not agree to go to an approved place of residence upon release. In a habeas corpus action, *Ex parte Endo*, the Authority contended that Congress had ratified this policy by appropriating funds for the continued operation of the relocation centers. Justice Douglas said:

> . . . Congress may of course do by ratification what it might have authorized. . . . And ratification may be effected through appropriation acts. . . . But the appropriation must plainly show a purpose to bestow the precise authority which is claimed. We can hardly deduce such a purpose here when a lump sum appropriation was made for the overall program of the Authority and no sums were earmarked for the single phase of the total program which is here involved. Congress may support the effort to take care of these evacuees without ratifying every phase of the program.*

Justice Owen J. Roberts concurred in the result, but he asserted that Congress had actually ratified the practice of detaining loyal citizens. He complained of the test applied by Douglas for calling "a specific item referring to that portion of the programme" essential.*

Quite possibly Justice Roberts was indignant that the Court relied on a proposition about ratification because he wished to press on to what he considered the central issue—the detention of citizens in violation of the due process clause. In any case, Douglas seems to have had the better opinion. An appropriation merely authorizes the expenditure of money. If any other legislative consequence is attributed to it, it should be clearly mandated by the appropriation.

The other case in which the Court denied that Congress had ratified an executive action by appropriation is *Greene v. McElroy*.* Here the Court held that the practice of denying security clearance without affording a hearing had not been ratified by the funding of the program, even though Congress knew of the practice. However, the opinion was somewhat narrower than that in *Ex parte Endo*. It emphasized the fact that denial of a hearing was of "doubtful constitutionality" and said: "Such decisions [as ratification] cannot be assumed by acquiescence or non-action. . . . They must be made explicitly . . . because explicit action, especially in areas of doubtful constitutionality, requires careful and purposeful consideration by those responsible for making and implementing our laws."

Such careful and purposeful consideration was not given by Congress when it enacted the legislation that has been adduced as authorization for the Vietnam War. Indeed, it appears that before entering the Vietnam War, the Johnson administration deliberately planned a legal strategy of deprecating the legal significance of legislation when it was requested and of magnifying its significance after it had been enacted. So it was with the Tonkin Gulf Resolution; so it has been with appropriation acts.

On February 7, 1965, President Johnson began his air attacks on North Vietnam. Without even requesting an invitation from the Saigon regime, he began to move substantial bodies of troops into South Vietnam; eventually the number reached 545,000. It would have been politically imprudent to take these momentous actions without making some gesture toward Congress. The normal procedure would have been to propose a bill specifying what the President was to do in Indochina. This bill would have been considered by the foreign relations and armed services committees, and these committees would have been obliged to review the policy proposed in the bill. They would have canvassed alternatives. The two houses would have debated the concrete recommendations of the President. Congress would have played its constitutional role in the exercise of the war power. But President Johnson merely asked for an appropriation; then he asserted that the appropriation would be interpreted by the North Vietnamese and by Communists everywhere as evidence of the stern resolution of the American people and their willingness to follow wherever President Johnson should lead. On May 4, he sent a message to Congress.

I ask the Congress to appropriate at the earliest possible moment an additional $700 million to meet mounting military requirements in Vietnam.

This is not a routine appropriation. For every member of Congress who supports this request is also voting to persist in our effort to halt Communist aggression in South Vietnam. Each is saying that the Congress and the President stand united before the world in joint determination that the independence of South Vietnam shall be preserved and Communist attack will not succeed. . . .

I do not ask complete approval for every phase and action of your Government. I do ask for prompt support of our basic course: resistance to aggression, moderation in the use of power, and a constant search for peace. Nothing will do more to strengthen your country in the world than the proof of national unity which an overwhelming vote for this appropriation will clearly show. To deny and delay this means to deny and delay the fullest support of the American people and the American Congress to those brave men who are risking their lives for freedom in Vietnam.*

On May 7, President Johnson signed into law a joint resolution of less than a hundred words which authorized the secretary of defense, "upon determination by the President that such action is in connection with military activities in southeast Asia," to transfer seven hundred million dollars from unappropriated funds to any existing military account.*

It was said in *Ex parte Endo* that to constitute a ratification "the appropriation must plainly show a purpose to bestow the precise authority which is claimed." The joint resolution of May 7 contained no other language than that authorizing the transfer of funds. It did not purport to alter the legal status of any past event. In view of this fact, and of President Johnson's denial that he asked "complete approval for every phase and action of your Government," it is hard to see how the appropriation can be read as a ratification of any particular action. The joint resolution had legal effect as an appropriation measure. It had no other legal effect.

Of course it had extralegal significance. President Johnson said that a vote for the appropriation was also a vote "to persist in our effort to halt Communist aggression in South Vietnam." This latter vote would not grant authority but would strike a posture. It would announce that "the Congress and the President stand united before the world"; it would be "proof of national unity." The striking of postures, however, is not an exercise of the legislative power of Congress; it does not take the place of the words *Be it enacted*.

Suppose, however, that we supply the words *Be it enacted* and that we further interpret into the resolution the entire statement of purpose in the President's message. Suppose we assume that the resolution authorizes the President to accomplish these purposes: halting of Communist aggression, preservation of the independence of South Vietnam, "resistance to aggression, moderation in the use of power, and a constant search for peace." Do these words prescribe a definite course of action? Do they supply standards to guide the President? Do they specify the means he is to employ? Clearly a resolution cast in these terms would be another attempt at the delegation of legislative power, which is forbidden by the Constitution.

When a supplementary defense appropriation bill came before the Senate in 1967, certain senators attempted to forbid further escalation of the war by amendment to the bill. From a legal point of view, the administration was ill-advised to oppose the amendment, for by accepting limits to presidential action it could easily have obtained a congressional mandate for action within those limits. But the administration preferred to retain the whole war power in the President's hands. Accordingly, in the amendment that emerged from debate in the two houses and from conference committee, and that passed both houses on March 8, Congress declared neither for war nor for peace. As before, it left the conduct of affairs entirely in the hands of the President, who might either abandon the war or further escalate it into a war with China without violating the amendment.

> The Congress hereby declares:
> (1) Its firm intentions to provide all necessary support for members of the armed forces of the United States fighting in Viet Nam;
> (2) its support of efforts being made by the President of the United States and other men of good will throughout the world to prevent an expansion of the war in Viet Nam and to bring that conflict to an end through a negotiated settlement which will preserve the honor of the United States, protect the vital interests of this country, and allow the people of South Viet Nam to determine the affairs of that nation in their own way; and
> (3) its support for the convening of the nations that participated in the Geneva Conferences or any other meeting of nations similarly involved and interested as soon as possible for the purpose of pursuing the general principles of the Geneva accords of 1954 and 1962 and for formulating plans for bringing the conflict to an honorable conclusion.*

The first paragraph is not an exercise of the war power of Congress. It does not instruct the President to prosecute the war; it is merely a statement of the intention of Congress, which of course is not legally binding, to pass other appropriation acts if he does. Nor does it appear that the second and third paragraphs have any legal effect. The most general principles of the Geneva accords of 1954, which the third paragraph adopts as the basis of a settlement, were the insistence that Vietnam was one state and the agreement upon the unification of the north and south military withdrawal zones by nationwide elections.[1] But the second paragraph calls "South Viet Nam" a nation and endorses its independence.

But even if the implied endorsement of unification in the third paragraph did not conflict with the second paragraph, it could not be argued that

---

[1]The so-called Geneva accords were the "Agreement on the Cessation of Hostilities in Vietnam," signed by the commanders in chief of the French Union Forces in Indochina and the People's Army of Vietnam on July 20, 1954, and the "Final Declaration of the Geneva Conference" of July 21, 1954. These are published in The Consultative Council of the Lawyers Committee on American Policy towards

Congress, by approving the Geneva accords—which, incidentally, forbade the introduction of foreign troops in Vietnam—had forbidden the President to prosecute the war. The words are merely precatory. In the amendment Congress resolutely maintained its position of interested bystander. It refused to discharge its constitutional duty of determining whether there should be war or peace. Representative William H. Bates, the minority floor leader, was quite right when he said of the amendment: "It is almost innocuous. It is barely a pious preachment."*

On June 11, 1968, when a motion to strike from a supplemental appropriations bill the "Emergency Fund, Southeast Asia" of $6,136,000,000 was before the House, Chairman George H. Mahon of the Appropriations Committee assured the House that the passage of the appropriation would not imply an endorsement of the war.

> This amendment does not involve a test of one's basic views with respect to the war in Vietnam. We have more than 500,000 troops in Vietnam. The question here is that they are entitled to our support as long as they are there, regardless of our views otherwise. . . .
>
> This proud nation of ours just must not do anything other than fully support our men who are under attack. Regardless of one's philosophic views on the war, we just must provide support for the 500,000 men who are in Southeast Asia. . . .*

Until January 12, 1971, both the Johnson and the Nixon administrations had relied principally on the Tonkin Gulf Resolution when they had recognized the right of Congress to participate in war. But with the repeal of the resolution on that date, no legislative authorization of war in Indochina was available except appropriation acts and the current Service Act—the latter, of course, was merely the continuation of a policy begun in 1940. In 1971 Solicitor General Erwin Griswold argued that these would do the work without the Tonkin Gulf Resolution. Congress had made available to the President both men and money without which he would have been unable to carry on wars in Indochina, and this had been done "in full knowledge of the situation in Southeast Asia, and in support of the President's actions."* But if these appropriation acts and the renewal of the draft in 1967[2] were viewed as authorizing the President to conduct war, they were an even more

---

Vietnam, *Vietnam and International Law* (Flanders, N.J.: O'Hare Books, 1967), pp. 137–49. Paragraph 5 of the "Final Declaration" said that "the essential purpose of the agreement relating to Vietnam is to settle military questions with a view to ending hostilities and that the military demarcation line is provisional and should not in any way be interpreted as constituting a political or territorial boundary." Paragraph 6 provided for general elections to unify the two zones in 1956; it is well known that Diem of the Saigon regime, with the encouragement of the United States, frustrated these elections.

[2]The renewal of the Selective Service Act in 1967, if viewed as a delegation or

outrageous delegation of legislative power than the Tonkin Gulf Resolution. They required neither war nor peace but permitted the President to choose either; they named no antagonist but allowed him a free hand. In fact, they named no friend. It was said that we were engaged in supporting the government of South Vietnam, but the executive had overthrown—or had sanctioned the overthrow of—a long series of governments in South Vietnam which had previously enjoyed our support. Until 1955 the executive took the position that Vietnam was a member of the French Union and was headed by the Emperor Bao Dai. But it forced Ngo Dinh Diem on Bao Dai as prime minister and assisted Diem in expelling Bao Dai and withdrawing Vietnam from the French Union. (24, II, 880–81) Diem established a dictatorship with American money, but when oppression of the population under his control made him so intolerable that he was no longer useful, the American executive assisted in a military coup that overthrew and led to the murder of Diem and his brother.[3] The executive then supported the military dictatorship of General Duong Van Minh until another coup, in which the American role is obscure, replaced Minh with General Nguyen Khanh. (198, 232–34; 148, II, 277, 334–35, 340) The Khanh government was apparently overthrown without American consent, but the executive readily adopted the Nguyen Cao Ky regime that replaced it. (148, II, 342–48, 361–69) Politics thereafter were dominated by a clique of officers in which Nguyen Van Thieu bested Ky; Thieu staged two pro forma elections in order to make it appear that he had a popular, as well as a military and American, base. Without violating any word in any appropriation act, the President might have thrown his weight behind the Hanoi regime and ousted Thieu's government at Saigon; he might have supported Norodom Sihanouk and ousted Lon Nol in Cambodia. If the appropriation acts had any legal effect other than the appropriation of funds, they had this entire effect. One can imagine no more complete delegation of legislative power to the President.

But let us suppose that Griswold was right and that appropriation acts legalized the Vietnam War. Whatever endorsement they may have given to

---

ratification, is exposed to the objections already canvassed; in addition, it presents its own peculiar problems. The power of Congress to raise armies and the power to make war are distinct. Never before had it been suggested that by raising an army Congress had authorized the President to make war. As we have seen, the President may not make use of the army that Congress has created without statutory authorization for the specific use.

It is curious that anyone should undertake to justify war in terms of the exercise of the power to raise armies and not in terms of the power to make war; if there were interdependence, it would seem more natural to ground the draft on the power to make the war. But in fact the two powers are distinct, and the exercise of either does not entail the other.

[3]See Bouscaren, 19, Chapter 9; Lacoutoure, 98, 95–101; Shaplen, 198, 200–212.

the war was withdrawn when Congress repealed the Tonkin Gulf Resolution on January 12, 1971.*

What is called, after the language of a note by Edmund Plowden,* the doctrine of "the equity of the statute" goes back at least to the fifteenth century. (40, 1, 2, 21; 59, I, 24) It is firmly established in English and American law. (211, III, 137) This doctrine proposes that the meaning of a statute is not found solely within the literal text. The statute is intruded into an existing legal order and must be read in such a way as to harmonize with related features of the law. On the other hand, to give effect to the intention of the legislature, it may be necessary to make adjustments in the existing body of the law, even when the text of the statute does not explicitly call for these changes.

Sometimes the doctrine of the equity of the statute has been pushed to what may appear unnecessary extremes. Both the House of Lords and the United States Supreme Court have held that the cumulation of statutes recognizing and regulating labor unions have in effect converted these voluntary associations into corporations liable for the torts of their members.* In 1939, in *Keifer & Keifer v. Reconstruction Finance Corp.*, the Supreme Court held that because Congress had created forty governmental corporations and had waived sovereign immunity in all but two cases, it implicitly waived immunity in the case of regional agricultural credit corporations created by the RFC, especially since it had explicitly waived immunity in the case of the parent corporation.*

A less debatable situation is presented by a statute that repeals earlier legislation. In 1919, the House of Lords held that the repeal of named acts aimed at the Roman Catholic religion repealed all laws against that faith, including the prohibition on bequests for superstitious uses, although this topic was not mentioned in any of the acts of repeal.*

In the United States, a series of decisions has established the proposition that an act of repeal that inaugurates a new policy repeals all acts inconsistent with that new policy although they are not named. In 1845, in *United States v. Freeman*, the Supreme Court held that an act of 1818 that in terms abolished brevet pay and rations only for army officers applied also to marine officers in the same position, because other acts had treated all brevet officers alike.

> The correct rule of interpretation is that if diverse statutes relate to the same thing, they ought all to be taken into consideration in construing any one of them, and it is an established rule of law, that all acts in pari materia are to be taken together, as if they were one law.*

In *The Paquete Habana*, in 1900, the Court was called upon to interpret an act of Congress that revised the law governing the appellate jurisdiction of the Supreme Court. In general, the new scheme made the right to appeal turn on the nature of the case rather than on the amount in controversy, but Congress did not explicitly repeal an earlier act limiting appeals in prize cases to suits where the matter in dispute exceeded two thousand dollars or where the district judge certified that the adjudication involved a matter of general importance. Justice Gray reviewed the law and concluded that Congress, by establishing a general policy governing review, had implicitly repealed the two–thousand–dollar limitation in prize cases.

> And it is a well settled rule in the construction of statutes, often affirmed and applied by this court, that "even where two acts are not in express terms repugnant, yet if the latter act covers the whole subject of the first act, it will operate as a repeal of that act."*

The most famous statement on the question is that of Justice Holmes.

> A statute may indicate or require as its justification a change in the policy of the law, although it expresses that change only in the specific cases most likely to occur to the mind. The Legislature has the power to decide what the policy of the law shall be, and if it has intimated its will, however indirectly, that will should be recognized and obeyed.*

United States v. Hutcheson was a criminal prosecution of a labor leader under the Sherman Act for calling a jurisdictional strike.* In the Clayton Act, Congress had exempted labor disputes from the Sherman Act, but in *Duplex Printing Co. v. Deering*, the Court drastically limited the definition of labor dispute. Finally, in the Norris–LaGuardia Act, Congress forbade the use of injunctions in labor disputes, defining this term so broadly as to include jurisdictional strikes. The question in *Hutcheson* was whether the abolition of injunctive relief in the Norris–LaGuardia Act also abolished the criminal penalty of the Sherman Act in labor disputes. It was a problem, said Justice Frankfurter, of the interpretation of the "three interlacing statutes."

> . . . we need not determine whether the conduct is legal within the restrictions which Duplex Printing Co. v. Deering gave to the immunities of §20 of the Clayton Act. Congress in the Norris–LaGuardia Act has expressed the public policy of the United States and defined its conception of "labor dispute" in terms that no longer leave room for doubt. . . .
>
> To be sure, Congress expressed this national policy and determined the bounds of a labor dispute in an act explicitly dealing with the future withdrawal of injunctions in labor controversies. But to argue, as it was urged before us, that the Duplex case still governs for purposes of a criminal prosecution is to say that that which on the equity side of the Court is allowable conduct may in a criminal proceeding become the road to prison. . . . This is not the way to read the will of Congress, particularly when expressed by a statute which, as we have already indicated, is practically and historically one of a series of enactments touching one of the most sensitive national problems. Such legislation must not be read in a spirit of mutilating narrowness. On matters far less vital and far less interrelated we have had occasion to point out the importance of giving "hospitable scope" to Congressional purpose even when meticulous words are lacking.*

According to administration theory, the Tonkin Gulf Resolution was an explicit delegation of the war power to the President; appropriation acts were implied delegations. When Congress repealed the explicit delegation, it repealed all implied delegations. The appropriation acts were merely tributary to the Tonkin Gulf Resolution and could not survive its repeal.

Nor did Congress leave this question open to doubt. In the National Procurement Authorization Act of November 13, 1971, it enacted an affirmative policy for Indochina.* This statement advised the President to take two, and only two, actions: to negotiate an immediate cease-fire; and to negotiate a phased withdrawal of all American forces by a certain date, subject to the release of all American and allied prisoners of war. No imaginary emanation from an earlier appropriation act could enlarge the terms of this subsequent explicit declaration of congressional purpose. It follows that President Nixon's statement of January 25, 1972—that he would subscribe to no agreement that did not provide for a stipulated political settlement in South Vietnam—could claim no authorization by any act of Congress. On the contrary, it collided with an act of Congress. It represents the high-water mark of the claim of presidential power, asserting that the President may carry on a war not only without the support of Congress but also in defiance of Congress.

In one of the last decisions, or rather nondecisions, on the legality of the war in Indochina, the court of appeals for the District of Columbia, on March 20, 1973, held that even before the repeal of the Tonkin Gulf Resolution, there had been no endorsement of the Indochina war by appropriation acts.* Writing for himself and Chief Judge David L. Bazelon, Judge Charles Edward Wyzanski renounced the opinion that he and some other inferior court judges had expressed earlier—"that the appropriation, draft extension, and cognate laws enacted with direct or indirect reference to the Indo-China war . . . did constitute a constitutionally permissible form of assent."

> This court cannot be ignorant of what every schoolboy knows: that in voting to appropriate money or to draft men a Congressman is not necessarily approving of the continuation of a war no matter how specifically the appropriation or draft act refers to that war. A Congressman wholly opposed to the war's commencement and con-tinuation might vote for the military appropriations and for the draft measures because he was unwilling to abandon without support men already fighting. An honorable, decent compassionate act of aiding those already in peril is no proof of consent to the actions that placed and continued them in that dangerous posture. We should not construe votes cast in pity and piety as though they were votes freely given to express consent.*

Chapter 15

THE DOCTRINE
OF POLITICAL QUESTIONS

Although legal scholars debated the nature of justiciability prior to the Indochina War as part of an ongoing discussion of the nature and legitimacy of judicial review, the refusal of the federal courts to rule on the legality of the war spawned a new and intensified examination of the concept of justiciability generally and the political question doctrine in particular.[1] In the past, scholars had agreed that the political question doctrine involved the avoidance of issues through a technique of nondecision and deference to the judgment of another branch. According to this classic view, "[i]n political question decisions . . . the Court refuses to apply legal principles which are relevant to the disposition of the case. . . . [T]he Court does not hold that legal rules do not apply; it holds that competence to apply them should rest with the political departments." (*191*, 560) The pre–Vietnam debate thus assumed that a body of case law provided authority for the view that the Court might on occasion refuse to decide the legal issues before it; the issue became whether the Court might legitimately invoke the doctrine only when it had determined that the Constitution itself had demarcated certain issues to be resolved by a nonjudicial branch, or whether, instead, the Court might take account of certain prudential factors in determining to abstain.

Scholars have generally agreed that the fundamental constitutional concept of separation of powers, which keeps the various branches balanced

[1]See, e.g., Tigar, *218*, 1135; Henkin, *77*, 284; Schwartz and McCormack, *195*, 1033.

and in check, lies at the base of the political question doctrine. (*101*, 386) The separation of powers doctrine is invoked whether one accepts a classical view of political questions or one of several prudential theories. The classical view has come to be identified with the formulation of Herbert Wechsler.

> I submit that . . . the only proper judgment that may lead to an abstention from decision is that the Constitution has committed the determination of the issue to another agency of government than the courts. Difficult as it may be to make that judgment wisely, whatever factors may be rightly weighed in situations where the answer is not clear, what is involved is in itself an act of constitutional interpretation, to be made and judged by standards that should govern the interpretation process generally. That, I submit is *toto caelo* different from a broad discretion to abstain or intervene. (*234*, 9)

Other commentators have contended that the Court might invoke the doctrine on the basis of more discretionary and pragmatic considerations. Some factors that have been isolated are the lack of adequate legal standards to apply (*54*, 511–12); the possibility that a judgment, if rendered, would not be enforced;[2] or the absence of sufficient information available through the limited fact–finding techniques available to the judiciary. (*60*, 38; *191*, 566–67) In addition, Professor Alexander Bickel presented what has been described as a "normative" theory of the political question doctrine, which rests upon the view that extralegal considerations—economic, political, military, international—*ought* to be allowed to guide the decisions of the political branches on particular occasions as much as constitutional principles.[3]

In *Baker v. Carr*, Justice Brennan articulated the concept of separation of powers as the touchstone for the determination of political questions and lent support to proponents of classical and prudential views.

> It is apparent that several formulations which vary slightly according to the settings in which the questions arise may describe a political question,

[2]Strum, *209*; Finkelstein, *55*, 338. See also Duncan v. Kahanamoku, 327 U.S. 304 (1946) (Burton, dissenting) (warning of the rule of nonenforcement).

[3]See Bickel, *15*, 183–98. Bickel's theory is described as "normative" by Scharpf (*191*, 558–66). Bickel's view that the Court should occasionally abstain from reaching the merits, rather than use techniques of broad interpretation to uphold questionable acts by the political branches, is based on his belief that the Court exists primarily to uphold principle. Even if the Court determines that various considerations should prevent judicial intervention against acts of the political branches, the Court should not uphold such act if it cannot do so in a principled way. Instead, Bickel would have the courts refrain from making an independent determination while praising the principles that the branches should consider. Scharpf objects that this approach might provide grounds for expanded use of the doctrine and would ultimately undermine the effectiveness of the Court in both its functions as arbiter of the Constitution and as "teacher to the citizenry." (*191*, 561–66)

although each has one or more elements which identify it as essentially a function of the separation of powers. Prominent on the surface of any case held to involve a political question is found a textually demonstrable constitutional commitment of the issue to a coordinate political department; or a lack of judicially discoverable and manageable standards for resolving it; or the impossibility of deciding without an initial policy determination of a kind clearly for non-judicial discretion; or the impossibility of a court's undertaking independent resolution without expressing lack of the respect due coordinate branches of government; or an unusual need for unquestioning adherence to a political decision already made; or the potentiality of embarrassment from multifarious pronouncements by various departments on one question.*

That Brennan used the term *several formulations* and noted that only a slight variation might exist between his various descriptions of political questions indicates that he recognized the substantial redundancy that existed among his criteria. All are connected to separation of powers. The first criterion, a "textually demonstrable constitutional commitment," represents the clearest statement of a classical or Wechslerian position. The political question doctrine is linked to a textual constitutional delegation to a political branch. This avoids the erosion of the legitimacy of judicial review that could result from recognizing discretion in political questions and hence in judicial review itself. The second, "judicially discoverable and manageable standards," is ambiguous enough to be interpreted either as simply referring to the constitutionally mandated elements of "cases" and "controversies"—concreteness and justiciability—or as including discretionary criteria related thereto but not necessarily demanded by the Constitution. Brennan's third criterion, involving issues the resolutions of which demand discretionary policy determinations by the political branches, simply combines the first two criteria—i.e., the Court may find not only a broad textual grant to the political branches to formulate policy, but also a lack of specific limitations on the means of implementing that policy. The next formulation, the impossibility of attempting independent judicial resolution without "expressing lack of the respect due" the political branches, sounds much more discretionary or "prudential" in nature but is no less tied to consequences stemming from the separation of powers. The same can be said for the final two formulations relating to adherence to an existing political decision and the necessity of the national government to speak with one voice under certain circumstances: prudential judgment about the limits of judicial competence is recognized as legitimate, but the focus is on the spirit of separation of powers. Thus, it has been observed that the most "definitive" judicial statement on the nature of the doctrine leaves the scholarly debate where it was found, in a state of confusion and disagreement. (*220*, 71 n.1)

Baker v. Carr recognized, however, what had become the one generally accepted proposition about the political question doctrine: whatever its dimensions and scope, the most common application of the political question doctrine is in cases raising legal issues related to the conduct of the foreign relations of the United States. After noting prior judicial statements to the effect that all questions involving foreign relations are political questions, Justice Brennan went on to demonstrate that the Court will often independently decide many such cases. Nevertheless, he acknowledged that the major responsibilities in the conduct of foreign relations were given to the political branches and pointed to several factors that would lead the Court to defer to those branches.

> Our cases in this field seem invariably to show a discriminating analysis of the particular question posed, in terms of the history of its management by the political branches, of its susceptibility to judicial handling in light of its nature and posture in the specific case, and of the possible consequences of judicial action.*

During the Vietnam era, scholars began to challenge the assumption that complete abstention from deciding constitutional issues is justified either historically or logically.[4] In particular, it has been argued that the great bulk of cases cited in support of a political question doctrine are merely separation of powers rulings about the scope of the political branches' power, rather than true examples of judicial abstention. More specifically, Professor Louis Henkin argues that most of the so-called political question rulings in the field of foreign relations actually ruled that the Constitution does not require the political branches to obey rules of international law in exercising their plenary power in foreign relations. (76, 286–87) Henkin argues, for example, that when the Court has held that Congress may abrogate a treaty in municipal law by enacting legislation that contradicts terms of the treaty, reasoning that the decision involved is a "political question," the Court has simply held that the Constitution does not require Congress to uphold the nation's treaty obligations.* The political question label, according to this view, adds nothing to the analysis of the issue but is merely a gratuitous phrase that has been twisted into a doctrine of justification for recent aberrations.

Professor Henkin and Professor Michael Tigar have applied the treaty abrogation paradigm to cases of judicial deference to executive action within its sphere of authority under the Constitution. (76, 289; 218, 1155–56, 1159 62) Thus, when the Court refuses to address the issue of whether a particular group is the sovereign power of a foreign country, in the absence of an executive pronouncement, it is merely pronouncing the rule of law that the executive has complete authority to determine whom to recognize as the sovereign of a nation, which authority is simply not subject to the traditional

---

[4]Tigar, 218; Henkin, 77; see also Albert, 5, 1139; Henkin, 76, 597.

standards of customary international law for determining sovereignty.* In these cases, according to Henkin and Tigar, the Court is not refusing to apply the law to the facts; rather, it is treating the executive acts as "legislative" in character, as indeed establishing the law that is to be applied. Henkin and Tigar conclude that the source of this law–declaring power in the executive is not an act of judicial abstention but a judicial determination of the scope of the foreign affairs powers of the executive branch in these particular areas.

These scholars do not deny that the judicial determination of these issues reflects, in part, judicial awareness of the sensitive setting in which foreign relations decisions are made and a corresponding deference to the branches that hold the preponderant grants of power over foreign relations under the Constitution. (76, 605 n.27; 218, 1156) But deference to another branch is a frequent part of the determination of constitutional issues, including, for example, the presumption of constitutionality accorded most enactments and the Court's deferential standard of what constitutes "commerce" for purposes of determining whether congressional enactments fall within the scope of the commerce power. The Court's perception of the leeway required by another branch affects its judgment in fixing the limits of that branch's power, but the rulings still establish that certain questions are considered to involve policy, not law, and that the political acts in question are the law to be applied in the case. They are not, according to this argument, refusals to decide the merits of the controversies before the Court.

Certainly it is true that not all the foreign affairs cases cited as illustrations of the political question doctrine are true political question cases. And virtually none of the cases traditionally cited to support the political question doctrine fit Professor Henkin's restrictive definition. Henkin would limit discussion of the doctrine to cases in which the Court in effect tells the litigants that although a constitutional provision may have been violated, the Court may not address the question because of its political character. (76, 599) Most foreign affairs cases to which the label political question has been attached did not involve the contention that a political branch had acted ultra vires under the Constitution. To understand why these cases have been characterized as political question cases, one must begin with a broader definition, one that views the hallmark of political questions to be "a judicial refusal to decide a relevant issue because it is, for some reason, not appropriate for judicial handling, even though there are [relevant] legal standards which could be applied to decide the issue." (127, 526) The distinction between this kind of ruling and a typical ruling on the scope of another branch's power is that the focus here is on the limits of judicial competence rather than on the meaning and effect of constitutional language. As we shall see, it is only an understanding of this distinction that adequately explains the selective invocation of the political question doctrine. Any historical case must be confronted individually to determine if this test is met, but many foreign affairs cases seem to fit.

We should first briefly consider a class of cases that are clearly analogous to political question cases but which should perhaps be viewed as involving a separate (though related) doctrine. Although a number of these cases have frequently been cited as political question cases, they actually involve the issue of whether review of administrative action is precluded in a given set of circumstances. (*39*, 80; *12*, 965) These cases are closely related to the political question doctrine because they are frequently rooted in separation of powers concerns and reflect a sensitivity to the critical nature of the decision-making area involved. They should perhaps be separated from political question analysis, however, because such rulings frequently involve statutory interpretation as to the intent of Congress and thus are not always justiciability rulings. They are, in any event, instructive.

Cases refusing to review administrative action have, like the political question cases, stirred much controversy and debate. In particular, considerable debate has focused on the implications of the language in the Administrative Procedure Act that precludes review of actions "committed to agency discretion."* Since a related provision provides for review to determine if there has been "an abuse of discretion," the issue is whether the statute sanctions complete preclusion of review in some instances or provides for limited review for "abuse" of discretion in all cases.[5] Although the clear trend is away from refusing review because of statutory language granting discretionary decision-making authority,* considerable case law authority backs the proposition that there is no review even for abuse of discretion in some areas. (*39*, 80)

A number of these cases are very old. For example, in *Decatur v. Pauling*, decided in 1840, the Court held that executive discretion precluded judicial review of the secretary of the navy's refusal to pay a pension. Chief Justice Taney stated that "[t]he interference of the courts with the performance of the ordinary duties of the executive departments, would be productive of nothing but mischief; and we are quite satisfied that such power was never intended to be given to them."*

The early case of *Martin v. Mott* provides an example of the Court's approach to the discretionary exercise of the war power by the executive.* In *Martin*, the New York militia had been summoned by the governor pursuant to orders of the President in the prosecution of the War of 1812. Jacob Mott refused to report for duty and was convicted and fined by court-martial. A 1795 act of Congress authorized the President to call up the militia "whenever the United States shall be invaded, or be in imminent danger of invasion from any foreign nation or Indian tribe."* Justice Story for the Court found that the President's decision was not reviewable.

We are all of the opinion, that the authority to decide whether the exigency has arisen, belongs exclusively to the President, and that his

[5]Compare Berger, *12*, with Davis, *38*, 823.

decision is conclusive upon all other persons. We think that this construction necessarily results from the nature of the power itself, and from the manifest object contemplated by the Act of Congress.*

More recently, the Supreme Court considered whether courts could review an award of an international air route by the President. Despite a statute apparently granting judicial review, the Court declined review because the statutory scheme placed decision–making authority in the President himself and the question related to foreign affairs. Justice Jackson stated:

> [T]he very nature of executive decision as to foreign policy is political, not judicial. Such decisions are wholly confided by our Constitution on the political departments of the government, Executive and Legislative. They are delicate, complex, and involve large elements of prophecy. They are and should be undertaken only by those directly responsible to the people whose welfare they advance or imperil. They are decisions of a kind for which the Judiciary has neither aptitude, facilities, nor responsibility and which has long been held to belong in the domain of political power not subject to judicial intrusion or inquiry.*

Although we have a much bolder judiciary today, the courts continue to balk at issues deemed sensitive and beyond the realm of judicial competence. In *United States ex rel. Schonbrun v. Commanding Officer*, the court of appeals for the second circuit refused to review the decision of a commanding officer denying a hardship exemption from a call to active reserve duty.* Noting that the legislative history "made clear that the courts were 'not to direct or influence the exercise of discretion of the officer . . . in the making of the decision,'" the court, nevertheless, acknowledged the general view that "official conduct may have gone so far beyond any rational exercise of discretion as to call for mandamus even when the action is within the letter of the authority granted."* Although the legislative history was thus not decisive of itself, in this case the court concluded that judicial abstention was called for.

> . . . administration of the hardship exemption necessarily involves a balancing of the individual's claims against the nation's needs, and the balance may differ from time to time and from place to place in a manner beyond the competence of a court to decide.*

Focusing on §10(e) of the Administrative Procedure Act, which provides for review of "abuse of discretion," the court stated that its holding "that the correctness of a discretionary refusal to grant the hardship exemption is not subject to review by the courts necessarily represents a determination that such a refusal 'is by law committed to agency discretion' so far as to render §10(e) inapplicable. . . ." *

In addition to the cases refusing to review administrative action, other foreign affairs cases defy classification as mere separation of powers rulings. It is interesting to note that critics of the political question rulings of the 1960s went to great lengths to demonstrate that courts have not been foreclosed from deciding cases in the foreign affairs area. (*218*, 1168–70) As they have observed, the courts have in fact applied rules of customary international law to decide controversies before them, and the Supreme Court has held that international law is among the sources of law that courts should draw upon.* What these critics have not addressed is why the Supreme Court has selectively declined to decide questions of international law in settings where it was felt that deference to coordinate branches was required.

Questions that were deemed political when courts perceived the dangers of "multifarious pronouncements" have often been decided in a complete absence of pronouncements. For example, in *The Rogdai* a federal court stated and applied the traditional rule that courts are forbidden from acknowledging the existence of a foreign group exercising power that has not been formally recognized by the executive.* The case should be compared with *The Ambrose Light*. In that case, a federal district court recognized belligerent status, despite the refusal of the State Department expressly to recognize such status, on the basis of "long acquiescence by the United States in belligerent acts affecting another nation's interest."* Similarly, when the particular factual setting has seemed less sensitive, the Court has decided on a question that generally would have been deemed political, even though its decision was inconsistent with the prior determination of another branch. In *Foster v. Neilson*, the Supreme Court held that a political interpretation of a treaty is binding on the judiciary.* But one hundred years later, the same Court rejected a State Department treaty interpretation that would have allowed the involuntary expatriation of an American citizen.[6]*

Commenting on the treaty interpretation cases just discussed, Professor Fritz W. Scharpf observed, "It seems that the Court is paying much more attention to the political and legal implications of the concrete case than to the logic of any theory which might derive from the constitutional grant of the treaty power." (*191*, 546 n.102) This insight is consistent with Justice Brennan's statement that the Court focuses on "*the particular question posed*, in terms of the history of its management by the political branches, of its susceptibility to judicial handling in the light of its nature *and posture in the*

---

[6]The distinction between *Perkins* and Foster v. Neilson, 27 U.S. (2 Pet.) 253 (1829), may be traced in part to the traditional doctrine that courts are empowered to give direct legal effect only to treaties that are deemed "self-executing." See Head Money Cases, 112 U.S. 580, 598–99 (1884). It has been acknowledged, however, that courts also show unusual deference to executive interpretations of treaties, particularly in those areas in which the political branches are viewed as having the dominant interest. (*42*, 167) Cf. Z. & F. Assets Realizations Corp. v. Hull, 311 U.S. 470, 489 (1941), construing treaty implementation statute as precluding judicial review of whether award of international commission comported with treaty, relying in part on "the nature of the questions presented and their relation to the conduct of foreign affairs within the province of the Secretary of State."

specific case, and of the possible consequences of judicial action."* In many cases, the refusal of the courts to apply international law standards to resolve issues between individual litigants has not involved necessary logical inferences from the Constitution's grant of power to the political branches in foreign affairs; rather, the decisions have been practical inferences based on judicial self-awareness of inherent limitations on the judicial process.

Even when the Court has reached the merits of cases raising issues related to foreign affairs and the war powers, it has shown great deference to the political branches. (57, 81–89) This is appropriate in light of the preponderant commitment of these issues by the Constitution to the political branches, particularly to Congress. When the Court has reached the merits, it has been especially unwilling to second-guess the decisions of the political branches when it appeared that Congress and the President had been in accord on the act in question. (57, 80) The Japanese–American relocation cases, in particular, demonstrate most pointedly and painfully the expansive limits of the joint, cooperative use of the war powers by the political branches. In *Korematsu v. United States*, the Court upheld the evacuation program primarily on the grounds that it could not "reject as unfounded the judgment of the military authorities and of Congress" and that the exclusion was necessitated by urgent needs of national defense.* The Court thus deferred to the combined discretionary judgment of the political departments, even though that judgment involved a classification based on race.

Duncan v. Kahanamoku, on the other hand, lends support to a complementary thesis that the Court is less likely to defer if it appears that the political branches have not acted in unison.* Here, a civilian in Hawaii had been convicted by a military tribunal established pursuant to a declaration of martial law. The Supreme Court held that the Hawaiian Organic Act, which authorized the territorial governor to suspend the writ of habeas corpus and declare martial law, did not allow the armed forces to substitute military trials for judicial trials of civilians not charged with violations of the laws of war. The Court avoided a decision on the constitutionality of the Organic Act by finding that Congress had not authorized petitioners' trials by military tribunal.

When the political branches do not act in unison in regard to a war powers issue, the Court is more inclined to uphold the congressional act due to the preponderant textual grant of war powers to Congress.[7] The historic intrusion of the executive into this area during a time of congressional acquiescence is not likely to prevail as a legitimating factor for the

---

[7]With reference to executive action inconsistent with congressional authority, the remarks of Justice Jackson, concurring in Youngstown Sheet & Tube Co. v. Sawyer, 343 U.S. 579, 637–38 (1952), are instructive.

When the President takes measures incompatible with the expressed or implied will of Congress, his power is at its lowest ebb, for then he can rely only upon his own constitutional powers minus any constitutional powers of Congress over the

continuation of such practices in a judicial proceeding when the practices are opposed by the potent combination of subsequent congressional action and constitutional text.[8]

Illustrative of the Court's recognition of congressional predominance is *Youngstown Sheet & Tube Co. v. Sawyer*, decided during the Korean hostilities (see earlier discussions, pp. 137-38, 171-73).* In 1947 Congress rejected an amendment to the Taft-Hartley Act that would have authorized govern-mental seizure of major industries during a national emergency. In 1952 President Truman, by executive order, seized most of the nation's steel mills to avoid a work stoppage after a general strike had been called by the United Steelworkers of America. Justice Black, writing for the Court, denied any notion of extraconstitutional "executive power." No enlargement of the scope of constitutional power afforded the President as commander in chief or as the nation's executive could be claimed by virtue of an emergency of undeclared war.* The concurring opinions of Justices Frankfurter, Douglas, Jackson, Burton, and Clark identify more clearly the critical connection between congressional action and judicial willingness to scrutinize and overturn presidential acts performed, allegedly, under the war powers.* Justice Burton stated:

> The controlling fact here is that Congress, within its constitutionally delegated power, has prescribed for the President specific procedures, exclusive of seizure, for his use in meeting the present type of emergency. Congress has reserved to itself the right to determine where and when to authorize the seizure of property in meeting such an emergency. Under these circumstances, the President's order of April 8 invaded the jurisdiction of Congress. It violated the essence of the principle of the separation of governmental powers.*

Early in the Indochina War, legal challenges were routinely dismissed on standing, sovereign immunity, or political question grounds. (57, 91-92) Dialogue in the courts gradually evolved from an initial refusal under any circumstances to speak to the substance of the questions raised, to an increasingly fertile exchange on the nature of standing, political question,

---

matter. Courts can sustain exclusive presidential control in such a case only by disabling the Congress from acting upon the subject. Presidential claim to a power at once so conclusive and preclusive must be scrutinized with caution, for what is at stake is the equilibrium established by our constitutional system.

[8]For examples of occasions in which the Court was willing to view the acts as not being in the nature of the joint action found in *Korematsu*, see Kent v. Dulles, 357 U.S. 116 (1958) (secretary of state powerless to deny passports to American citizens who refused to submit affidavit concerning membership in Communist Party); Valentine v. United States *ex rel*. Neidecker, 299 U.S. 5 (1936)(executive without power to extradite fugitive criminals in absence of authority from treaty or congressional act); Brown v. United States, 12 U.S. (8 Cranch) 110 (1814); United States v. Guy W. Capps, Inc., 204 F.2d 655 (4th Cir. 1953), *aff'd on other grounds*, 348 U.S. 296 (1955).

justiciability, and substantive issues of constitutional delegation of the war powers.

The earliest political question decisions failed to provide any reasoned explanation for that result. For example, in *Luftig v. McNamara*, a circuit court justified its political question ruling without acknowledging that a serious constitutional issue had been raised.* Instead, the court simply stated that under our constitutional system it is not for the courts to "oversee the conduct of foreign policy or the use and disposition of military power."* This statement would present an obvious commonplace if the litigants were asking the court to make a policy decision that the war should be stopped because its continuation was inconsistent with the military and foreign affairs interests of the nation. But the litigants in *Luftig* were not asking the court to oversee the nation's foreign policy or military strategy; they were asking it to perform the traditional judicial function of demarcating the division of constitutional authority between the other two branches in the decision to go to war. Thus, the court effectively held that it was for the political branches to determine the scope of their own war powers under the Constitution, yet the court did not directly address why this should be. Such early cases so completely failed to provide any rationale for the invocation of the political question doctrine that they were described as "non-decisions leading to a non-law of justification." (*218*, 1178)

Other cases provided a somewhat more sophisticated exposition of the grounds for refusal to review. An example is *Atlee v. Laird*, in which a three-judge district court addressed the following issues:

> (1) whether our military participation in Southeast Asia ought to be classified as a "war"; (2) whether, assuming a formal declaration of war is for some reason unnecessary, Congress has taken sufficient action to authorize the "war"; and (3) whether the President, under his war powers and regardless of congressional action, has the authority to keep American forces in that area.*

In contrast to the *Luftig* court, the court in *Atlee* made clear that its political question determination involved a refusal to decide constitutional issues.

> The precept that federal courts do not decide political questions does not arise . . . from the text of the Constitution. It is instead a rule born of pragmatic considerations, based on the separation of powers concept and our system of checks and balances. Unlike general concepts of justiciability stemming from the constitutional "case and controversy" restriction on judicial power, the political question doctrine limits the exercise, not the existence, of federal judicial power.*

The court then articulated several factors, mainly prudential in nature, that "demonstrate the need for federal courts to move with extreme caution in the sensitive area of foreign policy." Although the balance of the opinion focused mainly on the *Baker v. Carr* formulation that looks for "judicially discoverable and manageable standards,"* the reasoning of the court made it apparent that the "unmanageability" of the proposed standards stemmed more from pragmatic considerations than from any inherent inability to articulate standards to apply.* The court's articulation is reminiscent of Professor Bickel's "normative" theory of the political question doctrine alluded to above.

> [W]hile a court could possibly devise a manageable set of standards for answering the question in 1972, world politics today change so rapidly that it might, by setting forth rules, create a rigid matrix that would unnecessarily restrict the executive some time in the future when the powers denied today may be essential to the well-being of the United States then.*

To a proponent of the classical theory of the political question doctrine, *Atlee* represents an unprincipled and unjustified refusal to exercise the judicial power. A dissenting opinion and scholarly commentators argued that standards existed for determining the issues raised in the case. (*218; 156*) Chief Justice Joseph S. Lord argued in dissent that there was no question that the Indochina conflict was to be considered "war" for purposes of the Constitution.* Scholars generally agreed. (*242*, 682; *126*, 1803) Prior case law on ratification suggested that there were standards for determining whether various acts of Congress "provide sufficient congressional authorization under the war making clause." Finally, Judge Lord contended that there were sufficient standards based on historical evidence to find that the President had no independent authority to keep American forces in Vietnam.*

There is, indeed, little question that adequate standards existed to enable courts to decide the constitutionality of war.

> There are no standards for going to war, and therefore the war power was given to Congress. No suitor may complain because Congress has declared war; and the courts may not take an action because Congress has declared war; and the courts may not take an action that resembles an act of war. But the standards to determine whether Congress has exercised its war power are simple and easy to apply. Similarly, in *Marbury v. Madison*, Chief Justice Marshall said that deciding whom to appoint was a political question, but whether an appointment had been made was a justiciable question. The legality of the Vietnam War is a justiciable question. (*242*, 680)

Moreover, the Supreme Court has ruled on the nature of the war power on several occasions in the past.* As early as the congressionally authorized maritime war with France, the Supreme Court ruled in *Bas v. Tingy* and *Talbot v. Seeman* that Congress could authorize hostilities without declaring general war.* Several years later, in *Little v. Barreme*, the Court held that the President is bound by restrictions placed upon executive war making by authorizing legislation.* Later, the Supreme Court applied principles of American constitutional law in *The Prize Cases* to determine the legality of President

Lincoln's blockade of southern ports at the beginning of the Civil War.* These cases go a long way toward dispelling the idea that the meaning and scope of the war clause is completely foreclosed from judicial scrutiny or is inherently nonjusticiable. For the classical theorist, this is conclusive of the political question issue. For prudential theorists, however, prior cases holding that the war clause is not out-of-bounds for the judiciary do not determine whether the judicial power should be exercised in the setting of the Indochina War. Their response would be that none of these prior cases occurred in circumstances portending direct confrontation with the executive branch during time of war. Nevertheless, one of the ironies of the refusal of the Court to hear legal challenges to the Indochina War is that the only Supreme Court precedents to guide future courts still point to the justiciability of issues relating to the authority of Congress and the President to wage war.

The Supreme Court's role during the Vietnam War was routinely to refuse to grant certiorari to consider the validity of the lower court decisions.* For the most part, these nondecisions provide no hint or clue as to the particular rationale upon which the members of the Court were relying. A notable exception is *Massachusetts v. Laird*, in which Justice Douglas dissented from the Court's refusal to grant a motion for leave to file a complaint.* His opinion suggests that members of the Court were concerned about standing and justiciability, although it provides no basis for concluding the breakdown of the Court between the two grounds. Justice Douglas's opinion summarized the issue under justiciability and adopted a classical view of political questions. He provided the most effective response to the Baker criterion of "the impossibility of a court's undertaking independent resolution without expressing lack of the respect due coordinate branches of government." Douglas noted, "It is far more important to be respectful to the Constitution than to a coordinate branch of government."* In the same vein, Justice Douglas characterized several of the Baker criteria as involving simply "a commitment of a problem and its solution to a coordinate branch of government," adopting the view, discussed below, that political question rulings of the past were really separation of powers rulings rather than refusals to decide.*

The court of appeals for the second circuit developed a different approach to cases challenging the war. In *Orlando v. Laird*, servicemen attacked the authority of the executive to wage war in Vietnam. The court stated that

> the constitutional delegation of the war-declaring power to the Congress contains a discoverable and manageable standard imposing on the Congress a duty of mutual participation in the prosecution of war. Judicial scrutiny of that duty, therefore, is not foreclosed by the political question doctrine. . . . As we see it, the test is whether there is any action by the Congress sufficient to authorize or ratify the military activity in question.*

The court in *Orlando* then found that Congress had given its approval to American participation in the Indochina War, as manifested in the Tonkin

Gulf Resolution, military appropriations, extensions of the draft, and other supportive acts. The court also stated, however, that the *form* of congressional authorization was a political question. A number of commentators have focused on the requirement that the congressional action be "sufficient" to ratify the military action, concluding that the case is therefore properly analyzed under the law of ratification and not as a political question case. This would make the case a classic example of a "false" political question, in Professor Henkin's terminology, in which the label adds nothing to the analysis.

It may be, however, that the court was recognizing and avoiding serious constitutional objections to its own approach. The court stated that "the *constitutional propriety* of the means used to ratify and approve the protracted military operations in Southeast Asia is a political question."* This statement may represent more than a judicial determination that the political branches, Congress in particular, had met all cognizable constitutional requirements in authorizing war; it may represent, instead, a tip of the hat, at least, to those who contend that the Tonkin Gulf Resolution represented an unconstitutional delegation of the war power (*226*, 19–27; *242*, 683–703) and that mere supportive legislation does not constitute legal ratification.* In short, the court's willingness to find "sufficient" authorization in circumstances that would allow the President to lead us into war by handing Congress a *fait accompli* suggests that the *Orlando* court was willing to defer to Congress on whether its constitutionally mandated role was one of policy making or one of abdication. Put another way, the court may have been willing to recognize congressional predominance in controlling the nation's power to go to war, and to serve notice on the President that in the event of a head–on clash, Congress would prevail. But the court may have been unwilling to scrutinize further to insure that Congress was actually fulfilling its intended role. This interpretation explains not only the court's own emphasis that it must find only "*some* mutual participation,"* which implies that more participation might arguably have been required by the Constitution, but also the court's argument that the "highly complex considerations of diplomacy, foreign policy and military strategy," which are necessarily involved in the war–making decisions, make the political branches an appropriate forum for resolving the constitutional question of the manner in which Congress may authorize war. (*127*, 537–88)

Whether or not *Orlando* is properly analyzed, at least in part, as a political question ruling, the dominant theme emerging from the cases decided near the end of the war was that courts might properly decide such cases in the event of a direct clash between the two branches. In the words of Judge Coffin:

> The war in Vietnam is a product of the jointly supportive actions of the two branches to whom the congeries of the war powers have been committed. Because the branches are not in opposition, there is no

necessity of determining boundaries. Should either branch be opposed
to the continuance of hostilities, however, and present the issue in clear
terms, a court might well take a different view.*

This approach, of course, has not been without its opponents. In *United States
v. Sisson*, Judge Wyzanski asserted that "cooperative action" by the political
branches in foreign policy "is the very essence of what is meant by a political
question."* "Thus," it was remarked, "the unconstitutionality of the action
[of delegating the war power] becomes the reason for not inquiring into its
constitutionality." (*242*, 686) This deference to the political branches,
however, is rooted in both a judicial concern that Congress and the President
not be unduly restricted in their joint responses to international crises and
in a judgment that a too narrowly fashioned rule might create dangerous
inflexibility in American foreign policy. Whether or not such concerns should
determine the propriety of judicial review, it seems likely that policy concerns
of these kinds would largely disappear if the courts confronted a direct clash
between Congress and the President.

Two years after the *Orlando* decision, one federal court would question
the holding that Congress had adequately ratified the war in Indochina, and
another would issue an injunction against bombing in Cambodia.* Although
the court in the former case still found a political question in the discretion
required to end prolonged conflict, and the injunction decision was reversed
on appeal, these cases demonstrated the rift that separated members of the
federal judiciary on the role of the courts in deciding the constitutional
boundaries of the war powers.

The injunction case, *Holtzman v. Schlesinger*, grew out of congressional
opposition to President Nixon's bombing of Cambodia. Congressional
opposition to military activity in Cambodia was predominant. After the
failure to override the President's veto of the Eagleton Amendment, a
compromise measure was passed that prohibited the use of appropriated
funds in Cambodia after August 15, 1973. In *Holtzman*, the district court used
the ratification theory analysis and concluded that the President had not been
authorized by Congress to bomb in Cambodia and therefore was acting
beyond his legal authority. In a real sense, the bombing of Cambodia was
as much out of harmony with a majority in Congress—against the "implied
will" of Congress, to use Justice Jackson's phrase—as was President Truman's
seizure of the steel mills. The district court reasoned not only that Congress
had expressed opposition to the bombing but also that the "forced"
compromise amendment could hardly represent an authorization of
continued bombing until August 15, 1973. Nevertheless the circuit court of
appeals reversed.* *Holtzman*, then, raises perhaps the most serious challenge
to the thesis that the courts will independently review war powers acts of
the executive when those acts are out of harmony with congressional will.

Several factors must be considered, however, to understand the reversal
by the circuit court. First, the Cambodia bombing represented final stages
in a protracted conflict that the courts had systematically refused to find

unconstitutional. The appellate court undoubtedly recognized the practical distinction between the relative ease of initiating war and the difficulty of ending it. The circuit court in *Holtzman* was convinced that the judiciary was incompetent to draw the line between tactical decisions that the President might make as commander in chief without congressional approval and those for which he needs new congressional authorization.* The circuit court was also unwilling to go behind the face of the compromise amendment and find that Congress did not intend to authorize a temporary continuation of the bombing.* The court was hesitant to interpose itself in accommodations being worked out between the branches. This hesitancy may suggest that the more sensitive the area of the war power involved, the more direct must be the clash between the branches to bring about judicial intervention. As helpful a precedent as the *Youngstown* case may be, it should be remembered that the Court's position was strengthened because it was a labor case as well as a war powers case. Finally, there were extralegal factors in *Holtzman* that probably motivated the court of appeals, particularly an affidavit by Secretary of State Rogers to the effect that a holding against the administration would do "irreparable harm" to the conduct of American foreign relations.* Such considerations undoubtedly would have been less persuasive if congressional opposition had been clear, formal, and unequivocal.

The thesis that formal congressional action may be the key to unleashing judicial power is lent some additional support by the Supreme Court's recent decision in *Goldwater v. Carter*.* In *Goldwater*, the Supreme Court refused to review whether the President may unilaterally terminate a treaty with a foreign nation. A plurality of the Court would have found that Senator Goldwater's challenge to President Carter's termination of a mutual defense treaty with Taiwan posed an inherently nonjusticiable political question. Nevertheless, at least two considerations suggest that the political question analysis of the plurality in *Goldwater* may not control the Court's willingness to consider the legality of presidential war making.

First, it is significant that the political question analysis did not command the assent of a majority of the Court. Second, much of the analysis of even the plurality opinion does not apply to the question of whether the President may wage unauthorized war. The first major component of the plurality's political question analysis was the absence of constitutional text speaking to the issue raised. Justice Rehnquist stated that "while the Constitution is express as to the manner in which the Senate shall participate in the ratification of a treaty, it is silent as to that body's participation in the abrogation of a treaty."* The plurality thus analogized *Goldwater* to *Coleman v. Miller*, in which the Supreme Court held that in the absence of a specific textual provision governing when, if ever, a proposed constitutional amendment lapses, the question should be resolved in the political forum.* As in *Coleman*, the plurality in *Goldwater* concluded that the means of treaty termination might appropriately vary according to the nature of the treaty involved and that the particular method of termination should be resolved in the political forum. But the issue raised by executive war making, particularly in the face of formal congressional opposition, does not at all require interstitial law making for which the political branches would be better suited. The historical evidence is clear that the textual power of Congress to declare war was specifically intended to give it exclusive power to initiate war on behalf of the United States.

The plurality's second rationale distinguished *The Steel Seizure Case* because the question there had involved real consequences for private litigants rather than purely an interbranch dispute. Whereas the effect of President Carter's termination of the treaty was "entirely external to the United States," President Truman's seizure of the steel mills had "a profound and demonstrable domestic impact."* To the extent that the Court will deem the locus of the impact as relevant to a prudential political question determination, it seems likely that a private litigant could demonstrate that illegal presidential war making has a profound and demonstrable domestic impact. Surely the stake of one resisting enlistment in such an illegal war would compare favorably to the interest of the private litigants in *The Steel Seizure Case*, so that such litigation could not fairly be characterized as presenting a purely interbranch dispute.

On the other hand, Justice Powell's concurring opinion in *Goldwater*, based on ripeness rather than political question analysis, may be suggestive of what is required to assure judicial review of executive war making.* Admittedly based on prudential considerations, Justice Powell's ripeness analysis in *Goldwater* is highly reminiscent of the political question cases decided near the end of the Indochina War. Justice Powell did not contend that Senator Goldwater lacked sufficient personal stake to claim standing, or that the issues were not sufficiently clear or the record sufficiently developed. Rather, his theory appeared to be based exclusively on deference to coordinate branches of government, the traditional underpinning of the political question doctrine. Declaring that "[i]f the Congress chooses not to confront the President, it is not our task to do so," Justice Powell concluded that "[t]he judicial branch should not decide issues affecting the allocation of power between the President and Congress until the political branches reach a constitutional impasse."*

Perhaps recognizing the tension between the prudential theories of the political question doctrine and the well-entrenched judicial teaching that the doctrine goes to issues rather than cases, Justice Powell preferred to use the language of ripeness analysis.* Nevertheless, it seems clear that it was similar instincts that motivated the lower federal courts to avoid the sensitive separation of powers issues posed by the Indochina War when the branches themselves did not seem clearly to be at odds. Although Justice Powell's analysis in *Goldwater* did not control any other vote, similar basic instincts may also move the Court even when the particular theory does not command its jurisprudence.

The War Powers Resolution is a strong congressional restatement of the constitutional moorings of the war powers, and it provides a significant definition of political questions and the exercise of the war powers for the courts. Specifically, congressional authorization for the introduction of American armed forces into "hostilities or into situations wherein involve- ment in hostilities is clearly indicated by the circumstances shall not be inferred from any provision of law . . . including any provision contained in any appropriation Act, unless such provision specifically authorizes" such introduction.* Nor shall said inference be drawn from "any treaty . . . un- less said treaty is implemented by legislation specifically authorizing the introduction" of armed forces into hostilities or into situations likely to result in hostilities.* The War Powers Resolution thus brings congressional interpretation of its own act of authorization or ratification of executive actions under the war powers very close to the position taken by Judges Bazelon and Wyzanski in *Mitchell*.

Congress has, through the War Powers Resolution, provided the executive and the courts with an interpretation of part of the war powers: a declaration of war or specific statutory authorization is necessary before the commander in chief may introduce United States forces into hostilities for any substantial length of time. The criteria often cited by the courts as indicating congressional assent to executive use of the war powers—appro- priation acts and the SEATO treaty, for instance—do not, by themselves, constitute congressional authorization. The War Powers Resolution's requirement of specificity in congressional authorization disowns any past congressional delegation of its war powers and warns the executive and the courts not to rely upon such techniques in the future.

Chapter 16

THE WAR POWER AND
THE REAGAN PRESIDENCY

> You know, there was a time when our national security was based on
> a standing army here within our own borders and shore batteries of
> artillery along our coasts. . . . The world has changed. Today, our
> national security can be threatened in faraway places.*
>
> —Ronald Reagan

Previous chapters of this book have traced the shift of the war power from
Congress to the President. That shift has continued in the Reagan
administration. Indeed, in a sense the Reagan presidency epitomizes what
Arthur Schlesinger has termed "The Imperial Presidency," a salient feature
of which is the unilateral control of the war power. During the Reagan
administration American forces have been actively involved in conflicts
around the globe, usually in the absence of—and often directly contrary
to—congressional authority.

The Reagan administration is determined to counter "worldwide Soviet
interventionism that poses an unprecedented challenge to the free world."
(215, 18) That interventionism is rarely, however, as blatant as in Afghanistan
and Poland; rather, it is accomplished by an alleged worldwide Communist
conspiracy operating through a "network of surrogates and terrorists."*
Ironically—and tragically—the Reagan administration itself has not hesi-
tated to intervene both overtly and covertly, and in so doing it has further
usurped the war power of Congress. This chapter examines the Reagan
administration's military actions in Central America, the Caribbean, and the
Middle East.

Reagan's actions in Central America were preceded by events occurring during the Carter administration. In Nicaragua, a bloody civil war resulted in the ouster of brutal right-wing dictator Anastasio Somoza Debayle. The leaders of Somoza's opposition were the Sandinistas, named after Augusto Sandino, who had opposed United States interventions in Nicaragua in the early part of the century. The Sandinistas—with the Carter administration's cautious support—promised economic, social, and political reforms.

Reagan had not been in office long before the Sandinista leadership began to renege on its promises and started to consolidate its own power through Somoza-like tactics. Several of the original leaders resigned in protest. The resulting junta developed close ties with Cuba and the Soviet Union, alienating the Reagan administration and precipitating a cutoff of American aid in April 1981. Several developments in Nicaragua alarmed the Reagan administration. First, according to the administration, Nicaragua was undertaking an unprecedented military buildup that far exceeded legitimate defense needs. Second, the administration found evidence that Nicaragua was fomenting insurgencies in other Central American countries, especially El Salvador. And third, the administration feared that Nicaragua was becoming another Communist satellite in this hemisphere, threatening American interests in the Caribbean, Panama, and elsewhere.

Meanwhile, developments in nearby El Salvador were producing similar concerns. That country, too, had long been the battleground for clashes between extremist ideologues. Right-wing forces prevailed after 1979 with a civilian-military junta which replaced deposed General Humberto Romero, but leftist guerillas continually mounted bloody forays against the government. The Carter administration granted limited military aid to the new right-wing government and sent five military advisors to El Salvador. The aid was cut off in late 1980, however, following a series of brutal attacks on civilians, including four American churchwomen, allegedly carried out by right-wing government security forces.

Nevertheless, the Reagan administration made good its post-election promises to increase military aid to the beleaguered country. After leftist insurgents in El Salvador announced a "final offensive" to topple the government in January 1981, the Reagan administration dispatched an additional twenty military advisors and requested substantial increases in other military aid, stating that arms supplied by the Soviet Union, Cuba, Ethiopia, and Vietnam were reaching the leftist rebels in a "textbook case of indirect armed aggression by Communist powers."[1]

The constitutional and legal issues involved in the assignment of military advisors to El Salvador were brought to light in *Crockett v. Reagan*,* an action by twenty-nine members of Congress against the President, the secretary

---

[1] *New York Times*, Feb. 20, 1981, p. A1, col. 1 (quoting text of a State Department Document).

of defense, and the secretary of state for violations of the War Powers Clause of the Constitution and the War Powers Resolution.* The complaint was based on a requirement in the War Powers Resolution that, lacking a declaration of war, the President must report to Congress within forty-eight hours of any deployment of United States Armed Forces in a situation of actual or imminent hostilities and that, if Congress thereafter fails to authorize the deployment, the troops must be withdrawn within sixty days. While more than sixty days had passed since the military advisors had been assigned to El Salvador, the administration argued that it had received the necessary authorization by the passage in December 1981 of the International Security and Development Cooperation Act of 1981.* Section 728 of that act specifically authorizes military aid to El Salvador. However, because that section does not specifically constitute statutory authorization within the meaning of Section 8(a) of the War Powers Resolution, the district court correctly concluded that congressional authorization cannot be inferred.

Unfortunately, the court dismissed the suit without reaching the merits, deferring to the political forum for a solution. Nevertheless, the merits are easily argued and seem to weigh in favor of the Congressmen's case. The administration argued that the War Powers Resolution did not apply to military advisors in El Salvador because the advisors had not been "introduced into hostilities or into situations where imminent involvement in hostilities is clearly indicated by the circumstances." Indeed, the legislation authorizing the assignment of armed forces to El Salvador limited their functions to those under the Foreign Assistance Act of 1961 or the Arms Export Control Act, and the State Department assured that the advisors would not have a combat role.*

The definition of "hostilities" in the War Powers Resolution, however, was intended to be sufficiently broad to cover any assignment of military advisors to a country engaged in a civil war. The Senate report on its version of the War Powers Resolution makes clear the evil sought to be remedied.

> The purpose of this provision is to prevent secret, unauthorized military support activities and to prevent a repetition of many of the most controversial and regrettable activities in Indochina. The ever deepening ground combat involvement of the United States in South Vietnam began with the assignment of U.S. "advisors" to accompany South Vietnamese units on combat patrols; and in Laos, secretly and without congressional authorization, U.S. "advisors" were deeply engaged in the war. . . .*

Although President Reagan continually denied any comparison between El Salvador and Vietnam, the parallels are obvious and disconcerting. Revelations in the press indicated that United States troops were fighting "side by side" with government troops battling the leftists. In February 1982 a senior military advisor was filmed carrying an M-16 rifle; he was summarily dismissed, and four other advisors were severely reprimanded for disobeying orders not to carry offensive weapons. Even after one serviceman was injured in February 1983 and another killed by unidentified gunmen in San Salvador later that year, the administration maintained that those casualties were due to terrorist acts, not hostilities.

Congress initially acquiesced in the President's sending of the military advisors. However, when the State Department planned to increase the number of military advisors in El Salvador to 125, various legislative measures were introduced to ensure the participation of Congress in any decision to increase American involvement. Two House resolutions sought to amend the War Powers Resolution to require specific statutory authorization for the further introduction of United States troops into El Salvador.* A similar proposal before the Senate provided that United States troops could not be introduced into El Salvador for combat except under constitutionally recognized circumstances: a congressional declaration of war, specific legislative authorization, humanitarian evacuation of United States citizens, or defense of an imminent attack on the United States.* Another resolution sought to require the President to report to Congress under Section 4(a) of the War Powers Resolution, which would start the sixty-day clock ticking.* Although these resolutions did not pass, the President subsequently announced that the limit of American advisors in El Salvador would remain at fifty-five. Thus, Congress was able at least to preclude further executive excesses.

American involvement in Nicaragua presents equally pressing war powers issues as it becomes increasingly clear that the Reagan administration is waging a covert war in Nicaragua. The objectives of that war are unclear. President Reagan has stated:

> . . . let us be clear as to the American attitude toward the government of Nicaragua. We do not seek its overthrow. Our interest is to insure that it does not infect its neighbors through the export of subversion and violence. Our purpose, in conformity with American and international law, is to prevent the flow of arms to El Salvador, Honduras, Guatemala, and Costa Rica.*

On the other hand, a senior Pentagon official has stated: "We must prevent consolidation of a Sandinista regime in Nicaragua. . . . We seek victory for the forces of democracy."[2] Whatever the objectives, the Reagan administration has chosen means that violate the Constitution and laws of the United States.

In March 1982 the Reagan administration revealed aerial reconnaissance photographs showing a massive military buildup in Nicaragua. At the same time, the President authorized a nineteen-million-dollar CIA plan for covert

---

[2]*New York Times*, Sept. 12, 1983, p. A3, col. 1; *Washington Post*, Sept. 13, 1983, p. A12a (quoting the address by Fred C. Ikle, under-secretary of defense for policy, to Baltimore Council on Foreign Affairs).

operations. While the covert operations supposedly were limited to stopping the flow of arms from Cuba and Nicaragua to other Central American countries, mounting evidence indicated that the covert activities constituted the largest surreptitious CIA operation since Vietnam. (*New York Times*, July 25, 1983) Initially, the CIA was believed to have indirectly supported, through funds and training, Nicaraguan rebel forces known as "Contras," whose activities include sabotage against strategic bridges, oil storage and pipeline facilities, power stations, and military installations. Later, however, it was revealed that the CIA was directly involved in many of those activities, including even the mining of Nicaraguan harbors. (*New York Times*, July 25, 1983) President Reagan had approved a plan calling for CIA recruits to work with Contras on a "mother ship" from which speedboats carrying the primitive undersea mines accomplished the mining. The mines damaged vessels from several countries, and the operation was eventually discontinued, but not in time to prevent an international and domestic uproar.

Nicaragua proceeded against the United States in the World Court; the Soviet Union accused the United States of "piracy"; and members of Congress, including some of the Reagan administration's staunchest supporters, decried the mining as "an act violating international law . . . an act of war."[3] The United States responded by denying the jurisdiction of the World Court and offering the following justification for its admitted role in the harbor mining:

> The use of naval mines is one legitimate means of exercising [the] right of individual and collective self-defense in appropriate circumstances. For example, the proportionate use of naval mines can be a legitimate means of interrupting a flow of arms destined for infiltration into the territory of the victim, or to disrupt the flow of military and other materials essential to the attack's overall aggressive effort.*

That justification pushes the concept of self-defense beyond the limit and ignores the fact that mining harbors is an act of war justified, if at all, only between belligerents. (*237*, X, 676-79) The harbor mining here involved could also be construed as a blockade (*237*, X, 869-70)—clearly an act of war. The United States government has yet to produce evidence that its individual or collective security was threatened by arms flowing through Nicaragua's ports or that the mining had any success in interdicting the flow of arms. The mining was an unjustifiable violation of international law and was so recognized by the World Court in a ruling prohibiting further mining, as well as sanctioning the United States for its role in the illegal acts. (*New York Times*, May 11, 1984)

---

[3] Quoting letter by Senator Barry Goldwater to William Casey, director of the CIA, reprinted in *Congressional Quarterly Weekly Reports* (April 14, 1984), p. 833.

Besides violating international law, the harbor mining also violated United States constitutional and statutory law. As a unilateral executive act of war, it violated the doctrine of separation of powers, and as an interference with the government of a country with which the United States was at peace, it violated United States neutrality laws. In addition, although the facts are murky, it appears that Congress was not informed of the mining, as required by the Intelligence Oversight Act of 1980.* On April 10 the Senate passed a nonbinding resolution expressing its outrage at the incident and deploring further United States participation in such activities; an identical resolution passed the House two days later.* A supplemental aid package of twenty-one million dollars for CIA operations, which passed the Senate before the Nicaraguan explosion, was rejected in the House after the mining news became public. In the wake of the Nicaraguan harbor mining, the President faced an uphill battle to convince Congress that his Central American goals were attainable and his means desirable.

Another particularly egregious aspect of American support for anti-Sandinista rebels in Nicaragua is the training of hundreds of Cuban and Nicaraguan exiles in California and Florida. Press reports indicate that the exiles are given sophisticated paramilitary training using American weapons, then are sent to Nicaragua to carry out guerilla operations.

In December 1982 Congress attempted to curb covert training activities by amending the Defense Appropriations Bill to prohibit funding in support of any forces aiming to overthrow the Nicaraguan government.⁴ And in *Sanchez–Espinoza v. Reagan,** several members of Congress and several Nicaraguan and Floridian citizens challenged United States actions in Nicaragua as violations of, *inter alia*, the War Powers Resolution and the neutrality laws.* As in *Crockett v. Reagan*, the court dismissed the action as a political question and therefore did not reach the merits. The dismissal here was perhaps less justified, however, as Congress was left essentially without a remedy short of impeachment. In *Crockett*, the court felt that Congress could still enact legislation to curb the President's excesses; in *Sanchez–Espinoza*, the legislation was in place. The only alternative to a judicial determination that the President's acts were illegal was a congressional determination in an impeachment proceeding.

If the court had considered the merits of *Sanchez–Espinoza*, it could have found American involvement in Nicaragua illegal on several grounds,

---

⁴Known as the Boland Amendment, the measure states:

None of the funds provided in this Act may be used by the Central Intelligence Agency or the Department of Defense to furnish military equipment, military training or advice, or other support, for military activities, to any group or individual not part of a country's armed forces for the purpose of overthrowing the Government of Nicaragua or of provoking a military exchange between Nicaragua and Honduras. (Further Continuing Appropriations Act, 1983, Pub. L. No. 97–377, §793, 96 Stat. 1830, 1865 [1983]) although the War Powers Resolution would not have been particularly helpful. Indeed, while the resolution's backers sought to include language that would have "restricted the practice of employing regular or irregular forces to engage in 'proxy' wars to achieve policy objectives never specifically approved by Congress," that language was dropped before the resolution finally was adopted.* American training camps for exiles and covert operations in Nicaragua do, however, violate United States neutrality laws.[5] The Intelligence Authorization Act* empowers the President to undertake covert operations without congressional approval, but that authorization must be construed in the context of neutrality laws dating back to the foundation of the Republic.[6] One purpose of neutrality acts past and present is to insure congressional knowledge of, and participation in, decisions that might lead to war. That purpose was reiterated in the 1974 Hughes–Ryan Amendment requiring the President, in most instances, to give a full report of intelligence activities to the Senate and House Select Committees on Intelligence.*

During the 1984 presidential campaign, it was revealed that the CIA had been involved in the publication and distribution of a training manual for Nicaraguan contra rebels. (New York Times, Oct. 15, 1984) The manual instructed rebels regarding sabotage, blackmail, and "neutralization" of public officials through the "selective use of violence." Former intelligence officials and critics of the Reagan administration charged that such language referred to political assassinations as a means of undermining the Sandinista government, but President Reagan insisted that the manual contained no such instructions and that the whole incident was "much ado about nothing." (Facts on File, Oct. 19, 1984, p. 852) Six lower–echelon CIA employees allegedly responsible for the manual were dismissed, and the "teflon President" escaped another potentially disastrous situation en route to an unprecedented landslide election victory.

American involvement in Nicaragua is a case study in unilateral presidential war making. The confusion of Congress concerning the administration's policy illustrates the failure of the reporting requirements and highlights the continuing need for congressional involvement and authorization. Although Congress consistently has sought to play such a role, the President has used means that preclude congressional participation,

---

[5]For a thorough analysis of United States violation of neutrality laws by covert operations in Central America, see J. Lobel, "The Rise and Decline of the Neutrality Act: Sovereignty and Congressional War Powers in United States Foreign Policy," 24 Harv. Int'l L. J. (Summer 1983).

[6]The first neutrality law was enacted in 1794. One of its basic provisions imposed criminal sanctions on anyone who organized or initiated an attack from United States territory against any country with which the United States was at peace. Act of 5 June 1794, ch. 50, 1 Stat. 381, 383–84 (1794); see Lobel, "The Rise and Decline," p. 28.

violating a time–honored notion implied in the constitutional requirement that Congress declare war: the notion that war should be waged openly, not secretly. War should be conducted "not in an underhand and illicit way, but in a way consistent with the laws of war and becoming our national character."[7] Most recently, reports have surfaced that American military troops in civilian attire are heavily involved in the contra insurgency, in violation of every congressional directive. Bitter memories of Indochina remind us of the foolishness of war entered by stealth and waged without popular support.

Other United States military activities in Central America also raise constitutional issues. Most of those activities revolve around Honduras, which has become the staging area for United States involvement in the region. In addition to harboring United States–supplied insurgents for their sorties into neighboring Nicaragua, Honduras was the site of the largest United States military exercises ever conducted in Central America. Dubbed "Big Pine II," the series of exercises involved some 6,000 army and marine combat troops, 19 warships, and 140 fighter planes in mock amphibious landings and joint maneuvers with Honduran troops. The Big Pine exercises immediately elicited congressional concern, although the President repeat- edly claimed the maneuvers were "routine." Among the fears in Congress was that the naval exercises in the adjacent Caribbean would develop into a "military quarantine" to cut off arms shipments to Nicaragua, an act of war that the President refused to rule out to achieve the administration's Central American objectives. (New York Times, July 19, 1983) The Sandinistas expressed fears that Big Pine II was but another step toward an imminent United States invasion of Nicaragua.

Given those fears, Congress debated the applicability of the War Powers Resolution to the maneuvers. Senator Robert Byrd and others felt that the President at least should have consulted with Congress about the exercises. The only event approaching "consultation" was a luncheon on July 25 in which Senate Majority Leader Howard Baker and House Minority Leader Robert Michel were given the reasons for the President's planning of the exercises. Other congressional leaders felt that the President should be required to report maneuvers of that magnitude conducted in volatile regions like Central America. Senator Gary Hart introduced the War Powers in Central America bill, requiring a joint resolution of Congress or a written statement of the President requesting an increased military involvement in Central America. The bill would have allowed the escalation only if necessary to protect American lives or to respond to the danger of an attack on the United States.*

---

[7]H. R. Doc. No. 1282, 60th Cong., 2d Sess. 364 (1909) (quoting remarks of James Madison), reprinted in Lobel, "The Rise and Decline," p. 29.

Congress is partially to blame for executive excesses in Central America. Almost none of the corrective measures discussed above were enacted; rather, Congress has allowed the fifty–five military advisors to remain in El Salvador and has continued to fund the Americanization of civil wars in Central America, by at least half the amounts requested by the administration. However, the administration has exceeded even those overbroad grants of authority. The General Accounting Office has found evidence in Central America and the Caribbean that money appropriated for "operations and maintenance" of United States armed forces has in fact been used to establish permanent military sites in those areas. Apparently Congress authorized money for the temporary exigencies of Big Pine II, but several members of Congress, led by Senator James Sasser, believe those funds went to construct permanent air fields and support facilities in Palmerola and La Ceiba, Honduras, as well as on Tiger Island and other Caribbean locations. (*Salt Lake Tribune*, Feb. 28, 1983, p.4) Those installations reveal the administration's intentions to establish a long–term military presence in Central America—a presence that could eventually lead to all–out, undeclared, presidential war.

In short, the Reagan administration seems committed to do whatever is necessary to counter Communist influence in Central America, apparently including, if necessary, the use of American combat troops. Now is the time for Congress to act, to insure that any decision to unleash the dog of war in Central America is made only after deliberation and debate in a representative forum. In response to President Reagan's statement of Central American policy, Senator Christopher Dodd said:

> We can take the road of military escalation. But we really don't know what the next step will be, where it will lead or how much it will cost. This much, however, we do know. It will mean greater violence. It will mean greater bloodshed. It will mean greater hostilities. And, inevitably, the day will come when it will mean a regional conflict in Central America. When that day comes—when the "dogs of war" are loose in Central America . . . —we will know where the President's appeal for more American money and a deeper American commitment has taken us.[8]

The Reagan administration's battle against Communist expansionism rages on another front in our hemisphere—the Caribbean. The paramount interest of the United States in that region is the maintenance of vital shipping lanes and strategic military positions. But there are also political and ideological interests. While the Reagan administration tolerates—for the time being—the Soviet-backed Marxist regime in Cuba, it is determined not to tolerate any more "Cubas" in the Caribbean. On October 25, 1983, the strength of the administration's resolve became obvious.

[8]*New York Times*, April 28, 1983, p. A13, col. 1 (text of 9).

Grenada is a tiny Caribbean island known primarily—until recently—for its tranquil beaches and nutmeg. After gaining independence in 1974, Grenada was ruled by Sir Eric Gairy, a charismatic but authoritarian figure often compared to Haiti's notorious François "Papa Doc" Duvalier. Deteriorating social and economic conditions due to Gairy's excesses led to his downfall in 1979. Maurice Bishop, leader of the New Jewel (Joint Endeavor for Welfare, Education and Liberation) Movement, seized power and immediately undertook a pro-Communist, anti-American campaign. President Reagan's dislike for such Soviet-Cuban functionaries was already evident from the administration's Central American policy. Soviet and Cuban military activities in Grenada, as well as in Central America, were spotlighted in a March 10 Reagan address to the nation. The President showed photographs of various Soviet-style military installations under construction in Grenada. Of gravest concern was a 9,800-foot airstrip capable of accommodating military aircraft. While Bishop insisted that the airstrip was designed to expand Grenada's tourist industry, the administration suspected that the island "was a Soviet-Cuban colony being readied as a major military bastion to export terror and undermine democracy."*

After President Reagan announced the Caribbean Basin Initiative—the "Marshall Plan" of the Caribbean—Prime Minister Bishop began to seek improved relations with the United States. Perhaps in part because of those overtures, Bishop was ousted and eventually killed during a week-long coup in October 1983. The military council that replaced him, a stridently Marxist group which Reagan called "a brutal group of leftist thugs," suspended travel and communications and imposed a twenty-four hour, shoot-to-kill curfew.* The specter of the Iranian hostage crisis immediately rose to haunt administration officials concerned for the safety of about one thousand American citizens on the island. But perhaps more frightening was the possibility of another Communist stronghold in the Caribbean.

On October 22, 1983, a ten-ship United States task force enroute to Lebanon circled south toward Grenada. Three days later, an invasion force composed largely of crack United States combat troops, but including about three hundred constables and militiamen from eastern Caribbean nations, seized the island in a well-planned and skillfully executed early morning landing. Despite unexpected resistance from Cuban "construction workers" near the airstrip, the troops quickly took control of that site and moved to rescue American citizens near St. George's. Within a week the United States forces, which had swelled to about six thousand, flushed out remaining pockets of resistance and secured the island. The official toll of American forces: 19 dead and 115 wounded. "Operation Urgent Fury" was considered an unmitigated military success.

Because the government excluded media coverage of the invasion, news of the event came slowly and measuredly. At an early morning news conference on the day of the invasion, President Reagan announced only that United States and Caribbean forces had conducted "a landing or landings" in Grenada. The *caso belli*: "to protect our own citizens . . . and to aid in the restoration of . . . government institutions in Grenada."* Because information was scarce, the initial reaction, even from the administration's critics, was cautious and subdued. But as the story unfolded, legitimate questions surfaced.

The strongest justification for the intervention was to protect American citizens. The administration astutely emphasized that justification, invoking memories of blindfolded American hostages in Iran and charred bodies of United States soldiers in the Iranian desert. President Reagan said: "I believe our Government has a responsibility to go to the aid of its citizens if their right to life and liberty is threatened. The nightmare of our hostages in Iran must never be repeated."*

That belief has some legal foundation. Humanitarian intervention is a doctrine of international law allowing a state to intervene in the territory of another state in order to protect its nationals.[9] Extreme exigency must exist to justify what would otherwise be the most blatant possible violation of a state's sovereignty. There must be an immediate threat to the lives of the would-be intervenor state's nationals without any concomitant likelihood that the territorial state can or will protect those lives. Further, such intervention must be "non-political"; that is, it must not be aimed at toppling or otherwise affecting the government of the territorial state. In short, the intervening state must move quickly to rescue its own citizens and then withdraw.[10]

Since World War II, the doctrine of humanitarian intervention has fallen into disrepute because of its misuse by former colonial powers in attempting to reassert or continue influence over former colonies. The doctrine also has been used by the United States in its attempts to increase and justify its influence in the Caribbean. (The Soviet Union has justified its far more brutal interventions—whether by direct military invasion in Czechoslovakia and

[9]On the doctrine of humanitarian intervention, see: E. de Vattel, "Civil War"; J. S. Mill, "A Few Words on Non-Intervention"; M. Halpern, "The Morality and Politics of Intervention"; and W. Friedmann, "Intervention, Civil War and the Role of International Law"; in R. Falk, comp., *The Vietnam War and International Law*, vol. 1 of 4 vols. (Princeton: Princeton University Press, 1968). See also Clark, *28*.

[10]See I. Brownlie, "Humanitarian Intervention," and R. Lillich, "Humanitarian Intervention: A Reply to Dr. Brownlie and a Plea for Constructive Alternatives," in J. N. Moore, ed., *Law and Civil War in the Modern World* (Baltimore: Johns Hopkins Press, 1974). The paradigms of legitimate humanitarian intervention are found in the Israeli raid at Antebbe airport in Uganda and in the United States and Belgian rescue of their nationals from the Congo. See also E. B. Firmage, "Summary and Interpretation," in R. Falk, ed., *The International Law of Civil War* (Baltimore: Johns Hopkins Press, 1971), p. 405.

Afghanistan, or threat of the same in Poland—by different notions not based upon threats to its own nationals, notions such as the "Brezhnev Doctrine of Limited Sovereignty.")

In determining the legality of the American intervention in Grenada, an important issue is whether the United States nationals were in such danger as to require that drastic action. The administration's concerns centered on the "climate of fear and violence" that followed the October coup.* Intelligence reports were confused. No one seemed to know the true state of affairs on the island. Although General Hudson Austin, the putative leader of the revolutionary military council, had sent a note to the United States Embassy in Barbados assuring the safety of American citizens and also had released a statement promising continued efforts to improve relations with the United States, it was unclear whether he was in any position to make good those promises.

Still there were many indications that the Americans were in no immediate danger. Charles Modica, the chancellor of St. George's medical school where most of the Americans were located, was in New York during the coup and the subsequent invasion, but he reported having received repeated assurances that the students were safe. Modica initially said the invasion was "very unnecessary." (New York Times, Oct. 26, 1983) He was much less sure of himself after a private State Department briefing; that briefing apparently convinced him that the students were not, in fact, safe. Initial reports from the students themselves were likewise mixed, but those interviewed on their return to the United States seemed relieved and grateful to be out of Grenada, although they were unsure whether the intervention was necessary to save their lives. (New York Times, Oct. 27, 1983)

In retrospect, one might conclude that although the United States citizens may not have been in immediate danger, the administration was nonetheless justified to intervene on their behalf out of an understandable abundance of caution. The nature of the intervention, however, belies that conclusion. Such a wholesale invasion leaves little doubt about the administration's true motives. As one administration strategist observed, "There was no way this administration was going to miss a chance to kick Fidel where it hurts and take one back from the Communists." (82, 75) As early as March 1983 the Grenadian government had expressed fears that it was the target of an imminent American invasion. The Big Pine military maneuvers in August gave the United States forces timely training for their mission. The invasion itself was brilliantly staged and flawlessly performed. All of those facts raise doubts about the administration's claims that the intervention was initially considered only after the violent coup cast in doubt the safety of American citizens. More likely, the administration had been anticipating an opportunity to intervene and overthrow the regime for some time; the presence of American citizens in Grenada furnished that opportunity.

The President did not rely on the humanitarian intervention doctrine alone. His second justification was the urgent request of Grenada's eastern

Caribbean neighbors that the United States join them in an attempt to restore democracy to Grenada. That rationale does not comport with international law, and it clearly is not among the constitutionally recognized bases for unilateral presidential war making.

Congressional debate of the invasion's legality naturally centered on the War Powers Resolution. Section 3 of that resolution requires the President to consult with Congress "in every possible instance" before introducing United States troops into actual or imminent hostilities. That the invasion entailed actual or imminent hostilities is undeniable, so the issues were whether the President "consulted" with Congress and, if not, whether consultation was impossible in this instance.

Testimony by a senior State Department official confirmed that the President signed the directive ordering the invasion at 6:00 P.M. on October 24.* At 8:00 P.M. the President met with the bipartisan leadership of Congress to inform them of his decision. The invasion began at 5:30 A.M. the next day. The administration insisted that the President's meeting with the bipartisan congressional leadership satisfied the consultation requirement. But one ranking member of the Senate Foreign Relations committee who was not even invited to the meeting commented, "There is a world of difference between being consulted and being asked do we think this is wise or not, or being informed, saying we are doing this at 5 A.M. tomorrow."*

A stronger justification for the President's failure to consult is that consultation was not possible in the circumstances. In his address to the nation the President said, "We knew that we had little time and that complete secrecy was vital to insure both the safety of the young men who would undertake this mission and the Americans they were about to rescue."* Even many high-level administration officials seem to have been unaware of the planned invasion. Congressional leaders were summoned to the White House secretly and in person. Thus the media was effectively kept in the dark. Secrecy indeed was essential to the success of the invasion. However, the President at least should have consulted secretly with members of Congress, as he did with his own staff and executive branch officers. In that way the decision to undertake the invasion could have followed more closely the constitutional procedure.

Even if secrecy demanded unilateral executive action before the invasion, the President should have sought congressional ratification after the invasion. Therefore, the real war powers issue centers on the reporting requirement of Section 4(a) (1), which triggers the sixty-day time limit of Section 5(b). The former section requires the President to report to Congress any time troops are introduced into actual or imminent hostilities and to remove the troops within sixty days of that report unless Congress indicates otherwise. The Reagan administration refused to acknowledge the validity of that requirement—a refusal that was to be a major issue in the executive-legislative tug-of-war over the marines in Lebanon, discussed later in the chapter.

President Reagan did report to Congress after the invasion of Grenada. That report stated:

> In accordance with my desire that the Congress be informed on this matter, and consistent with the War Powers Resolution, I am providing this report on the deployment of the United States Armed Forces. . . . This deployment . . . is being undertaken pursuant to my constitutional authority with respect to the conduct of foreign relations and as Commander–in–Chief. . . .*

The report did not refer to Section 4(a) (1), indicating that the President did not recognize any duty to withdraw the troops within sixty days if Congress had not acted. The administration was able to avoid challenging that provision directly by insisting that the troops would be withdrawn well within the sixty–day limit. When asked whether the administration asserted the authority to keep the troops in Grenada beyond the sixty–day limit should the President so decide, an administration official said: "The administration position is that we do not have a position on that question. We think there are very serious constitutional issues involved that should not be debated in the abstract in hypothetical questions."*

When the President failed to report specifically under Section 4(a) (1), the House adopted a measure declaring that the resolution's time limit became operative on October 25, 1983, giving the President until December 25 to withdraw the troops. Concerned that such a measure acknowledged a unilateral war–making power in the President, several members of Congress, led by Congressman Ted Weiss of New York, urged more Draconian measures. One declared that the President had violated the constitutional prerogative of Congress to declare war and demanded that United States troops be withdrawn immediately from Grenada. Another impeached President Reagan for "the high crime or misdemeanor of ordering the invasion of Grenada in violation of the Constitution of the United States."*

The impeachment resolution never really had a chance to pass. Nevertheless, it illustrates the frustration of those who understand the Constitution's allocation of the war powers and seek to restore Congress with its proper role. The invasion of Grenada was not only a military success but also a political success for the Reagan administration. A majority of Americans polled after the invasion approved of the United States participation.[11] Introducing the impeachment resolution, Congressman Weiss stated: "Perhaps as distressing as the constitutional violations engaged in by Mr. Reagan is the seeming acceptance of his actions by so many Americans. I hope that introduction of the impeachment resolution will help

---

[11]According to a *Newsweek* poll, fifty–three percent of those questioned approved of the invasion. *Newsweek* (Nov. 7, 1983), p. 65.

to stir a broad public debate on the constitutional principles on which America is founded."*

The invasion of Grenada showed the Reagan administration's resolve to preserve democracy in the hemisphere. Its success should not dim its serious constitutional and practical ramifications. Indeed, if the operation had not been successful, the public and political reaction might well have been much different. The legality and wisdom of the President's foreign policy decisions that involve the war powers should not be determined by immediate popular, nationalistic response to military success.

That unilateral executive war making can result in disaster is painfully obvious from the Reagan administration's placing of United States Marines in Lebanon. The President committed those troops to a hopeless cause without authorization from, or discussion with, Congress. The result was a two-year tug-of-war and a complete foreign policy failure.

President Reagan first deployed United States troops to war-ravaged Lebanon in August of 1982. About eight hundred United States Marines were sent to Beirut, the nation's capital, as part of a multinational force whose mission was to oversee the evacuation of Palestinian guerillas. The Palestinians were one of several foreign influences in Lebanon's continuous struggle to restore peace and democracy to the one Middle Eastern country that had enjoyed both until a bloody civil conflict erupted in the mid-1970s. Claiming constitutional authority to conduct foreign affairs and to act as commander in chief of the armed forces, President Reagan notified Congress that the marines would serve a short-lived, peaceful mission and then be withdrawn.*

Although the marines successfully completed that mission and left Beirut within about three weeks, three tragic events led to their return a month later. Bashir Gemayel, a rightist Christian leader, had been elected President of Lebanon, bringing hope for moderation and compromise among the country's various foreign-backed factions. But in September Gemayel was assassinated in a bomb blast at his party headquarters. The following day Israeli tanks and troops rolled into West Beirut, the city's Moslem stronghold, disregarding the protestations of the Lebanese government, the United States, and the United Nations. Then, on September 17, hundreds of Palestinian refugees were executed at two camps outside Beirut. Christian militiamen were responsible for the slaughter, but the advancing Israelis were also implicated. Lebanon was in crisis.

The Italian government, which had contributed troops to the earlier evacuation effort, asked the United States and France to join it in sending a "multinational peacekeeping force" (MNF) back to Beirut. The Lebanese government joined in the request. On September 20 President Reagan announced that about 1200 United States Marines would be redeployed in Lebanon as part of the MNF. On September 29, the day the first detachment arrived in Beirut, the President informed Congress of the marines' mission.

In identical letters to the House and Senate, the President said:

> Consistent with the War Powers Resolution, I am hereby providing a report on the deployment and mission [of the marines]. This deployment . . . is being undertaken pursuant to the President's constitutional authority with respect to the conduct of foreign relations and as Commander-in-Chief of the United States Armed Forces.*

It is worth noting here that the asserted basis for this deployment, as well as for the invasion of Grenada, does not pass constitutional muster. The President's authority with respect to the conduct of foreign relations is collegial authority to be exercised in concert with, not contrary to, congressional foreign policy authority. The President's constitutional authority as commander in chief is limited to the direction and conduct of hostilities following a congressional declaration of war or other congressional authorization. Also, as he had done when reporting the invasion of Grenada, the President refused to refer specifically to Section 4(a)(1) of the War Powers Resolution. The administration's position was that the resolution's "clock" did not start ticking when the marines were redeployed because the marines would not be involved in hostilities or imminent hostilities.

The original agreement for United States involvement in the MNF provided for an "interposition force" whose purpose was "to provide the multinational presence requested by the Lebanese Government to assist it and the Lebanese Armed Forces in the Beirut area."[12] That broad description of the marine role gave Congress no indication of whether the situation involved hostilities or imminent hostilities. The President's report to Congress, however, did guarantee that the marines would not engage in combat, although they would be equipped and authorized to act in self-defense.

After the marines had been in Lebanon nearly a year, intense fighting erupted among the warring factions. The marines were fired upon, and several were killed. The President again reported to Congress "consistent with the War Powers Resolution" but refused to acknowledge "hostilities" that would trigger the Section 4(a)(1) time limit. On September 1, 1983, the President instructed a large and potent naval task force to position itself off the coast of Lebanon. As the fighting in Beirut intensified, and the marines came under increasing fire, the President authorized tactical air strikes and artillery fire from the navy gunboats against Syrian positions in the mountains east of Beirut, positions that seemed to be the origin of the attacks on the marines. Congress, which until then had acquiesced in the President's deployment of the marines, began to stir.

The constitutional crisis that the President had deftly avoided in Grenada was now imminent. Although Congress had passed the Lebanon Emergency

[12]*Department of State Bulletin* 84 (September 1982), p. 4.

Assistance Act of 1983 on June 27, 1983, that act, by its own terms, did not constitute congressional authorization within the meaning of the War Powers Resolution.[13] Therefore, the President technically was in a situation where the War Powers Resolution would require him to withdraw the marines from Lebanon. That, he consistently said, he would not do. The President and his political allies wanted unfettered discretion over the use of the marines in Lebanon; his political foes wanted the marines withdrawn, or at least wanted the President to report specifically under Section 4(a) (1). Neither alternative seemed possible, so a compromise was reached in the Multinational Force in Lebanon Resolution on September 29, 1983.* To satisfy the President, the resolution authorized the marines' continued participation in the MNF for a period of eighteen months. The administration considered that length of time sufficient to assure the Lebanese government of American support and to signal to Syria and other foreign forces in Lebanon the strength of bipartisan American resolve. To satisfy Democrats in Congress, the resolution specified that Section 4(a)(1) of the War Powers Resolution became operative on August 29, 1983, the day two American marines were killed in Beirut. The resolution also limited the marines' role to that outlined in the original MNF agreement but allowed "such protective measures as may be necessary to insure the safety of the Multinational Force in Lebanon." That provision was designed to permit continued tactical air support and offshore artillery barrages in defense of the marine positions, but it did not allow such support for the Lebanese Armed Forces. (*Washington Post*, Sept. 9, 1983)

President Reagan signed the Multinational Force in Lebanon Resolution into law on October 12, 1983. In doing so, however, he expressed grave doubts as to the constitutionality of certain of its provisions. His statement is worth quoting at length.

> I would note that the initiation of isolated or infrequent acts of violence against United States Armed Forces does not necessarily constitute actual or imminent involvement in hostilities, even if casualties to those forces result. I think it reasonable to recognize the inherent risk and imprudence of setting any precise formula for making such determinations.
>
> Nor should my signing be viewed as any acknowledgment that the President's constitutional authority can be impermissibly infringed by statute, that congressional authorization would be required if and when the period specified in Section 5(b) of the War Powers Resolution might be deemed to have been triggered and the period had expired or that Section 6 of the Multinational Force in Lebanon Resolution may be

[13]The Act provides, "Nothing in this section is intended to modify, limit, or suspend any of the standards and procedures prescribed by the War Powers Resolution." Pub. L. No. 98–43, 97 Stat. 214, 98th Cong., 1st Sess. (1983).

interpreted to revise the President's constitutional authority to deploy United States armed forces.*

Thus, President Reagan refused to concede that congressional authorization is required before the President constitutionally can deploy the United States Armed Forces in situations like those in Central America, Grenada, and Lebanon.

Although Congress did authorize continued United States participation in the MNF, it cannot truly be said to have done so voluntarily. Once the President unilaterally committed the Marines, Congress faced a no-win situation. To authorize continued participation was in a way to acknowledge the President's power to deploy the armed forces, but to demand withdrawal was either to precipitate a standoff between coordinate branches of government or to signal weakness to Lebanon, the other multinational force members, and Lebanon's foreign invaders. As Senator Paul E. Tsongas of Massachusetts lamented when the marines were redeployed: "There's a sense that we're getting into a quagmire. We don't have a choice, but how are we going to get those troops out again once they go in?" (*Washington Post*, Sept. 9, 1983)

A quagmire indeed. In the early morning hours of October 23, 1983, a truck bulging with explosives penetrated the United States Marine compound and exploded into the barracks, killing over two hundred sleeping marines and injuring many others. That single act at once epitomized both the danger and helplessness the marines faced. Their leaders were frustrated and ashamed at placing crack United States troops, known for their skill and bravery, in a situation where they could do nothing but invite disaster. In the wake of the attack, artillery once again roared, this time in the form of the huge 16mm guns of the battleship *New Jersey*.

President Reagan viewed the attack not for what it was—an act of civil war directed against what had now tragically and unnecessarily become an obviously partisan participant—but as another manifestation of the worldwide Communist conspiracy. The vital and natural role for the United States as a neutral peacemaker offering itself as mediator had been destroyed in a spectacular act of presidential ignorance and misjudgment. In a nationwide address after the fateful week that saw crises involving American troops on both sides of the globe, the President charged:

> The events in Lebanon and Grenada, though oceans apart, are closely related. Not only has Moscow assisted and encouraged the violence in both countries, but it provides direct support through a network of surrogates and terrorists.*

Such a Manichean mindset not only demonstrates ignorance of the complexities of world history and the causes of world conflict but also borders on paranoia. In addition, it furnishes a too-convenient rationale for presidential war making whenever the ubiquitous "enemy" rears its head and threatens American "interests."

The marines eventually withdrew from Lebanon early in 1984. As was inevitable, the United States–backed Christian government was forced to the bargaining table with Moslems and other groups seeking representation in their country's government. In a final, unconstitutional act of war, the battleship *New Jersey* opened fire in a futile attempt to bolster Lebanon's rapidly defecting armed forces. When the secretary of the navy carelessly acknowledged that the shelling was not to protect American troops but to aid the Lebanese Army, he was quickly brought back into line. He then asserted that the guns were in fact defending the marines, who by that time were largely evacuated, or "redeployed," to ships offshore. (*Facts on File*, Feb. 10, 1984, p.84)

The administration refused to admit that it had failed in Lebanon. Indeed, administration officials blamed Congress for interfering by using the War Powers Resolution and thus preventing the outcome that the President had desired.* More probably, had Congress "interfered" from the beginning, the United States might have been able to perform a role for which it was ideally suited—neutral peacemaker offering good offices and mediation through diplomatic means, rather than through military adventurism, for peaceful resolution of disputes. And hundreds of Americans would still be alive.

In summary, both the President and Congress are responsible for the continued violations of the war power in the Reagan administration. The President has acted unconstitutionally by unilaterally exercising the war power in the following instances: sending "military advisors" to El Salvador; conducting covert paramilitary operations in Nicaragua; sponsoring American-trained Central American exiles to destabilize the Nicaraguan government; ordering extraordinary, large–scale military facilities with funds authorized for other purposes; invading Grenada; and committing the marines to Lebanon. Congress, for its part, has been unconstitutionally generous in allowing the military advisors to remain; funding covert activities; failing to condemn by resolution or even to impeach the President for the invasion of Grenada; and bargaining away its rightful control over the marines in Lebanon.

Chapter 17

THE WAR POWER
IN THE NUCLEAR AGE

The modern shift in the balance of the war power from Congress to the President in disregard of the Constitution raises weighty practical questions. For example, given that the nature of war has changed radically from what the founders envisioned when drafting the Constitution, is their Whiggish bias relevant and practical today? If so, how might the constitutional balance be restored? Answering the first question requires analyzing the nature of war in the nuclear age to determine whether secrecy and dispatch, inherent in the presidency, or deliberation and debate, hallmarks of Congress, are the most desirable decision-making attributes. Answering the second question requires scrutinizing the various ways Congress might reassert itself—the most fundamental, legitimate, and ultimately effective of which is impeachment. This chapter will pursue those two questions.

The advent of nuclear weapons poses a constitutional dilemma. As we have seen in previous chapters, the Constitution entrusts the war power to Congress, leaving the President only limited authority to act unilaterally in extraordinary situations, such as in repelling a surprise attack on United States territory. That allocation of the war power reflects the framers' desire that deliberation and debate be brought to bear on any decision so momentous as to commit the nation to war. On the other hand, the nature of war in the nuclear age seems to preclude the luxury of deliberation and debate, requiring instead secrecy and dispatch. Thus, many today advocate a strong President unfettered by the procedural formalities of what they consider to be an anachronistic allocation, ill-suited to the exigencies of the

modern world. "The heightened pace, complexity and hazards of contemporary events often require rapid and clear decisions. The Nation must be able
to act flexibly and, in certain circumstances, without prior publicity. The
institutional advantages of the presidency, which are especially important
in the area of foreign affairs, were pointed out in *The Federalist*: the unity of
office, its capacity for secrecy and dispatch, and its superior sources of
information."*

That argument, on its face, has a certain appeal. The Cuban missile crisis
is an example of the value of secrecy and dispatch in modern foreign
affairs—and of the seeming impracticability of the cumbersome constitutional allocation. Close analysis, however, reveals the need, now more than
ever, for deliberation and debate before committing the nation to war or
taking any step toward it. Although cumbersome, the constitutional
allocation reflects the framers' belief that war is a tremendous evil to be
avoided. That belief is greatly strengthened when war extends beyond the
field of combat to imperil innocent noncombatants and to threaten mankind
itself, as does nuclear war. The framers' judgment, inescapably value-laden,
was that, in matters of war and peace—now writ large, in matters of
extinction and survival—collective conscience, rather than individual whim,
must prevail. If the framers were chary of permitting the President to wield
muskets and sail ships, surely we must pause to consider the wisdom of
allowing him to unilaterally control the vast nuclear arsenal.

Nuclear weapons change the nature of war in several ways, all of which
point to the need for adherence to the constitutional allocation of the war
power. First and most obviously, nuclear weapons qualitatively differ from
any other weapons ever known. The destructiveness of nuclear weapons is
easy to state but difficult to comprehend. A single nuclear bomb from a single
bomber inflicted on Hiroshima a degree of devastation unequalled even by
the thousands of conventional bombs dropped on Tokyo from hundreds of
bombers over several weeks. That one bomb, however, packing the
equivalent explosive power of 12.5 kilotons of TNT, was small in comparison
to today's nuclear devices, which measure explosive force in megatons (the
equivalent of one thousand kilotons, or one million tons of TNT). The world's
nuclear arsenals contain about six thousand times the explosive power
unleashed during World War II—all the shells, all the incendiary bombs,
and all the Hiroshima and Nagasaki bombs combined. So powerful and
deadly are today's weapons that the warheads from a single modern
submarine could destroy 160 separate targets, unleashing some six megatons
of explosive force—more than twice as much as all the weapons of World
War II.[1]

---

[1]Excellent studies citing these and other data are found in *World Armaments and
Disarmament*, SIPRI Yearbook 1982 (London: Taylor & Francis, Ltd., 1982), and R.
L. Sivard, *World Military and Social Expenditures 1982* (Leesburg, Va.: World Priorities,
1982).

Not only nuclear weapons themselves, but also modern delivery systems have developed to an incredible degree. In the framers' day, transportation and communication were primitive; the war machine was slow and cumbersome. The railroad and the airplane revolutionized war in their respective eras, but even so, the *Enola Gay* (the B–29 bomber that delivered the A–bomb over Hiroshima) required six and a half hours to cover its 1,700–mile journey. By contrast, modern ICBM's (intercontinental ballistic missiles) can travel six to eight thousand miles in less than thirty minutes, and IRBM's (intermediate–range ballistic missiles) can reach Moscow from western Europe in just six minutes. In addition, sophisticated nuclear–powered submarines patrol the oceans with potent warheads just minutes from any major city, and long-range bombers sit ready to scramble at a moment's notice.

Nuclear weapons have changed the nature of war by these unique qualities, and also by their vast quantities and their diffusion among many countries. Vertical proliferation refers to the aggregation of nuclear weapons stockpiles far in excess of any arms race in history. Those stockpiles currently contain some fifty to sixty thousand nuclear weapons—a number that represents an overkill of many degress for every person on earth. Horizontal proliferation refers to the spread of nuclear weapons among many nations. Besides the six known nuclear actors—the United States, the Soviet Union, China, Great Britain, France, and India—several other nations, including many unstable regimes, probably have built nuclear weapons or could do so in the near future. As weapons proliferate vertically and horizontally, the likelihood of war by accident increases, as does the possibility of such weapons falling into the hands of terrorists.

Until recently, military planners and strategists calculated their scenarios on the basis of a scientific understanding of the direct effects of nuclear weapons. Hiroshima and Nagasaki furnish a text, albeit incomplete, for those effects.[2] The Hiroshima and Nagasaki bombs were exploded five hundred to six hundred meters in the air. The initial explosions each produced a supersonic shock wave followed by a powerful wind. Then, after an instant of deadly stillness, a fierce wind blew in the opposite direction. The flash of the explosions was so intensely hot that most people caught within a mile of the hypocenters were instantly vaporized. The intense heat spontaneously ignited hundreds of fires in both cities. Seventy to eighty thousand people in Hiroshima, and about forty thousand in Nagasaki, were killed immediately from flying debris, collapsing buildings, flash burns, burns from blazing structures, immediate irradiation, and instant vaporization. Extrapolating from Hiroshima and Nagasaki, and taking into account the vastly increased destructive power of modern weapons, recent studies estimate that an all–out

---

[2]See *The Effects of the Atomic Bombs on Hiroshima and Nagasaki*, The United States Strategic Bombing Survey (Washington, D.C.: U.S. Government Printing Office, 1946).

nuclear exchange would immediately kill approximately 1.1 billion people.[3]

Beyond the direct effects of an all–out nuclear exchange lies what has been called the "ultimate pandemic."[4] The unfortunate survivors of a nuclear war would contract radiation sickness, a debilitation symptomized by hair loss, scarring, vomitting, and, for many, death. Even non–lethal doses of radiation seriously impair the body's ability to recover from burns and other traumatic injuries. Various cancers can be expected to surface in the survivors and in their progeny. Facilities and personnel to treat immediate and lingering ailments caused by radiation would be woefully inadequate in the wake of a nuclear war due to the heavy concentration of hospitals and doctors in targeted urban areas. The effects of radiation nearly doubled the number of deaths in Hiroshima and Nagasaki by the end of 1945. Thus another billion or so people could be expected to die within months of a nuclear war. Combined with the immediate fatalities, one–half of the world's population would be wiped out.

As if such staggering destruction were insufficient to render nuclear war unthinkable, recent studies on the climatological and biological effects of nuclear war reveal that even a limited nuclear exchange—perhaps as small as one hundred megatons in the form of airbursts over cities—could plunge the world into a "nuclear winter" that surely would devastate civilization and perhaps would extirpate life on Earth.[5] The studies, spearheaded by Carl Sagan and Paul Ehrlich and inspired by *Mariner 9*'s discovery of the effects of a Martian duststorm on the surface and atmospheric conditions of that planet, used knowledge gathered from the study of volcanic eruptions on Earth to postulate the consequences of nuclear explosions. The studies indicate that dust–generating surface and near–surface detonations would loft tremendous quantities of radioactive debris into the atmosphere, creating a Mars–like dust cloud. In addition, attacks on urban centers would ignite

[3]See "Effects of the Use of Nuclear Weapons," Group of Experts, Report of the Secretary General of the United Nations, in B. H. Weston, ed., *Toward Nuclear Disarmament and Global Security: A Search for Alternatives* (Boulder: Westview Press, 1984), pp. 29–56.

[4]The expression "ultimate pandemic" was spawned by a seminal article in the 1962 *New England Journal of Medicine* which for the first time detailed the medical nightmare that would follow a nuclear war. Physicians for Social Responsibility, an international organization dedicated to preventing the ultimate pandemic, continues to study and speak out on the medical consequences of nuclear war. One need not be a physician, however, to understand that if our most modern burn and trauma centers are overwhelmed by relatively small fires and explosions, current medical facilities simply could not deal with the medical consequences of nuclear war.

[5]The studies appear in two articles in *Science* magazine: R. P. Turco, et al., "Nuclear Winter: Global Consequences of Multiple Nuclear Explosions," *Science* 222 (Dec. 23, 1983), p. 1283; and P. R. Ehrlich, et al., "Long–Term Biological Consequences of Nuclear War," *Science* 222 (Dec. 23, 1983), p. 1293.

vast fires fueled by oil and gas, coal, wood, and toxic chemicals, generating in a few days the rough equivalent of an entire year's worth of worldwide smoke emissions. Within one or two weeks, the individual plumes of dust and soot would coalesce into an enormous black cloud shrouding most of the Northern Hemisphere and blocking from ninety-five to ninety-nine percent of the Earth's sunlight. Dust particles, which are relatively heavy, could be expected to settle out of the atmosphere in a few weeks, but the lighter, more opaque smoke particles might remain aloft in the upper atmosphere for several months.

With most of the Earth's sunlight thus blocked, surface temperatures would plunge well below freezing in whatever season the exchange occurred. Because propagation of these atmospheric effects from the northern mid-latitudes to the tropics and even to the Southern Hemisphere is possible, the entire globe could become cold, dark, and inhospitable to all life. In addition, the enormous fireballs accompanying nuclear blasts would rend vast holes in the Earth's protective ozone layer, allowing nearly twice the normal penetration of ultraviolet radiation.

Given those atmospheric consequences, the studies concluded that "the environment that will confront most human beings and other organisms will be so altered and so malign that extreme and widespread damage to living systems is inevitable."[6] Under the smoke-shrouded skies of nuclear winter, light intensities would be too low to permit growth in plants, since photosynthetic activity is proportional to the amount of sunlight received. Marine ecosystems, long considered a viable resource for the survivors of even a massive nuclear exchange, would be similarly devastated, since marine phytoplankton, the photosynthesizing base of those ecosystems, are highly susceptible to prolonged darkness.

Unseasonably cold temperatures would severely damage even the hardiest of plants and animals. Ice one to two meters thick would form on inland bodies of water. Even after temperatures returned to normal, increased ultraviolet radiation through the rent ozone might blind many animals and burn many sensitive plants. Fallout would severely damage sensitive conifer forests of central importance in the biosphere, would severely affect even the hardiest crops, and would irradiate birds and mammals. Only pests and radiation-resistant insects would survive, carrying deadly plagues to the unfortunate survivors of the initial blasts. No society or species would be unaffected. As the studies grimly concluded, "extinction of the human species itself cannot be excluded."[7]

[6]A. Ehrlich, "Nuclear Winter: A Forecast of the Climatic and Biological Effects of Nuclear War," *Bulletin of the Atomic Scientists* 40 (April 1984), p. 18s (quoting P. R. Ehrlich).

[7]Ehrlich, "Long-Term Biological Consequences," p. 1293.

So frightening is the prospect of nuclear holocaust, so threatening to basic human instinct is the thought of extirpation of our species, that most people choose to dismiss nuclear war as "unthinkable." Yet world leaders do think about nuclear war. Such doctrines as "first use," "launch on warning," and "counterforce targeting," and such weapons as "first–strike" missiles, with sufficient accuracy and payload to destroy an enemy's land–based nuclear weaponry, have created a doomsday machine that could transform war into a catastrophe which no value system, no civilization, and, perhaps, no life on earth would survive. It is argued that no sane person would consider using nuclear weapons, yet war games act out the scenarios, and new offensive weapons systems make those scenarios more possible than ever. Surely the wisdom of the framers is unassailable: deliberation and debate are essential before this nation commits itself to those initial steps toward nuclear war that, once taken, may not be retraceable. Congressional powers over the conduct of foreign relations and, ultimately, the war power, must be invoked before the state becomes committed to a course of conduct that is deterministic and irreversible, a course that allows no alternative to nuclear war.

Obviously, however, in the face of a nuclear attack this country's political leadership would have only minutes to act. Congress simply could not assemble to debate the appropriate response. The constitutional allocation of the war powers does recognize the President's power to defend the country from imminent attack; indeed that power is essential if deterrence is to be at all effective. Still, once a nuclear attack is underway, deterrence has failed and defense is impossible. Thus Congress might perform a vital role in formulating policies that, in a time of crisis, will allow some degree of rationality to prevail. For example, while the threat of retaliation is essential to effective deterrence, it is not clear that actual retaliation would ever be a rational course of conduct. A top–level congressional committee could be formed to work closely with executive officers to secretly define the conditions, if any, under which a retaliatory strike should be ordered so that the fateful decision to destroy millions of innocent people will not be made unilaterally and irrationally.

More likely than the first–strike scenario is the first use of nuclear weapons by the United States in response to a conventional Soviet invasion of western Europe. In such a case the limited constitutional exception does not apply, and therefore Congress must be involved in any decision to order the first use of nuclear weapons. Jeremy Stone has argued that any decision to cross the nuclear threshold constitutes not merely an expansion of an ongoing conventional conflict but the commencement of a whole new war, thus necessitating a declaration of war or some other congressional authorization.[8] Stone encourages the formation of a "nuclear planning

[8] J. Stone, "Presidential First Use is Unlawful," *Foreign Policy* 56 (Fall 1984), pp. 94–112.

committee" of Congress to work closely with the President's coterie of national security advisors in a time of crisis. The committee could work expeditiously and, if necessary, secretly; it would also be vested with a veto power to prohibit first use pursuant to the war power of Congress.

Congress also can exercise considerable influence in lessening the threats—attributable to vertical and horizontal proliferation—of war by accident or by insanity. For example, Congress could freeze the number of nuclear weapons at present levels and enact policies against the spread of nuclear weapons technology. The President, as executive officer of congressional policies, would be bound to follow the leadership of Congress.

The need for quick, decisive executive action perhaps has been exaggerated in recent years to justify unilateral presidential war making under circumstances in which Congress might not otherwise acquiesce. With the possible and only partial exception of the Cuban missile crisis, an extraordinary situation, there have been few instances in our history "where the use of warmaking powers by the Executive without authority of Congress was clearly and incontrovertibly required by the nature of the emergency which the nation faced, . . . on the contrary in almost every instance the long run interests of the Nation would have been better promoted by consultation and delay."* Certainly speed was not the framers' goal. "It is important to keep in mind that speed and efficiency are not the proper ends of government; if they were the framers could have created a totalitarian state."*

As to the need for secrecy, no doubt many scenarios can be imagined where secrecy would be a paramount concern. But here too there is room for abuse by an executive afraid that, were his plans revealed, Congress simply would not acquiesce. Conceding that full-blown congressional involvement may be impractical in many foreign policy decisions, Congress still has established a few representative, bipartisan committees to act in conjunction with the executive branch on important foreign policy matters. The power and the number of such committees should be increased. And representatives of the executive administration should regularly report to Congress and submit to the most intimate and candid questioning. One need not move to "responsible government" on a British or continental model to see the need of this. Surely such a policy is congruent with a system of powers separated and balanced—especially in the conduct of foreign policy, which is based upon the presumption of collegial decision making by Congress and the President.

It is now more important than ever that Congress assume its proper constitutional role in controlling the war powers, yet how will it do so? Even if every constitutional argument is brought to bear against unilateral presidential war making, that practice is likely to continue. After nearly four decades of congressional acquiescence resulting in foreign policy disasters in Vietnam, Lebanon, and Central America, Congress must act soon to rein in the President, or further disasters surely will follow.

Congress possesses several means of controlling presidential excesses. First, Congress controls the budget. Refusing to fund certain projects can constitute a powerful bargaining chip. Perhaps more important, by its power to raise and support armies Congress theoretically can control United States troops and prevent the President's military forays. Unfortunately, that control often is ineffective because Congress must fund the armed forces to preserve America's legitimate defense needs, and those same forces remain at the President's disposal. The invasion of Grenada in October 1983 was neither authorized nor specifically funded by Congress, yet the President was able to employ the standing armed forces nonetheless. Even if Congress legitimately seeks to control the use of the armed forces by restricting funding to certain military activities, the President might go beyond congressional limits. For example, Government Accounting Office reports indicate that funds specifically approved for temporary training facilities in connection with the Big Pine II military exercises in Honduras were used instead for more permanent facilities, in violation of express congressional restrictions. Also, funds approved for covert CIA operations to halt the flow of arms from Nicaragua to El Salvador were diverted instead to activities, such as mining Nicaraguan harbors, that had little if any connection with the purpose for which the funds were authorized. Thus, although Congress controls the nation's purse strings, those strings furnish too weak a tether to effectively reign in the President.

Congress possesses another potentially important control over presidential excesses in foreign policy: the power of advice and consent. The Constitution (art. II, § 2) provides that the President is to make treaties and appoint foreign policy personnel with the advice and consent of the Senate. Thus, by withholding consent to important appointments and treaties, Congress could manifest its displeasure with the President's foreign policy. The framers intended that the President and the Congress act together in making foreign policy; therefore, they gave Congress a prominent role in the treaty process—the most important foreign policy process of their time. That prominent role increasingly has been undermined in recent years by the growing use of executive agreements, which are not subject to the advice and consent of the Senate. Congress should seek to restore its constitutional role in foreign policy matters by restricting the President's power to conduct foreign policy by executive agreement. But much more important, the general intent reflected in the mandate of collegial treaty making—that foreign policy generally be so conducted—is as wise and as much to be desired now as it was in the eighteenth century.

Congress also possesses various formal means of expressing its disapproval with executive conduct, including "sense of Congress" resolutions and formal censures. Throughout the ordeal of the United States Marines in Lebanon, some members of Congress urged such measures against the President for committing the troops without prior congressional approval. Similarly, following revelations of American involvement in the mining of Nicaraguan harbors, a flagrant violation of United States and international law, Congress overwhelmingly passed a nonbinding resolution deploring that involvement.* Such measures proved ineffective against President Reagan, however, who simply used them to illustrate the congressional "interference" to which he attributed his administration's foreign policy mistakes.

Until recently, the legislative veto proved a more or less effective means for Congress to exert control over the executive. The legislative veto allowed Congress to have the last word on the execution of its laws. Many pieces of legislation, including the War Powers Resolution, contained legislative veto provisions that allowed one or both houses of Congress to check execu-tive actions conducted contrary to the will of Congress. Often challenged as violative of the President's veto power and the doctrine of separation of powers, the legislative veto was held unconstitutional in *Immigration and Naturalization Service v. Chadha* which disallowed unicameral congressional reversal of a Justice Department nondeportation ruling.* The broad language of the case, however, probably prohibits Congress from using one of its most effective tools against presidential excesses.

Another means that Congress can and does use to control the President is legal action through the judicial system. A major obstacle to such action, however, is the political question doctrine. Unwilling to become involved in imbroglios between coordinate branches of government, the courts often cite the lack of judicially manageable standards or insufficient fact-finding capability to justify not hearing the merits of cases against the President. For example, on two recent occasions members of Congress sued President Reagan for alleged abuses of the war powers, and on both occasions the cases were dismissed as involving political questions.*

If congressional means of less magnitude and institutional significance fail to insure constitutional behavior by a President, perhaps the only remedy open to Congress is impeachment. Impeachment is of course the ultimate weapon in the arsenal of Congress. It is slow, cumbersome, and obtrusive. But when more subtle means fail, then unsubtle techniques must be used; gross departures require institutional corrections. Modern Presidents have strayed from the constitutional course in which peace is the norm, war is a last resort, and the people's representatives decide when to use the war power. Impeachment was included in the constitutional system to correct such deviations—not to punish the President (the criminal law exists for that purpose) but to preserve the nation.[9]

The Constitution provides, "The President, Vice President and all civil officers of the United States, shall be removed from office on impeachment for, and conviction of, treason, bribery, or other high crimes and misdemeanors." (art. II, §4) The phrase "high crimes and misdemeanors"

[9]See generally Firmage, 56; Firmage and Mangrum, 58.

embodies English precedents of which the framers were aware and which they understood to transcend criminal misconduct. Indeed, Sir William Blackstone defined the "first and principal" high misdemeanor as "maladministration of such high officers as are in public trust and employment." (*17*, 122) The framers extended the English precedents, inapplicable to the King, to the chief executive of the new Republic so that it might be a government of laws and not of men.

As provided for in the United States Constitution, impeachment was reserved for public offenses that, if not indictable crimes, were so egregious as to indicate gross personal corruption or so serious as to threaten the integrity of the state. Those offenses that have been found to be impeachable have been reduced to three broad categories:

> (1) exceeding the constitutional bounds of the powers of the office in derogation of the powers of another branch of government; (2) behaving in a manner grossly incompatible with the proper function and purpose of the office; and (3) employing the power of the office for an improper or for personal gain.*

And in perhaps the most discerning summary of the nature of American impeachment, Story wrote:

> Not but that crimes of a strictly legal character fall within the scope of the power . . . ; but that it has a more enlarged operation, and reaches what are aptly termed political offenses, growing out of personal misconduct or gross neglect or usurpation, or habitual disregard of the public interests, in the discharge of the duties of public office. These are so various in their character, and so indefinable in their actual involutions, that it is almost impossible to provide systematically for them by positive law. They must be examined upon very broad and comprehensive principles of public policy and duty. They must be judged . . . by the habits and rules and principles of diplomacy, of departmental operations and arrangements of parliamentary practice, of executive customs and negotiations, of foreign as well as domestic political movements; and, in short, by a great variety of circumstances, as well as those which aggravate as those which extenuate or justify the offensive acts which do not properly belong to the judicial character in the ordinary administration of justice, and are far removed from the reach of municipal jurisprudence. (*208*, 599)

English precedent and American practice support using impeachment to correct the current constitutional imbalance. Judged by the standards given above, modern presidential usurpations of the war power of Congress constitute impeachable offenses. Interestingly, however, some of the most egregious of those usurpations—the Vietnam War and the Cambodian offensives, in particular—were not cited in the articles of impeachment against Nixon. Those who drafted the articles apparently felt uneasy impeaching Nixon for continuing the constitutional practices of his predecessors. That uneasiness, which continues to be felt, arises from the basic notion of justice that the law should treat like situations alike. It is argued that impeachment should not be used against acts that previously have gone unpunished.

That argument, however, cannot prevail. In the American system, no one is above the law, even—and perhaps especially—the President, "that man . . . who can commit the most extensive injustice." (53, 65) Anyone who has contested a speeding violation understands the futility of using the defense that other offenders have escaped punishment. The President should fare no better. If we are ever to change an illegal course of conduct, we inevitably must break with the past. Increasing abuses must not become precedents for future illegal acts.

Recognizing the need for drastic action, several members of Congress introduced a resolution in the House to impeach President Reagan following the American invasion of Grenada.* The resolution charged that the President was guilty of "high crimes and misdemeanors" for introducing American troops into Grenada in violation of the Constitution and the War Powers Resolution; the invasion derogated from the congressional prerogative to declare war and breached the statutory requirement that the President consult with Congress before introducing troops into hostilities. Those are the very kinds of institutional usurpations for which impeachment historically would lie.

The President's approval of covert CIA activities without a full disclosure to Congress raises serious constitutional issues. Consider, for example, the covert mining of Nicaraguan harbors in light of the following statement by James Iredell, a member of the Constitutional Convention in Philadelphia and later a justice of the Supreme Court:

> [The President] must certainly be punishable for giving false information to the Senate. He is to regulate all intercourse with foreign powers, and it is his duty to impart to the Senate every material intelligence he receives. If it should appear he has not given them full information, but has concealed important intelligence which he ought to have communicated, and by that means induced them to enter into measures injurious to their country, and which they would not have consented to had the true state of things been disclosed to them,—in this case, I ask whether, upon an impeachment for . . . such an account, the Senate would probably favor him. (49, 127)

Many Senators, even some in high positions of leadership, complained that they were not told the full extent of the covert activities and would certainly not have approved of the harbor mining had they known all the facts. The nearly universal opprobrium that the United States incurred for its participation in the mining was the very kind of injurious result that Iredell would argue should lead to impeachment. This course of conduct, repeated, would constitute the sort of institutional harm to the fabric of government that impeachment was designed to prevent.

Chapter 18
THE PRESIDENCY
AS AN IDEAL TYPE

James MacGregor Burns, who has been one of the principal extollers of the strong presidency, said, "I do not contend that the White House exercises a kind of divine magic over the incumbent and invests him with magical powers." Rather, he said, the presidency brings out the "potentially great" in men. "We do have by now ample indication that the Presidency, with its spacious view of the world, its command of talent, and above all its historic role—does work its way on the men in the oval office." (24, 7–8)

The word *great* covers a broad territory. Churchill and Attila, Genghis Khan and Gandhi, Napoleon and Gladstone have been called great. Historians assign the adjective to two classes of American Presidents. A President identified with a great national crisis is great, not because of his conduct but because events have made him a symbol of the nation. Washington is not regarded as a great President because of his administration of the office (although he should be) but because he was commander in chief during the Revolution. Lincoln, whom Wendell Phillips called a "first-rate second-rate man," conducted the Civil War with a curious mixture of irresolution and imprudence, and he won the war only because the side he commanded enjoyed a great preponderance of men and resources—but he is called a great President. Wilson, although he was "too proud to fight," involved the country in the First World War and thereby achieved greatness. If the Mexican War and the Spanish–American War had put the nation in hazard, Polk and McKinley would also be regarded as great Presidents. Harold Laski said that in every crisis, the American people have found a

President equal to the occasion. Rather, it seems that in every tragic drama heroism is ascribed to the principals.

Second, greatness is attributed to Presidents who have magnified the office, whether by usurpation, self-assertion, or the sponsorship of an ambitious legislative program. Jackson is not known to have read more than one book in his life. (147, III, 695) John Quincy Adams did not exaggerate greatly when he said that Jackson "hardly could spell his own name." (1, 77) Nevertheless, a large literature of adulation has grown up about Jackson, and his name appears in every list of great Presidents. The reason seems to be that Jackson was arrogant and contentious and embroiled himself frequently with Congress, asserting his will over the other branches of government. The names of Wilson and Franklin Roosevelt are associated with ambitious domestic programs as well as with foreign wars. But it is not necessary that a President accomplish something significant in order to be called great. It is only necessary that he strike a dramatic posture—"Perdicaris alive or Raisuli dead"—and that this not produce an immediate failure. If by some miracle Lyndon Johnson's Vietnamese adventure had succeeded, he would be regarded as a great President. Of course other nations make their heroes in the same way.

Probably a more reflective view of greatness would emphasize other values and other traits of behavior. A great President would subordinate personal interests and personal fame to a larger social interest. He would not support predatory groups in the exploitation of the public at large. He would judge policies in terms of an accurate long-range calculation of social consequences rather than a short-range calculation of political advantages. He would be a man of personal integrity. Perhaps no one would deny that George Washington and John Quincy Adams at least approximated this definition of greatness. Probably everyone would agree that the majority of our Presidents have not come within bowshot of it.

The early literature of republicanism argued that the electoral process would bring to office men possessed of republican virtue, whereas in hereditary monarchies the character of the King was a matter of chance. But though one need not agree with H. L. Mencken that servility and opportunism are the sole qualities of the politician, nevertheless one who lacks these qualities enters upon a political career under a great competitive disadvantage. Moreover, politics is conflict. A combative personality is an initial asset; the practice of politics confirms and reinforces this trait. For the combative man, because victory in the struggle is the central issue, ruthlessness is added to servility and opportunism.

When Theodore Roosevelt declared for the Republican nomination for the presidency in 1912, his close friend Elihu Root wrote sorrowfully in a private letter:

He is essentially a fighter and when he gets into a fight he is completely dominated by the desire to destroy his adversary. He instinctively lays hold of every weapon which can be used for that end. Accordingly he is saying a lot of things and taking a lot of positions which are inspired by the desire to win. I have no doubt he thinks he believes what he says, but he doesn't. He has merely picked up certain popular ideas which were at hand as one might pick up a poker or chair with which to strike. (*90*, II, 180)

And later he said of Roosevelt, "Combativeness was his essential characteristic." (*90*, II, 185)

Taft, who had been lifted up and thrust by Roosevelt into the presidency, could not hold his ground against his former sponsor, although he made pathetic boast of his resolution, "Even a rat in a corner will fight." (*90*, II, 181)

A schoolmate recalled of the young Nixon: "He was combative rather than conciliatory. He had a nasty temper."[1] Nixon's campaign style was always one of personal assault. He began by unseating first Jerry Voorhis and then Helen Gahagan Douglas by campaigns of vilification. His role in the 1952 campaign was to slander Truman's principal advisors. So unsavory did his reputation become that in 1967 Raymond K. Price, who was to be his most prominent speech writer, advised that publicity releases should portray Nixon as having grown, mellowed, and matured. (*110*, 193) Newspaper columnists speculated as to whether there was in fact a "new Nixon," and on television the candidate confirmed that he had indeed changed and matured. In the 1968 campaign the cruder tasks were assigned to his running mate Agnew, but Nixon's own campaign followed his usual pattern. He ran against the Supreme Court, and more especially against Johnson's attorney general, Ramsey Clark, whom he blamed for an alleged breakdown of law and order, although Nixon knew that the Department of Justice had neither the responsibility nor the authority to deal with "crime in the streets." He privately thought that "Ramsey Clark is really a fine fellow. And he's done a good job." (*73*, 64)

It is possible to achieve high office without the endowments of a Roosevelt or a Nixon. A candidate from an influential family may enter politics in a safe legislative district and may rise a certain distance without learning the nastier political skills. But he is defenseless when he encounters a practitioner of gutter politics, as Millard Tydings was defenseless when Joe McCarthy attacked him.

It is even possible to enter politics at the highest level, to become a candidate for President, without serving a political apprenticeship and

---

[1] L. Shearer, "Richard Nixon and Ola Florence Welch," *Parade* (June 28, 1970), p. 5. *Washington Watch* (May 1, 1973), p. 2, reported that an ex–Cabinet member had told Jack Anderson of "watching the President go through the pantomime of plunging an imaginary dagger into an opponent. 'After you get your knife in,' the President said gleefully, 'you twist it.' And he twisted his wrist to demonstrate."

becoming a politician. But such a man does not win the nomination; it is given to him by professional politicians, and they choose a man whom they expect to serve their purposes. Eisenhower was enlisted by Thomas E. Dewey, the political representative of eastern financial interests, to champion their foreign policy against the claims of midwestern industry represented by Robert A. Taft. Probably Eisenhower had encountered politics even in the structured bureaucratic life of the Army, but the skills he had acquired were not those of electoral politics. Nevertheless, he tolerated the sharp practice that won him the nomination at the Republican convention in 1952 and the red-baiting his party carried on in the ensuing campaign; he even abandoned his friend General George Marshall, to whom he owed his military career, when Marshall was traduced by Senators Joseph McCarthy and William Jenner.

Machiavelli said:

> For there is such a difference between the way men live and the way they ought to live that he who prefers what ought to be done to what is actually done learns the way to ruin rather than to self-preservation; for a man who may desire to profess virtue in every matter insures his ruin among so many who are not virtuous. Whence it is necessary for a prince who wishes to survive to learn to be dishonest, and to be honest or dishonest according to the circumstances.[2]

An elective prince already will have learned this lesson. But is there not, as Burns says, something in the presidency that produces change in the man, that evokes new behavior, that liberates "potential greatness"?

Since Aristotle, we have known that character is formed incrementally, by a long succession of decisions. The politician who remains in the race is obliged to make a series of choices between principle and expediency. He must reward his followers at the public expense. On one or more occasions, he may be forced to break faith with his friends and allies. Like the boy in Grimm's fairy tale who paid his way with his golden brains, the politician pays his way with his character. He may arrive at the presidency with his heritage entirely spent. Henry Adams, "stable companion to statesmen," as he called himself, recorded the regret with which he saw John Hay yield to McKinley's summons to come to Washington as secretary of state. "No one in his experience had ever passed unscathed through that malarious marsh." Office was poison; this "poison was that of the will—the distortion of sight—the warping of mind—the degradation of tissue—the coarsening of taste—the narrowing of sympathy to the emotions of a caged rat." (2, 365)

Once formed, character is not very malleable. A psychiatrist does not undertake to reform it entirely but to undo a single quirk, and even in this he is not likely to succeed. However, behavior is a function not only of

[2]Machiavelli, *The Prince*, p. xv.

character but also of the situation; a change in status may alter the problems which face a man and thus may elicit new behavioral patterns. When a politician is appointed to the Supreme Court he often turns out better than most observers had expected. He abandons the combative posture, and his role is now dictated by the value system of the law. He will see this system, to be sure, through personal spectacles, but it will have a stability altogether lacking in the kaleidoscopic environment to which the politician must continually adjust himself. Here, in this sense at least, the office changes the man.

But the President does not escape from political life into another system of values. Rather, his political life rises to a higher pitch of intensity. Henry Adams explained Theodore Roosevelt in impersonal terms:

> Power is poison. Its effect on Presidents had always been tragic, chiefly in an almost insane excitement at first, and a worse reaction afterwards; but also because no mind is so well balanced as to bear the strain of seizing unlimited power without habit or knowledge of it; and finding it disputed with him by hungry packs of wolves and hounds whose lives depend on snatching the carrion. (2, 418)

But men are individuals. Each one is unique, so we can make no confident forecast about an unidentified individual case, though this need not terminate inquiry. The question regards the office, not the man. Can we offer a sociological account of the character structure appropriate to the official role, the behavioral pattern the office may be expected to generate, leaving aside questions of personal biography? An ideal type, as Max Weber described it, is an abstract description of the implications of a social situation, constructed by the use of our empirical knowledge of human nature, our emphatic understanding. (232, 91-114) It is a tool for calculating the consequences of adopting institutions of one sort or another—not an instrument of prediction, but an account of tendencies.

The man who achieves the presidency does change his status and does acquire greatness of a special sort: he stands at the pinnacle of power, not only in the nation but also in the world; he is flattered and adulated. Lord Acton said that all power corrupts. Adam Smith gave a description of the process that is worth quoting at length.

> Of the persons who, in estimating their own merit, in judging of their own character and conduct, direct by far the greater part of their attention to the second standard, to that ordinary degree of excellence which is commonly attained by other people, there are some who really and justly feel themselves very much above it, and who, by every intelligent and impartial spectator, are acknowledged to be so. The attention of such persons, however, being always principally directed, not to the standard of the ideal, but to that of ordinary perfection, they have little sense of their own weaknesses and imperfections; they have little modesty; are often assuming, arrogant and presumptuous, great

admirers of themselves, and great contemners of other people. Though their characters are in general much less correct, and their merit much inferior to that of the man of real and modest virtue, yet their excessive presumption, founded upon their own excessive self–admiration, dazzles the multitude, and often imposes even upon those who are much superior to the multitude. The frequent, and often wonderful, success of the most ignorant quacks and imposters, both civil and religious, sufficiently demonstrates how easily the multitude are imposed upon by the most extravagant and groundless pretensions. But when these pretensions are supported by a very high degree of real and solid merit, when they are displayed with all the splendour which ostentation can bestow upon them, when they are supported by high rank and great power, when they have often been successfully exerted, and are, upon that account, attended by the loud acclamations of the multitude; even the man of sober judgment often abandons himself to the general admiration. The very noise of those foolish acclamations often contributes to con-found his understanding, and while he sees those great men only at a certain distance, he is often disposed to worship them with a sincere admiration, superior even to that with which they appear to worship themselves. . . .

Great success in the world, great authority over the sentiments and opinions of mankind, have very seldom been acquired without some degree of this excessive self–admiration. The most splendid characters, the men who have performed the most illustrious actions, who have brought about the greatest revolutions, both in the situations and opinions of mankind; the most successful warriors, the greatest statesmen and legislators, the eloquent founders and leaders of the most numerous and most successful sects and parties; have many of them been not more distinguished for their very great merit, than for a degree of presumption and self–admiration altogether disproportioned even to that very great merit. This presumption was, perhaps, necessary, not only to prompt them to undertakings which a more sober mind would never have thought of, but to command submission and obedience of their followers to support them in such undertakings. When crowned with success, accordingly, this presumption has often betrayed them into a vanity that approached almost to insanity and folly. Alexander the Great appears, not only to have wished that other people think him a god, but to have been at least very well disposed to fancy himself as such. Upon his death–bed, the most ungodlike of all situations, he requested of his friends that to the respectable list of deities, into which he himself had long before been inserted, his old mother Olympia might likewise have the honour of being added. Amidst the respectful admiration of his followers and disciples, amidst the applause of the public, after the oracle, which probably had followed the voice of that applause, had pronounced him the wisest of men, the great wisdom of Socrates, though it did not suffer him to fancy himself a god, yet was not great enough to hinder him from fancying that he had secret and frequent intimations from some invisible and divine Being. The sound head of Caesar was not so perfectly sound as to hinder him from being much pleased with his divine genealogy from the goddess Venus; and, before the temple of this pretended great–grandmother, to receive without rising from his seat the Roman senate, when that illustrious body came to present him with some decrees, conferring upon him the most extravagant honours. This insolence, joined to some other actions of an almost childish vanity, little to be expected from an understanding at once so very acute and comprehensive, seems, by exasperating the public jealousy, to have emboldened his assassins and to have hastened the execution of their conspiracy. The religion and manners of modern times give our great men little encouragement to fancy themselves either gods or even prophets. Success, however, joined to great popular favour, has often so far turned the heads of the greatest of them, as to make them ascribe to themselves both an importance and an ability much beyond what they really possessed; and, by this presumption, to precipitate themselves into many rash, and sometimes ruinous adventures. . . .

In the humble projects of private life, as well as in the ambitious and proud pursuits of high stations, great abilities and successful enterprise in the beginning, have frequently encouraged to undertakings which necessarily led to bankruptcy and ruin in the end. (*200*, II, 107–10)

No special dispensation exempts Presidents from the intoxication of power. David Lloyd George has recorded the "most extraordinary outburst" of Wilson at the Paris Peace Conference.

"Why," he said, "has Jesus Christ so far not succeeded in inducing the world to follow His teachings in these matters? It is because He taught the ideal without devising any practical means of attaining it. That is the reason why I am proposing a practical scheme to carry out His aims." Clemenceau slowly opened his dark eyes to their widest dimensions and swept them round the Assembly to see how the Christians gathered around the table enjoyed this exposure of the futility of their Master. (*103*, I, 142)

In *The Twilight of the Presidency*, George Reedy, who served as press secretary and special assistant to President Johnson, says that the office itself engenders such an attitude. The President "is treated with all the reverence due a monarch." (*160*, 4) He is a "semidivinity"; consequently he regards himself with awe and "can easily slide into a feeling of divinity." (*160*, 16, 160) All too often, those who surround him are sycophants, and he is isolated from the people. Unless he is a "weak President," or an unusually wise one, his advisers will merely reflect his own opinions and biases. (*160*, 98)

Probably the self–made man is more vulnerable to megalomania than one born to the purple. He ascribes to his personal character or destiny the preeminence that the latter man is satisfied to ascribe to his station. Consequently the self–made man is led on to further and further adventures; in the end he is likely to come to disaster. Napoleon Bonaparte and Adolf Hitler are examples. But perhaps we should distinguish between different kinds of self–made men. Machiavelli said that "the prince must know how to play the beast as well as the man" and that he should emulate both the lion and the fox. The lion is strong but is vulnerable to snares; the fox, although physically weak, succeeds by deceit. Vilfredo Pareto made the lion and the fox alternative types of statesmen. (146) The lion characteristically employs frontal assault; the fox relies upon cunning. There is something to this. Caesar Augustus and Oliver Cromwell were extraordinarily clever manipulators; in our own day, Joseph Stalin. It does not appear that Stalin himself was deceived by the "cult of personality" which virtually deified him. Rather the emergence of such a cult seems to be a condition of the survival of a nation that is in a process of rapid social change. In a stable society, the coherence of the society is guaranteed by settled institutions and cultural practices which give the citizenry assurance and security. But in Stalin's day the institutions and the culture of the Soviet Union were in a state of rapid and bewildering transformation. The only focus for social cohesion was the figure of Stalin himself. The very ruthlessness with which Stalin destroyed the impersonal supports of the social order threw the society into depen-dence upon his person for emotional orientation and confidence. The same phenomenon is observable in other colonial countries in a period of rapid dissolution of institutions. The cult of personality emerged in China with Mao Tse-tung, in Indonesia with Sukarno, in Egypt with Gamal Abdal Nasser, in Cuba with Fidel Castro, in Ghana with Kwame Nkrumah, and in other African countries with other leaders. A similar development has occurred in industrialized societies in times of social collapse. The great depression destroyed the economic supports of the petty bourgeoisie in Germany, reducing them, to use Leon Trotsky's striking expression, to "human dust." Unanchored and lost, they accepted the leadership principle and restored social structure in the form of a Hitler cult.

If we accept the types of the lion and the fox, self-confidence and recklessness are more likely to characterize the lion than the fox. The fox succeeds by intrigue, which means that he consciously employs the strength of others. Stalin, who achieved power by manipulation, was enormously cautious. His goal was "socialism in one country," and often this seemed to entail opposition to socialism in any other. He actively attempted to discourage the rebellion of partisans and Communists against the British and against the monarchy in Greece in 1947; the latter occasion resulted in the Truman doctrine, which called for the repression of the supposedly insatiable expansionist appetite of Stalin. Stalin endorsed Chaing Kai-shek in China and tried to hold back Mao Tse-tung. But if supreme power did not induce megalomania in Stalin, it worked other unfortunate consequences. Acutely aware of the precarious tenure of power in a state such as the Soviet Union, in which power was so little routinized by institutions, Stalin developed suspicion and fear of his colleagues which progressed into paranoia, producing bloody purges.

On the other hand, there is certainly no assurance that a man whose career has hitherto been that of a fox will not upon achieving supreme power develop the hubris of a Caesar or a Napoleon. Johnson had been a skillful manipulator and achieved the presidency by the arts of the fox. But apparently his staggering victory over Goldwater in 1964 induced a self-confidence that led him to catastrophe. His language became as rash as his actions. Speaking at Omaha, Nebraska, on June 30, 1966, he laid claim to the war power of Congress: "Now there are many, many who can recommend, advise, and sometimes a few of them consent. But there is only one that has been chosen by the American people to decide." (*158*, I, 685) At Des Moines, Iowa, on the same day, he seems to have felt that he was being crucified by the "strident voices" that opposed his war, for he said: "I am not angry; I am not even sorrowful. I sometimes think of the words, 'God forgive them, for they know not what they do.'" (*158*, I, 693) He was in better spirits in Lancaster, Ohio, on September 5, 1966, when he assured the American people, "If you make these sacrifices for your country, you make these sacrifices for me."³

Power and responsibility entail other consequences. The duties of office produce exhaustion, which may have immediate effect. Theodore Sorensen says, "I saw first-hand, during the long days and nights of the Cuban crisis, how brutally physical and mental fatigue can numb the good sense as well as the senses of normally articulate men." (*203*, 78) Over a long term, the strain of effort and of hope, apprehension, and uncertainty induces tension. Physical and mental health are eroded.

The physical demands of a chief magistracy exceed the resources of most men. Before he was elected to the presidency, Wilson said that we must choose the President "from among wise and prudent athletes." (*16*, 74) Harold Macmillan said that a prime minister must have the constitution of an ox. (*16*, 76) But ordinarily a man achieves a leading position in politics only in his later fifties or even his sixties, an age at which most men, even athletes, have incurred permanent maladies of one sort or another. These maladies, aggravated by the strain of office, may have not merely physical but psychological consequences as well. They may distort perception or impair the judgment. In 1960 Dean Rusk, later secretary of state, said that "the international list of those who have carried great responsibility while ill is a long one and there are fleeting glimpses of decisions which good health might have turned another way." (*100*, 9) An English physician, Dr. Hugh L'Etang, who has canvassed all the available sources, summarized his findings:

³These were the words actually spoken live over television, but the printed text of the speech reads, "When you do what is best for your country, you will do what is best for me." (*158*, II, 977)

The list of international statesmen, senior officials who have borne supreme responsibility, while in the grip of disabling and debilitating illness, is certainly long and forbidding. In many cases a plausible case can be made for a link between their physical and mental handicaps and impairment of performance, judgement and powers of decision. (*100*, 9)

L'Etang points out that "since 1908 eleven out of thirteen British premiers and six out of ten American Presidents have had illnesses in office which have incapacitated them to some degree." (*100*, 10) He discusses the tragic case of Wilson, who was advised to retire as early as 1906 because of arterial degeneration. In 1913, Wilson's doctor advised him that it was doubtful he could retain his health through his first term. (*100*, 43) Personality change seems to have begun as early as 1917. (*100*, 48ff.) In 1919, on the platform at Pueblo, Colorado, Wilson was disabled by what may not have been his first stroke. (*100*, 51) The remainder of his career was tragic. "Wilson, isolated by his intimates and handicapped by increasing obstinacy, mental deterioration and failure of judgment, destroyed any hope of attaining even some of the objectives for which he had ruined his health." (*100*, 52) So distorted was his judgment that he attempted to obtain the Democratic nomination for an unprecedented third term in 1920, at a time when he was ill and partially paralyzed and had suffered decisive political defeat in the Senate. (*100*, 53)

Franklin D. Roosevelt was seriously ill by 1944 and died, apparently from a cerebral hemorrhage, in 1945. (*100*, 94) President Eisenhower had a heart attack and a stroke while in office. (*100*, 179, 181) He worried about his capacity to perform the duties of his office and made arrangements to be replaced by the Vice-President in case of total disability.

James Forrestal, secretary of defense under President Truman, resigned at the President's request in 1949. For some months, at least, he had believed that he was the victim of a conspiracy of Communists, Jews, and sinister figures in the White House. (*186*, 5) Drew Pearson reported that a few days after his removal Forrestal, upon hearing a fire engine, rushed into the street in his pajamas shouting that the Russians were attacking. (*186*, 13) If so, it was a fortunate accident that he was not secretary of defense at that time. Forrestal committed suicide a few days later.

From 1930 on, Ramsay MacDonald suffered physical and mental impairment; he continued as prime minister until 1935, although in June of 1933 his friend Lord Salter considered, "He was already no longer in a mental and physical condition to be capable of the continuous and exacting responsibilities of high office." (*100*, 71)

Churchill was sixty-five when he became prime minister in 1940. He suffered various illnesses but did not begin to lose his physical and mental powers until 1944. (*100*, 149) He lost his office in 1945. He held the premiership again from 1951 to 1955, but he had had a mild stroke in 1949 and then suffered a serious one in 1952. His physician's report seemed to indicate that he was not equal to his responsibilities in 1951, and after another stroke in 1953 he was clearly unfit to hold office. However, he resisted all advice and pressure to retire to the House of Lords until 1955. His successor, Anthony Eden, experienced illness and political crises which apparently aggravated each other, and he was forced to retire in 1957.

Dr. L'Etang surveys a multitude of similar cases and concludes with the modest proposition that great men are no less prone to illness than others. It does seem that the pressure and tensions of office make principal political figures considerably more vulnerable than ordinary men to disorders of the circulatory and nervous systems. It is precisely these diseases that threaten the capacity of a ruler to weigh a multitude of factors and make a wise judgment in a difficult case.

Where there is illness, there is medication. L'Etang quotes Malcolm Muggeridge to the effect that Eden was overcome "by excessive doses of sedatives, pep-pills, and John Foster Dulles." (100, 167) It appears that the administration of tranquilizers, not only to chiefs of state but also to other political figures, has now become standard medical practice. But the official must meet people, he must make decisions; for these purposes he is roused and sharpened with stimulants. In times of great trial he bounces back and forth like a ping-pong ball. We find ourselves governed by a "chemical man." And some medications have side effects. In many cases, for example, cortisone produces a false euphoria and unfounded optimism, and abuse of cortisone can cause messianic delusions. According to L'Etang, President Kennedy was treated regularly with cortisone after 1954. (100, 187–88) He may also have been treated with amphetamines. (Time, Dec. 18, 1972)

The fear that the President may become hopelessly irrational was the unexpressed motive for the proposal of the Twenty-fifth Amendment. (160, 171) Unfortunately, the amendment does not meet the problem. Either the President, or the Vice-President together with a majority of the department heads, may certify his disability. But the President may resume office simply by giving notice to the two houses of Congress. He can be overruled only if the Vice-President and a majority of the department heads make a report of continuing disability to Congress and if two-thirds of both houses confirm this finding. There seems to be no likelihood that a President will willingly surrender office, nor is a majority of the department heads—who are his appointees and his political partisans and whose tenures of office depend on the President—likely to vote him out unless his disability is as notorious as that of George III, whose insanity was recognized by act of Parliament. Moreover, the President may overrule any adverse finding and maintain his tenure of office unless two-thirds of both houses vote against him, which is improbable in the extreme.

In the British system, the cabinet colleagues of the prime minister could surely displace him in case of disability, although a tense political situation might arise if he appealed to the House of Commons. But this has never occurred. Sir Henry Campbell-Bannerman was incapacitated by a heart attack as early as November 1907, but he continued to hold the premiership. After a second heart attack on February 12, 1908, he was confined to his bed, but he did not resign until April 3, nineteen days before his death. (*100*, 59-60) As early as 1952 some of Churchill's associates tried to persuade him to surrender the premiership and take a seat in the House of Lords, but he refused to do so until April 6, 1955, by which time he was spending most of the day in bed. (*100*, 153, 155)

After much experience with politics and intimate acquaintance with the White House, Reedy wrote powerfully of the problem:

> A highly irrational personality, who under other circumstances might be medically certifiable for treatment, could take over the White House and the event never be known with any degree of assurance.
>
> I do have some experience with the reaction of human beings to irrational behavior, and it is clear to me that where presidents are concerned, the tolerance level for irrationality extends almost to the point of gibbering idiocy or delusions of identity.
>
> To put it more simply, no one is going to interfere with the presidential exercise of authority unless the president drools in public or announces on television that he is Alexander the Great. And even in these extreme cases, action would be taken hesitantly indeed.
>
> He will still have the authority to drop the atomic bomb on another nation even though in the privacy of Senate cloakrooms experienced men are whispering that "the president is nuts." (*160*, 168)

What this means is that the presidency, like other autocracies and semi-autocracies, embodies a permanent danger. But this danger is *in posse* rather than *in esse*; and in fact we have never, so far as we know, had a President who was authentically mad. Obviously it is possible and it does occur that some men survive the political struggle without collapsing into insanity or moral bankruptcy; they may win contests without becoming mere fighting cocks. An acute and dispassionate intelligence, a firm footing in humility, perhaps even a well-developed sense of humor may save a leader from megalomania. The leader may have an unusually sound body. But in contriving an ideal type we cannot take into account the unknown good qualities of unknown future incumbents. We must expect that incumbents will in the main fulfill rather than frustrate the potentialities of the institutions.

We should also recognize that a President may have personal traits that are not necessitated by the office but that may work damage in the office. The arrogance and self-righteousness of Wilson were sources of weakness rather than strength. The character of Harding colored his whole administration. Coolidge was temperamentally inclined to inactivity. Despite the cult of the "strong President," a Coolidge is likely to be less dangerous than a President given to self-dramatization. Theodore Roosevelt was addicted to posturing; this was clearly an overcompensation for childhood feelings of inadequacy. In the early years of the twentieth century Roosevelt's taste for the rash and the theatrical did little harm, but similar traits in Kennedy, fostered by ambition, produced very grave problems. The British journalist Louis Heren identified one of them.

> The President often feels compelled to initiate a new policy, even when one is not absolutely called for or when insufficient time has been given for consideration. . . . If this is regrettable, it is a fact of American political life that a President has a set period in which to make his mark, theoretically four years, or eight years at most, but it can be less if he loses majority support in Congress or public confidence. Moreover, he ascends to his awful throne of power with little or no intimate experience of foreign affairs. Unlike a British Prime Minister, he has not shared collective Cabinet responsibility and experience. He has rarely been a party to decision-making. Professor Schlesinger claimed for President Kennedy a more varied and extensive international experience. As a young man, the professor solemnly reported, he has talked to Franklin D. Roosevelt, Neville Chamberlain, and Stanley Baldwin. Unimpressive as this early experience may strike readers, it was more than that of some other Presidents. (*78*, 143–44)

Heren illustrates this weakness of the system in which "a new President finds that he is to be tested in a field of which he has little or no experience, under the compulsions of public expectation and the personal desire to make his mark" by referring to the very instructive case of the Bay of Pigs. It is not true that responsibility lay with Kennedy's subordinates.

> The fact of the matter, as admitted by one member of his staff who did not seek quick fame and fortune in memoir writing, was that President Kennedy, although new to office and with almost no experience, wanted to invade Cuba. When a President wants to do something badly, it is very difficult for a subordinate to oppose him. (*78*, 144)

John E. Ullmann believes that this initial motivation persisted. "Kennedy, of course, did give up on the Bay of Pigs when it flopped, but there is strong evidence that his escalation of the defense budget, his intervention in Vietnam and his enthusiasm for the space race were all attempts to prove his *machismo*." (*223*, 11)

Of course, this may be a misreading. Schlesinger assures us that Kennedy drifted into the Vietnam war because "he had never really given it his full attention." (*78*, 194) But this confirms our central point. It means that the most fateful decisions are functions of the perceptions, the misperceptions, even the inattention of a single man. Neither the recruitment process nor the office provides any defense against the idiosyncratic weaknesses that are bound to be a part of the personality of any individual.

In the middle ages the literature of advice to Kings urged upon them humility and self-abnegation. This probably did little good, but it did no harm. The contemporary literature of the presidency extols self-assertion and domination. The public at large applauds these traits. Unless he is immunized by an unusual character structure, as was Eisenhower, the President responds to this heady brew. The twentieth century has seen Mussolini, Hitler, Franco, Stalin, and a host of lesser figures faithfully fulfill the promises of power. We should expect that sooner or later a conjunction of the circumstances, the office, and a man may produce the same consequence in the United States. Our Constitution offers the nation and the world some protection from the potential of such a conjunction, through the dispensation of the power to declare and make war, but that protection is only as strong as the will of the legislative and judicial branches to invoke and enforce it.

Appendix A
VIEWS OF LEADING AUTHORITIES ON THE POWER TO INITIATE WAR

Joseph Story, *Commentaries on the Constitution of the United States* (edited by Thomas M. Cooley, 4th ed., Boston: Little, Brown and Co., 1873), Vol. 2, p. 87, assimilated the power of Congress to declare war to the "similar exclusive power under the Articles." Concerning Charles Pinckney's proposal in the Constitutional Convention that the power to make war be given to the Senate for the sake of dispatch, secrecy, and vigor, Story commented:

> On the other hand, it may be urged in reply, that the power of declaring war is not only the highest sovereign prerogative, but that it is, in its own nature and effects, so critical and calamitous, that it requires the utmost deliberation, and the successive review of all the councils of the nation. . . . The representatives of the people are to lay the taxes to support a war, and therefore have a right to be consulted as to its propriety and necessity. The executive is to carry it on, and therefore should be consulted as to its time, and the ways and means of making it effective. The co-operation of all branches of the legislative power ought, upon principle, to be required in this highest act of legislation as it is in all others.

William Whiting, *War Powers under the Constitution of the United States* (10th ed., Boston: Little, Brown and Co., 1864), pp. 38–40, said that war might arise by foreign attack or by insurrection.

> A state of war may exist, in either of the modes above mentioned, without a declaration of war by either of the hostile parties. Congress has the sole power, under the constitution, to make that declaration, and to sanction or authorize the commencement of *offensive* war. . . . But this is quite a different case from

a defensive or a civil war. The constitution establishes the mode in which this government shall *commence* wars, and what authority shall ordain, and what declarations shall precede, any act of hostility; but it has no power to prescribe the manner in which others should begin war against us. Hence it follows, that when war is commenced against this country, by aliens or by citizens, no declaration or war by the government is necessary. The fact that war is levied against the United States, makes it the duty of the President to call out the army or navy to subdue the enemy, whether foreign or domestic. . . . The constitution, made as it was by men of sense, never leaves the nation powerless for self-defence. That instrument, which gives the legislature authority to declare war, whenever war is *initiated* by the United States, also makes it the duty of the President, as commander–in–chief, to engage promptly and effectually in war; or, in other words, to make the United States a belligerent nation, whenever he is legally called upon to suppress rebellion, repel invasion, or to execute the laws against armed and forcible resistance thereto. . . . It must not be forgotten that by the law of nations and by modern usage, no formal *declaration* of war *to the enemy* is necessary. All that is now requisite is for each nation to make suitable declarations or proclamations to their own citizens, to enable them to govern themselves accordingly.

John Norton Pomeroy, the author of several important treatises, said in *Introduction to the Constitutional Law of the United States* (10th ed., Boston: Houghton, Mifflin, 1888), p. 373:

It is sufficient to know that the people considered the act and state of war a matter of such transcendent importance and magnitude, involving such untold personal and material interests, hazarding the prosperity, and perhaps the very existence of the body politic, that they committed its formal inception to that department of the government which more immediately represents them,—the Congress.

But Pomeroy quoted *The Prize Cases*, "If a war be made by an invasion of a foreign nation, the President is not only authorized, but bound to resist force by force." (376) And he agreed that the same rule applied in the case of an insurrection.

Thomas McIntyre Cooley, chief judge of the Supreme Court of Michigan and one of the top legal authorities of the nineteenth century, in *The General Principles of Constitutional Law in the United States of America* (3d ed., Boston: Little, Brown and Co., 1898), p. 316, said of the President as commander in chief, "The power to declare war being confided to the legislature, he has no power to originate it, but he may in advance of its declaration employ the army and navy to suppress insurrection or repel invasion."

Hermann von Holst, *The Constitutional Law of the United States of America* (Chicago: Callaghan and Co., 1887), pp. 164–65, said:

The right to declare war belongs to congress alone (art. I., sec. 8, §11). Of course, the United States may get into a war without congress' having declared war. War is, in the first place, a state of fact, the appearance of which cannot be made wholly dependent, by any constitutional provisions whatever, upon the pleasure of one of the nations concerned. As far as that is possible, however, congress has the exclusive right of the initiative. If a foreign power brings war against the United States, then it is not only the right, but the duty, of the president to oppose the enemy with all the means placed at his disposal by the constitution and the laws. But he is not to regard every act of hostility as the opening of an aggressive war and thereupon begin on his own part actual war. It is for congress to decide whether he has exceeded his constitutional authority in this respect, or has actually found himself face to face with an accomplished fact by the initiative of a foreign state. That the latter may be the state of the case is expressly acknowledged by the constitution's providing that without the consent of congress "no state shall . . . engage in war, unless actually invaded, or in such imminent danger as will not admit of delay." (art. I., sec. 10, §3) The states can no more begin war than can the president; they can take into account the presence of actual facts only as far as the inalienable right and imperious necessity of self-defense demand it.

Westel W. Willoughby, *The Constitutional Law of the United States* (New York: Baker, Voorhis and Co., 1929), Vol. 3, p. 1560, quoted with approval from Justice Nelson's dissenting opinion in *The Prize Cases* to the effect that "the right of making war belongs exclusively to the supreme or sovereign power of the State. This power in all civilized nations is regulated by the fundamental laws or municipal constitution of the country. By our Constitution, the power is lodged in Congress." Willoughby agreed with the majority in *The Prize Cases* that the President had acted properly in attempting to suppress the rebellion of the southern states, but he denied that any of the President's actions could institute the legal state of war. "That no war can exist between the United States and a foreign State, except by the declaration of Congress, there has never been any doubt."

Appendix B

STATUTES
DIRECTING THE PRESIDENT

1 Stat. 403 (1794) authorized President Washington to call forth no more than 2500 militiamen to be stationed in the four western counties of Pennsylvania following the suppression of the Whiskey Rebellion.

2 Stat. 206 (1803) authorized the President to procure four ships of war and to build fifteen gunboats "for the protection of the seamen and commerce of the United States in the Mediterranean and adjacent seas, and for other purposes, as the public service may require, and to build fifteen gunboats to be employed for such purposes as in his opinion the public service might require."

2 Stat. 245 (1803) authorized the President to take possession of the territory ceded by France and "in order to maintain in the said territories the authority of the United States, employ any part of the army and navy of the United States" and of the militia.

2 Stat. 424, 428 (1807) authorized the President to use the armed vessels of the United States to prevent the importation of slaves after January 1, 1808.

2 Stat. 445 (1807) provided that the President might direct a United States marshal to employ "such military force as he may judge necessary and proper" to remove unauthorized persons from land ceded to the United States by a foreign nation or state. Attorney General Caesar Rodney advised President Jefferson that in reliance on this act he might use military force to take possession of alluvial lands in front of the suburb St. Mary, New Orleans, since they belonged to the United States.

2 Stat. 528 (1809) authorized the President to use part of the land or naval forces or the militia, as he deemed necessary, to force a vessel to depart if it had entered the United States contrary to the Nonintercourse Act.

3 Stat. 332, 333 (1816) authorized the President to use the military force of the United States to seize goods carried by an unlicensed foreigner trading in Indian lands and also to seize all goods purchased by the foreigner from Indians.

3 Stat. 447 (1818) authorized the President to use the land or naval forces or the militia to detain any vessel that should not depart from the United States under the neutrality law, or to compel any vessel to depart that ought not to be allowed to remain under treaties of the United States. The statute was reenacted in 35 Stat. 1090–91 (1909) and 40 Stat. 223 (1917). See also 38 Stat. 1226 (1915).

3 Stat. 449 (1818) authorized the President to use land or naval forces or the militia to enforce process of court under the laws concerning foreign armed vessels and prizes and the laws fitting out or carrying out a military expedition.

3 Stat. 510 (1819) authorized and requested the President to employ as many of the public armed vessels as he judged were needed to protect merchant vessels of the United States from piratical aggression.

3 Stat. 524 (1819) authorized the President to take possession of East and West Florida when the King of Spain ratified the treaty of cession and, "in order to maintain in said territories the authority of the United States, employ any part of the army and navy of the United States, and the militia of any state or territory which he shall deem necessary."

3 Stat. 532 (1819) authorized the President to use armed vessels of the United States to cruise on the coasts of the United States, Africa, and elsewhere and to seize American vessels that had taken aboard, or were intending to take aboard, slaves for transportation to the United States in violation of law. 3 Stat. 600 (1820) extended the act, and 3 Stat. 721 (1823) extended it without limit.

3 Stat. 597 (1820) provided that after July 1, 1820, it should be unlawful for any foreign armed vessel to enter any but nine named harbors of the United States, unless forced in elsewhere by distress or danger of the sea or pursuit of an enemy, and authorized the President to use the land and naval forces or the militia to enforce the act and to prevent such vessels from entering or remaining in the waters of the United States except to enter or leave one of the nine named ports. The act expired by its own terms on July 1, 1822.

3 Stat. 651 (1822) authorized the President to employ as much of the land and naval forces as might be necessary to prevent the cutting and transportation of timber on lands of the United States in Florida.

3 Stat. 682 (1822) authorized the President to instruct army officers and other specified officials to search the stores of traders with the Indians for alcoholic liquors.

3 Stat. 720 (1822) authorized the President to augment the navy for service against pirates in the Gulf of Mexico and "the seas and territories adjacent."

4 Stat. 411 (1830) provided that the President might establish districts in land west of the Mississippi, not lying in any state or organized territory, to which the Indian title had been extinguished, for the reception of tribes willing to remove there; he might supply aid and assistance to enable them to remove and might "cause such tribe or nation to be protected, at their new residence, against all interruption or disturbance from any other tribe or nation of Indians, or from any person or persons whatever." By 1 Stat. 50 (1789) the secretary of war had been put in charge of such Indian affairs as the President should refer to him.

4 Stat. 730 (1834) provided that the President might direct the use of military force in the removal of unauthorized persons and settlers from Indian country, and in the apprehension of Indians and all other persons who had committed crimes or other offenses in any state or territory and had fled into Indian territory. He might also use the military in preventing or terminating hostilities between Indian tribes. At the direction of the superintendent of Indian affairs or his agents or subagents, the military was to break up any distillery in Indian country.

By *9 Stat. 647* (1851) the President was requested to authorize one of the public vessels in the Mediterranean to bring Louis Kossuth and his associates from Turkey to the United States. Kossuth was the principal figure in the Hungarian revolution of 1848.

11 Stat. 119 (1856) authorized citizens to claim unowned guano islands and the President in his discretion to annex these; he might in his discretion use the land and naval forces to protect the rights of the discoverer.

12 Stat. 255, 256 (1861) authorized the President to use the army, navy, militia, or citizen volunteers as was necessary to retain a vessel taken in custody by officers of the customs when, because of unlawful combinations of persons, it was impracticable to execute the laws otherwise.

12 Stat. 314, 315 (1861) authorized the President to instruct the commanders of naval vessels and privateers to seize piratical vessels built, purchased, or fitted out in whole or in part in the United States.

12 Stat. 334 (1862) authorized the President, when he judged the public safety to require it, to take possession of any or all telegraph lines and railroads in the United States and place their officers, agents, and employees under military control.

14 Stat. 27 (1866), the First Civil Rights Act, authorized the President to use "such part of the land or naval forces of the United States, or of the militia, as may be necessary" to enforce the act.

15 Stat. 337 (1869) provided that the President might employ the land or naval forces or the militia for the safekeeping of any person delivered up by a foreign government for trial in the United States for crime.

17 Stat. 13 (1871) authorized the President to suppress combinations for the denial of rights that citizens enjoy at national law by the use of the militia or the land or naval forces.

23 Stat. 321 (1885) authorized the President to employ civil or military force to remove and destroy unlawful enclosures on public lands.

25 Stat. 1009 (1889) said that "it shall be the duty of the President" annually to make proclamation warning all persons against entering the American waters of the Bering Sea in order to take certain furbearing animals and to "cause one or more vessels of the United States to diligently cruise said waters and arrest all persons and seize all vessels found to be in or to have engaged in any violation of the laws of the United States therein."

28 Stat. 52 (1894) was passed to "give effect to the award of the Tribunal of Arbitration at Paris under the treaty concluded at Washington February

29, 1892, for submitting to arbitration certain questions concerning the preservation of the fur seals." It provided that "it shall be the duty of the President to cause a sufficient naval force to cruise in the waters to which this act is applicable" and that it should be the duty of the commanding officer of any vessel belonging to the naval or revenue service, when so instructed by the President, to seize any vessel of the United States employed in those waters in violation of the act.

39 Stat. 223 (1916) authorized the President, in his discretion, to detail officers and enlisted men of the navy and marines to serve the government of Haiti.

39 Stat. 799 (1916) provided that when, during a war in which the United States was not engaged, the President became satisfied that there was reasonable ground to believe that any vessel, American or foreign, was discriminating against United States citizens or firms, he might detain the vessel. When he became satisfied that a belligerent nation was not giving United States ships or citizens facilities of commerce that its vessels or citizens enjoyed in the United States, or was giving more favorable treatment to vessels or citizens of another nation than to those of the United States, the President might withhold clearance of one or more vessels of that nation until equality of treatment was restored. He might employ such part of the land or naval forces of the United States as should be necessary to carry out the act.

44 Stat. 565 (1926) authorized the President, on the application of one of the republics of the two Americas or of Cuba, Haiti, or the Dominican Republic, whenever in his discretion the public interests rendered such a course advisable, to detail officers and enlisted men of the United States Army, Navy, and Marine Corps to assist such government "in military and naval matters." 49 Stat. 218 (1935) added the Philippines to the list of eligible governments. 56 Stat. 763 (1942) added to the list, "and, during a war or declared national emergency, the governments of such other countries as the President deems it in the interest of national defense to assist." The Philippines were dropped in the reenactment in 70A Stat. 32 (1956), and the services of the Air Force were made available. It was under this legislation that President Harry S. Truman, after declaring that the Korean war had created a national emergency, sent "military advisers" to South Vietnam. Presidents Eisenhower, Kennedy, and Johnson made successive enlargements of the number of military advisers, all on the pretext of the Korean emergency, until Johnson assumed the principal role in the war. The War Powers Resolution, 87 Stat. 555, 558 (1973), forbade the assignment of members of the United States armed forces, in the absence of a state of war or the authorization of Congress, "to command, coordinate, participate in the movement of, or accompany the regular or military armed forces of any foreign country or government when such forces are engaged, or there exists an imminent threat that such forces will become engaged, in hostilities." By 90 Stat. 729, 731 (1976), Congress enacted that without the specific authorization of Congress "no military assistance advisory group, military mission, or other organization of United States military personnel performing similar advisory functions under this Act may operate in any foreign country," with two exceptions: three members of the armed forces might be assigned to the chief of each United States Diplomatic Mission; and, regular units of the armed forces might be sent to engage "in routine functions designed to bring about the standardization of military operations and procedures between the Armed Forces of the United States and allies of the United States."

In the foregoing statutes Congress has conferred upon the President the power to use the armed forces for one purpose or another. In the following list the orders of Congress run directly to members of the armed forces, or subject members of the armed forces to some authority other than the President.

1 Stat. 145, 154 (1790) provided that a naval officer assigned to a port should assist the collector of the port in the collection of customs. The same statute authorized collectors, naval officers, and sundry others to board vessels within four leagues—twelve miles—of the United States coast to make search with a view to preventing evasion of the customs duties. Such a provision was included in 1 Stat. 627, 668 (1799) and in subsequent acts to this day.

1 Stat. 469 (1796) provided: "That it shall be lawful for the military force of the United States, to apprehend every person, who shall, or may be found in Indian country . . . in violation of . . . this act, and him or them immediately to convey . . . to the civil authority of the United States . . . to be proceeded against, in due course of law. . . ." The act was periodically renewed: 1 Stat. 743, 748 (1799); 2 Stat. 139, 144 (1802). This feature of the act ran directly to the military without using the President as an intermediary. But the same statutes (1 Stat. 470; 1 Stat. 745; 2 Stat. 142) authorized the President to use "such military force, as he may judge necessary" to remove persons unlawfully making settlement on Indian lands.

1 Stat. 619 (1799) "authorized and required" the officers of revenue cutters and military officers commanding in any fort or station on the coast to enforce the quarantine and health laws of any state, "according to their respective powers and precincts, as they shall be directed, from time to time, by the Secretary of the Treasury of the United States."

2 Stat. 70 (1800) provided that commissioned vessels of the United States might seize as a prize any vessel, owned in whole or in part by citizens of the United States, used in carrying slaves from one foreign country to another.

2 Stat. 339 (1805) provided that if a crime against the United States should be committed by anyone found on a foreign armed vessel in any port or harbor of the United States, a United States judge, if satisfied that a posse comitatus could not execute judicial process, might "issue his order, directed to any officer having command of militia, or having command of regular troops or armed vessels of the United States in the vicinity, requiring him to aid the United States marshal in the execution of the process, with all the force at his command, or such part thereof as may be necessary." Furthermore, under the same circumstances the governor of the state in which the crime was committed might "issue his order directed to any officer having command of regular troops or armed vessels of the United States," requiring him to give aid in the apprehension of the fugitive. The same act authorized the President "to permit or interdict at pleasure, the entrance of the harbors and waters of the United States to all armed vessels belonging to any foreign nation, and by force to repel and move them from the same"; if such a vessel should refuse to depart, the President "might employ such part of the land and naval forces of the United States, or the militia thereof, as he shall deem necessary to compel the said armed vessel to depart." The act was to continue for two years, and thereafter until the end of the next session of Congress; it was renewed for a similar period by 2 Stat. 484 (1808).

2 Stat. 379 (1806) forbade the importation of certain articles from Great Britain or any of its dependencies and provided that every collector, navy officer, surveyor, or other officer of customs might seize goods whose importation violated the act.

3 Stat. 151 (1814) made it the duty of officers of the army, when acting in cooperation with personnel of the navy or marines, to supply the latter, upon requisition by their commanding officer, with rations, equipage, and transportation.

5 Stat. 409 (1840) "authorized and instructed" the secretary of the navy to transport Horatio Greenough's statue of George Washington from Florence, Italy, to Washington, D.C.

12 Stat. 72, 77 (1860), an act to carry into effect treaties with China, Japan, and Siam, authorized the United States minister to each of these countries "to issue all manner of writs, to prevent the citizens of the United States from enlisting in the military or naval service of either of the said countries, to make war upon any foreign power with whom the United States are at peace, or in the service of one portion of the people against any other portion of the same people; and he may carry out this power by a resort to such force as may at the time be within his reach, belonging to the United States."

A civil appropriations act of June 25, 1860 (12 Stat. 104, 106) provided $500,000 for the completion of the Washington Aqueduct, "to be expended according to the plans and estimates of Captain Meigs and under his superintendence." Captain Montgomery C. Meigs had lobbied for this appointment against the wishes of the secretary of war. On the same day President Buchanan sent a message to the House of Representatives in which he said that he had signed the bill but protested that if this feature were regarded as mandatory it would be an invasion of the President's authority as commander in chief. If Congress "could withdraw an officer from the command of the President and select him for the performance of an executive duty, they might upon the same principle annex to an appropriation bill to carry on a war a condition requiring it not to be used for the defense of the country unless a particular person of its own selection should command the Army." Therefore Buchanan assumed that Congress had "merely designated Captain Meigs as its preference for the work. But he assigned Captain Meigs to his statutory task.

Equally striking is 19 Stat. 92 (1876), which said that "the President of the United States be, and he is hereby, directed to detail General H. C. Wright and General Q. A. Gillmore, of the Engineer Corps of the Army, who, with Edward Clark of Washington, D.C., shall form a commission, whose duty it shall be to select and determine the best kind of pavement to be used in paving Pennsylvania avenue. . . ." In 1893 the Supreme Court upheld an act that appointed the commissioners who were to establish a public park in the District of Columbia: the chief of engineers of the army, the engineer commissioner of the District, and three civilians to be appointed with the advice and consent of the Senate. No objection was made to the designation of the ex officio members by Congress, but it was argued that since the civilians were subject to senatorial approval, the commissioners must be officers, and therefore the two ex officio members should be subjected to confirmation as well. The Court replied, "It cannot be doubted, and it has frequently been the case, that Congress may increase the power and duties of an existing office without thereby rendering it necessary that the incumbent should be again nominated and appointed."

The 1863 edition of the *United States Consul's Manual* authorized a consul to inform the commander of a naval vessel of facts making necessary "the protection of the lives and property of American citizens which might be endangered by delay." In 1862, by 12 Stat. 561, 565 (1862), Congress had given the secretary of the navy rule–making power, and the *Regulations for the Government of the Navy*, which appeared in 1865, instructed the commanders of vessels to afford to diplomatic agents of the United States "such aid and co–operation in all matters for the benefit of the government as they may require, and as he may judge to be expedient and proper." The 1893 edition of the *Naval Regulations* made the authorization explicit: to prevent irreparable injury to the United States or its citizens a naval commander might find it necessary "to land an armed force in foreign territory on occasions of political disturbance where the local authorities are unable to give adequate protection to life or property"; he should first, if possible, obtain the consent of the local authorities, or of some of them.

14 Stat. 546 (1867) prohibited peonage in New Mexico or in any territory or state of the United States and provided that "it shall be the duty of all persons in the military or civil service of the Territory of New Mexico to aid in the enforcement" of the act.

16 Stat. 140 (1870), the Second Civil Rights Act, authorized commissioners of the federal courts to use the land or naval forces or the militia to aid in the execution of the judicial process issued under the act.

31 Stat. 588, 619 (1900) authorized and directed the secretary of war, at the request of the secretary of the interior, to make the necessary detail of troops to prevent intruders from entering the Sequoia National Park, the Yosemite National Park, and the General Grant National Park for the purpose of destroying game or objects of curiosity or for any other purpose forbidden by the regulations of the reservations, and to remove such persons from the parks.

40 Stat. 223 (1917) authorized the collectors, naval officers, surveyors, inspectors of customs, marshals, deputy marshals, and any other person designated for the purpose by the President to seize and detain arms or munitions or other articles when there was probable cause to believe that the articles were intended to be exported or taken out of the United States in violation of law.

The Tariff Act of 1922, *42 Stat. 858, 979* (1922), provided that officers of the customs or of the Coast Guard, and other persons authorized by the secretary of the treasury, might stop and search a vessel within four leagues of the coast of the United States to determine whether a violation of the laws of the United States had occurred. A similar provision was included in the Tariff Act of 1930, 46 Stat. 590, 747 (1930).

70A Stat. 33 (1956) provided that at the request of the secretary of state, the secretary of one of the military departments might detail members of the armed forces under his jurisdiction as inspectors of buildings under construction or repair abroad by or for the United States, and as couriers for the State Department.

Cases, Statutes, and
Various Government Documents

20	1 C. Rob 196, 199, 165 Eng. Rep. 146, 147.
21	United States v. Smith, 27 F. Cas. 1192, 1230 (C.D.N.Y. 1806).
25	The Prize Cases, 67 U.S. (2 Black) 635 (1863).
26	Ibid., 668.
	Ibid., 698–99.
	12 Stat. 255 (1861).
	1 Stat. 424 (1795).
	2 Stat. 443 (1807).
29	96 *Cong. Rec.* 9648 (1950).
	119 *Cong. Rec.* S14141 (daily ed. July 19, 1973).

Page	*Chapter 3*
35	32 *Annals of Cong.*, 15 Cong., 1st Sess., Col. 1500 (1818).
	Ibid., Col. 1591.
	3 Stat. 678 (1822).
36	5 Stat. 163, 170 (1837).
	42 Stat. 2122 (1922).
37	1 Stat. 743 (1799).
41	51 *Cong. Rec.* 6908–9 (1914).
42	38 Stat. 770 (1914).
	78 Stat. 384 (1964).
43	The Prize Cases, 67 U.S. (2 Black) 635, 666 (1863).
45	76 Stat. 697 (1962).
46	The *Antelope*, 23 U.S. (10 Wheat.) 66, 118 (1825).
	The *Exchange* v. McFaddon, 11 U.S. (7 Cranch) 116, 140–41 (1812).
	The Ship *Richmond* v. United States, 22 U.S. (9 Wheat.) 102 (1815).
47	The *Appollon*, 22 U.S. (9 Wheat.) 362, 370–71 (1824), *accord* 4 Op. Att'y Gen. 285 (1843).
	Davison v. Seal-skins, 7 F. Cas. 192, 196 (D. Conn. 1835).
51	87 Stat. 130, 134 (1973).
52	*Weekly Comp. Pres. Doc.*, 597 (May 4, 1970).

Page	*Chapter 4*
53	Miller v. The Ship *Resolution*, 2 U.S. (2 Dall.) 12, 21 (1782).
54	2 Stat. 755 (1812); 9 Stat. 9 (1846); 30 Stat. 364 (1898); 40 Stat. 1 (1917); 40 Stat. 429 (1917); 55 Stat. 795, 796, 797 (1941); 56 Stat. 307 (1942).
	5 Stat. 797 (1845).
	9 Stat. 108 (1845).
	Cong. Globe, 30th Cong., 1st Sess., App. 595 (1848).
55	9 Stat. 9 (1846).
	9 Stat. 2 (1845).
	Cong. Globe, 30th Cong., 1st Sess., 95 (1848).

56   9 Stat. 334 (1848).
     1 Stat. 370 (1858).
     26 Stat. 674 (1890).

57   28 Stat. 975 (1895).
     30 Stat. 738 (1898).
     30 Stat. 364 (1898).

58   1 Stat. 350 (1794).
     1 Stat. 453 (1796).
     1 Stat. 565 (1798), 1 Stat. 613 (1799); 1 Stat. 578 (1798); 1 Stat.
        553 (1798), 1 Stat. 709 (1799); 1 Stat. 594 (1798), 1 Stat. 729
        (1799); 1 Stat. 547 (1798), 1 Stat. 552 (1798), 1 Stat. 556
        (1798), 1 Stat. 569 (1798), 1 Stat. 576 (1798), 1 Stat. 595
        (1798), 1 Stat. 621 (1799); 1 Stat. 558 (1798), 1 Stat. 569
        (1798), 1 Stat. 604 (1798), 1 Stat. 725 (1799); see also 1 Stat.
        549 (1798), 1 Stat. 552 (1798), 1 Stat. 554 (1798), 1 Stat. 555
        (1798), 1 Stat. 604 (1798).
     1 Stat. 561 (1798).
     1 Stat. 574 (1798).
     1 Stat. 578 (1798).
     1 Stat. 743 (1799).
     Bas v. Tingy, 4 U.S. (4 Dall.) 37 (1800).

59   Talbot v. Seeman, 5 U.S. (1 Cranch) 1 (1801).
     Ibid., 28.
     Little v. Barreme, 6 U.S. (2 Cranch) 170 (1804).

60   Ibid.

61   2 Stat. 129 (1802).
     3 Stat. 472 (1813).

62   3 Stat. 230 (1815).

63   39 Op. Att'y Gen. 484 (1940).
     55 Stat. 31 (1941).
     55 Stat. 764 (1941).

64   3 Stat. 471 (1811).
     5 Stat. 355 (1839).

65   5 Stat. 356 (1839).
     1 Stat. 424 (1795).
     59 Stat. 619, 621 (1945), 63 Stat. 734, 735 (1949); 69 Stat. 7
        (1955); 71 Stat. 5 (1957).
     78 Stat. 384 (1964).

68   The Prize Cases, 67 U.S. (2 Black) 635 (1863).
     Ibid., 668. Compare 690–92 (Nelson, dissenting).

70   Ibid., 668.
     United States v. Mitchell, 6 U.S. (2 Dall.) 348, 355 (1795). See
        also United States v. Vogel, 6 U.S. (2 Dall.) 346 (1795).

71   United States v. Smith, 27 F. Cas. 1192, 1230 (C.D.N.Y. 1806).
     Ibid., 1230.

72   The Prize Cases, 67 U.S. (2 Black) 668 (1863) (emphasis added).
     Ibid.

Page   *Chapter 5*

78   *Cong. Globe*, 30th Cong., 1st Sess., 778 (1848); further debate
      reported in appendix, 590–643 (1848).

79   54 *Cong. Rec.* 2550 (1917).

80   Ibid., 4273.
      Ibid., 4399, 4715.
      55 *Cong. Rec.* 103 (1917).
      3 Stat. 510, 513 (1819).

Page   *Chapter 6*

88   United States v. Hosmer, 76 U.S. (9 Wall.) 432 (1870).
      12 Stat. 326 (1861).
      1 Stat. 95, 96 (1789).
      1 Stat. 264 (1792).
      12 Stat. 329 (1861).

89   12 Stat. 617 (1862).
      81 Stat. 760 (1868).
      22 Stat. 564, 565 (1833); 25 Stat. 489 (1888).
      10 Stat. 723 (1855).
      12 Stat. 279, 280 (1861).
      12 Stat. 326 (1861).

90   13 Stat. 11 (1864).
      14 Stat. 223 (1866).

91   32 Stat. 830, 831 (1903).
      38 Stat. 928, 929 (1915); see also 39 Stat. 556, 558 (1916).
      61 Stat. 503 (1947).
      7 Op. Att'y Gen. 453, 465 (1853).
      4 Op. Att'y Gen. 516 (1846).
      14 Stat. 485, 486–87 (1867).

92   15 Stat. 14 (1867).
      16 Stat. 315, 319 (1870).
      61 Stat. 500 (1947).
      1 Stat. 424 (1795).
      Houston v. Moore, 18 U.S. (5 Wheat.) 1 (1820).

93   35 Stat. 400 (1908).
      1 Stat. 302 (1793).
      Kentucky v. Denison, 65 U.S. (24 How.) 66, 107 (1861).

94   39 Stat. 223 (1916).
      10 Op. Att'y Gen. 11 (1861).
      10 Op. Att'y Gen. 413 (1862), *accord* 13 Op. Att'y Gen. 9
         (1869); 21 Op. Att'y Gen. 46 (1894).
      12 Op. Att'y Gen. 4 (1866).
      United States v. Perkins, 116 U.S. 483 (1886).
      United States v. Symonds, 120 U.S. 46 (1887); see also Glavey
         v. United States, 182 U.S. 595 (1901).
      United States *ex rel.* Hirschberg v. Cooke, 336 U.S. 210 (1949).
      2 Stat. 818, 819 (1813); 3 Stat. 297, 298 (1816).

United States v. Maurice, 21 F. Cas. 1211, 1215 (D. Va. 1823); see also United States v. Freeman, 44 U.S. (3 How.) 556, 567 (1845).

95   6 Op. Att'y Gen. 10, 14–26 (1853).
12 Stat. 561, 565 (1862); see also 10 Stat. 583, 587 (1854); 11 Stat. 407 (1859).
Smith v. Whitney, 116 U.S. 167 (1886); see also Johnson v. Sayre, 158 U.S. 115 (1895).
Little v. Barreme, 6 U.S. (2 Cranch) 170 (1804).
Jones v. Seward (40 Barb.) 563 (1863).
Ex parte Milligan, 71 U.S. (4 Wall.) 2 (1866).
Milligan v. Hovey, 17 F. Cas. 380 (D. Ind. 1871).
Bates v. Clark, 95 U.S. 204 (1877).
United States v. Ripley, 32 U.S. (7 Pet.) 18 (1833); see also United States v. Macdaniel, 32 U.S. (7 Pet.) 1 (1833).
Gratiot v. United States, 40 U.S. (15 Pet.) 371 (1841); see also Gratiot v. United States, 45 U.S. (4 How.) 80 (1846), and Minis v. United States, 40 U.S. (15 Pet.) 423 (1841).

96   Orloff v. Willoughby, 345 U.S. 83, 88 (1953).
27 Op. Att'y Gen. 259, 260–61 (1909).
30 Op. Att'y Gen. 234 (1913).
33 Op. Att'y Gen. 562, 567 (1923).
Auffmordt v. Hedden, 137 U.S. 310, 329 (1890).
Burrow-Giles Lithographic Co. v. Sarony, 111 U.S. 53, 57 (1884).
The *Laura*, 114 U.S. 411, 416 (1885).
Stuart v. Laird, 5 U.S. (1 Cranch) 299, 309 (1803).

97   1 Stat. 400 (1794).
2 Stat. 206 (1803).

98   70A Stat. 15 (1956); 10 U.S.C. §§331–34 (1959).

100   6 Op. Att'y Gen. 466 (1854).

102   41 Op. Att'y Gen. 313, 331 (1957).

103   83 Stat. 469, 487 (1969).
84 Stat. 2020, 2038 (1971); 85 Stat. 716, 735 (1971); 86 Stat. 1184, 1203 (1972).
84 Stat. 2020, 2037 (1971).
84 Stat. 1942, 1943 (1971).
85 Stat. 423, 430 (1971).
29 *Cong. Qtrly Wkly Rep.* 2371 (Nov. 20, 1971).

Page   *Chapter 7*

106   Mostyn v. Fabrigas, 1 Coup. 160 (1774) and cases reported; cases reported in Johnstone v. Sutton, 1 T.R. 536 (1783); Musgrave v. Pulido, 5 App. Cas. 102 (1879); Walker v. Baird, 1892 A.C. 491.

107   1 Stat. 558 (1798), *repealed by* 2 Stat. 132 (1802).

108   1 Stat. 749, 752 (1799).

Ex parte Bollman and Swartwout, 8 U.S. (4 Cranch) app. 455,
   459 (1807).
1 Stat. 709, 714, 715 (1799).
McConnel v. Hampton, 12 Johns. 234, 238 (N.Y. 1815).

111   Fleming v. Page, 50 U.S. (9 How.) 603, 615 (1850).
        United States v. Sweeny, 157 U.S. 281, 284 (1895).
        Hirota v. MacArthur, 338 U.S. 197 (1949).
        Ibid., 208.

112   36 Stat. 2259 (1910).
        Murray v. The *Charming Betsy*, 6 U.S. (2 Cranch) 64, 118
           (1804); The *Nereide*, 13 U.S. (9 Cranch) 388, 423 (1815); The
           Antelope, 23 U.S. (10 Wheat.) 66, 120 (1825).
        Ibid.
        Ex parte Milligan, 71 U.S. (4 Wall.) 2, 140 (1866).

113   1 Stat. 403 (1794).
        5 Stat. 29, 30 (1836).

114   54 Stat. 885, 886 (1940).
        83 Stat. 469, 487 (1969); 84 Stat. 1942 (1971); 84 Stat. 2020
           (1971); 85 Stat. 716 (1971).
        87 Stat. 130 (1973).
        Brown v. United States, 12 U.S. (8 Cranch) 110 (1814).
        United States v. Eliason, 41 U.S. (16 Pet.) 29 (1842).

115   *Ex parte* Vallandigham, 68 U.S. (1 Wall.) 243 (1864).
        Ex parte Milligan, 71 U.S. (4 Wall.) 2 (1866).
        Swaim v. United States, 165 U.S. 553 (1897).
        34 Op. Att'y Gen. 483 (1925).
        Ex parte Quirin, 317 U.S. 1, 26 (1942).
        United States v. Caltex, 344 U.S. 149 (1952); and see National
           Board of Y.M.C.A. v. United States, 395 U.S. 85 (1969).
        Mitchell v. Harmony, 54 U.S. (13 How.) 115 (1852).
        Ibid., 134.

116   See, e.g., United States v. General Motors Corp., 323 U.S. 373
           (1945); United States v. Petty Motor Co., 327 U.S. 372
           (1946); Kimball Laundry v. United States, 338 U.S. 1 (1949).
        Fleming v. Page, 50 U.S. (9 How.) 603 (1850).
        United States v. Alexander, 69 U.S. (2 Wall.) 417 (1864).
        Congress, on the other hand, has "the right to seize and
           confiscate all property of an enemy and to dispose of it at
           the will of the captor." [Miller v. United States, 78 U.S. (11
           Wall.) 268, 305 (1871).]
        In re Yamashita, 327 U.S. 341 (1946); cf. *In re* Egan, 8 F. Cas.
           367 (N.D.N.Y. 1866).
        Madsen v. Kinsella, 343 U.S. 341 (1952). By the time of Reid
           v. Covert, 354 U.S. 1 (1957), the military government of
           Germany had ended.
        Cross v. Harrison, 57 U.S. (16 How.) 164 (1853); Dooley v.
           United States, 182 U.S. 222 (1901).
        Leinsdorfer v. Webb, 61 U.S. (20 How.) 176 (1858); United
           States v. Diekelman, 92 U.S. 520 (1875).
        The Grapeshot v. Wallerstein, 76 U.S. (9 Wall.) 129 (1870);
           Burke v. Miltenberger, 86 U.S. (19 Wall.) 519 (1874); New

Orleans v. New York Mail S.S. Co., 87 U.S. (20 Wall.) 387 (1874); Lewis v. Cocks, 90 U.S. (23 Wall.) 466 (1874); Mechanics and Traders Bank v. Union Bank, 89 U.S. (22 Wall.) 276 (1875). However, the personnel of the occupying army are not subject to the jurisdiction of the provisional court civilly [Dow v. Johnson, 100 U.S. 158 (1880)] or criminally [Coleman v. Tennessee, 97 U.S. 509 (1879)].
Santiago v. Nogueras, 214 U.S. 260 (1909); Rose v. McNamara, 375 F. 2d 924 (D.C. Cir. 1967), *cert. den.* 389 U.S. 856 (1967).
Raymond v. Thomas, 91 U.S. 712 (1876).
Jecker v. Montgomery, 54 U.S. (13 How.) 498 (1851).
6 Stat. 248 (1820).

117   5 Stat. 651 (1844).
Johnson v. Duncan, 3 Mart. 530 (La. 1815).
Matter of Stacy, 10 Johns. 127 (N.Y. 1813).
Smith v. Shaw, 12 Johns. 257 (N.Y. 1814).
McConnel v. Hampton, 12 Johns. 234, 238 (N.Y. 1815).
Ex parte Milligan, 71 U.S. (4 Wall.) 2, 129 (1866).
Pierce v. United States, 74 U.S. (7 Wall.) 676–77 (1859).

118   16 *Annals of Cong.*, 16th Cong., 1st Sess., Pt. 1, Col. 43, 423 (1819–1820).
Ex parte Bollman and Swartwout, 8 U.S. (4 Cranch) 75, 101 (1807).

119   *Ex parte* Merryman, 17 F. Cas. 144, 149 (D. Md. 1861).
Ibid.

120   10 Op. Att'y Gen. 28 (1861).
Ex parte Merryman, 17 F. Cas. 144, 149 (D. Md. 1861); *Ex parte* Benedict, 3 F. Cas. 159 (N.D.N.Y. 1862); *Ex parte* Field, 9 F. Cas. 1 (D. Vt. 1862); *In re* Kemp, 16 Wis. 382 (1863). See also *Ex parte* Orozco, 201 F. Cas. 106 (W.D. Tex. 1912).
12 Stat. 755 (1863).
In re Fagan, 8 F. Cas. 947 (D. Mass. 1863); *In re* Dunn, 8 F. Cas. 83 (S.D.N.Y. 1863); *In re* Oliver, 17 Wis. 703 (1864).
Ex parte Milligan, 71 U.S. (4 Wall.) 2 (1866).
Ibid., 121.
Ibid., 140.
Kurtz v. Moffitt, 115 U.S. 487 (1888).
Ibid.

121   Reid v. United States, 211 U.S. 529 (1909).

Page   *Chapter 8*

123   Cherokee Nation v. Georgia, 30 U.S. (5 Pet.) 1, 16 (1831).
Marks v. United States, 161 U.S. 297, 302 (1896).

124   12 Stat. 528 (1862).
16 Stat. 544, 566 (1871).
19 Stat. 192 (1876); 19 Stat. 254 (1877).
United States v. Kagama, 118 U.S. 375 (1885).
23 Stat. 851, 855–56 (1891).

125   Scott v. United States, 33 Ct. Cl. 486, 489 (1898).

1 Stat. 50 (1789).

1 Stat. 123 (1790); 1 Stat. 549 (1798); 2 Stat. 58 (1800); 2 Stat. 399 (1805); 2 Stat. 514 (1809).

1 Stat. 95, 96 (1789).

1 Stat. 119 (1790).

126   1 Stat. 222 (1791).

127   Cherokee Nation v. Georgia, 30 U.S. (5 Pet.) 1, 16 (1831).

4 Stat. 214, 215 (1827); 4 Stat. 257, 258 (1828); 4 Stat. 348, 349 (1829); 4 Stat. 465, 466 (1831); 10 Stat. 218, 219 (1853); 10 Stat. 307 (1854); 10 Stat. 311 (1854); 11 Stat. 200, 204, 205 (1857).

22 *Annals of Cong.*, 11th Cong., 3d Sess., Col. 1259 (1810).

128   3 Stat. 471 (1811).

3 Stat. 472 (1813).

130   *S. Doc. No.* 100, 15th Cong., 2d Sess., 8 (1819).

34 *Annals of Cong.*, 15th Cong., 2d Sess., Pt. 1, Col. 518 (1819).

8 Stat. 252, 260 (1819).

3 Stat. 768 (1823).

6 Stat. 569 (1834).

Page   *Chapter 9*

133   Inland Waterways Corp. v. Young, 309 U.S. 517, 524 (1940).

134   Powell v. McCormack, 395 U.S. 486, 546 (1969).

Stuart v. Laird, 5 U.S. (1 Cranch) 299 (1803).

Ibid., 307–8.

Ibid., 309.

Burrow–Giles Lithographic Co. v. Sarony, 111 U.S. 53, 57 (1884).

135   Powell v. McCormack, 395 U.S. 486, 547 (1969).

136   *Ex parte* Grossman, 267 U.S. 87, 119 (1925).

Youngstown Sheet & Tube Co. v. Sawyer, 343 U.S. 579 (1952).

United States v. United States District Court, 407 U.S. 297 (1972).

United States v. Nixon, 418 U.S. 683, 707 (1974).

Train v. City of New York, 420 U.S. 35 (1975).

2 Stat. 206 (1803).

137   McPherson v. Blacker, 146 U.S. 1, 27 (1892); Walz v. Tax Commission, 397 U.S. 664, 678 (1970).

Youngstown Sheet & Tube Co. v. Sawyer, 343 U.S. 579 (1952).

Ibid., 584.

Ibid., 585–87.

Ibid., 610–11.

138   Ibid., 648.

Ibid., 683.

Edwards' Lessee v. Darby, 25 U.S. (12 Wheat.) 206, 210 (1827).

United States v. Bank of North Carolina, 31 U.S. (6 Pet.) 29 (1832); Union Ins. Co. v. Hoge, 62 U.S. (21 How.) 35 (1859); Peabody v. Stark, 83 U.S. (16 Wall.) 240 (1873); Smythe v.

Fiske, 90 U.S. (23 Wall.) 374 (1874); United States v. Moore, 95 U.S. 760 (1878); United States v. Pugh, 99 U.S. 265 (1879); Hahn v. United States, 107 U.S. 402 (1883); Brown v. United States, 113 U.S. 568 (1884); United States v. Philbrick, 120 U.S. 52 (1887); United States v. Hill, 120 U.S. 169 (1887); United States v. Johnston, 124 U.S. 236 (1888); Robertson v. Downing, 127 U.S. 607 (1888); United States v. Alabama G.S.R. Co., 142 U.S. 615 (1892); United States v. Union Pacific R. Co., 148 U.S. 562 (1893); Hewitt v. Schultz, 180 U.S. 139 (1901); United States v. American Trucking Associations, 310 U.S. 534 (1940); Billings v. Truesdell, 321 U.S. 542 (1944); Skidmore v. Swift & Co., 323 U.S. 134 (1944).

Swift and Courtney and Beecher Co. v. United States, 105 U.S. 691 (1882); United States v. Graham, 110 U.S. 219 (1884); United States v. Tanner, 147 U.S. 661 (1893); United States v. Alger, 152 U.S. 384 (1894); Webster v. Luther, 163 U.S. 331 (1896); Parsons v. United States, 167 U.S. 324 (1897).

United States v. Macdaniel, 32 U.S. (7 Pet.) 1, 15 (1833); *Cf.* Merritt v. Cameron, 137 U.S. 542 (1890).

139   United States v. Arrendondo, 31 U.S. (6 Pet.) 691, 713–14 (1832).

United States v. Alexander, 79 U.S. (12 Wall.) 177, 180 (1871); United States v. Dakota–Montana Oil Co., 288 U.S. 459, 466 (1933); McFeely v. Commissioner of Internal Revenue, 296 U.S. 102, 108 (1935); United States v. Safety Car Heating & Lighting Co., 297 U.S. 88, 95 (1936).

United States v. Midwest Oil Co., 236 U.S. 459 (1915).

Ibid., 474, 478.

Ex parte United States, 242 U.S. 27 (1916).

141   87 *Cong. Rec.* 5930–31 (1941).

142   *H.R. Doc. No.* 443, 84th Cong., 2d Sess. (1956).

143   117 *Cong. Rec.* 28977 (1971).

119 *Cong. Rec.* S14174 (daily ed. July 20, 1973).

144   42 Stat. 2122 (1922).

31 Stat. 897 (1901).

145   39 Stat. 1654 (1915).

39 Stat. 1659 (1916).

39 Stat. 223 (1916).

44 Stat. 2193, 2194 (1925).

146   68 *Cong. Rec.* 1326 (1927).

147   Davison v. Sealskins, 7 F. Cas. 192 (D. Conn. 1835).

Page   *Chapter 10*

151   Murray v. The *Charming Betsy*, 6 U.S. (2 Cranch) 64, 120 (1804).

The Slaughter-House Cases, 83 U.S. (16 Wall.) 36, 79 (1873); *In re* Neagle, 135 U.S. 1, 64 (1890).

15 Stat. 223 (1868).

152   Prigg v. Pennsylvania, 41 U.S. (16 Pet.) 539 (1842).
Durand v. Hollins, 8 F. Cas. 111 (1860).
In re Neagle, 135 U.S. 1, 64 (1890).
Cong. Globe, 33rd Cong., 1st Sess., 80, 82 (1854).
10 Stat. 594 (1854).
In re Neagle, 135 U.S. 64 (1890).

154   12 Stat. 561, 565 (1862).
Smith v. Whitney, 116 U.S. 167 (1886); Johnson v. Sayre, 158
U.S. 115 (1895).

158   Kent v. Dulles, 357 U.S. 116 (1958).
See, e.g., *In re* Chapman, 166 U.S. 661 (1897); Standard Oil
Co. of New Jersey v. United States, 221 U.S. 1 (1911); The
Abby Dodge v. United States, 223 U.S. (1912); A. A.
Schechter Poultry Corp. v. United States, 295 U.S. 495
(1935).
Rev. Stat. §1547.

159   *H.R. Exec. Doc. No.* 1, 43rd Cong., 2d Sess. (1874).

160   Durand v. Hollins, 8 F. Cas. 111 (1860).

Page   *Chapter 11*

161   1 Stat. 28 (1789).
1 Stat. 68 (1789).

162   Marbury v. Madison, 5 U.S. (1 Cranch) 137 (1803).
43 Stat. 5 (1924), approved in Sinclair v. United States, 297
U.S. 263 (1929).
5 Stat. 409 (1840); 5 Stat. 460 (1841).
United States v. Maurice, 26 F. Cas. 1211 (D. Va. 1823); 10
Op. Att'y Gen. 11 (1861).

163   Gelston v. Hoyt, 16 U.S. (3 Wheat.) 245, 330–32 (1818); see
also Hendricks v. Gonzalez, 67 F. 351 (2nd Cir. 1895); 29
Op. Att'y Gen. 247 (1911).
Muir v. Louisville & Nashville Railroad, 247 F. 888, 894 (W.D.
Ky. 1895).
Little v. Barreme, 6 U.S. (2 Cranch) 170 (1804).

164   Tracy v. Swartwout, 35 U.S. (10 Pet.) 80 (1836).
Bates v. Clark, 95 U.S. 204 (1877).
Hendricks v. Gonzalez, 67 F. 351 (2d Cir. 1895).
United States v. Nixon, 94 S. Ct. 390 (1974). This decision
undermines Mississippi v. Johnson (4 Wall.) 475 (1867).
1 Op. Att'y Gen. 624–26 (1823).
1 Op. Att'y Gen. 624 (1823); 1 Op. Att'y Gen. 678 (1824); 2
Op. Att'y Gen. 507 (1832); 2 Op. Att'y Gen. 307 (1829).
4 Op. Att'y Gen. 515 (1846).
2 Op. Att'y Gen. 482 (1831).
Myers v. United States, 272 U.S. 52 (1926). The authority of
the Myers case has been sapped by Rathbun v. United
States, 295 U.S. 602 (1935) and Wiener v. United States,
357 U.S. 349 (1958).
Ex parte Hennen, 38 U.S. (13 Pet.) 230, 261 (1839).

165   Kendall v. United States, 53 U.S. (12 Pet.) 524, 613 (1838).
       State Highway Commission v. Volpe, 479 F. 2d 1099 (8th Cir.
          1973); Train v. City of New York, 420 U.S. 35 (1975).

166   117 *Cong. Rec.* 28977 (1971).
       Youngstown Sheet & Tube Co. v. Sawyer, 343 U.S. 579, 682
          (1952).
       In re Neagle, 135 U.S. 1 (1890).

167   Ibid., 67–68.
       In re Debs, 158 U.S. 564 (1895).

168   United States v. Debs, 64 F. 724 (Ill. 1894).

169   *In re* Debs, 158 U.S. 591–93 (1895).
       United States v. Guest, 383 U.S. 745, 769 (1966).
       United States v. Midwest Oil Co., 236 U.S. 459 (1915).
       Ibid., 481.

170   United States v. Western Union Tel. Co., 272 F. 311 (S.D.N.Y.
          1921), *rev'd on stipulation*, 260 U.S. 754 (1922).
       Ibid., 315.

171   Youngstown Sheet & Tube Co. v. Sawyer, 343 U.S. 672 (1952).
       Ibid., 587.

172   *Dissenting* in Myers v. United States, 272 U.S. 177 (1926).
       Youngstown Sheet & Tube Co. v. Sawyer, 343 U.S. 629 (1952).
       Ibid., 646.
       Ibid., 652.
       Ibid., 659.

173   Mitchell v. Harmony, 54 U.S. (13 How.) 115 (1851).
       United States v. Russell, 80 U.S. (13 Wall.) 623 (1871).
       Youngstown Sheet & Tube Co. v. Sawyer, 343 U.S. 662 (1952).
       New York Times Company v. United States, 403 U.S. 713
          (1971).
       Ibid., 718.
       Ibid., 718–19.

174   Ibid., 730.
       Ibid., 732–40.

175   Ibid., 741–42.
       Ibid., 753–54.
       Myers v. United States, 272 U.S. 52 (1926).
       Wallace v. United States, 257 U.S. 541 (1922).
       Ex rel. Knauff v. Shaughnessy, 338 U.S. 537 (1950).

Page   *Chapter 12*

180   United States v. Curtiss–Wright Export Corp., 299 U.S. 304,
          316, 319 (1936).
       Youngstown Sheet & Tube Co. v. Sawyer, 343 U.S. 587 (1952).

181   Reid v. Covert, 354 U.S. 1, 16–17 (1957); see also Kinsella v.
          United States *ex rel.* Singleton, 364 U.S. 234, 261 (1960).
       10 *Annals of Cong.*, 6th Cong., 1st Sess., Col. 613 (1800),
          reprinted in 18 U.S. (5 Wheat.) 26 n.1.

182   United States v. Curtiss–Wright Export Corp., 299 U.S. 304
          (1936).

316   CASES, STATUTES, AND DOCUMENTS

Ibid., 319–20.
Youngstown Sheet & Tube Co. v. Sawyer, 343 U.S. 579,
635–36 (1952).
Zemel v. Rusk, 381 U.S. 1, 17 (1965).

184 *Cong. Globe*, 38th Cong., 2d Sess., 65–67 (1864).
40 *Cong. Rec.* 2132, 2134 (1906).
*Hearings on Separation of Powers before the Subcommittee on
Separation of Powers of the Senate Committee on the Judiciary,*
90th Cong., 1st Sess., 52 (1967).
Chae Chan Ping v. United States (Chinese Exclusion Case),
130 U.S. 581, 603–4 (1889).
Perez v. Brownell, 356 U.S. 44, 57 (1958).
Galven v. United States, 347 U.S. 522, 530 (1954); Harisiades
v. Shaughnessy, 342 U.S. 580, 587–88 (1952); MacKenzie v.
Hare, 239 U.S. 299, 311–12 (1915).
First National City Bank v. Banco Nacional de Cuba, 406 U.S.
759 (1972).

185 Ibid., 773.
Ibid., 776.
Ibid., 792.
90 Stat. 729 (1976); 90 Stat. 771 (1976).
90 Stat. 729, 758 (1976).
90 Stat. 729, 759–60 (1976).

186 33 Stat. 51 (1817); 35 Stat. 432 (1818); 35 Stat. 612 (1820).
The *Orinoco*, 18 F. Cas. 830 (D. Mass. 1812); Gelston v. Hoyt,
16 U.S. (3 Wheat.) 246 (1818).
84 Stat. 2053, 2055 (1971).
84 Stat. 910 (1970).
85 Stat. 716 (1971); 85 Stat. 423 (1971).
85 Stat. 20 (1972).
Eagleton Amendment, *H.R. Rep. No.* 7447, 93rd Cong., 2d
Sess. (1973); 87 Stat. 130, 134 (1973).

187 50 U.S.C. §1544(c).
Ibid., 1547.
See Orlando v. Laird, 433 F. 2d 1039 (2nd Cir.), *cert. denied,*
404 U.S. 864 (1971); but see Mitchell v. Laird, 488 F. 2d
611 (D.C. Cir. 1973), and also Firmage, 57, 93–96.

189 Chae Chan Ping v. United States (Chinese Exclusion Case),
130 U.S. 581 (1889).

190 50 U.S.C. §1544(c) (1973).

192 United States v. Belmont, 301 U.S. 324 (1937).
Ibid., 330–31.

193 Ibid.

194 22 U.S.C. §§801 *et seq.* United States v. Germain, 99 U.S. 508
(1878).
United States v. Hartwell, 73 U.S. (6 Wall.) 385, 393 (1868).

Page   *Chapter 13*

198 Schechter Poultry Corporation v. United States, 250 U.S. 495,
529–30 (1935).

Wayman v. Southard, 23 U.S. (10 Wheat.) 1, 42–43 (1825).

199   *S. Doc. No.* 105, 65th Cong., 1st Sess., 9 (1917).
The Brig *Aurora*, 11 U.S. (7 Cranch) 382 (1813).

200   Panama Refining Co. v. Ryan, 293 U.S. 388, 415 (1935).
Cong. Globe, 23d Cong., 2d Sess., 23 (1834).

202   Ibid., 35th Cong., 2d Sess., 1120 (1859).

204   59 Stat. 621 (1945), *amended* 63 Stat 735 (1949); 22 U.S.C. §287d (1964).

205   69 Stat. 5 (1955).
71 Stat. 5 (1957).
78 Stat. 384 (1964).
110 *Cong. Rec.* 18402–3 (1964).
Ibid., 18132.

206   Field v. Clark, 143 U.S. 649, 693 (1892).
Panama Refining Co. v. Ryan, 293 U.S. 388, 415 (1935).
Schechter Poultry Corporation v. United States, 250 U.S. 551 (1935).
United States v. Cohen Grocery Co., 255 U.S. 81 (1921).

207   United States v. Curtiss–Wright Export Corp., 299 U.S. 316 (1936).

208   Ibid., 316–17.
Reid v. Covert, 354 U.S. 1, 5–6 (1957).
Kinsella v. United States *ex rel.* Singleton, 361 U.S. 234, 261 (1960).
Stuart v. Laird, 5 U.S. (1 Cranch) 299 (1803).
Field v. Clark, 143 U.S. 649 (1892).

209   Ibid., 692–93.
Ibid., 691.
United States v. Curtiss–Wright Export Corp., 299 U.S. 324 (1936).

210   Ibid., 329.
Youngstown Sheet & Tube Co. v. Sawyer, 343 U.S. 579, 635–36n. (1952).
Zemel v. Rusk, 381 U.S. 1, 17 (1965).
United States *ex rel.* Knauff v. Shaughnessy, 338 U.S. 5, 37 (1950).
Fong Yue Ting v. United States, 149 U.S. 698, 728 (1893).

211   Kent v. Dulles, 357 U.S. 129 (1958).
Zemel v. Rusk, 381 U.S. 17 (1965).
Ibid., 21–22.

212   Hirabayashi v. United States, 320 U.S. 1, 104 (1943).
Yakus v. United States, 321 U.S. 414, 426 (1944).
Bowles v. Willingham, 321 U.S. 503, 514 (1944).
Woods v. Cloyd W. Miller Co., 333 U.S. 138, 144 (1948).
Lichter v. United States, 334 U.S. 742, 784 (1948).
Oestereich v. Selective Service System Local Board No. 11, 393 U.S. 233, 237, 238–39 (1968).

213   United States v. Robel, 389 U.S. 258, 272 (1967).
Morse v. Boswell, 289 F. Supp. 812 (D.C. Md. 1968), *aff'd per curiam*, 401 F. 2d 544 (4th Cir. 1969); Goldstein v. Clifford,

Citizens to Preserve Overton Park v. Volpe, 401 U.S. 402
(1971).
Decatur v. Pauling, 39 U.S. (14 Pet.) 496, 516 (1840).
Martin v. Mott, 25 U.S. (12 Wheat.) 19 (1827).
1 Stat. 424 (1795).

235   Martin v. Mott, 25 U.S. (12 Wheat.) 30 (1827).
Chicago & Southern Airlines, Inc. v. Waterman Corp., 333
U.S. 103, 111 (1948).
United States *ex rel.* Schonbrun v. Commanding Officer, 403
F. 2d 371 (2d Cir. 1968).
Ibid., 374.
Ibid., 374–75.
Ibid., 375 n.2.

236   The Paquete *Habana*, 175 U.S. 677 (1900); see discussion in
Baker v. Carr, 396 U.S. 186, 211–14 (1962).
The *Rogdai*, 278 F. 294, 296 (N.D. Cal. 1920).
The *Ambrose Light*, 25 F. 408 (S.D.N.Y. 1885).
Foster v. Neilson, 27 U.S. (2 Pet.) 253 (1829).
Perkins v. Elg, 307 U.S. 325 (1939).

237   Baker v. Carr, 396 U.S. 186, 211–12 (1962). For similar
analysis and conclusions, see *118*, 526–27.
Korematsu v. United States, 323 U.S. 214, 218 (1944).
Duncan v. Kahanamoku, 327 U.S. 304 (1946).

238   Youngstown Sheet & Tube Co. v. Sawyer, 343 U.S. 579 (1952).
Ibid., 587.
Ibid., 593, 629, 634, 655, 660.
Ibid., 660, 662.

239   Luftig v. McNamara, 373 F. 2d 664 (D.C. Cir. 1967), *cert.*
denied, 387 U.S. 945 (1967).
Ibid., 666.
Atlee v. Laird, 347 F. Supp. 689 (E.D. Pa. 1972) (three–judge
court), *aff'd* 411 U.S. 911 (1973).
Ibid., 701.

240   Baker v. Carr, 369 U.S. 186, 217 (1962).
Atlee v. Laird, 347 F. Supp. 707 (E.D. Pa. 1972).
Ibid., 707.
Ibid., 709.
Ibid., 711–12.
Ibid., 712–13.
For discussion of the Supreme Court case law, see
Massachusetts v. Laird, 400 U.S. 886, 897–99 (1970)
(Douglas, dissenting); Atlee v. Laird, 347 F. Supp. 689,
710–11 (1972) (Lord, dissenting).
Bas v. Tingy, 4 U.S. (4 Dall.) 36 (1800); Talbot v. Seeman, 5
U.S. (1 Cranch) 1 (1801).
Little v. Barreme, 6 U.S. (2 Cranch) 170 (1804).

241   The Prize Cases, 67 U.S. (2 Black) 635 (1863).
See, e.g., Velvel v. Johnson, 287 F. Supp. 846 (D. Kan. 1968),
cert. denied, 396 U.S. 1042 (1970).
Massachusetts v. Laird, 400 U.S. 886 (1971).

Ibid., 894.
Ibid., 895.
Orlando v. Laird, 443 F. 2d 1039 (2d Cir.), *cert. denied*, 404
    U.S. 869, 1042 (1971).

242   Ibid., 1043.
Ex parte Endo, 323 U.S. 283 (1944).
Orlando v. Laird, 443 F. 2d 1043 (2d Cir. 1971).

243   Massachusetts v. Laird, 451 F. 2d 26, 34 (1st Cir. 1971).
United States v. Sisson, 294 F. Supp. 511, 515 (D. Mass. 1968).
Mitchell v. Laird, 488 F. 2d 611 (D.C. Cir. 1973); Holtzman v.
    Schlesinger, 361 F. Supp. 553 (E.D.N.Y. 1973), *rev'd* 484 F.
    2d 1307 (2d Cir.), *cert. denied*, 416 U.S. 936 (1973).
Holtzman v. Schlesinger, 484 F. 2d 1307 (2d Cir. 1973).

244   Ibid., 1310.
Ibid., 1314.
Ibid., 1310 n.1.
Goldwater v. Carter, 100 S. Ct. 533 (1979).
Ibid., 537.
Coleman v. Miller, 307 U.S. 433 (1939).

245   Goldwater v. Carter, 100 S. Ct. 538 (1979) (Rehnquist,
    concurring).
Ibid., 533.
Ibid., 534.
See Baker v. Carr, 369 U.S. 186, 217 (1962).

246   50 U.S.C. §1547(a)(1).
Ibid., §1547(a)(2).

Page   *Chapter 16*

247   *Address to the Nation*, October 27, 1983, *Weekly Comp. Pres. Doc.*,
    1497 at 1502 (Oct. 31, 1983) [hereinafter *Address to the
    Nation*].
Ibid.

248   Crockett v. Reagan, 558 F. Supp. 893 (D.D.C. 1982).

249   50 U.S.C. §§1541–48 (1980).
21 U.S.C. §2151 (1980).
75 Stat. 424 (1961) (codified at scattered sections of 22 U.S.C.);
    22 U.S.C. §§2751 *et seq.* (1980).
S. Rep. No. 220, 93rd Cong., 1st Sess., 27 (1983).

250   *H.R.* 1619; *H.R.* 1777, 98th Cong., 1st Sess. (1983).
S. 2179, 98th Cong., 1st Sess. (1983).
H. Con. R. 67, 98th Cong., 1st Sess. (1983).
*Message from the President of the United States Transmitting his
    Central American Policy*, H. Doc. No. 53, 98th Cong., 1st Sess.
    (1983).

251   *Use of Naval Mines in the Exercise of Self–Defense*, State Dep't
    Document reprinted in 42 *Cong. Qrtly Wkly Rep.* 835 (April
    14, 1984).

252   50 U.S.C. §413 (1980).

Immigration and Naturalization Service v. Chadha, 103 S. Ct. 2764 (1983).

Crockett v. Reagan, 558 F. Supp. 893 (D.D.C. 1982); Sanchez–Espinoza v. Reagan, 568 F. Supp. 596 (D.D.C. 1983).

276   *Constitutional Grounds for Presidential Impeachment*, Staff of the Impeachment Inquiry of the House Judiciary Committee, 93rd Cong., 2d Sess. (Comm. Print 1974).

277   *H. Res.* 370, 98th Cong., 1st Sess. (1983).

Bibliography

1. Adams, B. "The Heritage of Henry Adams." In *Henry Adams, The Degradation of the Democratic Dogma* (1958).
2. Adams, H. *The Education of Henry Adams* (1931).
3. Adams, J. *Works*. Edited by C. F. Adams. 10 vols. (1850–56).
4. Adams, J. Q. *Memoirs of John Quincy Adams*. Edited by C. F. Adams. 12 vols. (1970).
5. Albert, L. "Justiciability and Theories of Judicial Review: A Remote Relationship." 50 *S. Cal. L. Rev.* 1139 (1977).
6. *American State Papers: Naval Affairs* (1860).
7. *Armed Actions Taken by the United States Without a Declaration of War, 1789–1967.* Department of State, Historical Studies Division (1967).
8. Armstrong, J. *The Life of Anthony Wayne* (1849).
9. Austin, J. *Philosophical Papers* (1970).
10. "Authority of the President to Repel the Attack in Korea." 23 *Dep't St. Bull.* (1950).
11. Bagehot, W. *The English Constitution* (1928).
12. Berger, R. "Administrative Arbitrariness: A Synthesis." 78 *Yale L.J.* (1969).
13. Berger. "The Presidential Monopoly on Foreign Relations." 71 *Mich. L. Rev.* (1972).
14. Berger. "War Making by the President." 121 *U. Pa. L. Rev.* (1972).
15. Bickel, A. *The Least Dangerous Branch* (1962).
16. Bingham, C. *Men and Affairs* (1967).
17. Blackstone, W. *Commentaries on the Laws of England*. Edited by W. C. Jones (1915).
18. *Bombing in Cambodia, Hearings before the Senate Committee on Armed Services.* 93d Cong., 1st Sess. (1973).

19. Bouscaren, A. T. *The Last of the Mandarins: Diem of Vietnam* (1965).

20. Bowett, D. W. *Self–Defense in International Law* (1958).

21. Branch, C. "The Trial of the CIA." *New York Times Magazine* (Sept. 12, 1976).

22. Brooks, N. C. *A Complete History of the Mexican War* (1849).

23. Brownlie, I. *International Law and the Use of Force by States* (1963).

24. Burns, J. M. *The Embattled Presidency*. 2 vols. (1964).

25. Buttinger, J. *Vietnam: A Dragon Embattled*. 2 vols. (1967).

26. Carter, C. E., ed. *The Territorial Papers of the United States*. 28 vols. (1936).

27. Chamberlain, W. H. *The Russian Revolution, 1917–1921* (1952).

28. Clark, J. R., Jr. *The Right to Protect Citizens in Foreign Countries by Landing Forces* (1912).

29. Clendenen, C. C. *Blood on the Border: The United States Army and the Mexican Irregulars* (1969).

30. Clode, C. M. *The Military Forces of the Crown*. 2 vols. (1869).

31. Comyns, J. *Comyns' Digest*. Edited by A. Hammond (5th ed. 1822).

32. Congressional Research Service, Library of Congress. *The Constitution of the United States of America: Analysis and Interpretation* (1973).

33. *Consular Regulations: A Practical Guide for Consular Officers* (1868).

34. Cooke, J., ed. *The Federalist* (1961).

35. Cooley, T. *The General Principles of Constitutional Law in the United States of America* (3d ed. 1898).

36. Crandall, S. B. *Treaties, Their Making and Enforcement* (1916).

37. Daniels, J. *The Wilson Era: Years of Peace—1910–1917* (1944).

38. Davis, K. C. "Administrative Arbitrariness—A Postscript." 114 *U. Pa. L. Rev.* (1966).

39. Davis. *Administrative Law Treatise* §28.16 (1958).

40. de Littleton, Sir Thomas. *Treatise on Tenures* (1896).

41. de Riencourt, A. *The Coming Caesars* (1957).

42. Deutsch, E. "The President as Commander in Chief." 57 *A.B.A.J.* (1971).

43. de Vattel, E. *The Law of Nations*. Translated by C. Fenwick (1916).

44. Dicey, A. V. *Introduction to the Study of the Law of the Constitution* (10th ed. 1959).

45. *Diplomatic History of the Panama Canal*. S. Doc. No. 474, 63d Cong., 2d Sess. (1918).

46. Dupuy, R. E. *The Compact History of the United States Army* (1961).

47. Eagleton, C. "The Form and Function of the Declaration of War." 32 *Am. J. Int'l L.* (1938).

48. Eisenhower, D. D. *Mandate for Change* (1963).

49. Elliot, J., ed. *The Debates in the Several State Conventions on the Adoption of the Federal Constitution*. 5 vols. (1907).

50. Ellsworth, H. A. *One Hundred Eighty Landings of United States Marines, 1800–1934* (1974).

51. Emerson, T. "War Powers Legislation." 74 *W. Va. L. Rev.* (1972).
52. Emerson. "The War Powers Resolution Tested: The Presidents Independent Defense Power." 51 *Notre Dame Law* (1975).
53. Farrand, M., ed. *The Records of the Federal Convention of 1787.* 4 vols. (1966).
54. Field, O. P. "The Doctrine of Political Questions in the Federal Courts." 8 *Minn. L. Rev.* (1924).
55. Finkelstein, M. "Judicial Self–Limitation." 37 *Harv. L. Rev.* (1923).
56. Firmage, E. B. "The Law of Presidential Impeachment." *Utah L. Rev.* (1973).
57. Firmage. "The War Powers and the Political Question Doctrine." 49 *U. Colo. L. Rev.* (1977).
58. Firmage and C. P. Mangrum. "Removal of the President: Resignation and the Procedural Law of Impeachment." *Duke LJ.* (1974).
59. Fortescue, Sir John. *De Natura Legis Naturae.* 2 vols. (1869).
60. Frank, J. "Political Questions." In *Supreme Court and Supreme Law* (1968).
61. Frei, D. *Risks of Unintentional War* (1983).
62. Fulbright, J. W. *The Arrogance of Power* (1966).
63. Fuller, H. B. *The Purchase of Florida* (1906).
64. Gibbs, G. *Memoirs of the Administrations of Washington and John Adams.* 2 vols. (1846).
65. Goldsmith, W., ed. *The Growth of Presidential Power.* 3 vols. (1974).
66. Goldwater, B. "The President's Ability to Protect America's Freedom." *Law & Soc. Ord.* (1971).
67. Goldwater. "The Presidents' Constitutional Primacy in Foreign Relations and National Defense." 13 *Va. J. Int'l L.* (1973).
68. Goodnow, F. J. *Politics and Administration* (1914).
69. Hackworth, G. H. *Digest of International Law* (1940).
70. Hamilton, A. *Papers.* Edited by H. Syrett. 17 vols. (1962).
71. Hamilton. *The Works of Alexander Hamilton.* Edited by H. C. Lodge. 12 vols. (2d ed. 1903).
72. Handin, O., and M. F. Handin. *The Popular Sources of Political Authority: Documents on the Massachusetts Convention of 1780* (1966).
73. Harris, R. "Annals of Politics (The Department of Justice—I)." *New Yorker* (Nov. 8, 1969).
74. *Hearings on Separation of Powers before the Subcommittee on Separation of Powers of the Senate Committee on the Judiciary.* 90th Cong., 1st Sess. 52 (1967).
75. Henkin, L. *Foreign Affairs and the Constitution* (1972).
76. Henkin. "Is There a 'Political Question' Doctrine?" 50 *Yale LJ.* (1976).
77. Henkin. "Vietnam in the Courts of the United States: Political Questions." 63 *Am. J. Int'l L.* (1969).
78. Heren, L. *The New American Commonwealth* (1968).
79. Hill, H. C. *Roosevelt and the Caribbean* (1965).

80. House Committee on Foreign Affairs, Committee Print. *Background Information on the Use of the United States Armed Forces in Foreign Countries* (1970).

81. Hughes, C. E. *War Powers under the Constitution.* S. Doc. No. 105, 65th Cong., 1st Sess. 7 (1917).

82. "The Invasion Countdown." *Newsweek* (Nov. 7, 1983).

83. Irwin, R. W. *The Diplomatic Relations of the United States with the Barbary Powers, 1776–1816* (1970).

84. Israel, F. L., ed. *The State of the Union Messages of the Presidents 1790–1966.* 3 vols. (1966).

85. Javits, J. *Who Makes War?* (1973).

86. Jefferson, T. *Notes on the State of Virginia.* Edited by W. Peden (1955).

87. Jefferson. *The Papers of Thomas Jefferson.* Edited by J. Boyd. 18 vols. (1954).

88. Jefferson. *The Writings of Thomas Jefferson.* 20 vols. (1895).

89. Jefferson. *The Writings of Thomas Jefferson.* Edited by A. Lipscomb and A. Bergh. 20 vols. (1903).

90. Jessup, P. C. *Elihu Root.* 2 vols. (1938).

91. Jessup. "Should International Law Recognize an Intermediate Status between Peace and War?" 48 *Am. J. Int'l L.* (1954).

92. *Journals of the Continental Congress.* 34 vols. (1904–37).

93. "Judgment." *The Trial of the German Major War Criminals: Proceedings of the International Military Tribunal Sitting at Nuremberg, Germany* (1950).

94. Kahn, H. *On Thermonuclear War* (1960).

95. Kappler, C., ed. *Indian Affairs: Laws and Treaties.* 5 vols. (1904).

96. Kent, J. *Commentaries on American Law.* Edited by O. W. Holmes. 4 vols. (12th ed. 1896).

97. Kohl, J. "The Secret War in Brazil." *Progressive* (Aug. 1977).

98. Lacoutoure, J. *Le Vietnam entre deux paix* (1965).

99. *The Legal Historian* (1958).

100. L'Etang, H. *The Pathology of Leadership* (1970).

101. Levi, E. H. "Some Aspects of Separation of Powers." 76 *Colum. L. Rev.* (1976).

102. Lincoln, A. *The Writings of Abraham Lincoln.* Edited by A. Lapsley. 8 vols. (1905–6).

103. Lloyd George, D. *Memoirs of the Peace Conference.* 2 vols. (1939).

104. Locke, J. *Two Treatises of Government.* Edited by P. Laswell (1967).

105. Lofgren, C. A. "United States v. Curtiss–Wright Export Corporation: An Historical Reassessment." 83 *Yale L.J.* (1973).

106. Lofgren, "War-Making Under the Constitution: The Original Understanding." 81 *Yale L.J.* (1972).

107. McCaleb, W. F. *The Aaron Burr Conspiracy* (1966).

108. McDougal, M. S. "Treaties and Congressional-Executive or Presidential Agreements: Interchangeable Instruments of National Policy." 54 *Yale L.J.* (1945).

109. McDougal and F. P. Feliciano. *Law and Minimum World Public Order* (1961).
110. McGinnis, J. *The Selling of the President, 1968* (1969).
111. Madison, J. *Letters and Other Writings.* 4 vols. (1884).
112. Meeker, L. "Defensive Quarantine and the Law." 57 *Am. J. Int'l L.* (1963).
113. Meeker. "The Legality of the United States Participation in the Defense of Vietnam." 54 *Dep't St. Bull.* (1966).
114. Meneely, A. H. *The War Department, 1861* (1928).
115. Monaghan, H. P. "Presidential War–Making." 50 *B.U.L. Rev.* (Special Issue 1970).
116. Montesquieu. *The Spirit of Laws.* Edited by D. Carrithers (1977).
117. Moon, P. T. "Self Defense and 'Unselfish Service' in the Caribbean." In *The United States and the Caribbean* (1929).
118. Moore, J. B. *The Collected Papers of John Bassett Moore.* 7 vols. (1944).
119. Moore. *A Digest of International Law.* 8 vols. (1906).
120. Moore. *International Law Digest* (1908).
121. Moore, J. N. "The National Executive and the Use of the Armed Forces Abroad." In *The Vietnam War and International Law.* Edited by R. Falk. 4 vols. (1969).
122. Munro, D. G. *The United States and the Caribbean Area* (1934).
123. Murphy, J. F. "Treaties and International Agreements Other than Treaties: Constitutional Allocation of Power and Responsibility Among the President, the House of Representatives and the Senate." 23 *U. Kan. L. Rev.* (1975).
124. Myers, W. S. *A Study in Personality: General George Brinton McClellan* (1934).
125. Nelson, R. H. "The Termination of Treaties and Executive Agreements by the United States: Theory and Practice." 42 *Minn. L. Rev.* (1958).
126. Note, "Congress, the President and the Power to Commit Forces to Combat." 81 *Harv. L. Rev.* (1968).
127. Note, "A Dialogue on the Political Question Doctrine." *Utah L. Rev.* (1978).
128. Note, "1973 War Powers Legislation: Congress Reasserts Its War-making Power." 5 *U. Loy. Chi. L. Rev.* (1974).
129. Office of Congressional Relations Memorandum, Department of State. *Presidential Authority to Terminate Treaties* (1979).
130. Offutt, M. *The Protection of Citizens Abroad by the Armed Forces of the United States* (1928).
131. Oppenheim, L. *International Law, A Treatise.* Edited by H. Lauterpacht. 2 vols. (7th ed. 1961).
132. *Papers Relating to the Foreign Relations of the United States, 1863.*
133. *Papers Relating to the Foreign Relations of the United States, 1864.*
134. *Papers Relating to the Foreign Relations of the United States, 1894.*
135. *Papers Relating to the Foreign Relations of the United States, 1899.*
136. *Papers Relating to the Foreign Relations of the United States, 1903.*

137. *Papers Relating to the Foreign Relations of the United States, 1904.*
138. *Papers Relating to the Foreign Relations of the United States, 1906.*
139. *Papers Relating to the Foreign Relations of the United States, 1910.*
140. *Papers Relating to the Foreign Relations of the United States, 1911.*
141. *Papers Relating to the Foreign Relations of the United States, 1912.*
142. *Papers Relating to the Foreign Relations of the United States, 1912* (1919).
143. *Papers Relating to the Foreign Relations of the United States, 1914.*
144. *Papers Relating to the Foreign Relations of the United States, 1915* (1922).
145. *Papers Relating to the Foreign Relations of the United States, 1917.*
146. Pareto, V. *The Mind and Society: A Treatise on General Sociology.* 4 vols. (1935).
147. Parton, J. *Life of Andrew Jackson.* 3 vols. (Boston 1860).
148. *The Pentagon Papers.* 4 vols. (Senator Gravel ed. 1971).
149. Polybius. *The Histories of Polybius.* Translated by E. S. Shuckburgh. 2 vols. (1962).
150. Pomeroy, J. *Introduction to the Constitutional Law of the United States* (10th ed. 1888).
151. *The Powers of the President as Commander in Chief of the Army and Navy of the United States.* H.R. Doc. No. 445, 84th Cong., 2d Sess. (1956).
152. Prucha, F. *The Sword of the Republic: The United States Army on the Frontier, 1783–1846* (1969).
153. *The Public Papers and Addresses of Franklin D. Roosevelt.* Vol. 9: 1940 (1941).
154. *The Public Papers and Addresses of Franklin D. Roosevelt.* Vol. 10: 1941 (1950).
155. *Public Papers of the Presidents of the United States: Dwight D. Eisenhower, 1954* (1960).
156. *Public Papers of the Presidents of the United States: John F. Kennedy, 1962* (1963).
157. *Public Papers of the Presidents of the United States: John F. Kennedy, 1963* (1964).
158. *Public Papers of the Presidents of the United States: Lyndon B. Johnson, 1966.* 2 vols. (1967).
159. Ratner, L. G. "The Coordinated Warmaking Power—Legislative, Executive, and Judicial Roles." 44 *S. Cal. L. Rev.* (1970–1971).
160. Reedy, G. E. *The Twilight of the Presidency* (1970).
161. *Regulations for the Government of the United States Navy: 1865* (1865).
162. *Regulations for the Government of the United States Navy: 1870* (1870).
163. *Regulations for the Government of the United States Navy: 1893* (1893).
164. *Regulations Prescribed for the Use of the Consular Service of the United States* (1874).
165. Rehnquist, W. H. "The Constitutional Issues—Administration Position." In *Vietnam and International Law.* Edited by R. Falk (1972).
166. *Report of Commander E. B. Boutwell to Commodore William Mervine Dec. 22, 1855.* H.R. Exec. Doc. No. 115, 34th Cong., 1st Sess.
167. *Report of Rear Admiral John J. Almy to the Hon. George M. Robeson, Oct. 6,*

1873. H.R. Exec. Doc. No. 1, 43rd Cong., 1st Sess. 263.

168. *Report of the Commandant of the U.S. Marine Corps, 1905*. H.R. Exec. Doc. No. 3, 59th Cong., 1st Sess. 1236.

169. *Report of the Secretary of the Navy, 1839*. S. Doc. No. 1, 26th Cong., 1st Sess. 385.

170. *Report of the Secretary of the Navy, 1854*. S. Doc. No. 1, 33rd Cong., 2d Sess. 385.

171. *Report of the Secretary of the Navy, 1859*. S. Exec. Doc. No. 2, 36th Cong., 1st Sess. 1145.

172. *Report of the Secretary of the Navy, 1867*. H.R. Exec. Doc. No. 1, 40th Cong., 2d Sess.

173. *Report of the Secretary of the Navy, 1868*. H.R. Exec. Doc. No. 1, 40th Cong., 3d Sess.

174. *Report of the Secretary of the Navy, 1871*. H.R. Exec. Doc. No. 1, 42d Cong., 2d Sess. 277–85.

175. *Report of the Secretary of the Navy, 1873*. H.R. Exec. Doc. No. 1, 43d Cong., 1st Sess. 8.

176. *Report of the Secretary of the Navy, 1874*. H.R. Exec. Doc. No. 1, 43d Cong., 2d Sess. 8, 181–85.

177. *Report of the Secretary of the Navy, 1883*. H.R. Exec. Doc. No. 1, 47th Cong., 2d Sess. 14.

178. *Report of the Secretary of the Navy, 1889*. H.R. Exec. Doc. No. 1, 50th Cong., 2d Sess. 20–21.

179. *Report of the Secretary of the Navy, 1891*. H.R. Exec. Doc. No. 1, 52d Cong., 1st Sess. 151.

180. *Report of the Secretary of the Navy, 1894*. H.R. Exec. Doc. No. 1, 53d Cong., 3d Sess. 24.

181. Richardson, J., ed. *A Compilation of the Messages and Papers of the Presidents*. 20 vols. (1911).

182. Rienow, R., and L. T. Reinow. *The Lonely Quest: The Evolution of Presidential Leadership* (1966).

183. Robertson, W. S. "South America and the Monroe Doctrine, 1824–28." 30 *Pol. Sci. Q.* (1915).

184. Rogers, J. G. *World Policing and the Constitution* (1945).

185. Rogers, W. P. "Congress, the President, and the War Powers." 59 *Calif. L. Rev.* (1971).

186. Rogow, A. *James Forrestal: A Study of Personality, Politics and Policy* (1963).

187. Ronan, W. J. "English and American Courts and the Declaration of War." 31 *Am. J. Int'l L.* (1937).

188. Rosenfeld, S. A. "The Power of Congress and the President in International Relations." 25 *Calif. L. Rev.* (1937).

189. Rostow, E. V. "Great Cases Make Bad Law: The War Powers Act." 50 *Tex. L. Rev.* (1973).

190. Russell, R.W. *The United States Congress and the Power to Use Military Force*

Abroad. Ph.D. dissertation, Fletcher School of Law and Diplomacy (1967).

191. Scharpf, F. W. "Judicial Review and the Political Question: A Functional Analysis." 75 *Yale L.J.* (1966).

192. Schlesinger, A. M., Jr. *The Imperial Presidency* (1973).

193. Schmidt, H. *The United States Occupation of Haiti, 1915–1934* (1971).

194. Schwartz, B. *A Commentary on the Constitution of the United States* (1963).

195. Schwartz, W. F., and W. McCormack. "The Justiciability of Legal Objections to the Military Effort in Vietnam." 46 *Tex. L. Rev.* (1968).

196. Schwarzenberger, G. "Jus Pacis Ac Belli?" 37 *Am. J. Int'l L.* (1943).

197. Scroggs, W. O. *Filibusters and Financiers* (1969).

198. Shaplen, R. *The Last Revolution* (1965).

199. Small, N. J. *Some Presidential Interpretations of the Presidency* (1932).

200. Smith, A. *The Theory of Moral Sentiments.* 7 vols. (1822).

201. Sofaer, A. D. *War, Foreign Affairs and Constitutional Power* (1976).

202. Sohn, L. B. *1969 Proceedings of the American Society of International Law* (1969).

203. Sorensen, T. C. *Decision-Making in the White House* (1963).

204. Spong, W. B., Jr. "The War Powers Resolution Revisited: Historic Accomplishment or Surrender?" 16 *Wm. & Mary L. Rev.* (1975).

205. Stanwood, E. *A History of the Presidency from 1897 to 1916* (1916).

206. Stebbins, R., ed. *Documents on American Foreign Relations, 1965* (1966).

207. Stimson, H. L., and M. Bundy. *On Active Service in Peace and War* (1948).

208. Story, J. *Commentaries on the Constitution of the United States.* Edited by T. Cooley. 2 vols. (4th ed. 1870).

209. Strum, P. *The Supreme Court and "Political Questions": A Study in Judicial Evasion* (1974).

210. Sutherland, G. *The Constitution and World Affairs* (1919).

211. Sutherland, J. *Statutes and Statutory Construction.* 3 vols. (1943).

212. Taft, W. H. "The Boundaries between the Executive, the Legislative and the Judicial Branches of the Government." 25 *Yale L.J.* (1916).

213. Taft. *Our Chief Magistrate and His Powers* (1925).

214. Tansill, C., ed. *Documents Illustrative of the Union of the American States* (1927).

215. "Terror Right and Left." *Time* (March 23, 1982).

216. Thomas, A.V.W., and A. J. Thomas, Jr. *The War-Making Powers of the President: Constitutional and International Law Aspects* (1982).

217. Thorpe, F., ed. *The Federal and State Constitutions, Colonial Charters, and Other Organic Laws.* 7 vols. (1909).

218. Tigar, M. E. "Judicial Power, the Political Question Doctrine and Foreign Relations." 17 *UCLA L. Rev.* (1970).

219. *Transmittal of Executive Agreements to Congress, Hearings on S. 596 before the Senate Foreign Relations Committee.* 92d Cong., 1st Sess. 26 (1971). Testimony of Professor Alexander H. Bickel cited in Murphy, "Treaties and International Agreements Other than Treaties."

220. Tribe, L. H. *American Constitutional Law* (1978).

221. Truman, H. S. *Memoirs, Years of Trial and Hope, 1946–1952* (1956).

222. Tucker, G. *Dawn Like Thunder* (1963).

223. Ullmann, J. E. "The Expert Mismanagement of the Vietnam War." *War/Peace Report* (Feb. 1970).

224. *The United States Consul's Manual: A Practical Guide for Consular Officers: 1865* (1863).

225. *Use of the United States Navy in Nicaragua, Hearing before the Senate Committee on Foreign Relations.* 70th Cong., 1st Sess. 42–43 (1928).

226. Van Alstyne, W. "Congress, the President, and the Power to Declare War: A Requiem for Vietnam." 121 *U. Pa. L. Rev.* (1972).

227. Van Bynkershoek, C. *Questionum Juris Publici Libii Duo.* Translated by T. Frank (1930).

228. Von Holst, H. *The Constitutional Law of the United States of America* (1887).

229. *War of Rebellion: Official Records of the Union and Confederate Armies.* 3 vols. (Series II, 1897).

230. *War Powers: A Test of Compliance, Hearings before the Subcommittee on International Security and Scientific Affairs of the Committee on International Relations.* 94th Cong., 1st Sess. 3–4 (1975).

231. Washington, G. *Writings of George Washington.* Edited by J. Sparks. 12 vols. (1834–47).

232. Weber, M. *The Methodology of the Social Sciences.* Translated by E. A. Shils and H. A. Finch (1949).

233. Webster, D. *The Works of Daniel Webster.* 6 vols. (1851).

234. Wechsler, H. "Toward Neutral Principles of Constitutional Law." 73 *Harv. L. Rev.* (1959).

235. Weigley, R. F. *History of the United States Army* (1967).

236. Wheaton, H. *Elements of International Law.* Edited by R. Dana (1936).

237. Whiteman, M. *Digest of International Law.* 14 vols. (1968).

238. Whiting, W. *War Powers under the Constitution of the United States* (10th ed. 1864).

239. Williams, M. W. *Anglo–American Isthmian Diplomacy* (1965).

240. Willoughby, W. W. *The Constitutional Law of the United States.* 3 vols. (2d ed. 1929).

241. Wisan, J. E. *The Cuban Crisis as Reflected in the New York Press* (1965).

242. Wormuth, F. D. "The Nixon Theory of the War Power: A Critique." 60 *Calif. L. Rev.* (1972).

243. Wormuth. *The Origins of Modern Constitutionalism* (1949).

244. Wright, Q. "Legal Aspects of the Vietnam Situation." 60 *Am. J. Int'l L.* (1966).

General Index

Act of Settlement, 7
Act of state doctrine, 184–85, 192
Acton, Lord [John Emerich Edward Dalberg], 283
Acts of war, 52, 72, 144, 151, 194–95, 219, 251–52, 254; defined, 34 (*see also* blockade; intervention; military trespass; recognition; reprisal; visitation and search); vs. state of war, 33–34, 71–73
Adair, John, 116
Adams, Henry, 282–83
Adams, John, 4, 11, 59, 107–8, 181
Adams, John Quincy, 64, 81, 140, 280
Administrative Procedure Act, 234, 235
Advice and consent, 189, 192, 274
Affirmative acts, 195, 228
Agnew, Spiro, 281
Agreements, international. *See* executive agreements
Algiers, 61–62
Alienage, law of, 210
Altgeld, John Peter, 98, 167
American Revolution, 106, 207
Angola, 185
Appollon (ship), 13, 46–47
Appropriation: acts of, 219–21, 228, 246; defined, 221; in Vietnam War, 222–25
Arbuthnot, Alexander, 129–30
Aristocracy, 4; House of Lords as, 2–3

Aristotle, 1, 282
Armbrister, Robert C., 129–30
Armed Actions Taken by the United States Without a Declaration of War, 1789– 1967, 142
Armed forces, 141, 225; authorized use of, 215; in Central America, 249–50, 254; forbidden uses of, 98–101, 187; under Foreign Assistance Act, 249; in Lebanon, 261–62; statutes of control over, 97–99. *See also* President, and power to command armed forces; United States Congress, control over armed forces by
Armed neutrality, 79–80
Arms Export Control Act, 249
Army of the Confederation, 88
Army of Virginia, 90
Army Warwick (ship), 25
Articles of Confederation, 4, 17
Articles of War, 88–90, 93, 106
Ashburton, Lord Alexander, 50
Ashmun, George, 55–56
Aury, Louis, 128
Austin, Hudson, 258
Austin, John L., 66
Austin, Warren, 44

Bacon, Augustus, 184
Bagehot, Walter, 3
Baker, Howard, 254

Case Index